I'M A BEHEMOTH, an S-Ranked MONSTER, but MISTAKEN for a CAT, I Live as an ELF GIRL'S PET

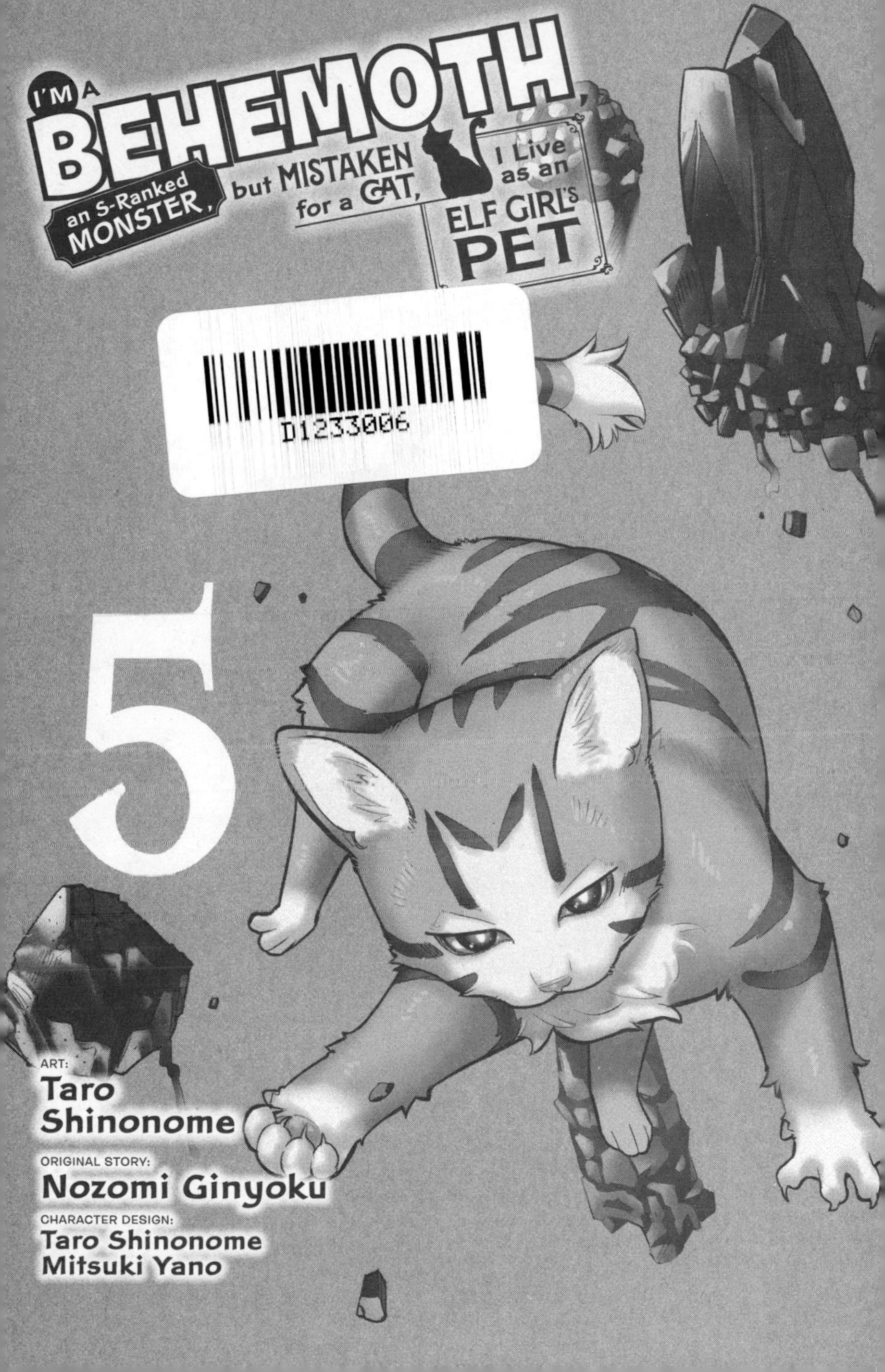

5

ART:
Taro Shinonome

ORIGINAL STORY:
Nozomi Ginyoku

CHARACTER DESIGN:
Taro Shinonome
Mitsuki Yano

Story & Characters

STORY

Our protagonist, a proud knight delving into the labyrinth, was slain by a mighty demonic assassin. Or so he thought...

When he came to, he had been reincarnated as an S-ranked behemoth cub! Not long after assuming this new form, he was on the brink of death from the wounds he received in a fierce battle, but a beautiful elf named Aria saved him and gave him a new name: Tama.

Now Tama has sworn on his honor as a knight to protect the woman who saved his life. With Aria's swiftness, her hammer-wielding friend Vulcan's raw power, and Tama's enormous variety of skills to guard them from danger, their party is making a name for itself! After Aria emerges victorious from an intense battle against a demon and recovers from the wounds she received during it, the party returns to action.

At that time, the earth dragon (another S-ranked monster) Tama slew reincarnates as a dragonewt girl. Seeking the "Strong One" who felled her, she runs into Tama and Aria in the labyrinth. Aria, unable to leave this strangely naive girl in such a perilous position, names her Stella and invites her to join the party.

Stella is obsessed with Tama, the Strong One, and doesn't hesitate to let him know that, but the normally kind and gentle Aria refuses to give him up. Their strained relationship has come to have a negative impact on their party's effectiveness in the dungeon...and may be putting the party in danger of splitting up!?

Welcome to the adventures of an adorable little fluffball of a kitten (with unfathomably great powers) and his gorgeous elf master (with astoundingly huge mammaries) in another world!

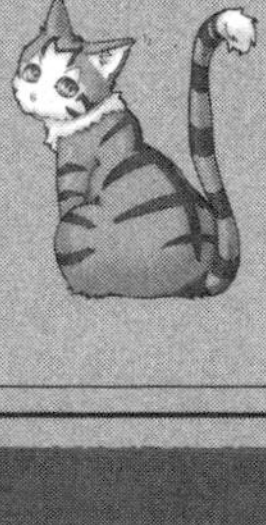

★★★ CHARACTERS ★★★

TAMA

In his former life as a knight, he crossed swords with many a monster, but he was suddenly reborn as one himself—an S-ranked behemoth. After he was dealt a mortal blow by an earth dragon, Aria saved him, and he started a new life. He supports Aria in battle with his knowledge from his years of knightly training and an array of new skills.

ARIA

A kind elf girl who took in a kitten she found passed out in a dungeon and named him Tama. After showing great talent with a skill that gives her incredible speed and teaming up with Tama, she has become a C-ranked adventurer. Her melon-sized breasts and beauty entrance people on the street, and her particular sexual disposition has led her deeper and deeper in love with Tama.

VULCAN

A member of the tiger-eared clan and a C-ranked adventurer who wields a war hammer and can use skills. She has a habit of wearing revealing overalls with nothing underneath. As an armorer, she used to create equipment for Aria, but now the two have formed a party together.

ANNA

Real name: Arnold Holzweilzenegger. A former B-ranked adventurer who could silence crying children with just a look, he's now the guild receptionist. His genuine first-rate strength has allowed him to resolve conflicts between many disagreeable adventurers. He's highly knowledgeable, and has theorized that the skill-using Tama is an elemental cat.

STELLA

This girl, who suddenly appeared in the labyrinth one day, wrapped in a tattered tunic, is the reincarnation of the earth dragon whom Tama slew. After she comes across Aria and company, the party takes her in, and she joins them on their adventures. She decides that Tama, the Strong One, will be her mate, and hounds him to impregnate her.

Contents

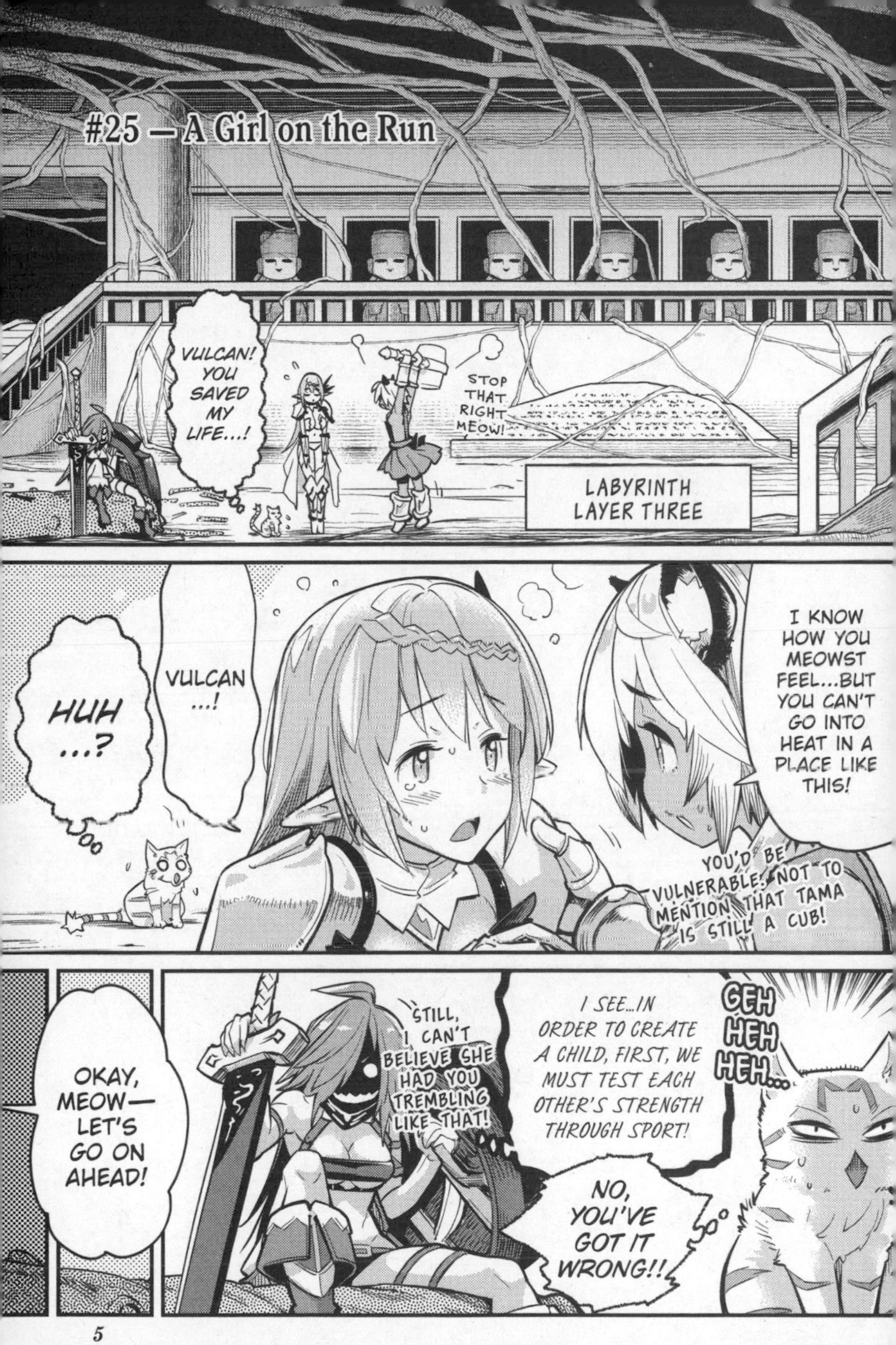
#25 — A Girl on the Run
LABYRINTH LAYER THREE
STOP THAT RIGHT MEOW!
VULCAN! YOU SAVED MY LIFE...!
I KNOW HOW YOU MEOWST FEEL...BUT YOU CAN'T GO INTO HEAT IN A PLACE LIKE THIS!
YOU'D BE VULNERABLE! NOT TO MENTION THAT TAMA IS STILL A CUB!
VULCAN ...!
HUH ...?
GEH HEH HEH...
I SEE...IN ORDER TO CREATE A CHILD, FIRST, WE MUST TEST EACH OTHER'S STRENGTH THROUGH SPORT!
NO, YOU'VE GOT IT WRONG!!
STILL, I CAN'T BELIEVE SHE HAD YOU TREMBLING LIKE THAT!
OKAY, MEOW— LET'S GO ON AHEAD!

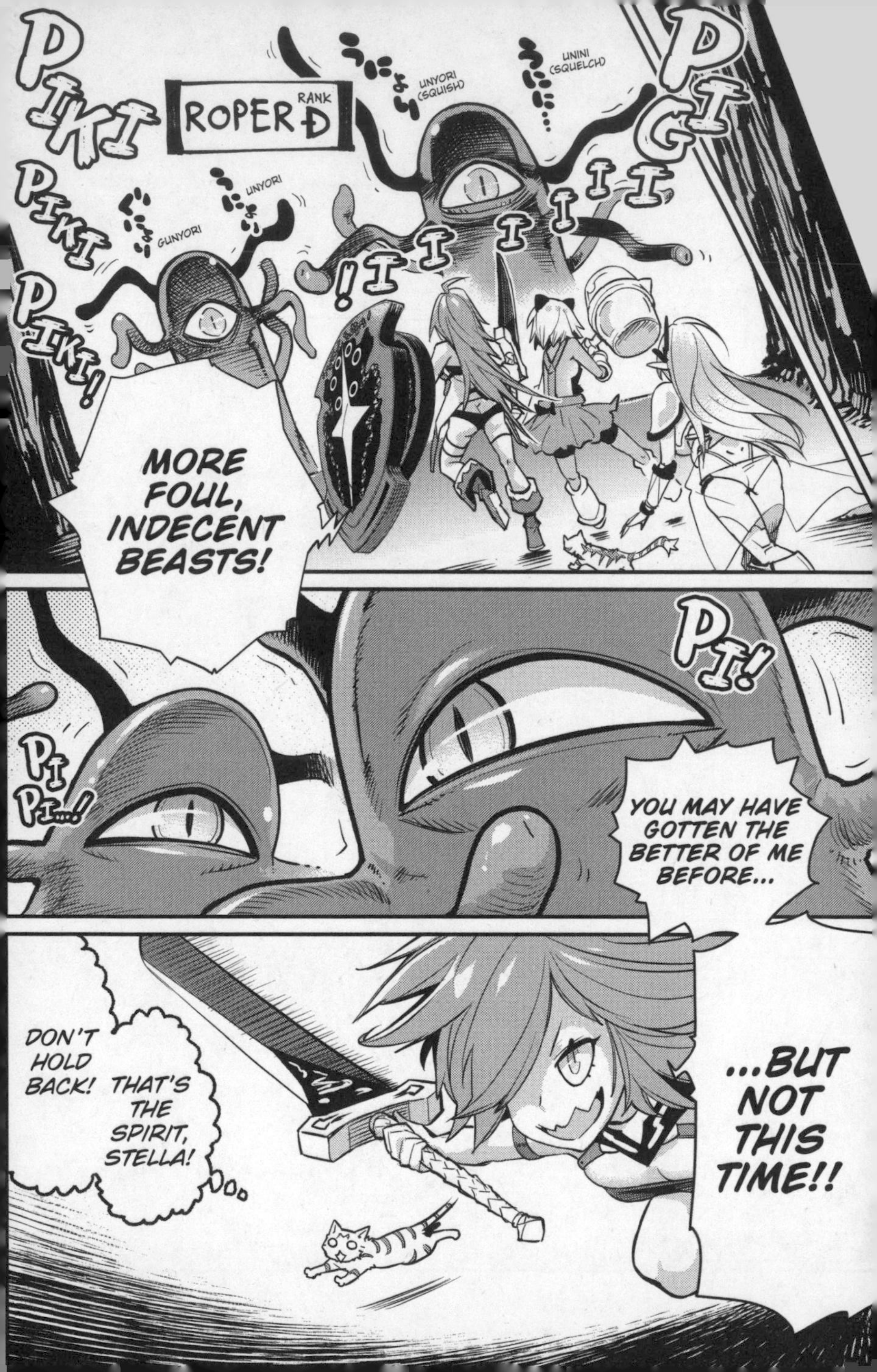
PIGIIIIIII!
うにに…
UNINI (SQUELCH)
うにょり
UNYORI (SQUISH)
ROPER RANK D
PIKI
PIKI PIKI PIKI!
うにょり
UNYORI
ぐにょり
GUNYORI
MORE FOUL, INDECENT BEASTS!
PI!
YOU MAY HAVE GOTTEN THE BETTER OF ME BEFORE...
PI PI...!
...BUT NOT THIS TIME!!
THAT'S THE SPIRIT, STELLA!
DON'T HOLD BACK!

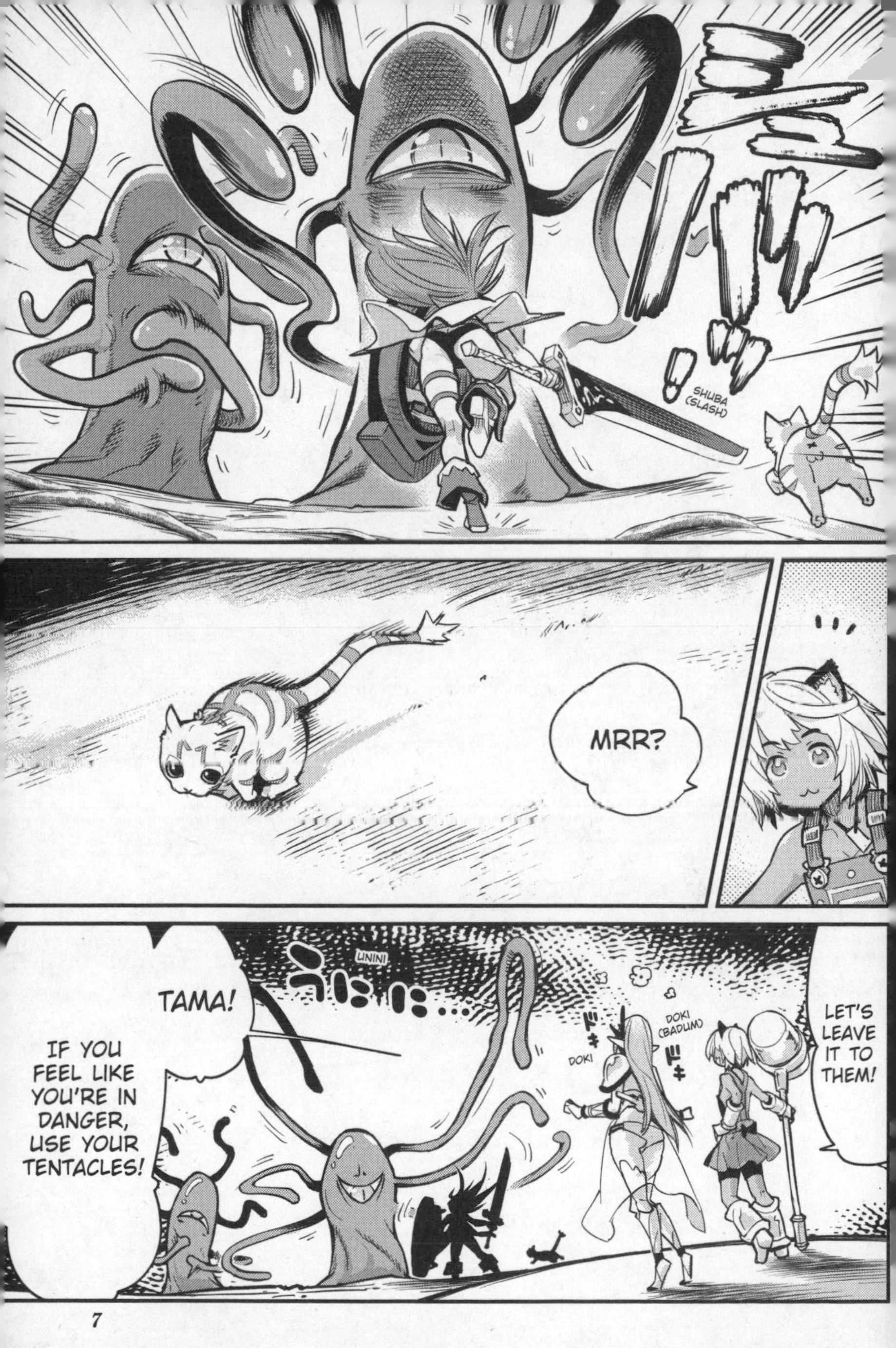
SHUBA (SLASH)
MRR?
LET'S LEAVE IT TO THEM!
DOKI (BADUMP)
DOKI
UNINI
TAMA!
IF YOU FEEL LIKE YOU'RE IN DANGER, USE YOUR TENTACLES!

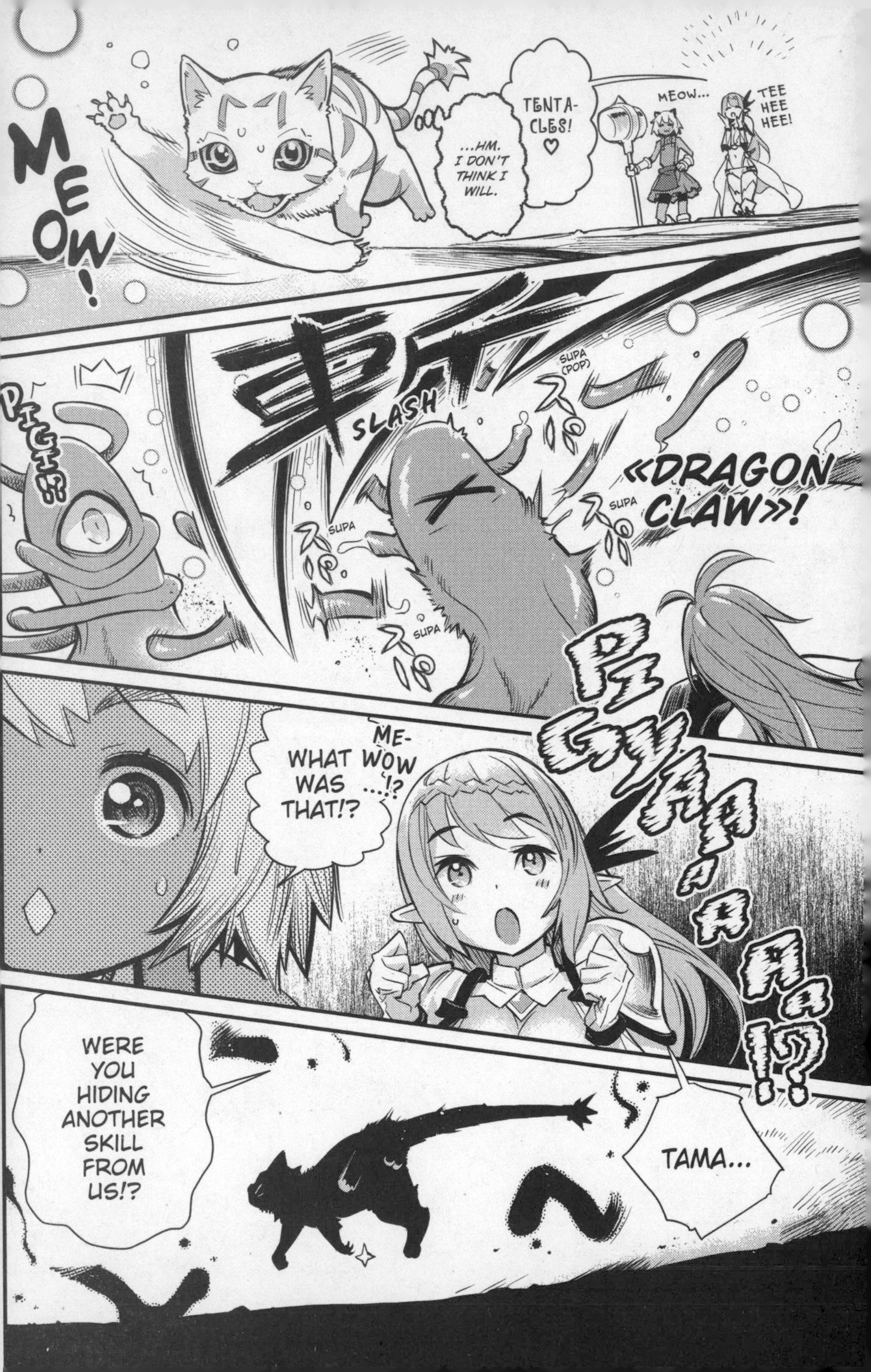
TEE HEE HEE!
MEOW...
TENTA-CLES! ♡
...HM. I DON'T THINK I WILL.
MEOW!
«DRAGON CLAW»!
SUPA (POP)
SLASH
SUPA
SUPA
SUPA
PIGI!!
PIGYAAAAA!?
ME-WOW...!?
WHAT WAS THAT!?
TAMA...
WERE YOU HIDING ANOTHER SKILL FROM US!?

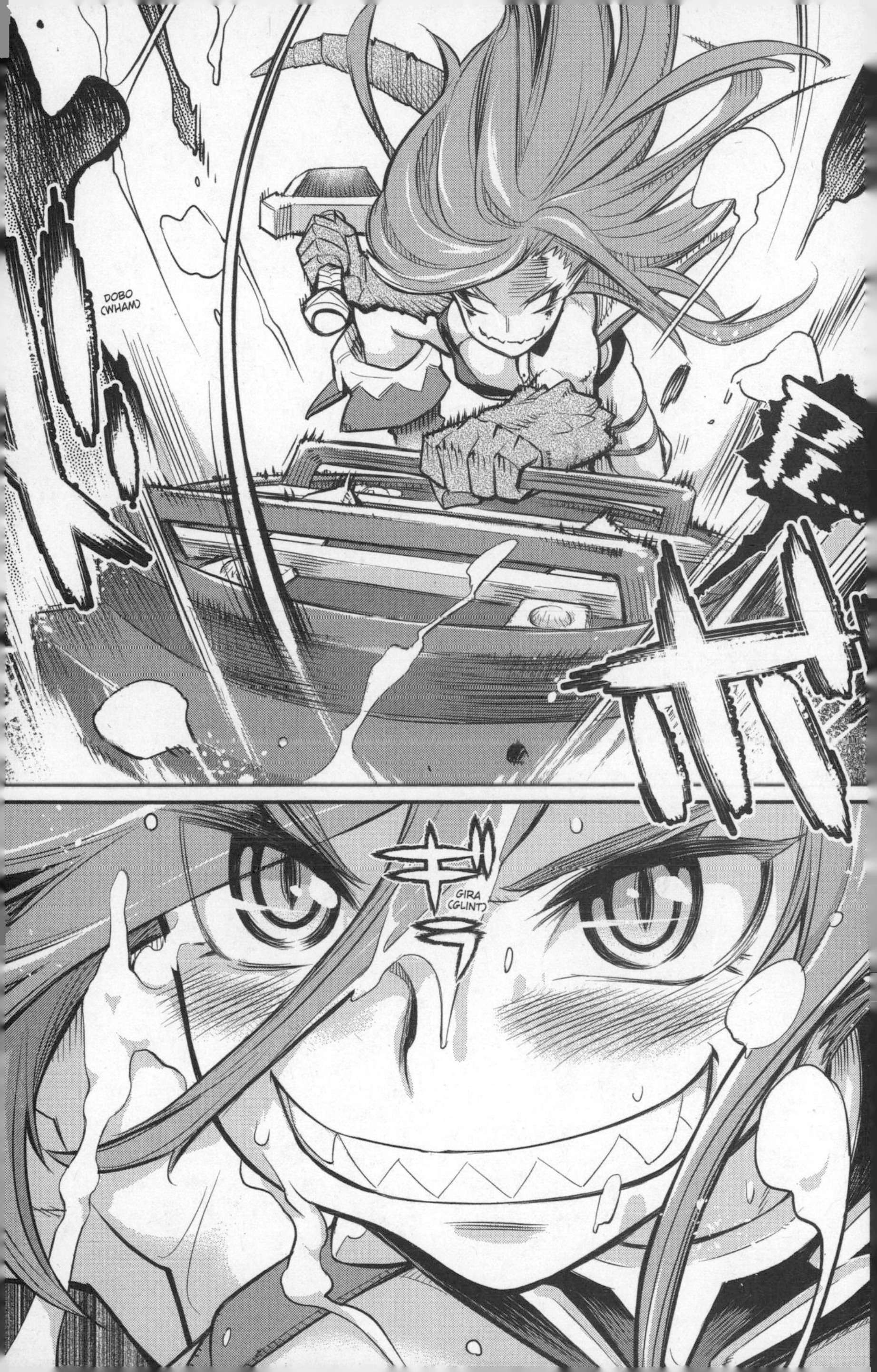
DOBO (WHAM)
GIRA (GLINT)

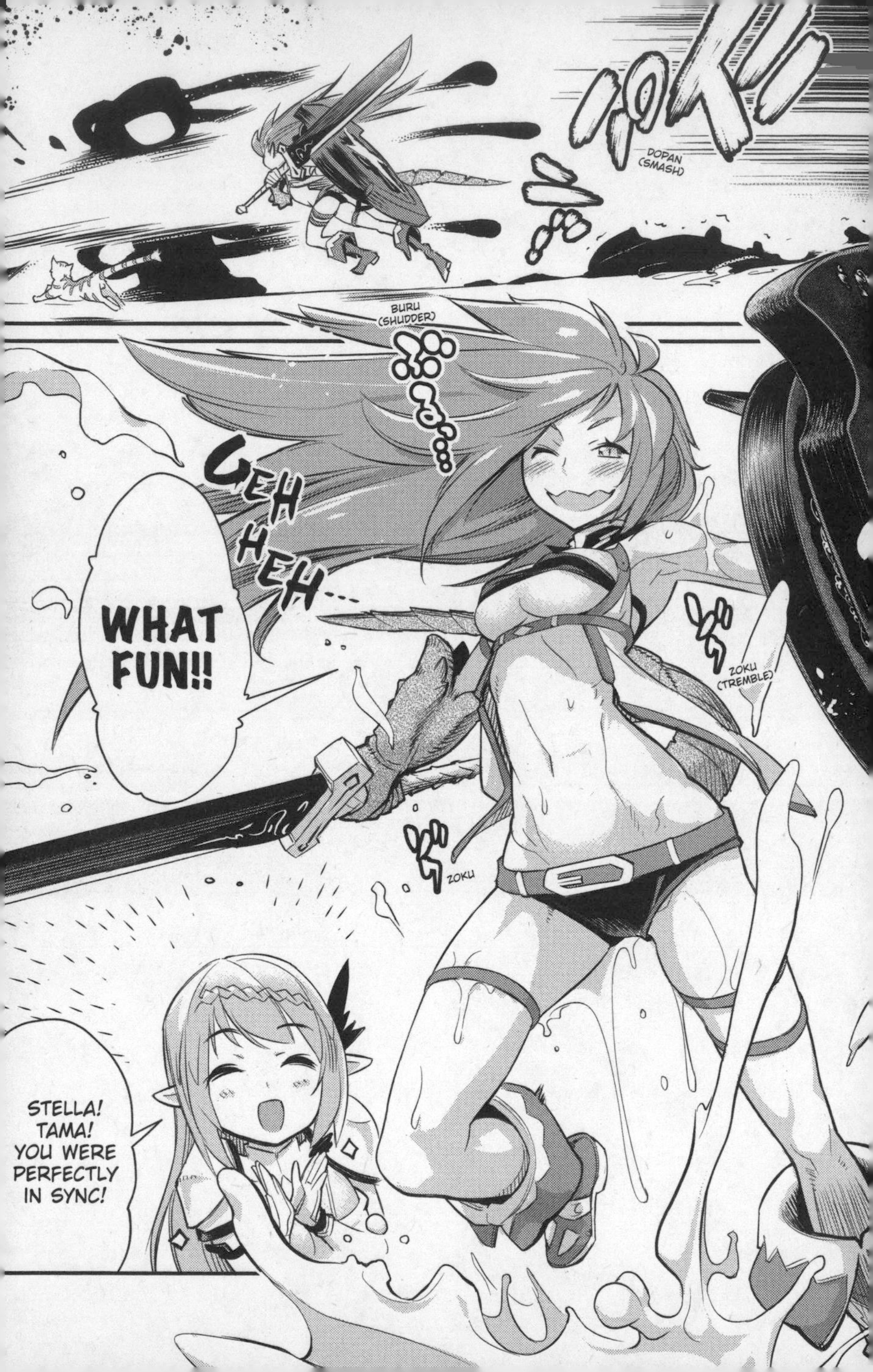
DOPAN (SMASH)
BURU (SHUDDER)
ZOKU (TREMBLE)
GEH HEH HEH...
WHAT FUN!!
ZOKU
STELLA! TAMA! YOU WERE PERFECTLY IN SYNC!

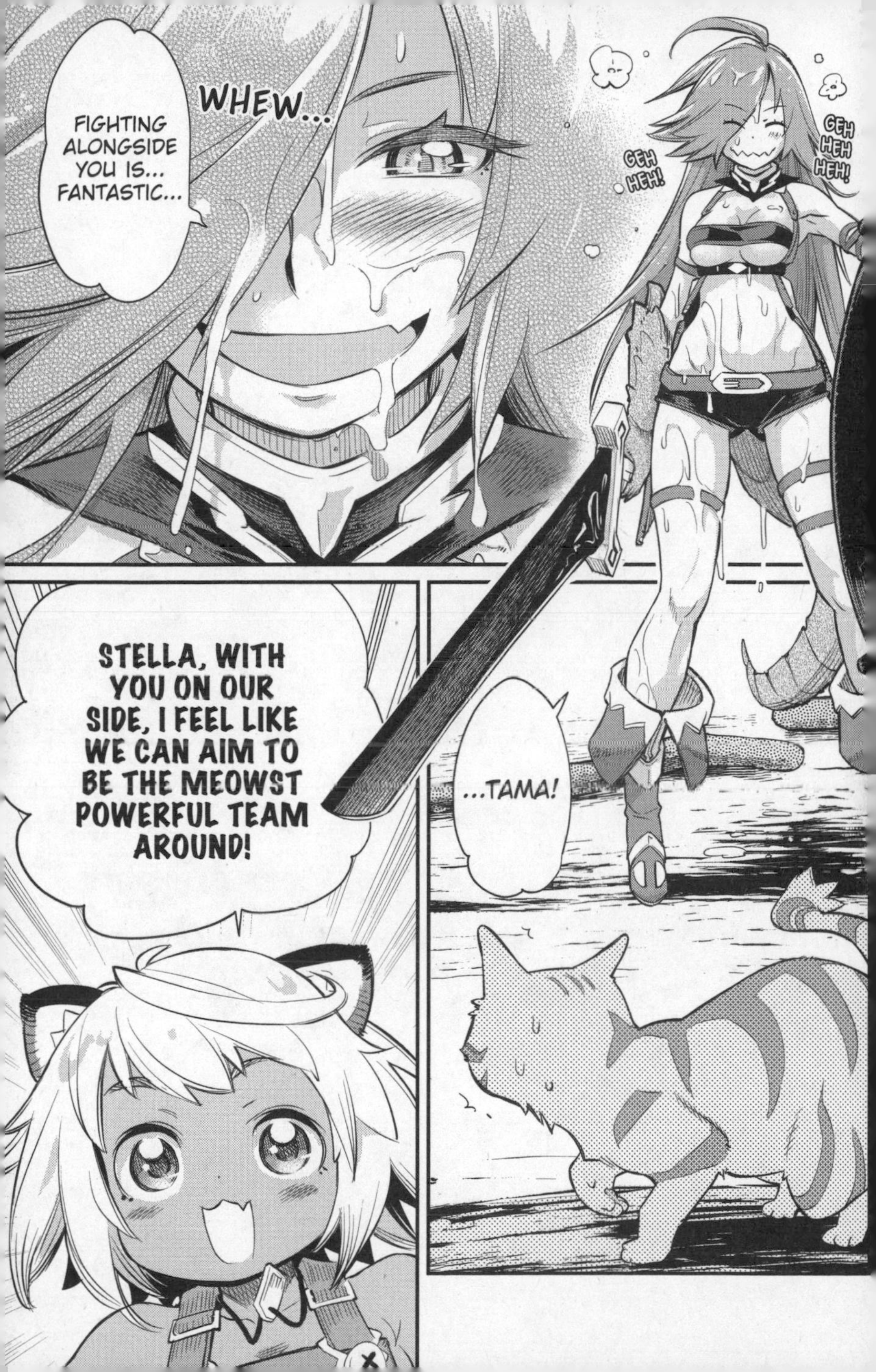
GEH HEH HEH!
GEH HEH!
WHEW...
FIGHTING ALONGSIDE YOU IS... FANTASTIC...
...TAMA!
STELLA, WITH YOU ON OUR SIDE, I FEEL LIKE WE CAN AIM TO BE THE MEOWST POWERFUL TEAM AROUND!

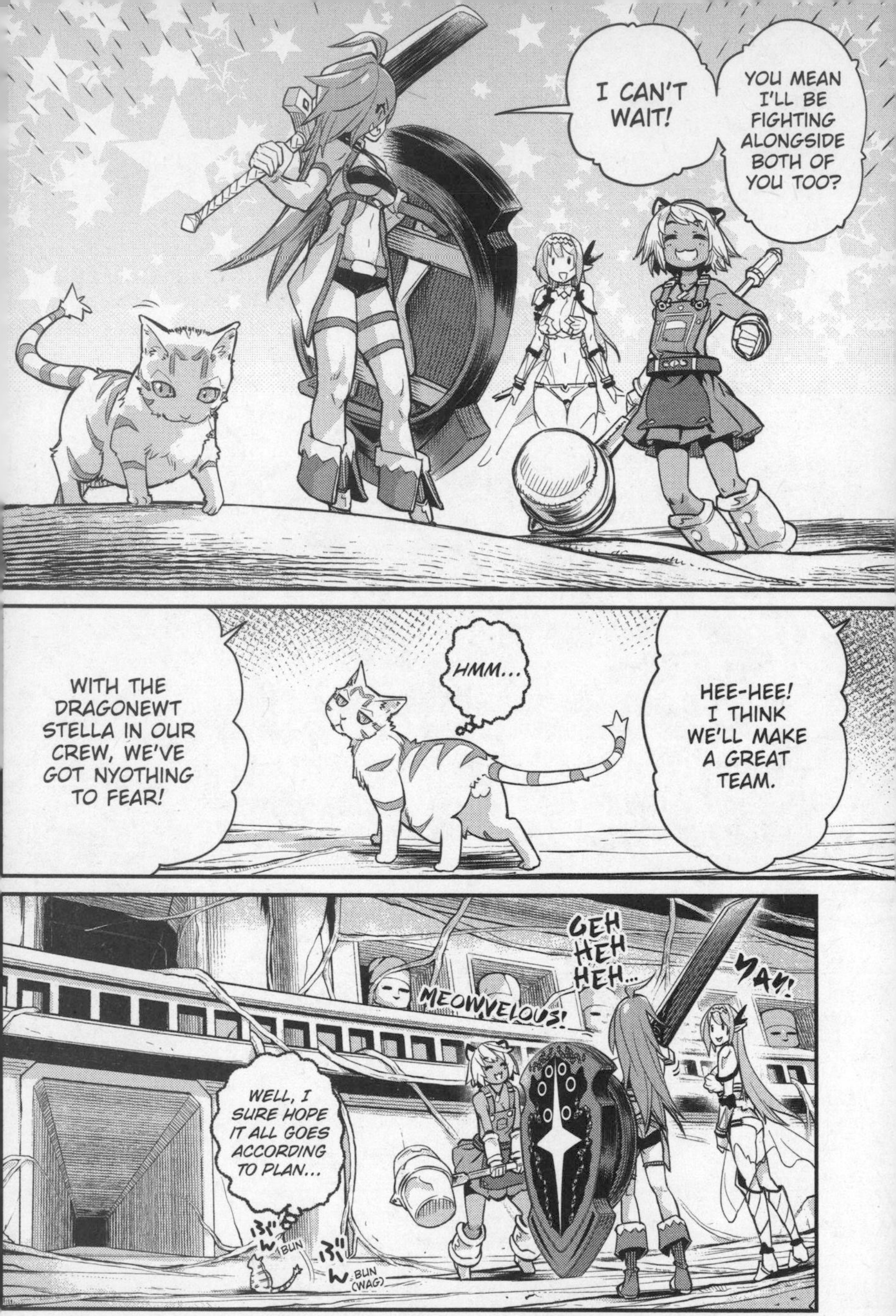
YOU MEAN I'LL BE FIGHTING ALONGSIDE BOTH OF YOU TOO?
I CAN'T WAIT!
HEE-HEE! I THINK WE'LL MAKE A GREAT TEAM.
HMM...
WITH THE DRAGONEWT STELLA IN OUR CREW, WE'VE GOT NYOTHING TO FEAR!
YAY!
GEH HEH HEH...
MEOWVELOUS!
WELL, I SURE HOPE IT ALL GOES ACCORDING TO PLAN...
ぶん BUN
ぶん BUN (WAG)

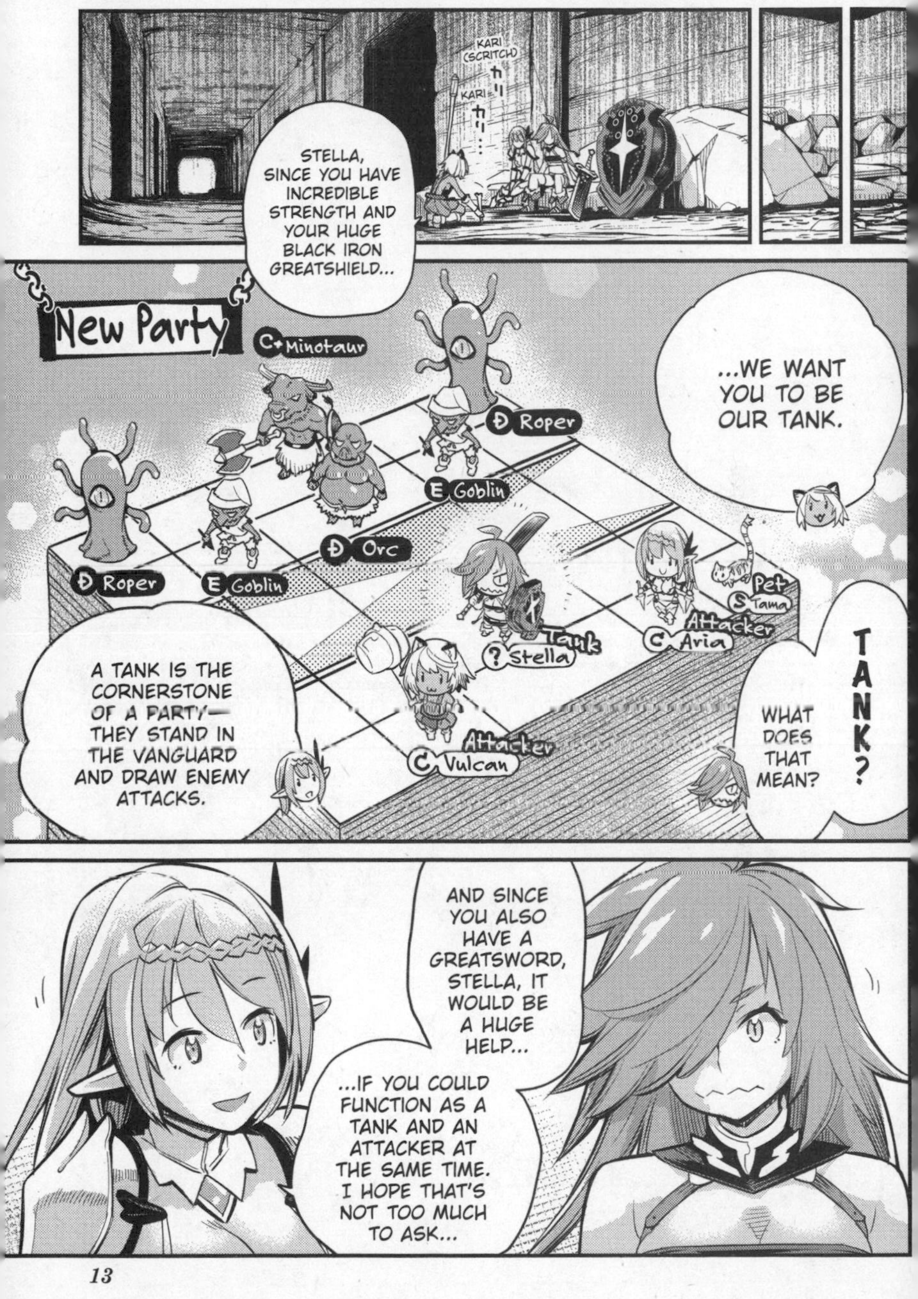
KARI (SCRITCH)
カリ
KARI
カリ…
STELLA, SINCE YOU HAVE INCREDIBLE STRENGTH AND YOUR HUGE BLACK IRON GREATSHIELD...
...WE WANT YOU TO BE OUR TANK.
TANK?
WHAT DOES THAT MEAN?
New Party
C+ Minotaur
D Roper
E Goblin
D Orc
D Roper
E Goblin
Pet S Tama
Attacker C Aria
Tank ? Stella
Attacker C Vulcan
A TANK IS THE CORNERSTONE OF A PARTY—THEY STAND IN THE VANGUARD AND DRAW ENEMY ATTACKS.
AND SINCE YOU ALSO HAVE A GREATSWORD, STELLA, IT WOULD BE A HUGE HELP...
...IF YOU COULD FUNCTION AS A TANK AND AN ATTACKER AT THE SAME TIME. I HOPE THAT'S NOT TOO MUCH TO ASK...

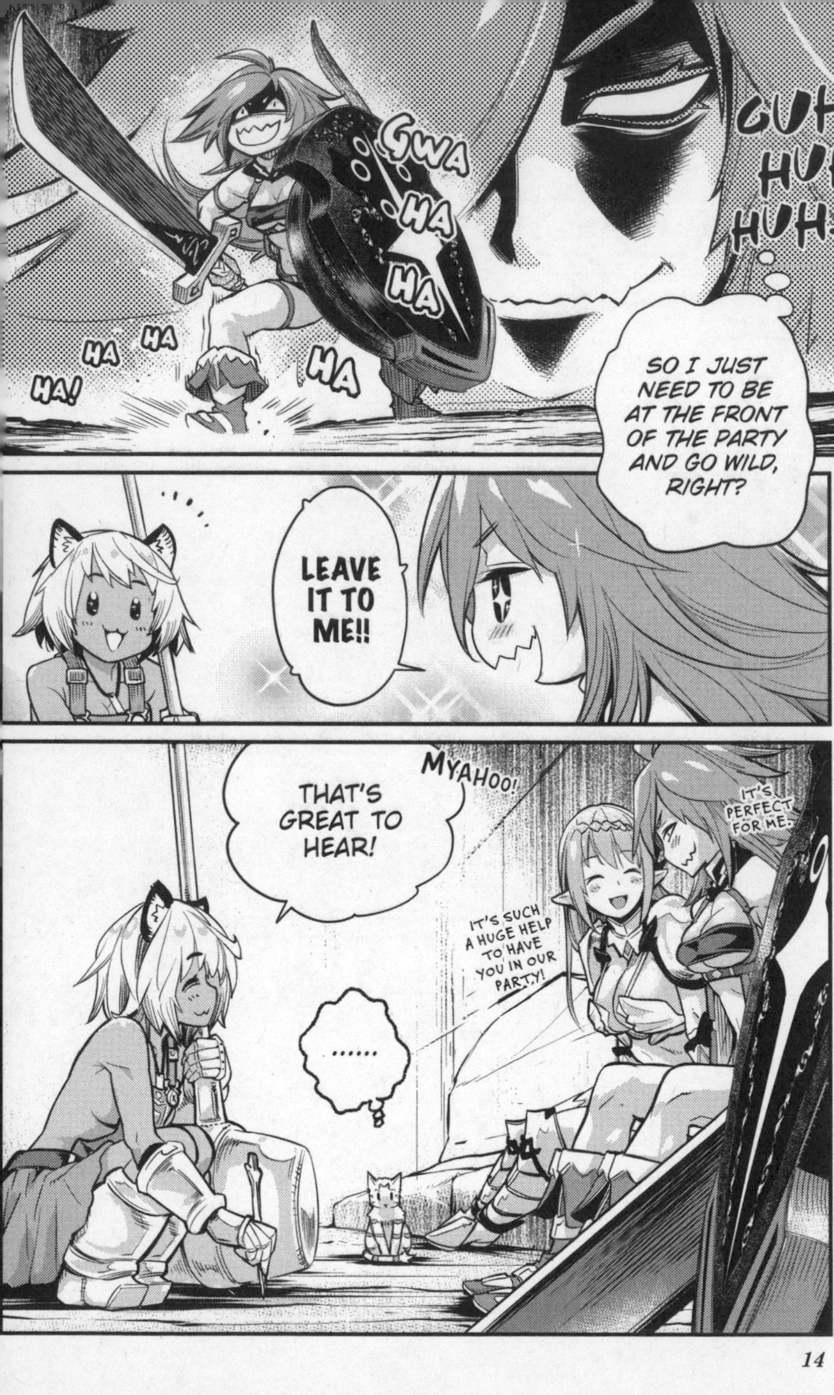
GUH HUH HUH...
SO I JUST NEED TO BE AT THE FRONT OF THE PARTY AND GO WILD, RIGHT?
GWA HA HA
HA HA HA! HA
LEAVE IT TO ME!!
IT'S PERFECT FOR ME.
MYAHOO!
THAT'S GREAT TO HEAR!
IT'S SUCH A HUGE HELP TO HAVE YOU IN OUR PARTY!
......

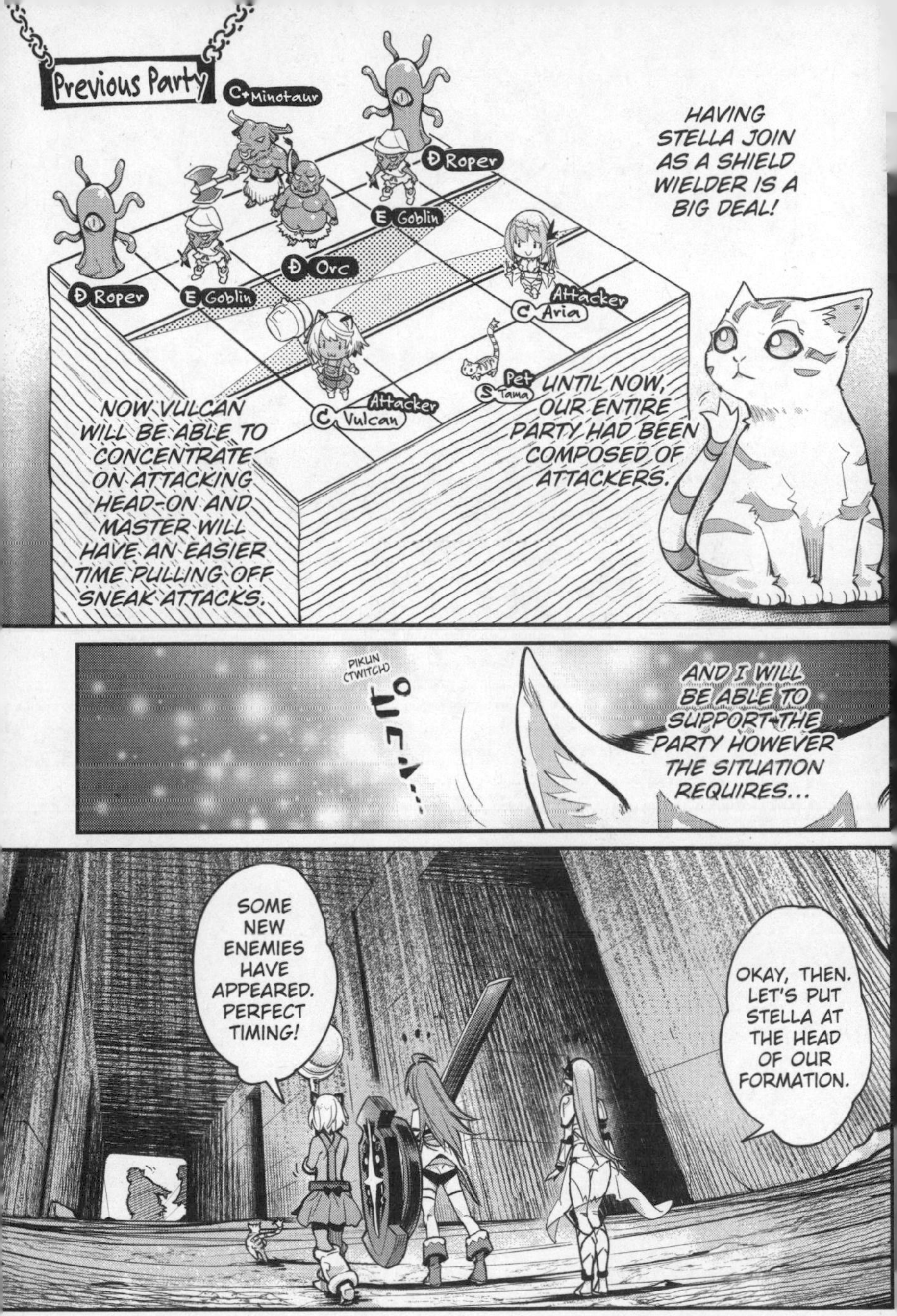
Previous Party
C Minotaur
D Roper
E Goblin
D Orc
D Roper
E Goblin
Attacker C Aria
Pet S Tama
Attacker C Vulcan
HAVING STELLA JOIN AS A SHIELD WIELDER IS A BIG DEAL!
UNTIL NOW, OUR ENTIRE PARTY HAD BEEN COMPOSED OF ATTACKERS.
NOW VULCAN WILL BE ABLE TO CONCENTRATE ON ATTACKING HEAD-ON AND MASTER WILL HAVE AN EASIER TIME PULLING OFF SNEAK ATTACKS.
AND I WILL BE ABLE TO SUPPORT THE PARTY HOWEVER THE SITUATION REQUIRES...
PIKUN (TWITCH)
OKAY, THEN. LET'S PUT STELLA AT THE HEAD OF OUR FORMATION.
SOME NEW ENEMIES HAVE APPEARED. PERFECT TIMING!

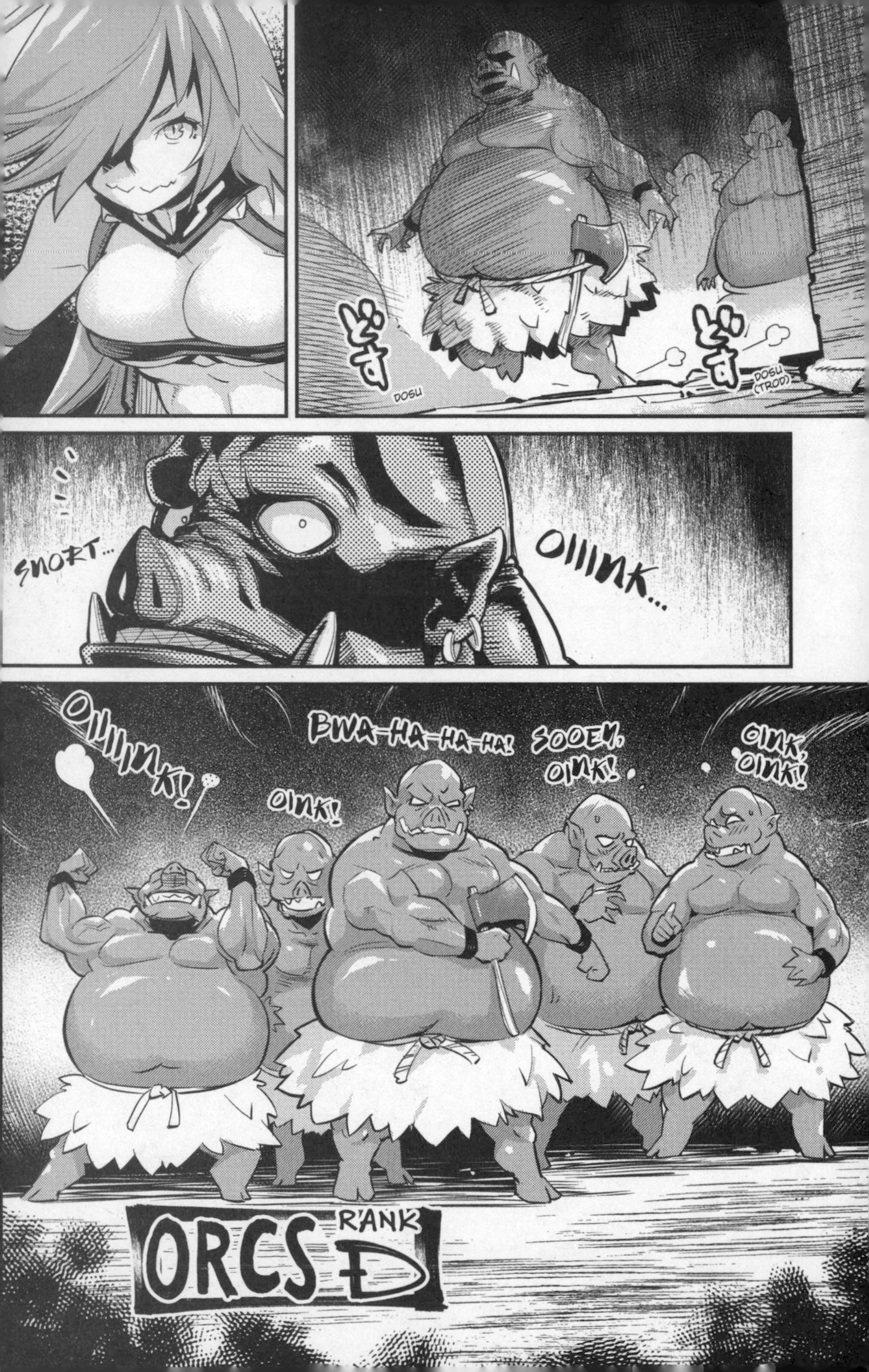
どす
DOSU (TROD)
どす
DOSU
OIIIINK...
SNORT...
OINK, OINK!
SOOEY, OINK!
BWA-HA-HA-HA!
OIIIINK!
OINK!
ORCS
RANK D

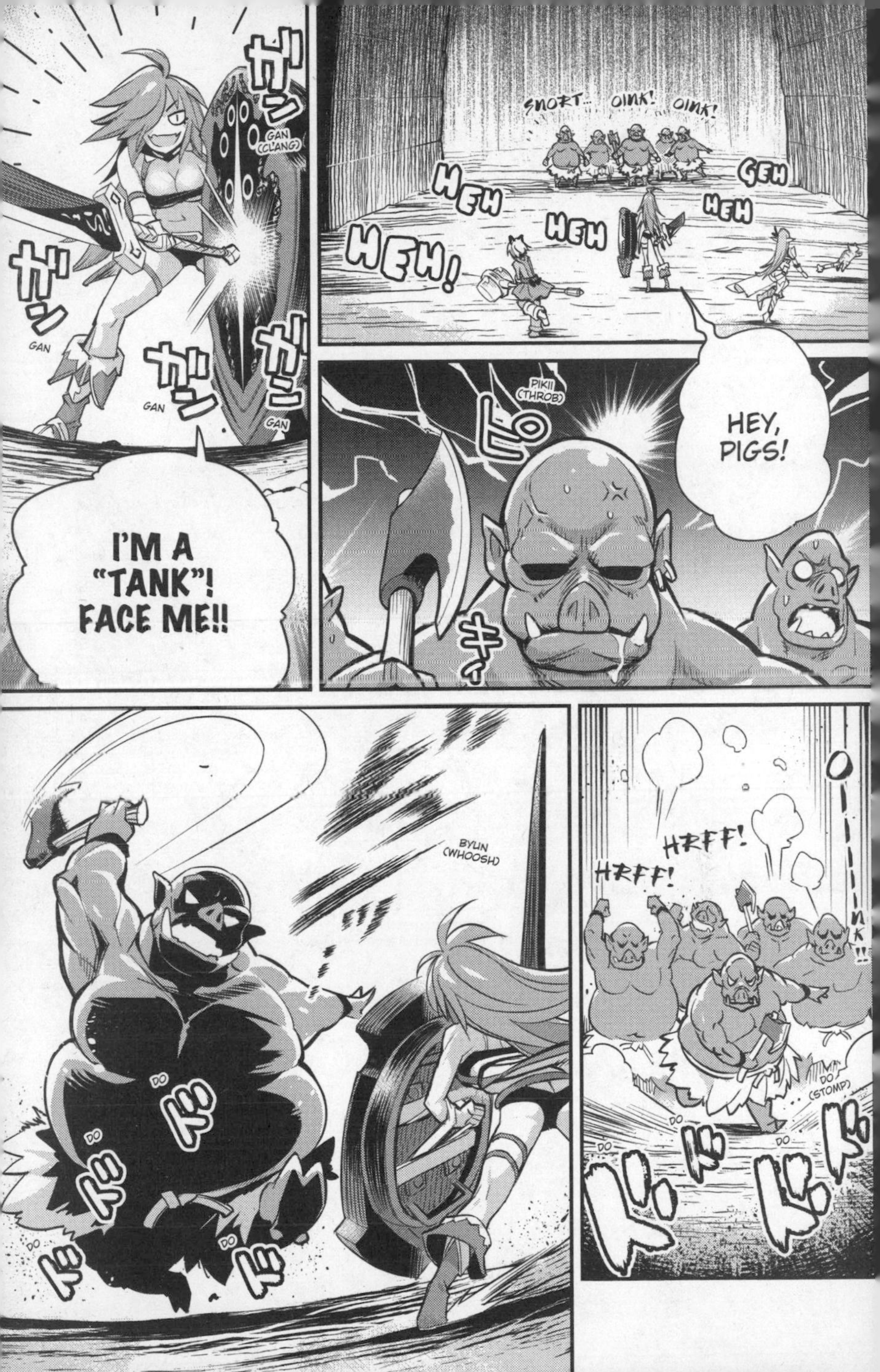
SNORT... OINK! OINK!
GEH
HEH
HEH
HEH
HEH!
HEY, PIGS!
PIKII (THROB)
GAN (CLANG)
GAN
GAN
GAN
I'M A "TANK"! FACE ME!!
...NK!!
HRFF!
HRFF!
DO (STOMP)
DO
DO
BYUN (WHOOSH)
DO
DO
DO
DO

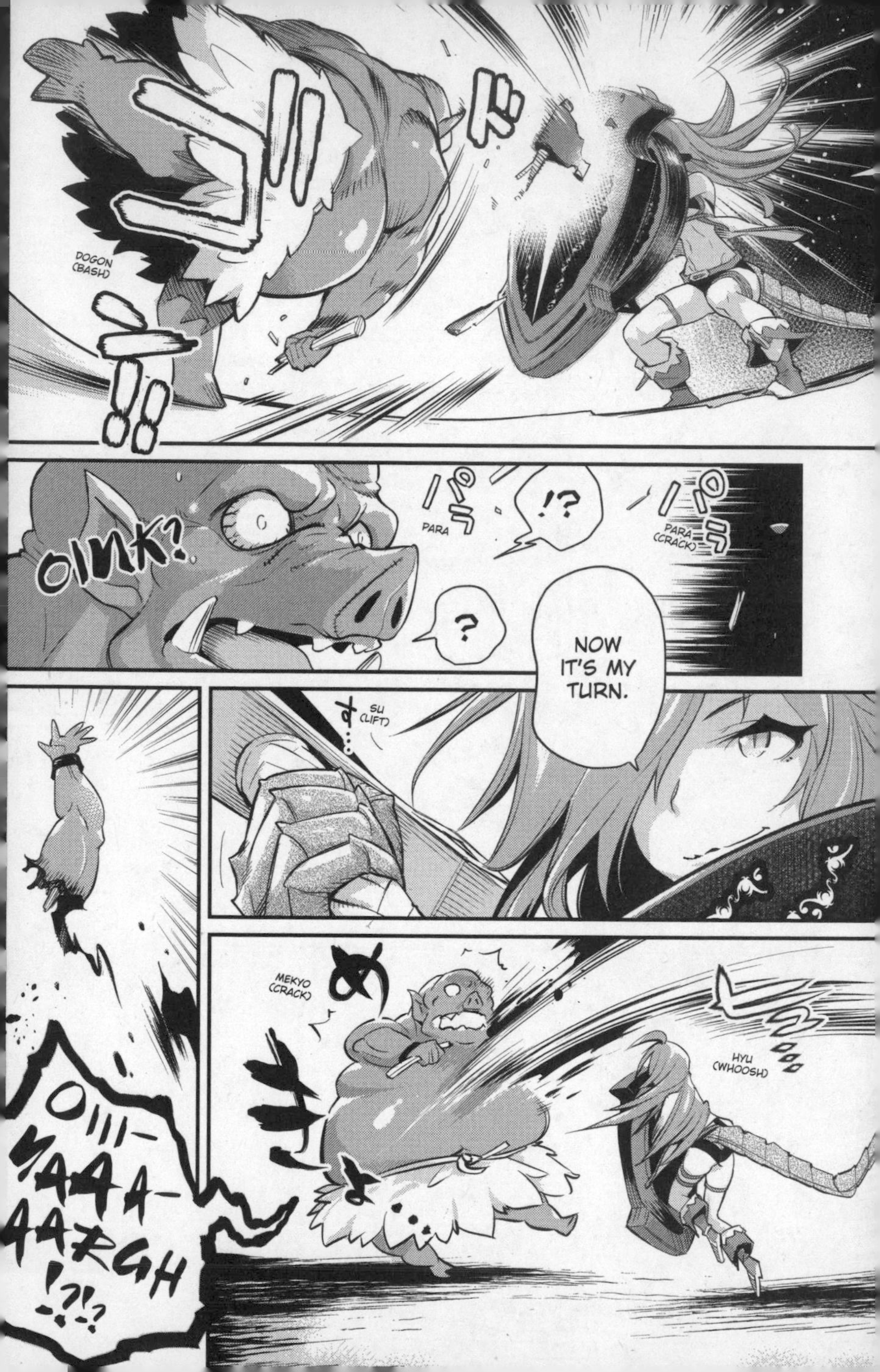
DOGON (BASH)
PARA (CRACK)
!?
PARA
NOW IT'S MY TURN.
OINK?
?
SU (LIFT)
HYU (WHOOSH)
MEKYO (CRACK)
OIII-AAAA-AARGH!?!?

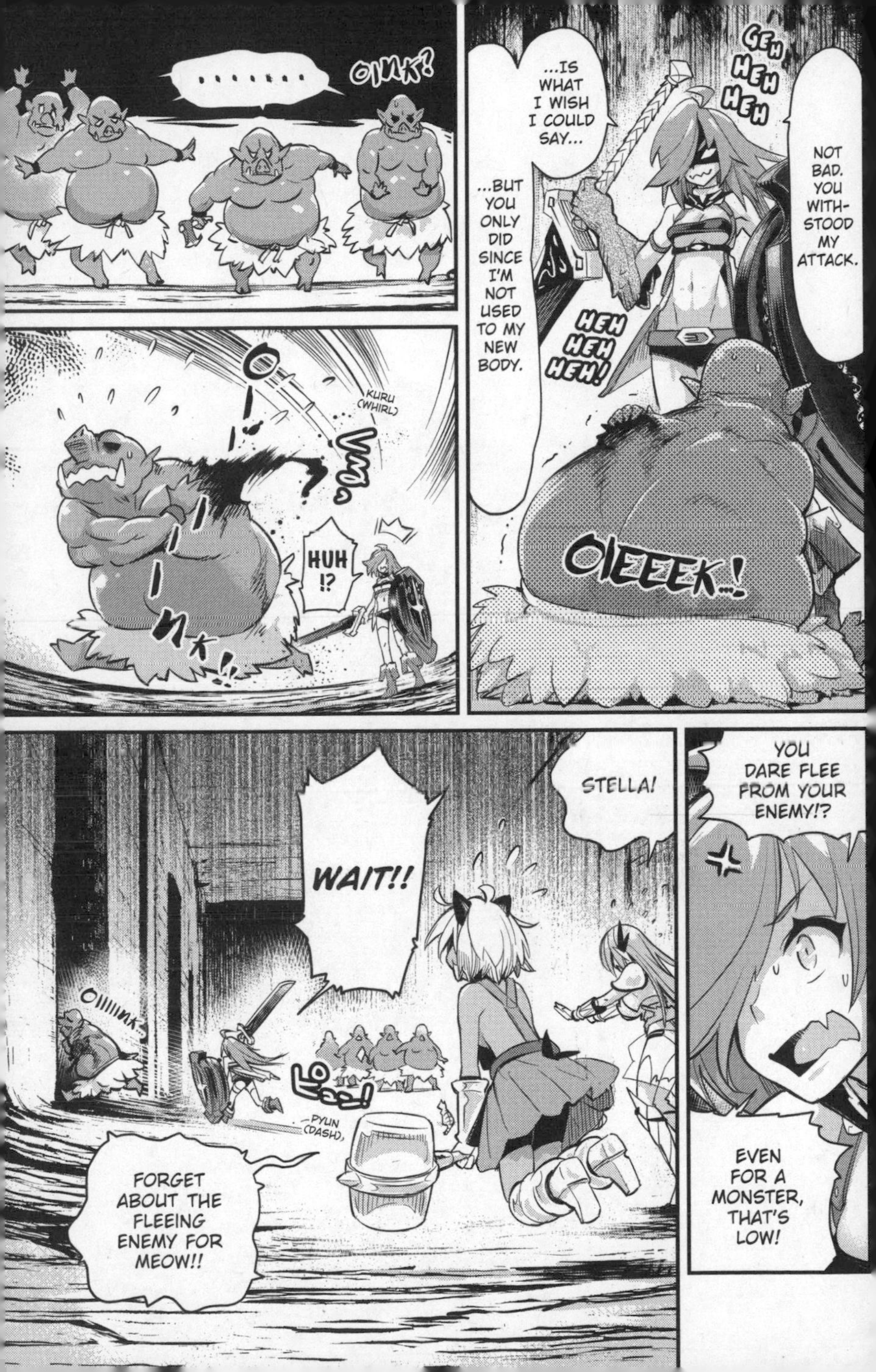
GEH HEH HEH
NOT BAD. YOU WITHSTOOD MY ATTACK.
...IS WHAT I WISH I COULD SAY...
...BUT YOU ONLY DID SINCE I'M NOT USED TO MY NEW BODY.
HEH HEH HEH!
OIEEEK...!
OINK?
....
OI---NK!!
KURU (WHIRL)
HUH!?
YOU DARE FLEE FROM YOUR ENEMY!?
EVEN FOR A MONSTER, THAT'S LOW!
STELLA!
WAIT!!
OIIIINK...
PYUN (DASH)
FORGET ABOUT THE FLEEING ENEMY FOR MEOW!!

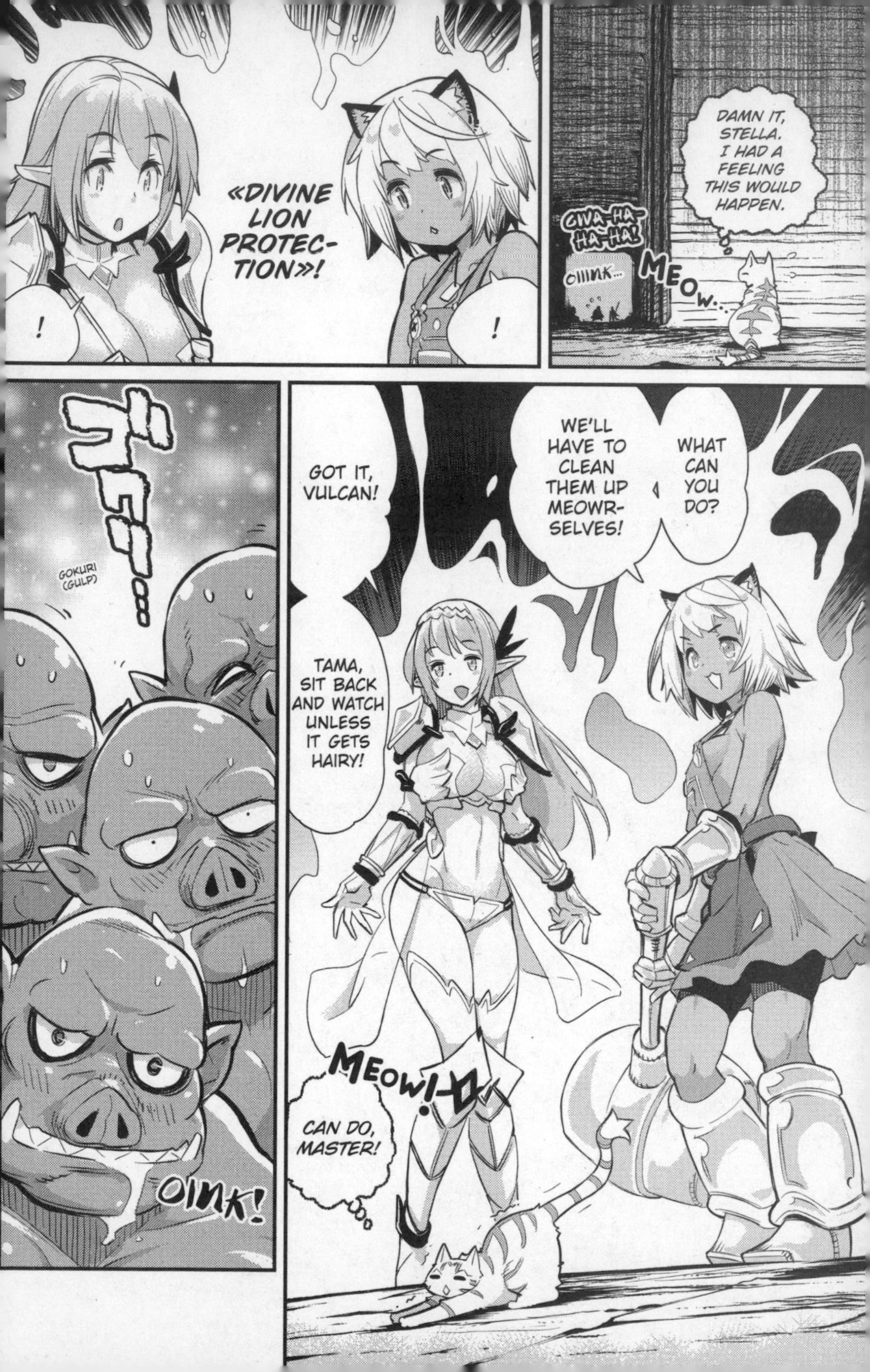
DAMN IT, STELLA. I HAD A FEELING THIS WOULD HAPPEN.
GWA-HA-HA-HA!
OIIIINK...
MEOW...
«DIVINE LION PROTECTION»!
!
!
WHAT CAN YOU DO?
WE'LL HAVE TO CLEAN THEM UP MEOWRSELVES!
GOT IT, VULCAN!
TAMA, SIT BACK AND WATCH UNLESS IT GETS HAIRY!
MEOW!-O
CAN DO, MASTER!
GOKURI (GULP)
OINK!

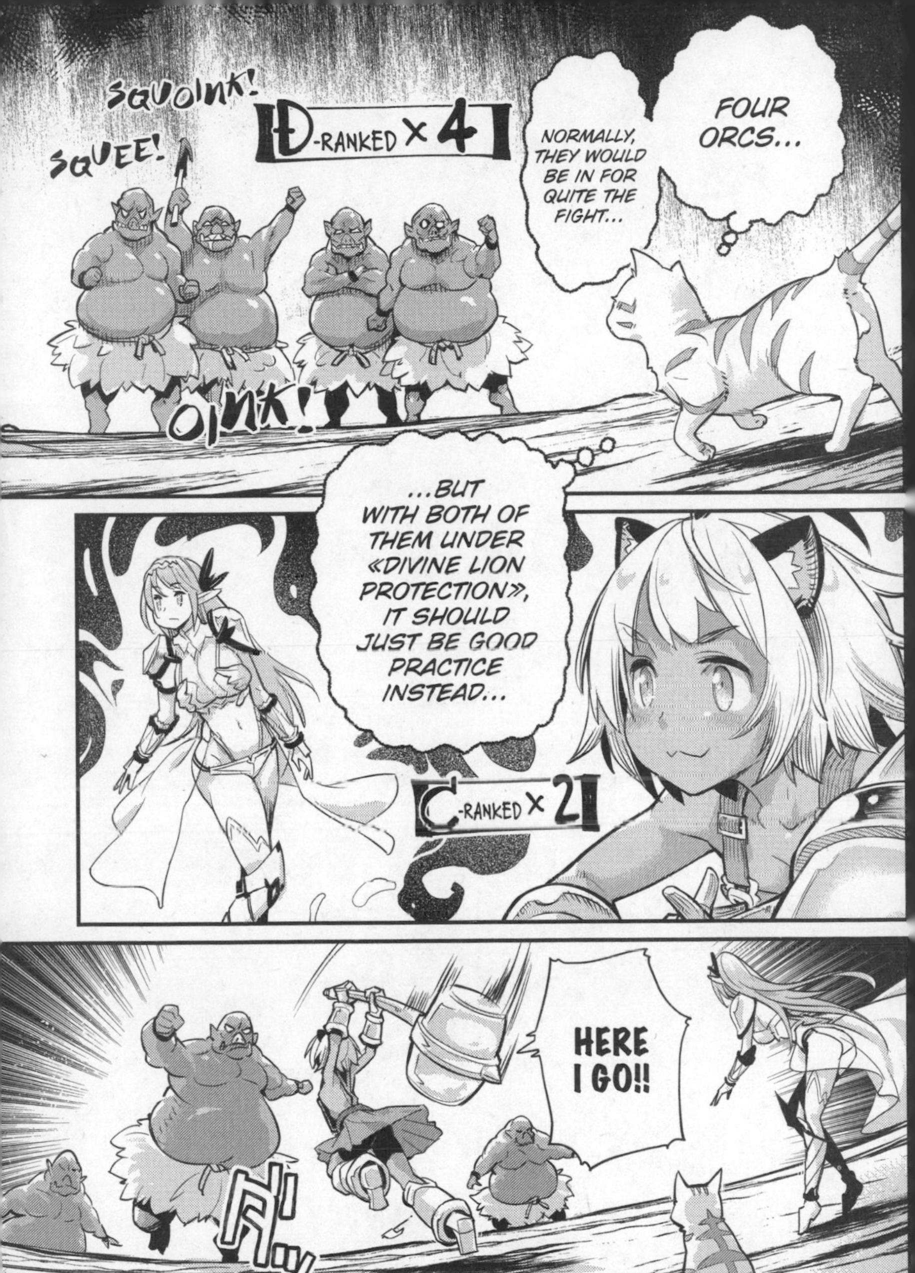
FOUR ORCS...
NORMALLY, THEY WOULD BE IN FOR QUITE THE FIGHT...
D-RANKED × 4
SQUOINK!
SQUEE!
OINK!
...BUT WITH BOTH OF THEM UNDER «DIVINE LION PROTECTION», IT SHOULD JUST BE GOOD PRACTICE INSTEAD...
C-RANKED × 2
HERE I GO!!
DA (DASH)

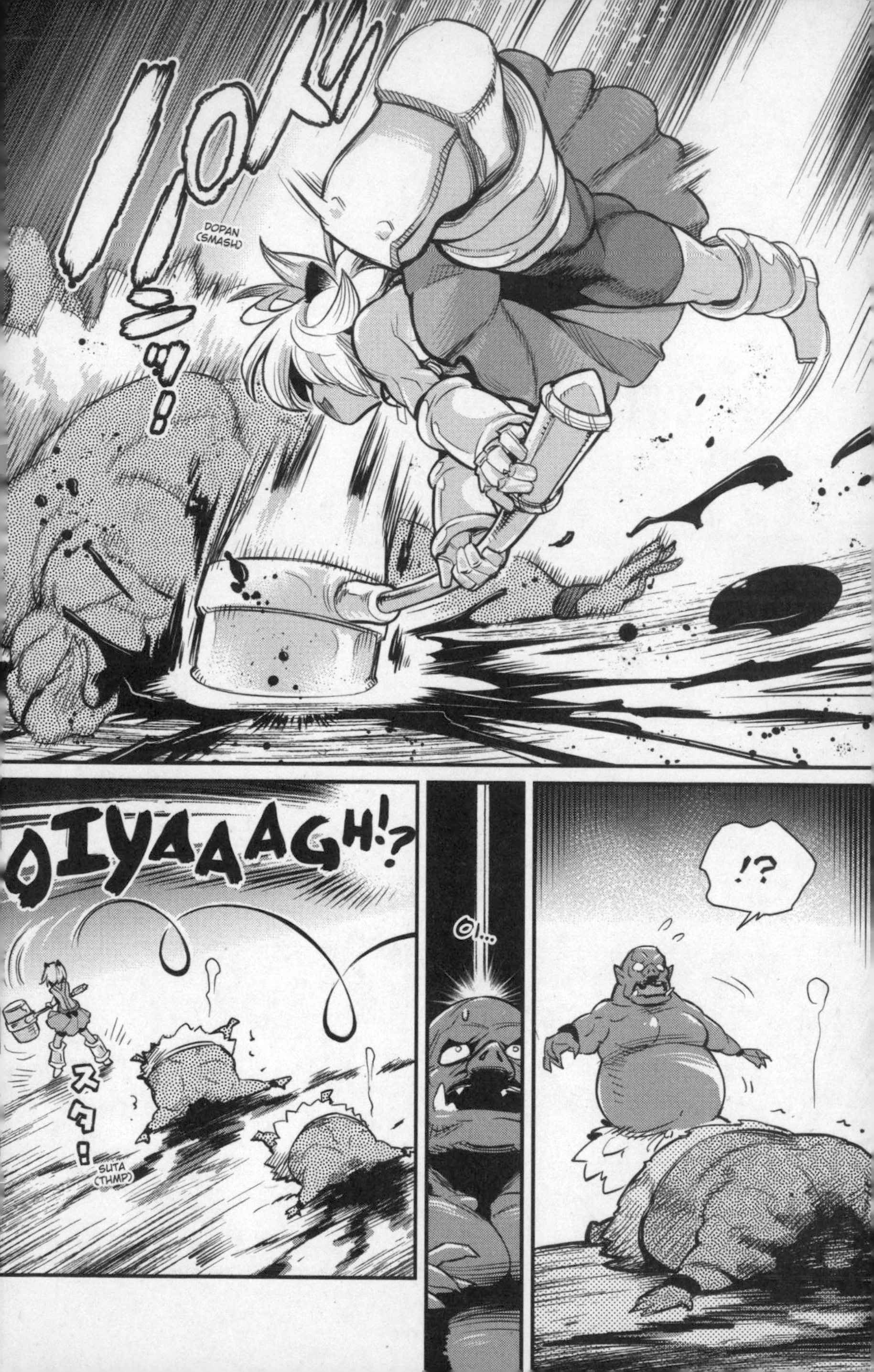
DOPAN (SMASH)
!?
OI...
OIYAAAGH!?
SUTA (THMP)

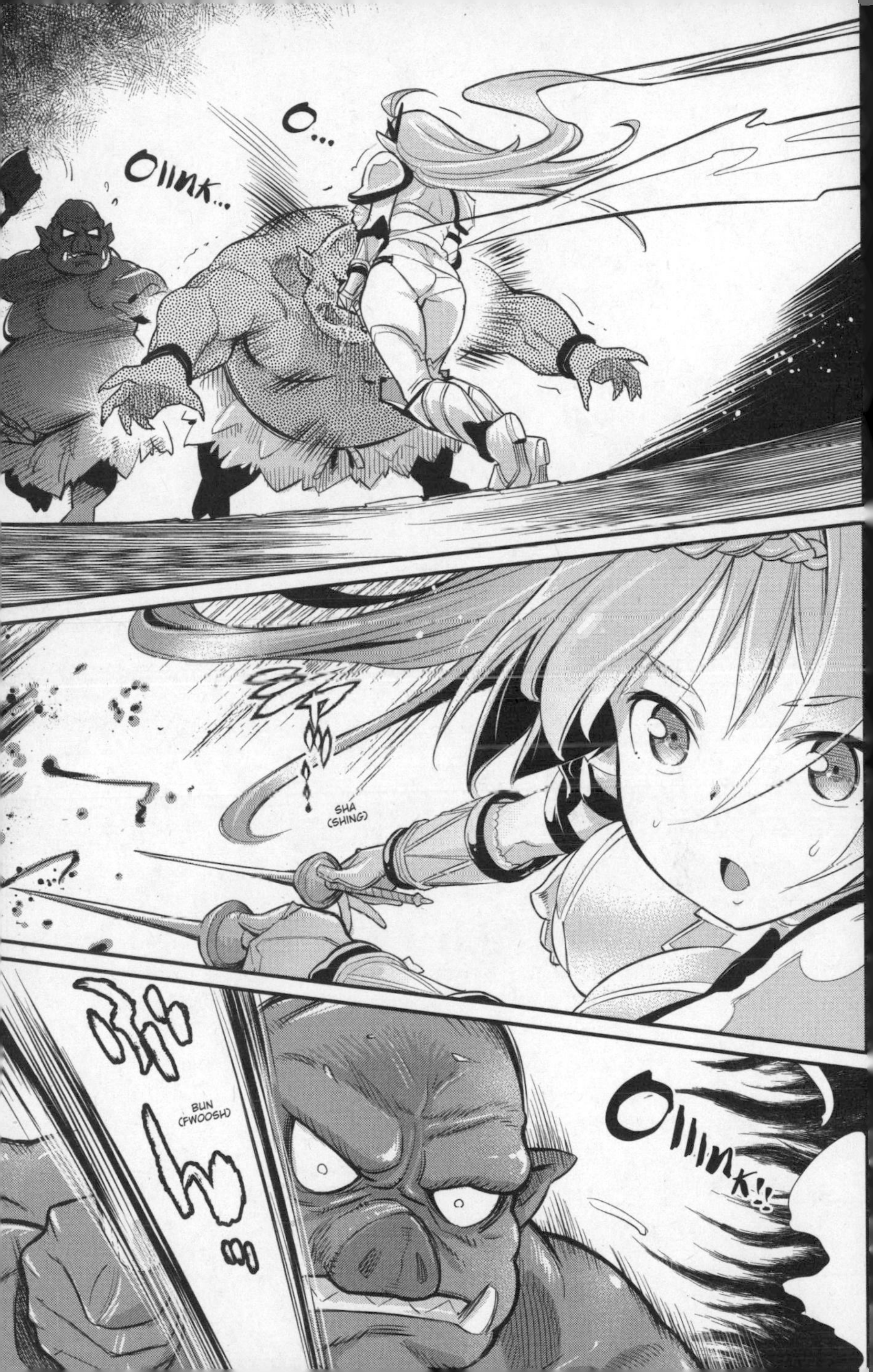
O...
Ollnk...
SHA (SHING)
Olllnk!!
BUN (FWOOSH)

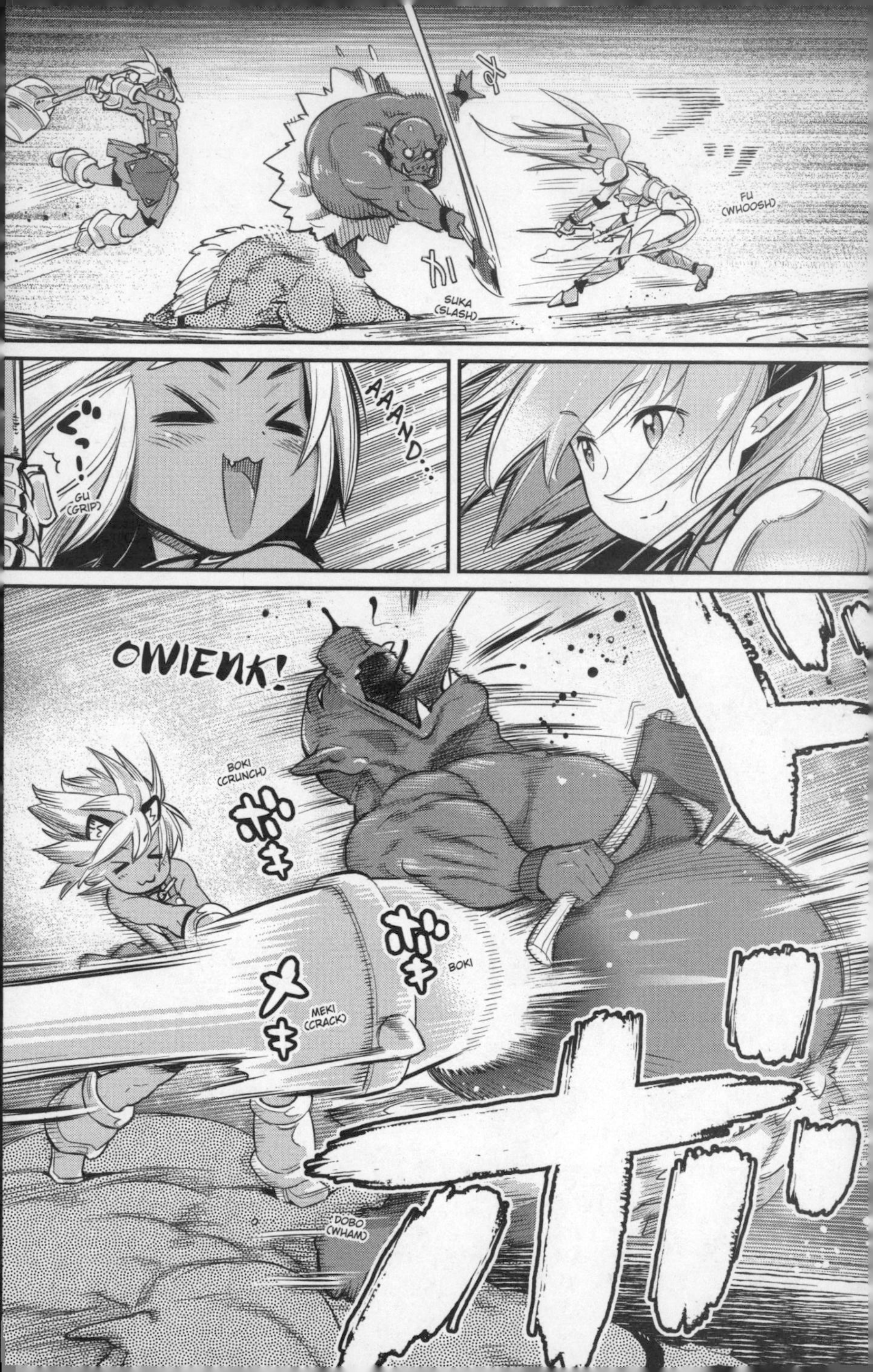

FU (WHOOSH)
SUKA (SLASH)
AAAND...
GU (GRIP)
OWIENK!
BOKI (CRUNCH)
BOKI
MEKI (CRACK)
DOBO (WHAM)

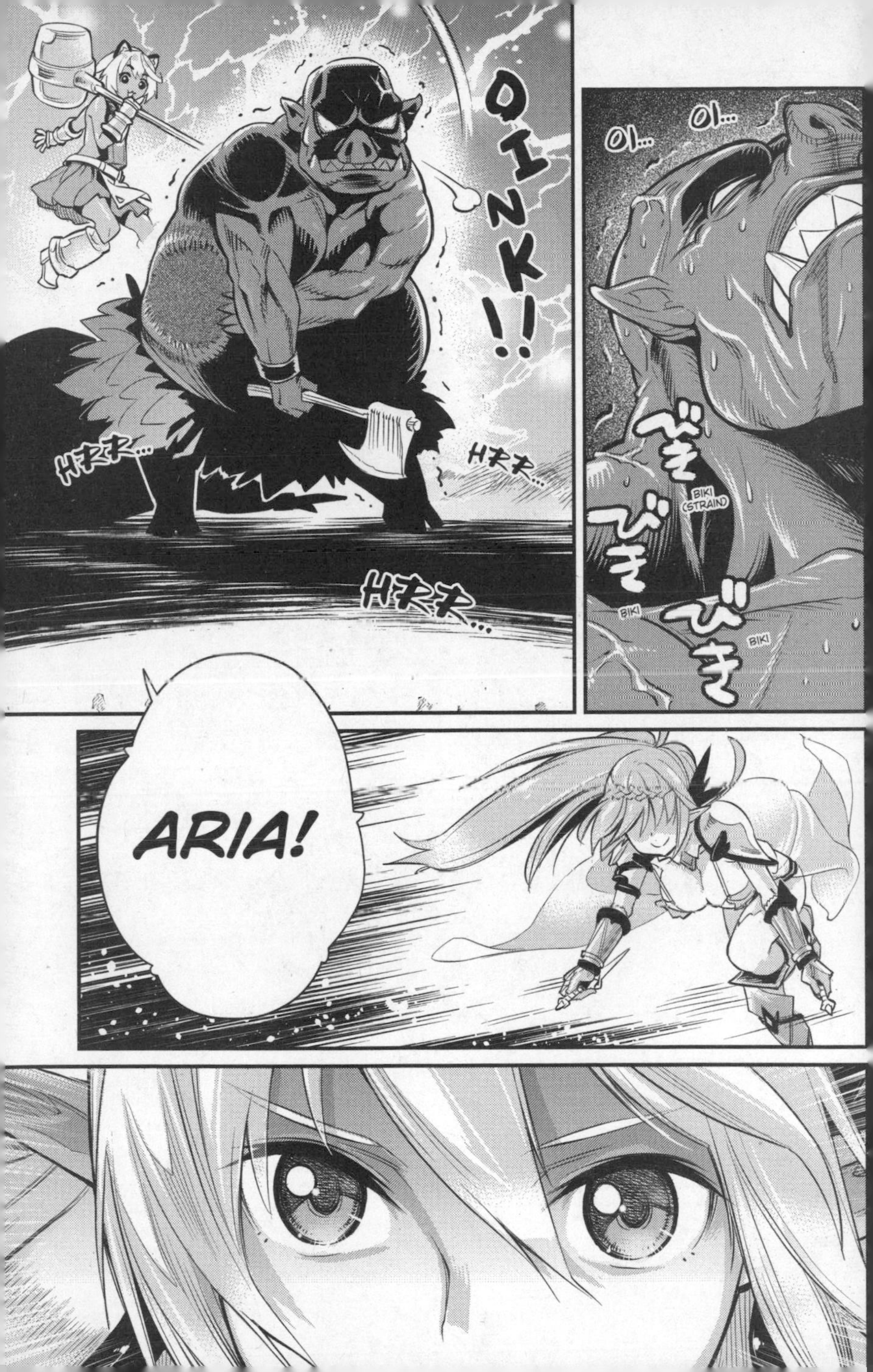
OI... OI...
べき
BIKI (STRAIN)
びき
BIKI
びき
BIKI
OINK!!
HRR...
HRR...
HRR...
ARIA!

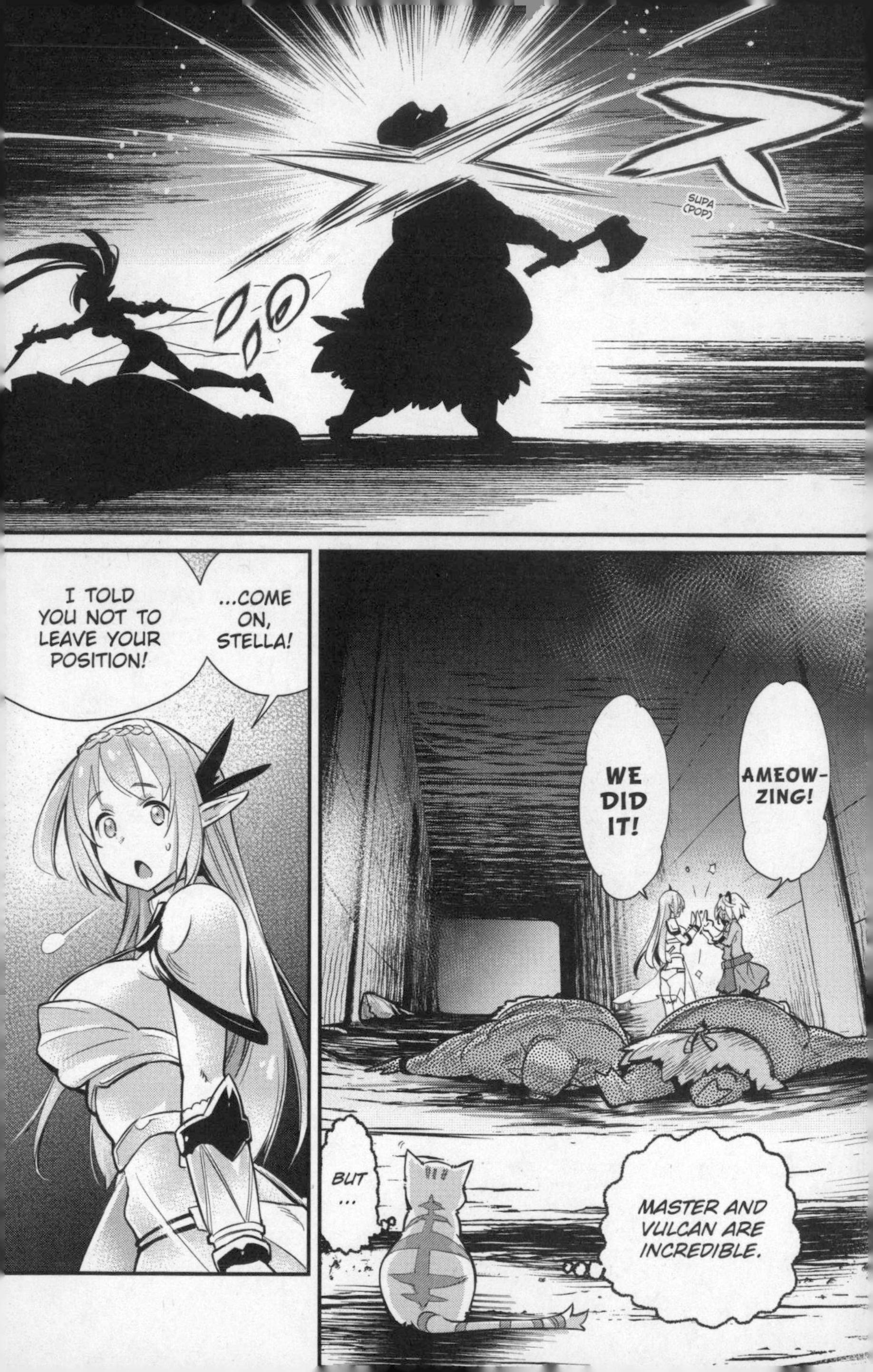
SUPA (POP)
AMEOW-ZING!
WE DID IT!
MASTER AND VULCAN ARE INCREDIBLE.
BUT ...
...COME ON, STELLA!
I TOLD YOU NOT TO LEAVE YOUR POSITION!

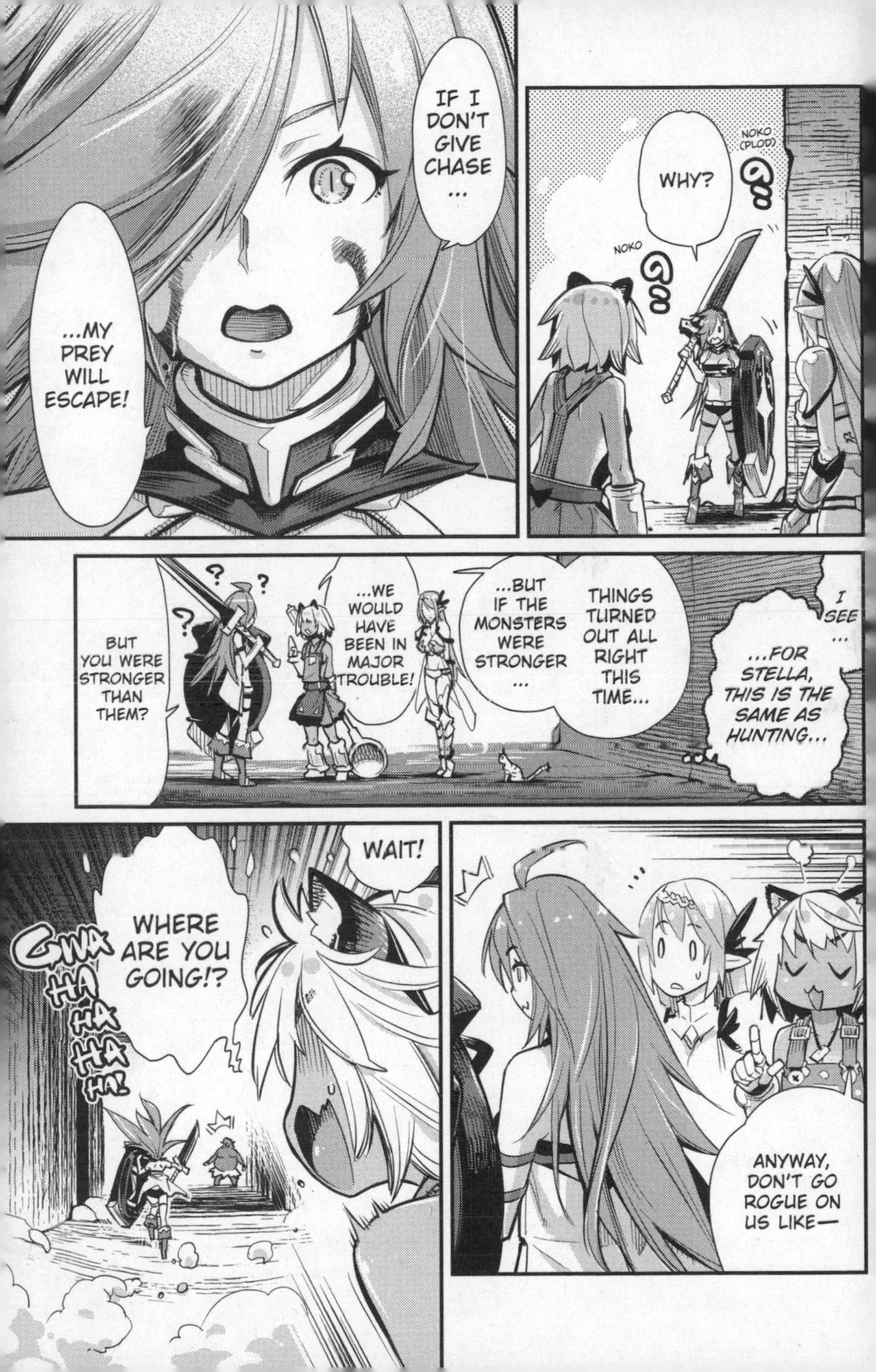
WHY?
NOKO (PLOD)
NOKO
IF I DON'T GIVE CHASE...
...MY PREY WILL ESCAPE!
I SEE...
...FOR STELLA, THIS IS THE SAME AS HUNTING...
THINGS TURNED OUT ALL RIGHT THIS TIME...
...BUT IF THE MONSTERS WERE STRONGER...
...WE WOULD HAVE BEEN IN MAJOR TROUBLE!
BUT YOU WERE STRONGER THAN THEM?
ANYWAY, DON'T GO ROGUE ON US LIKE—
WAIT!
WHERE ARE YOU GOING!?
GWA HA HA HA HA!

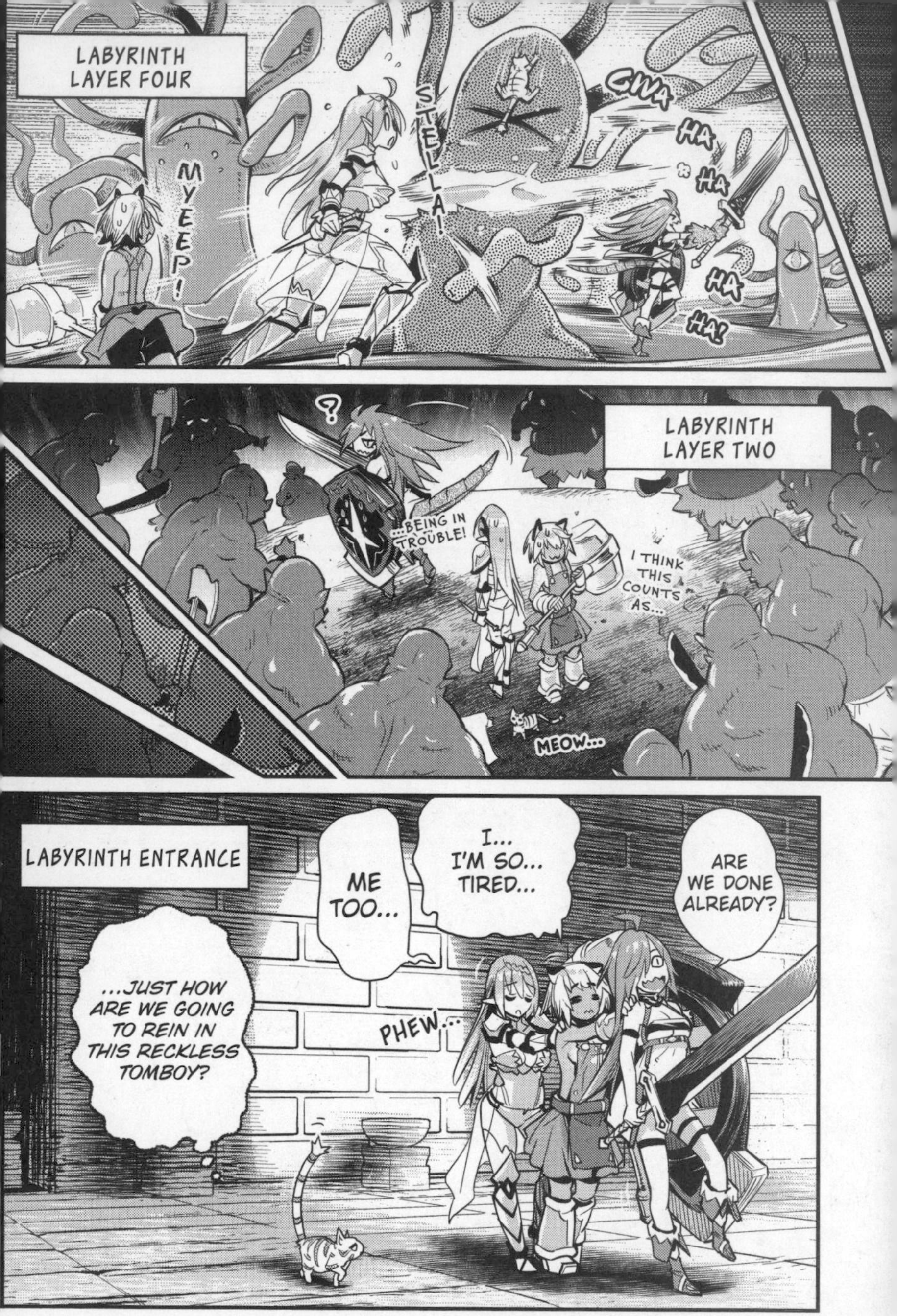
GWA HA HA HA HA!
STELLA!
LABYRINTH LAYER FOUR
MYEEP!
LABYRINTH LAYER TWO
I THINK THIS COUNTS AS...
...BEING IN TROUBLE!
MEOW...
ARE WE DONE ALREADY?
I... I'M SO... TIRED...
ME TOO...
LABYRINTH ENTRANCE
PHEW...
...JUST HOW ARE WE GOING TO REIN IN THIS RECKLESS TOMBOY?

#26 — A Special Mission

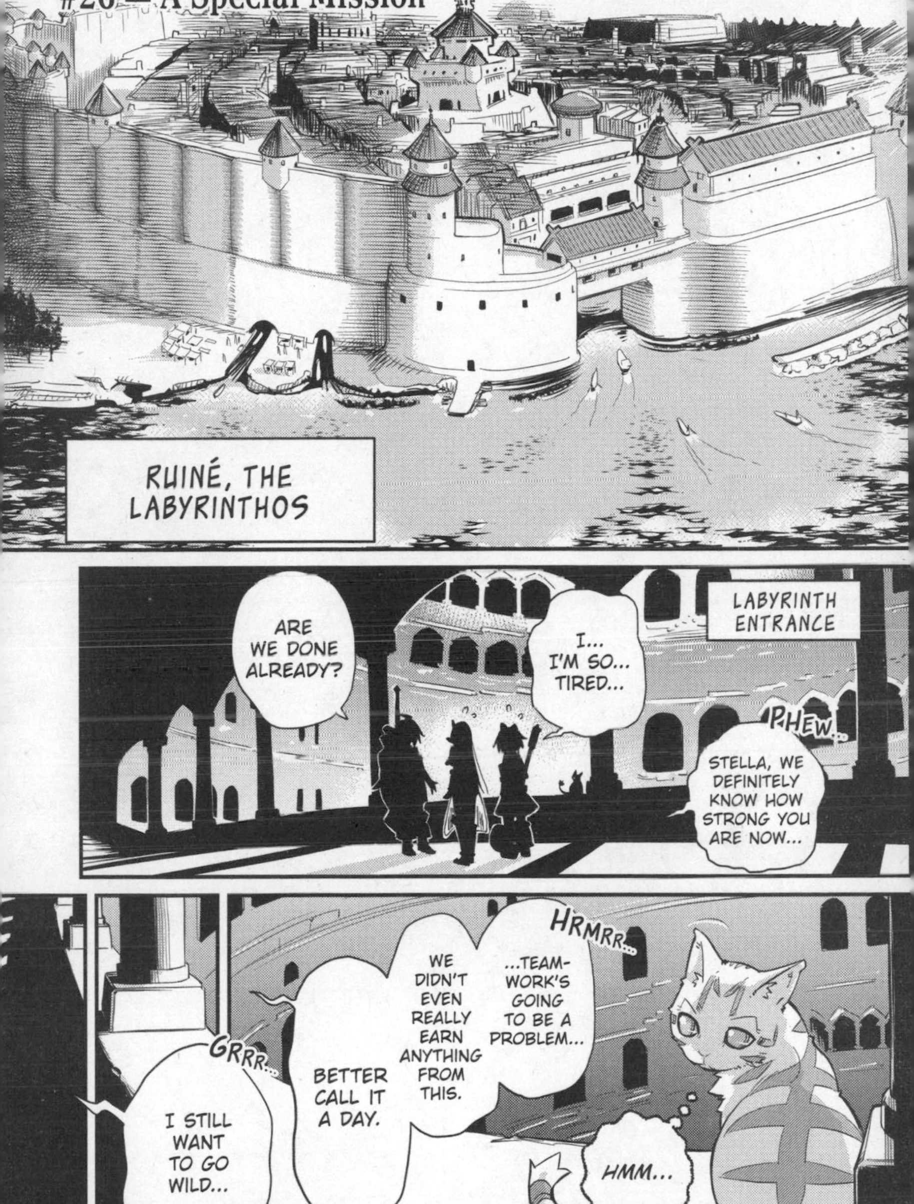
RUINÉ, THE LABYRINTHOS
LABYRINTH ENTRANCE
I... I'M SO... TIRED...
ARE WE DONE ALREADY?
PHEW...
STELLA, WE DEFINITELY KNOW HOW STRONG YOU ARE NOW...
HRMRR...
HMM...
...TEAM-WORK'S GOING TO BE A PROBLEM...
WE DIDN'T EVEN REALLY EARN ANYTHING FROM THIS.
BETTER CALL IT A DAY.
GRRR...
I STILL WANT TO GO WILD...

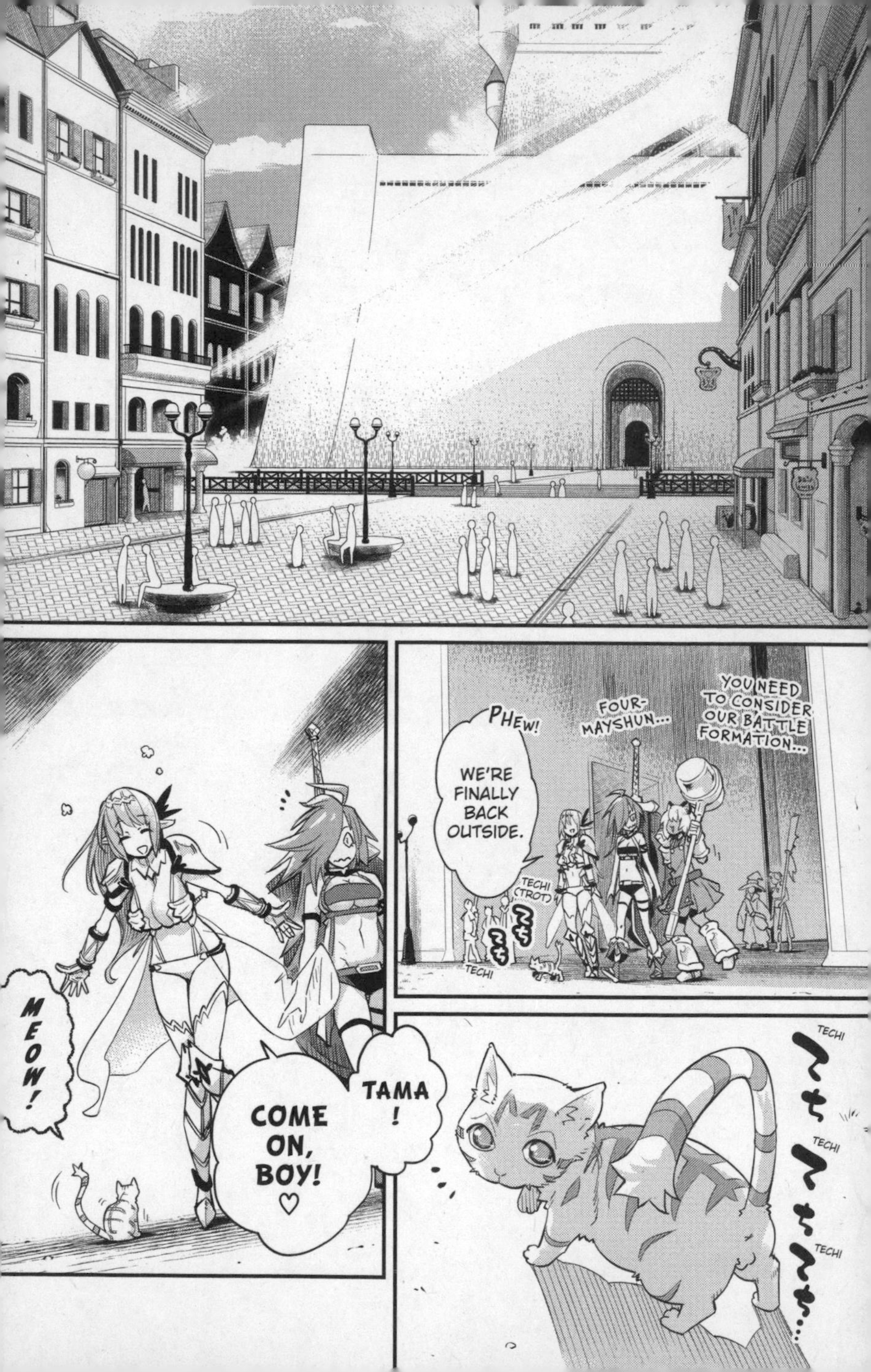

YOU NEED TO CONSIDER OUR BATTLE FORMATION...
FOUR-MAYSHUN...
PHEW!
WE'RE FINALLY BACK OUTSIDE.
TECHI (TROT)
TECHI
TECHI
TECHI
TECHI
TAMA!
COME ON, BOY! ♡
MEOW!

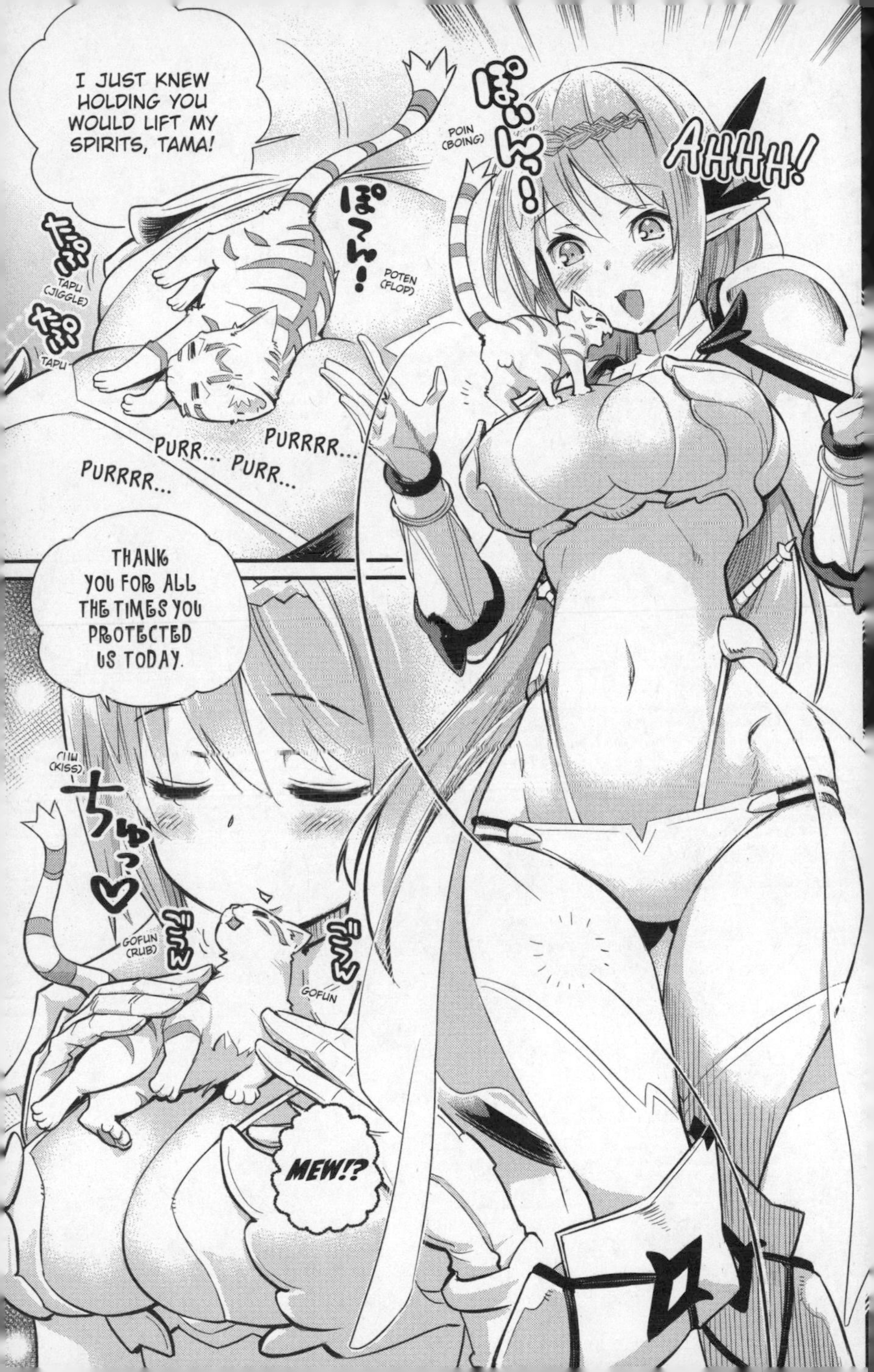
ぽいんっ!!
POIN (BOING)
AHHH!
ぽてん!
POTEN (FLOP)
I JUST KNEW HOLDING YOU WOULD LIFT MY SPIRITS, TAMA!
たぷ
TAPU (JIGGLE)
たぷ
TAPU
PURRRR...
PURR... PURR...
PURRRR...
THANK YOU FOR ALL THE TIMES YOU PROTECTED US TODAY.
ちゅっ♥
CHU (KISS)
ごふん
GOFUN (RUB)
ごふん
GOFUN
MEW!?

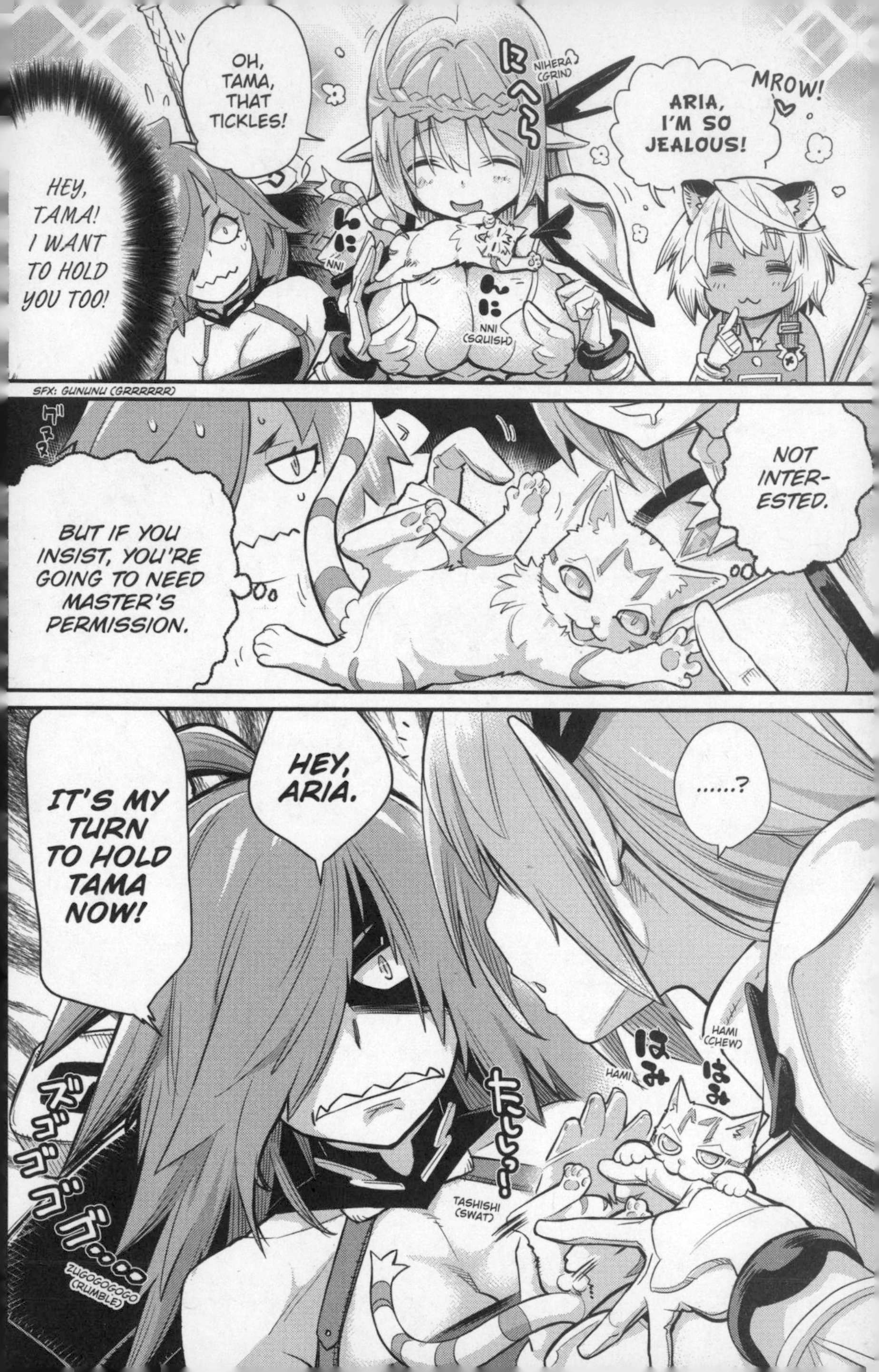
MROW!
ARIA, I'M SO JEALOUS!
にへら
NIHERA (GRIN)
OH, TAMA, THAT TICKLES!
んに
NNI (SQUISH)
んに
NNI
HEY, TAMA! I WANT TO HOLD YOU TOO!
SFX: GUNUNU (GRRRRRR)
NOT INTER-ESTED.
BUT IF YOU INSIST, YOU'RE GOING TO NEED MASTER'S PERMISSION.
......?
HEY, ARIA.
IT'S MY TURN TO HOLD TAMA NOW!
はみ
HAMI (CHEW)
はみ
HAMI
たしっ
TASHISHI (SWAT)
ズゴゴゴ…
ZUGOGOGOGO (RUMBLE)

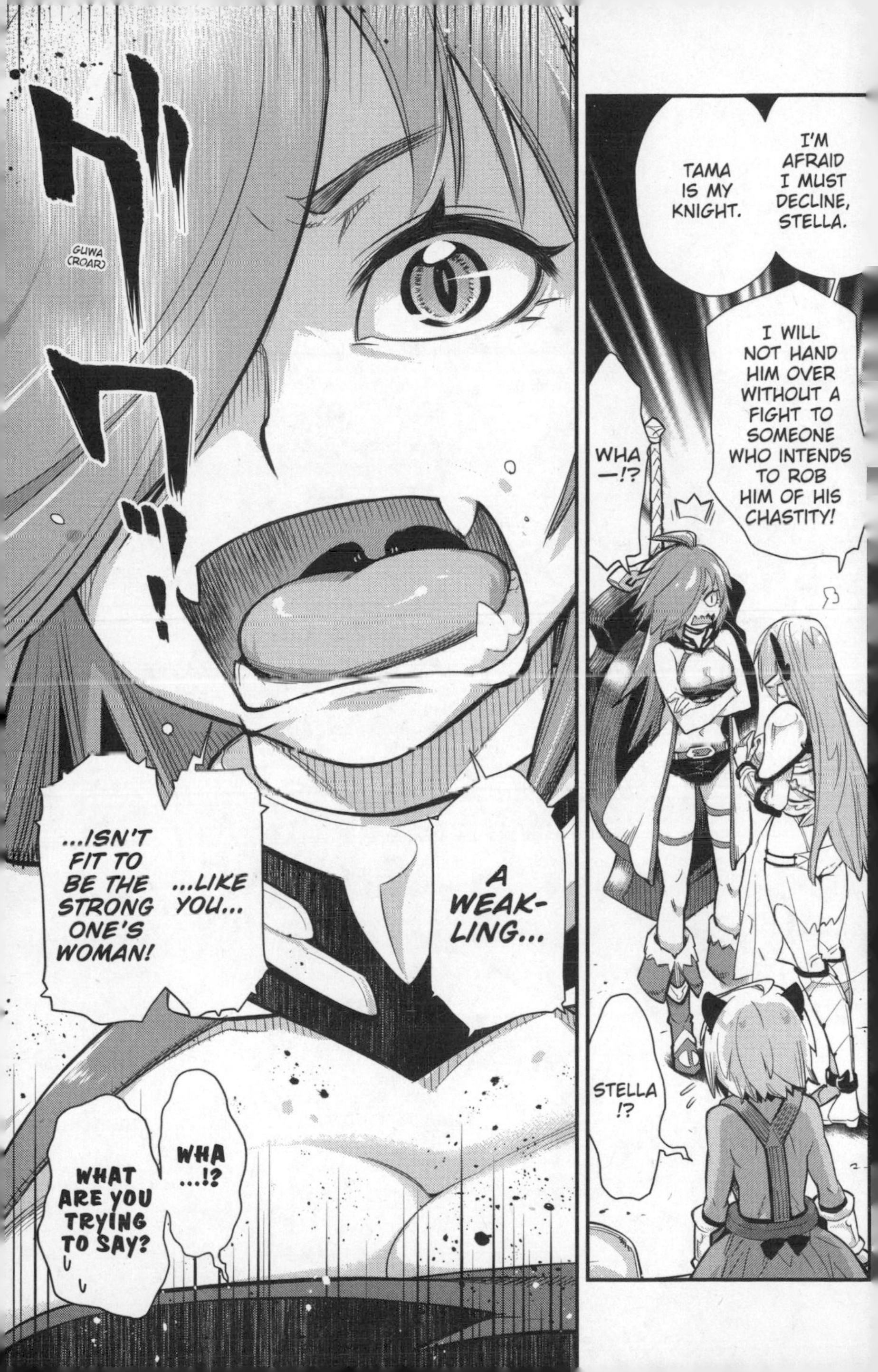
I'M AFRAID I MUST DECLINE, STELLA.
TAMA IS MY KNIGHT.
I WILL NOT HAND HIM OVER WITHOUT A FIGHT TO SOMEONE WHO INTENDS TO ROB HIM OF HIS CHASTITY!
WHA—!?
STELLA !?
GUWA (ROAR)
A WEAK-LING...
...LIKE YOU...
...ISN'T FIT TO BE THE STRONG ONE'S WOMAN!
WHA ...!?
WHAT ARE YOU TRYING TO SAY?

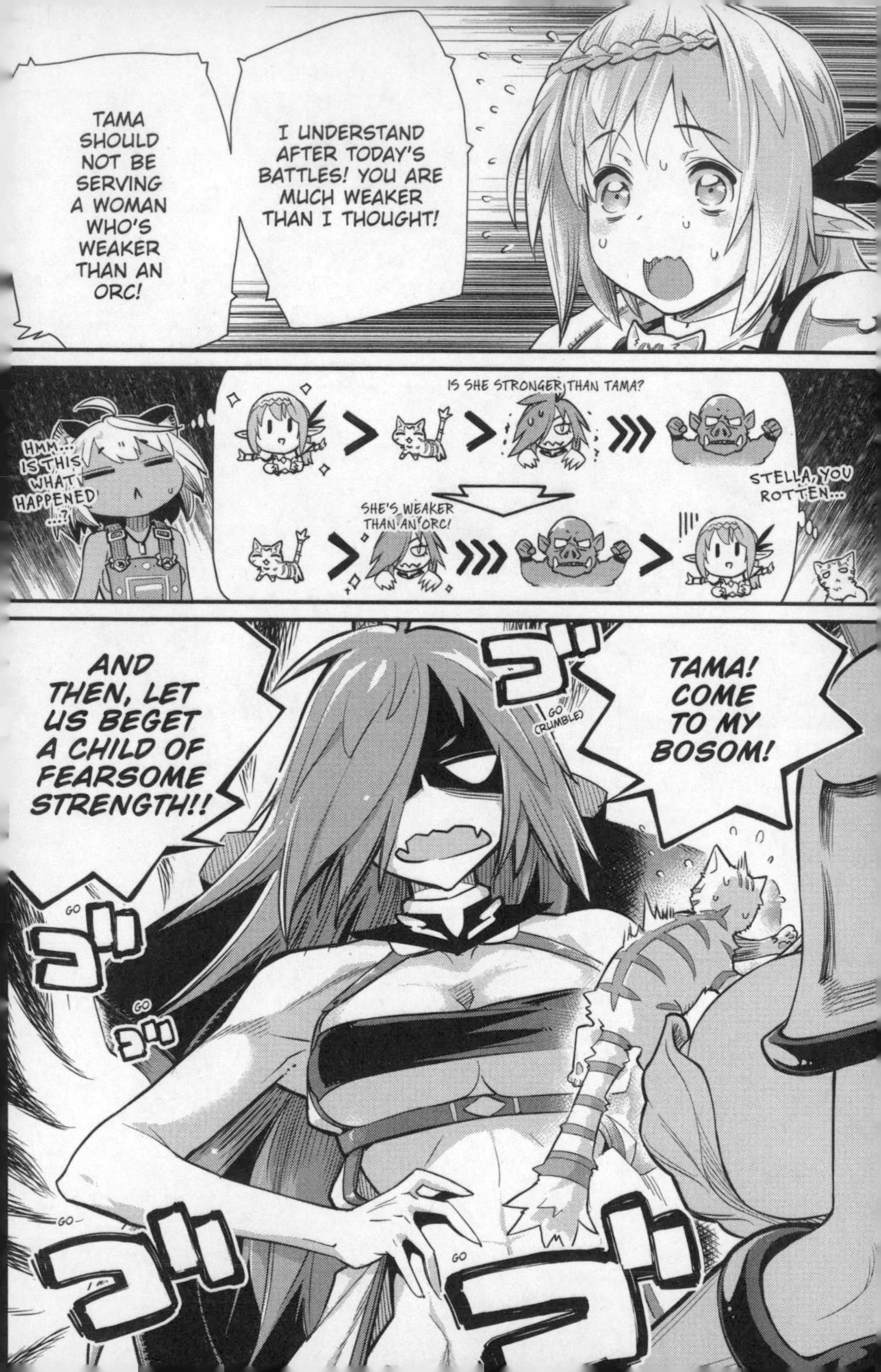
I UNDERSTAND AFTER TODAY'S BATTLES! YOU ARE MUCH WEAKER THAN I THOUGHT!
TAMA SHOULD NOT BE SERVING A WOMAN WHO'S WEAKER THAN AN ORC!
STELLA, YOU ROTTEN...
IS SHE STRONGER THAN TAMA?
SHE'S WEAKER THAN AN ORC!
HMM... IS THIS WHAT HAPPENED...?
TAMA! COME TO MY BOSOM!
ゴ
GO (RUMBLE)
AND THEN, LET US BEGET A CHILD OF FEARSOME STRENGTH!!
GO
ゴ
GO
ゴ
GO
ゴ
GO
ゴ

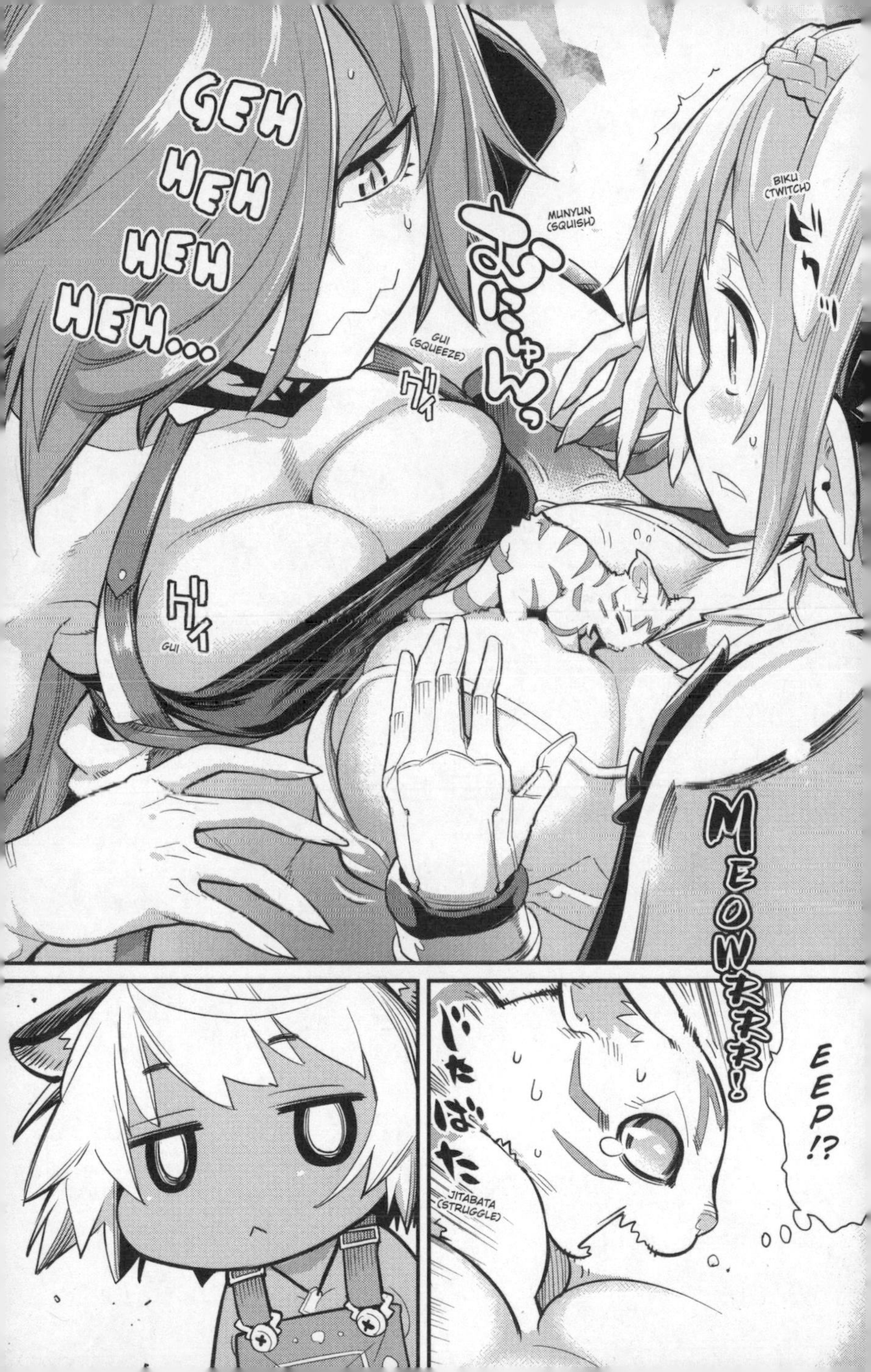
BIKU (TWITCH)
MUNYUN (SQUISH)
むにゅん
GEH HEH HEH HEH...
GUI (SQUEEZE)
グイ
グイ
GUI
MEOWRRR!
EEP!?
じたばた
JITABATA (STRUGGLE)

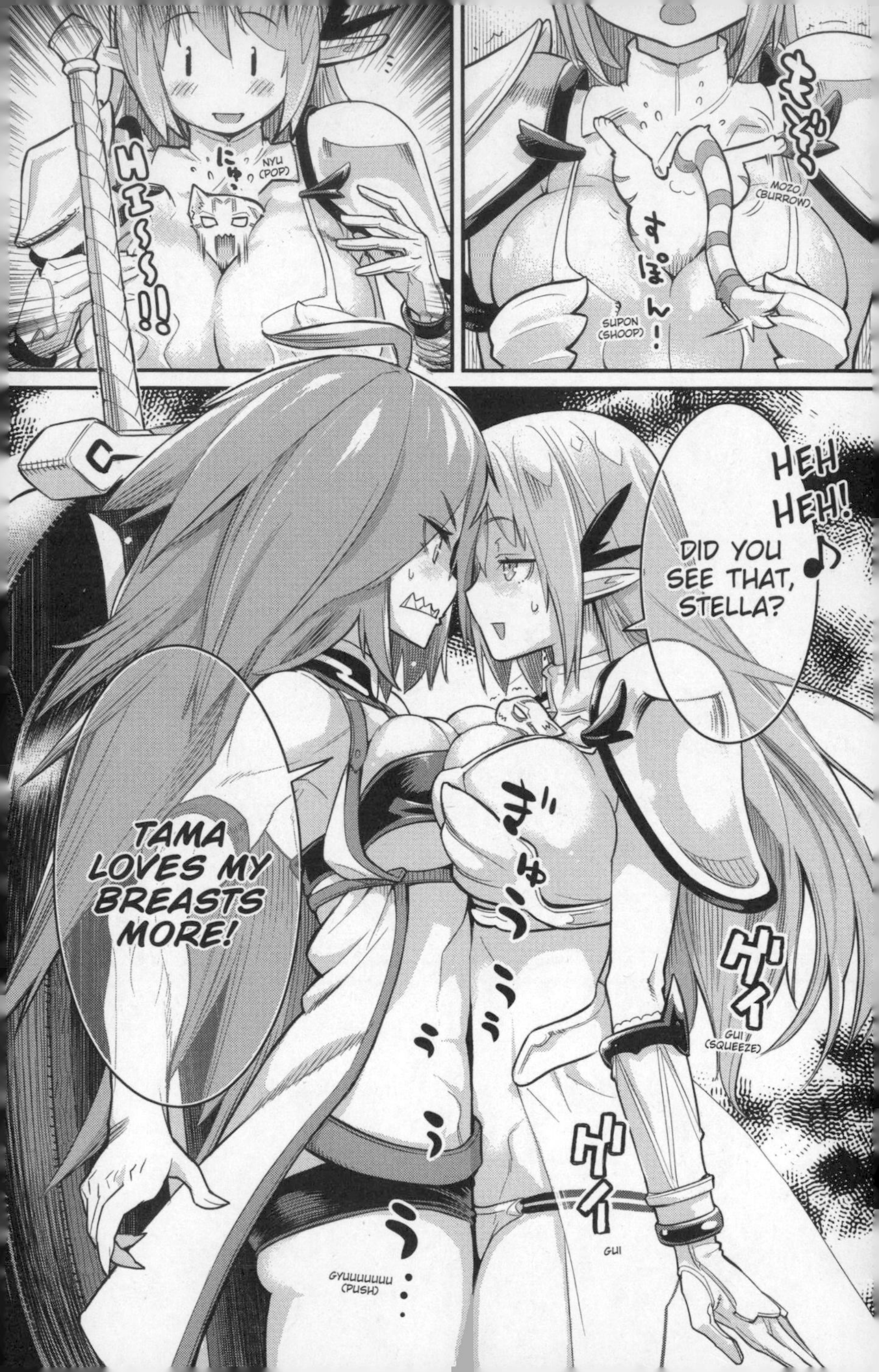
もぞ…
MOZO (BURROW)
すぽん！
SUPON (SHOOP)
にゅ
NYU (POP)
HI~~!!
HEH HEH! ♪
DID YOU SEE THAT, STELLA?
TAMA LOVES MY BREASTS MORE!
グイ
GUI (SQUEEZE)
グイ
GUI
ぎゅううう…
GYUUUUUUU (PUSH)

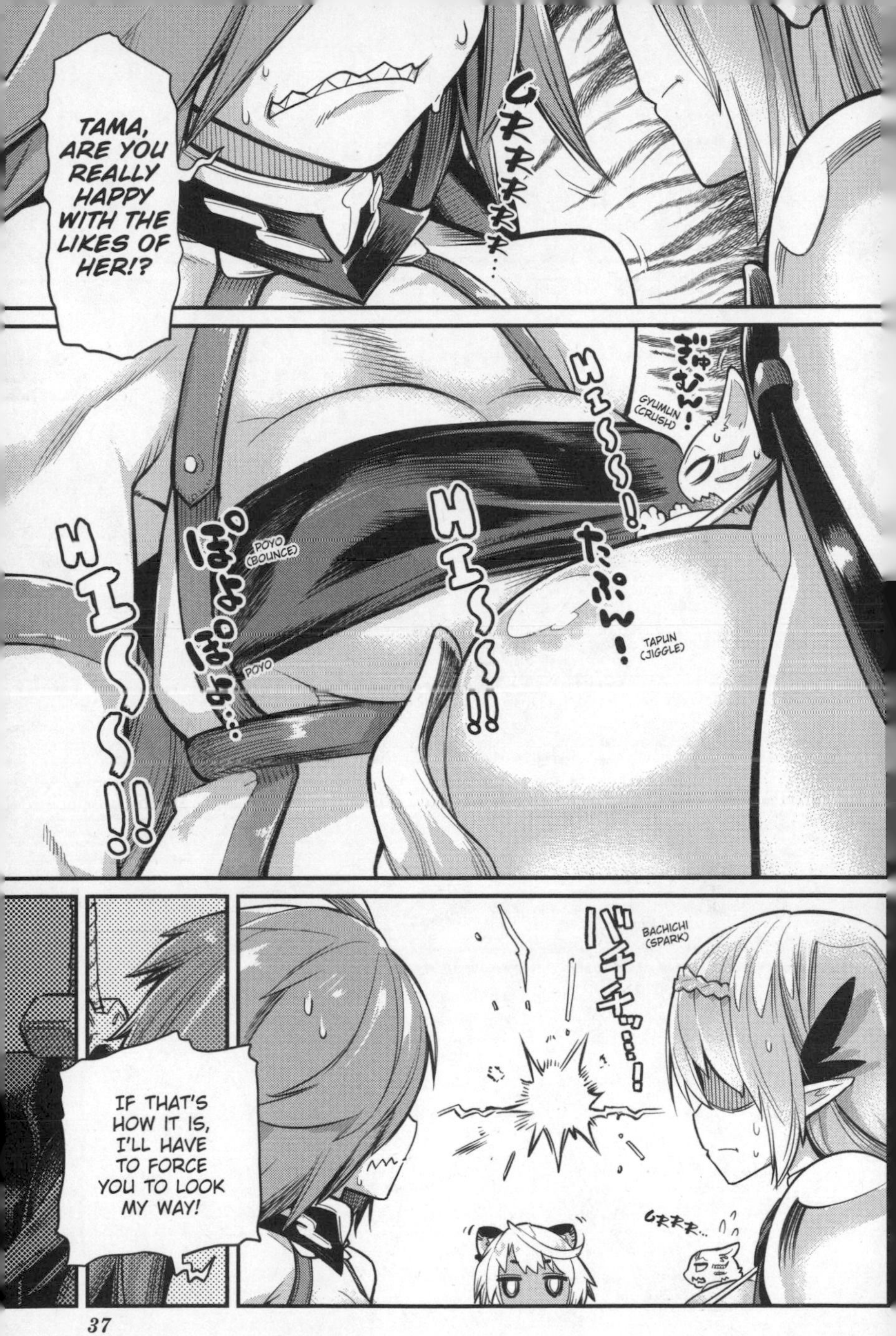
GRRRRRR...
TAMA, ARE YOU REALLY HAPPY WITH THE LIKES OF HER!?
ぎゅむん！
GYUMUN (CRUSH)
HII~~!
たぷん！
TAPUN (JIGGLE)
HII~~!!
ぽよぽよ…
POYO (BOUNCE)
POYO
HII~~!!
バチチッ…！
BACHICHI (SPARK)
GRRR...
IF THAT'S HOW IT IS, I'LL HAVE TO FORCE YOU TO LOOK MY WAY!

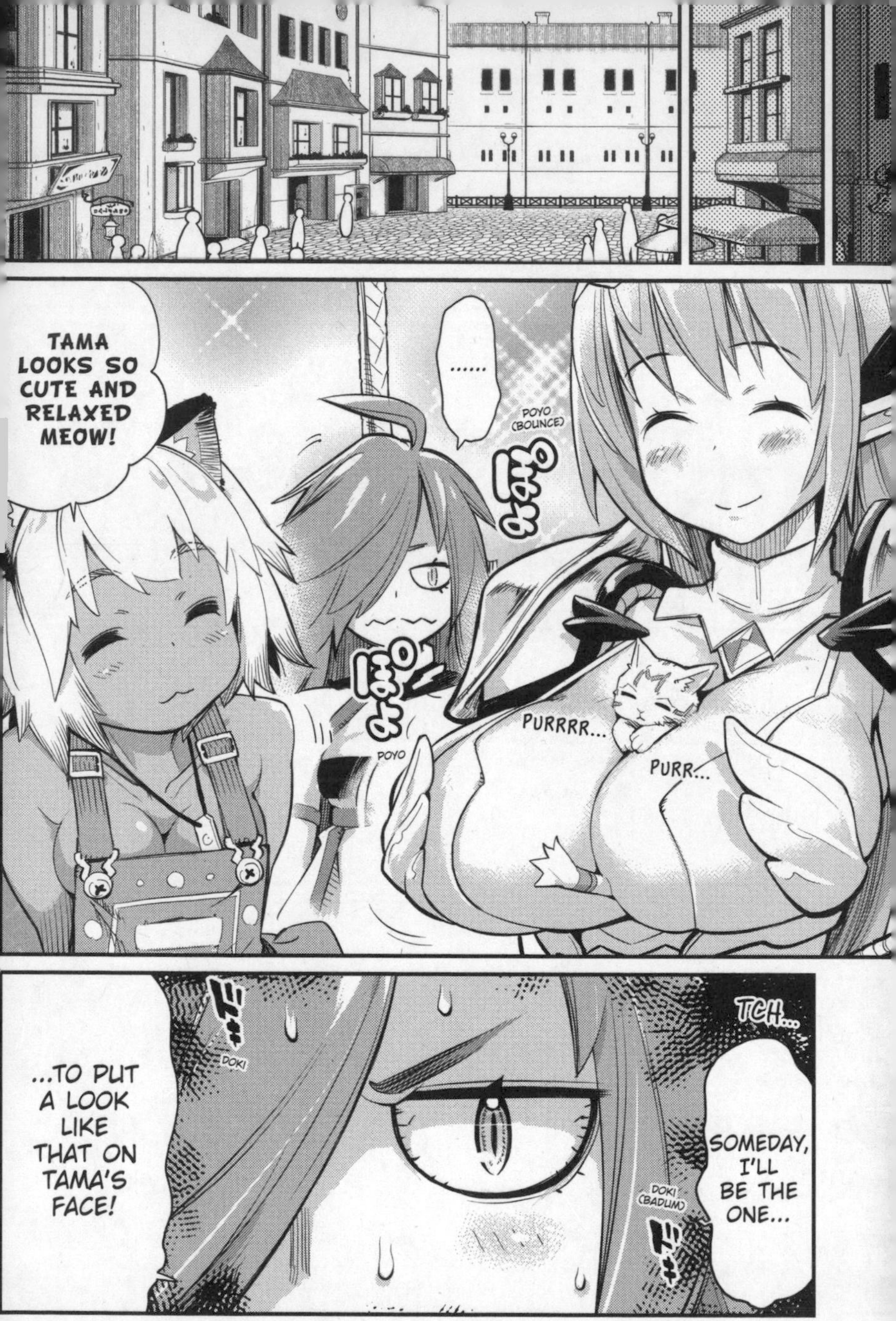
......
POYO (BOUNCE)
TAMA LOOKS SO CUTE AND RELAXED MEOW!
PURRRR...
PURR...
POYO
TCH...
SOMEDAY, I'LL BE THE ONE...
DOKI (BADUM)
DOKI
...TO PUT A LOOK LIKE THAT ON TAMA'S FACE!

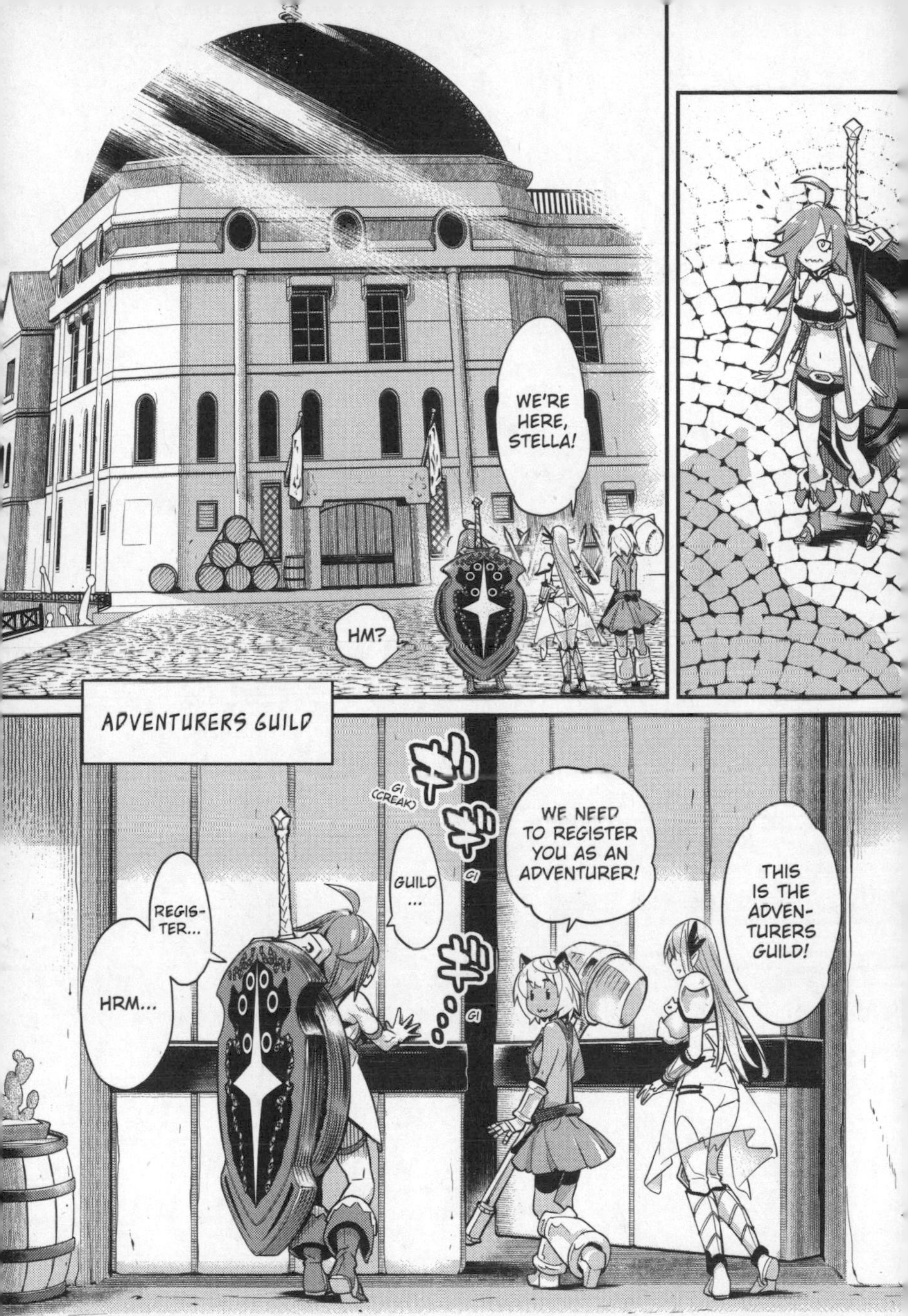
WE'RE HERE, STELLA!
HM?
ADVENTURERS GUILD
THIS IS THE ADVEN-TURERS GUILD!
WE NEED TO REGISTER YOU AS AN ADVENTURER!
GI (CREAK)
GI
GI
GUILD ...
REGIS-TER...
HRM...

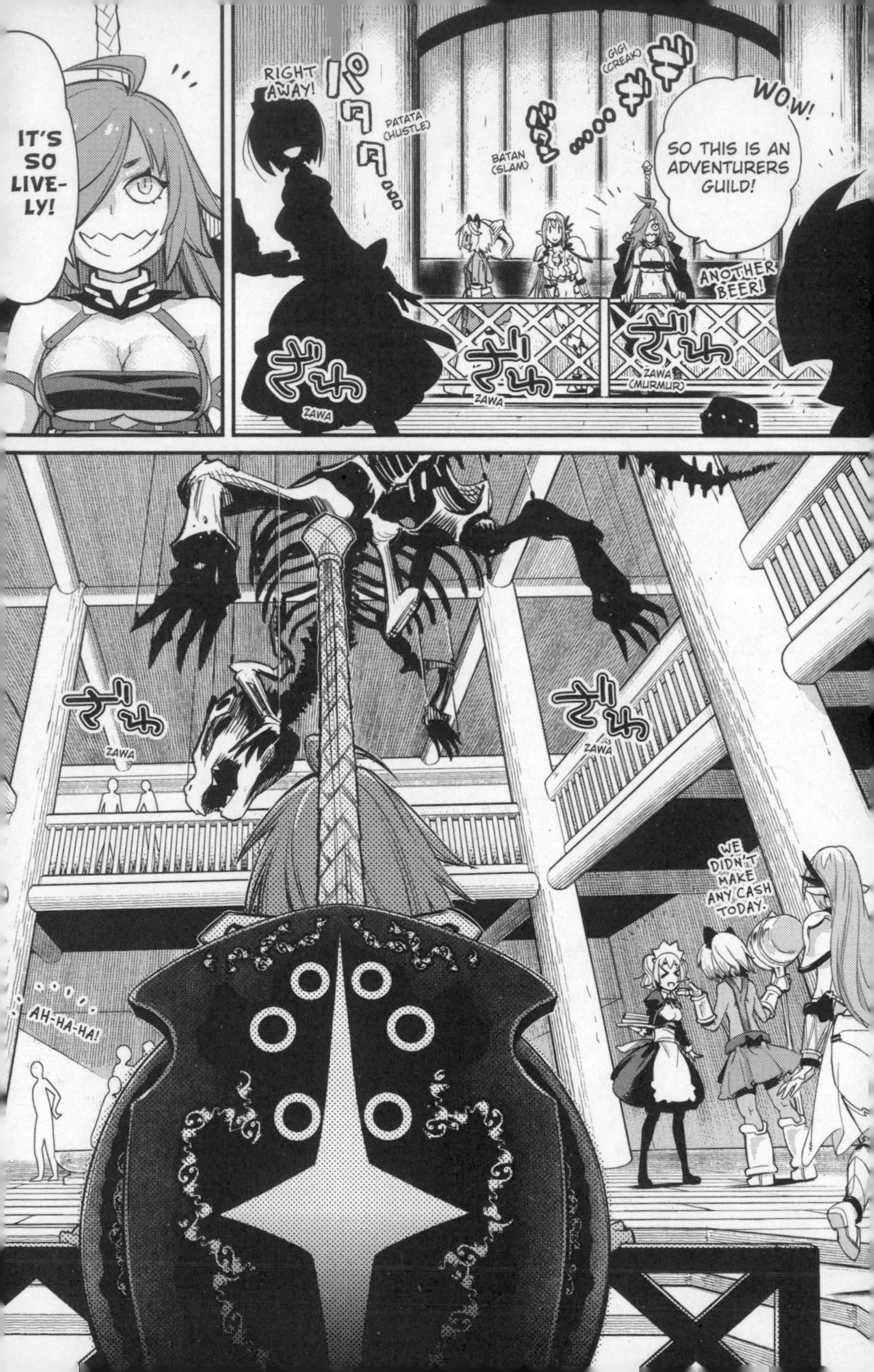
WOW!
SO THIS IS AN ADVENTURERS GUILD!
GIGI (CREAK)
BATAN (SLAM)
PATATA (HUSTLE)
RIGHT AWAY!
ANOTHER BEER!
ZAWA (MURMUR)
ZAWA
ZAWA
IT'S SO LIVE-LY!
ZAWA
WE DIDN'T MAKE ANY CASH TODAY.
ZAWA
AH-HA-HA!

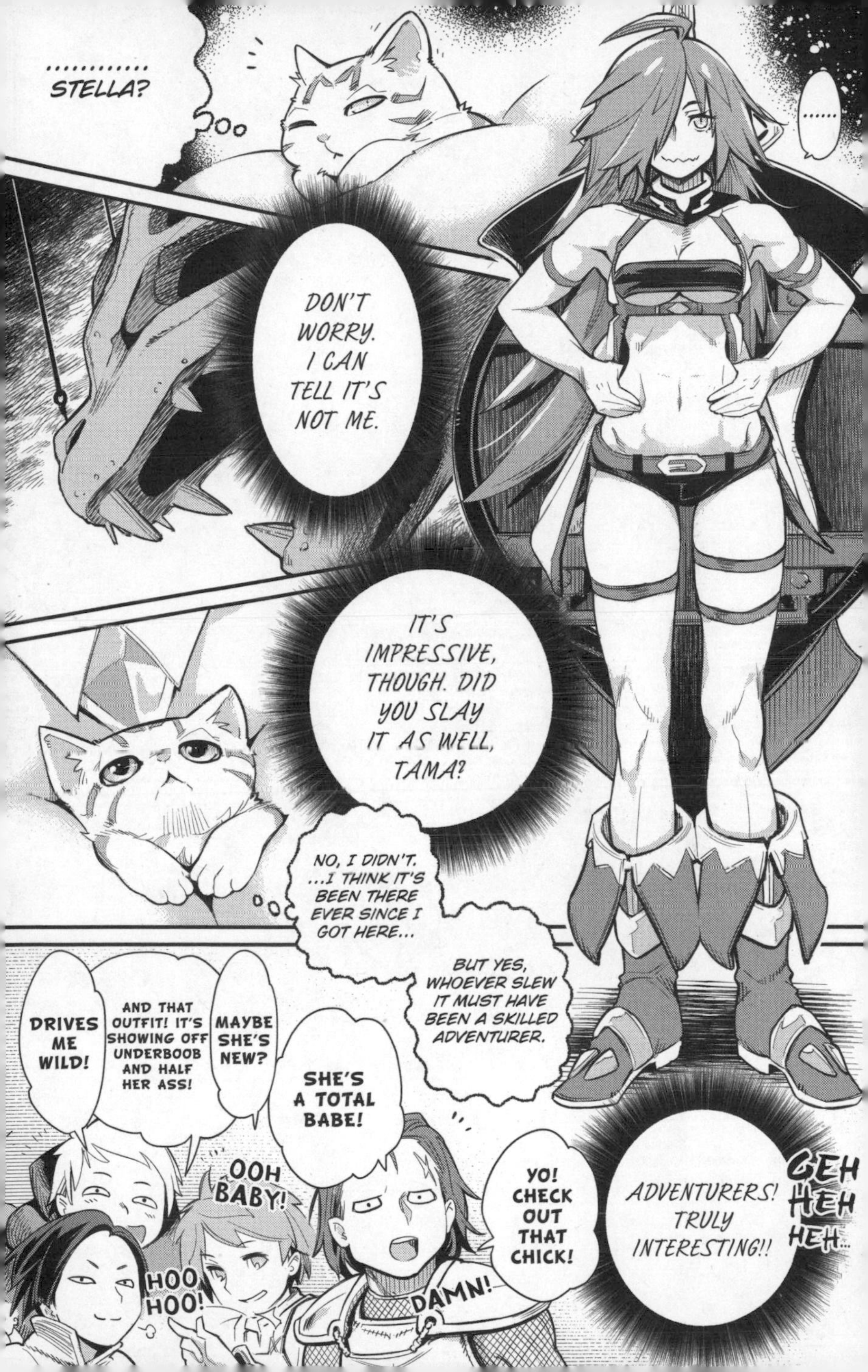
......
....
STELLA?
DON'T WORRY. I CAN TELL IT'S NOT ME.
IT'S IMPRESSIVE, THOUGH. DID YOU SLAY IT AS WELL, TAMA?
NO, I DIDN'T. ...I THINK IT'S BEEN THERE EVER SINCE I GOT HERE...
BUT YES, WHOEVER SLEW IT MUST HAVE BEEN A SKILLED ADVENTURER.
GEH HEH HEH...
ADVENTURERS! TRULY INTERESTING!!
YO! CHECK OUT THAT CHICK!
DAMN!
SHE'S A TOTAL BABE!
MAYBE SHE'S NEW?
OOH BABY!
AND THAT OUTFIT! IT'S SHOWING OFF UNDERBOOB AND HALF HER ASS!
DRIVES ME WILD!
HOO HOO!

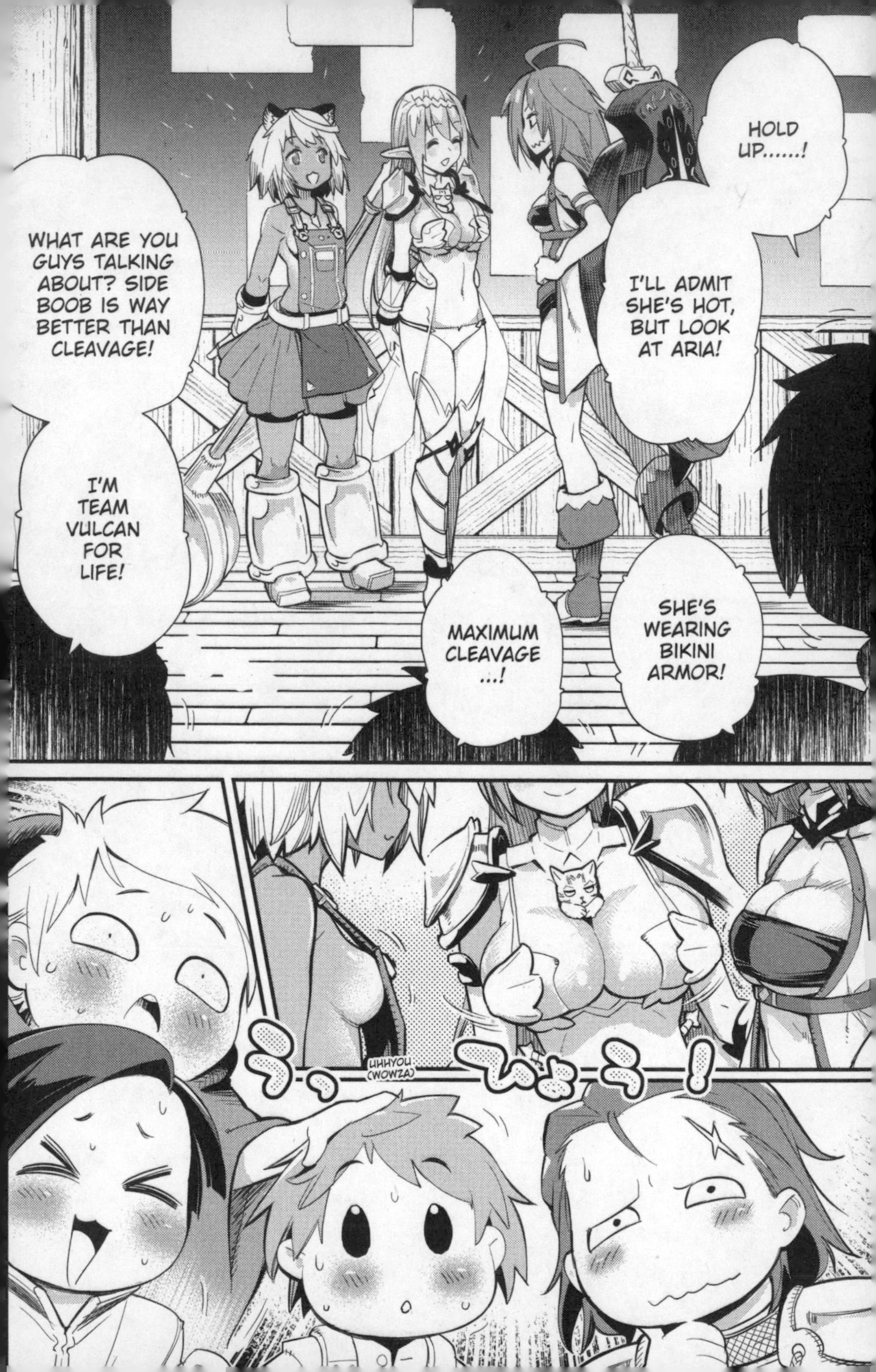
HOLD UP......!
I'LL ADMIT SHE'S HOT, BUT LOOK AT ARIA!
SHE'S WEARING BIKINI ARMOR!
MAXIMUM CLEAVAGE ...!
WHAT ARE YOU GUYS TALKING ABOUT? SIDE BOOB IS WAY BETTER THAN CLEAVAGE!
I'M TEAM VULCAN FOR LIFE!
UHHYOU (WOWZA)

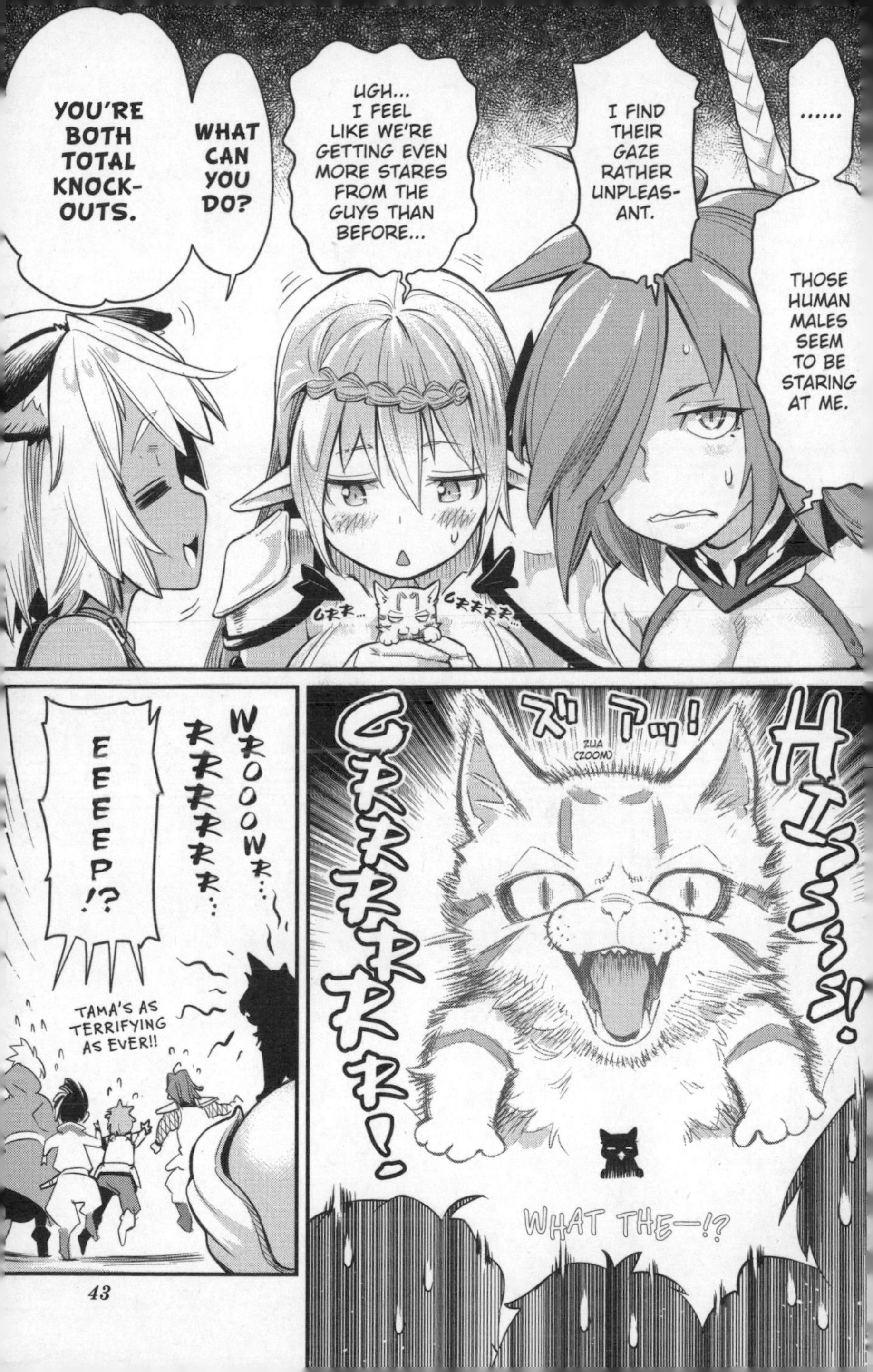
......
THOSE HUMAN MALES SEEM TO BE STARING AT ME.
I FIND THEIR GAZE RATHER UNPLEASANT.
UGH... I FEEL LIKE WE'RE GETTING EVEN MORE STARES FROM THE GUYS THAN BEFORE...
WHAT CAN YOU DO?
YOU'RE BOTH TOTAL KNOCK-OUTS.
HISSSSS!
ズアッ!
ZUA (ZOOM)
GRRRRRRR!
WHAT THE—!?
WROOOOWR... RRRRRRR...
EEEEEP!?
TAMA'S AS TERRIFYING AS EVER!!

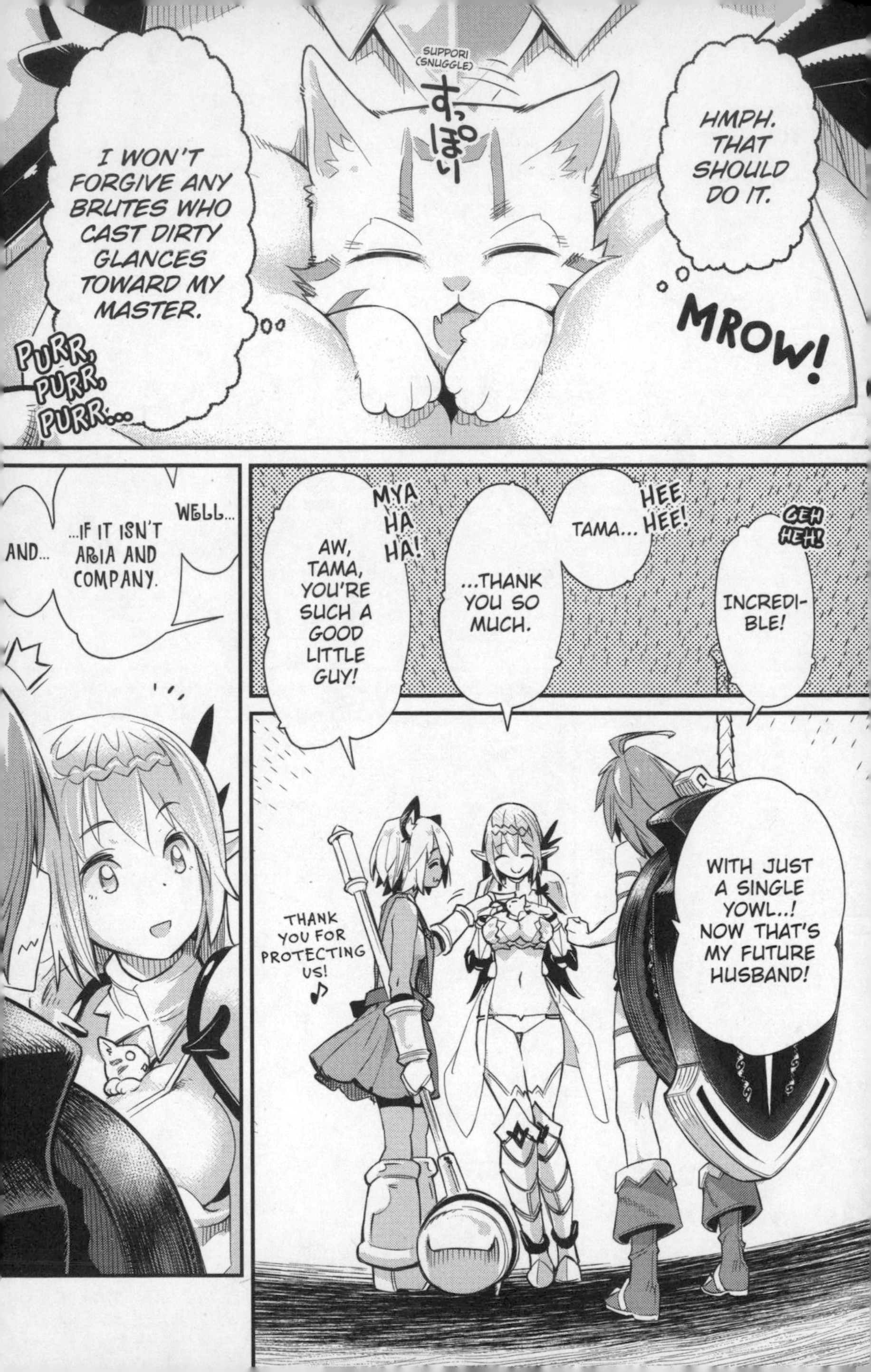
HMPH. THAT SHOULD DO IT.
MROW!
SUPPORI (SNUGGLE)
すっぽり
I WON'T FORGIVE ANY BRUTES WHO CAST DIRTY GLANCES TOWARD MY MASTER.
PURR, PURR, PURR...
GEH HEH!
INCREDIBLE!
HEE HEE!
TAMA...
...THANK YOU SO MUCH.
MYA HA HA!
AW, TAMA, YOU'RE SUCH A GOOD LITTLE GUY!
WELL...
...IF IT ISN'T ARIA AND COMPANY.
AND...
WITH JUST A SINGLE YOWL..! NOW THAT'S MY FUTURE HUSBAND!
THANK YOU FOR PROTECTING US! ♪

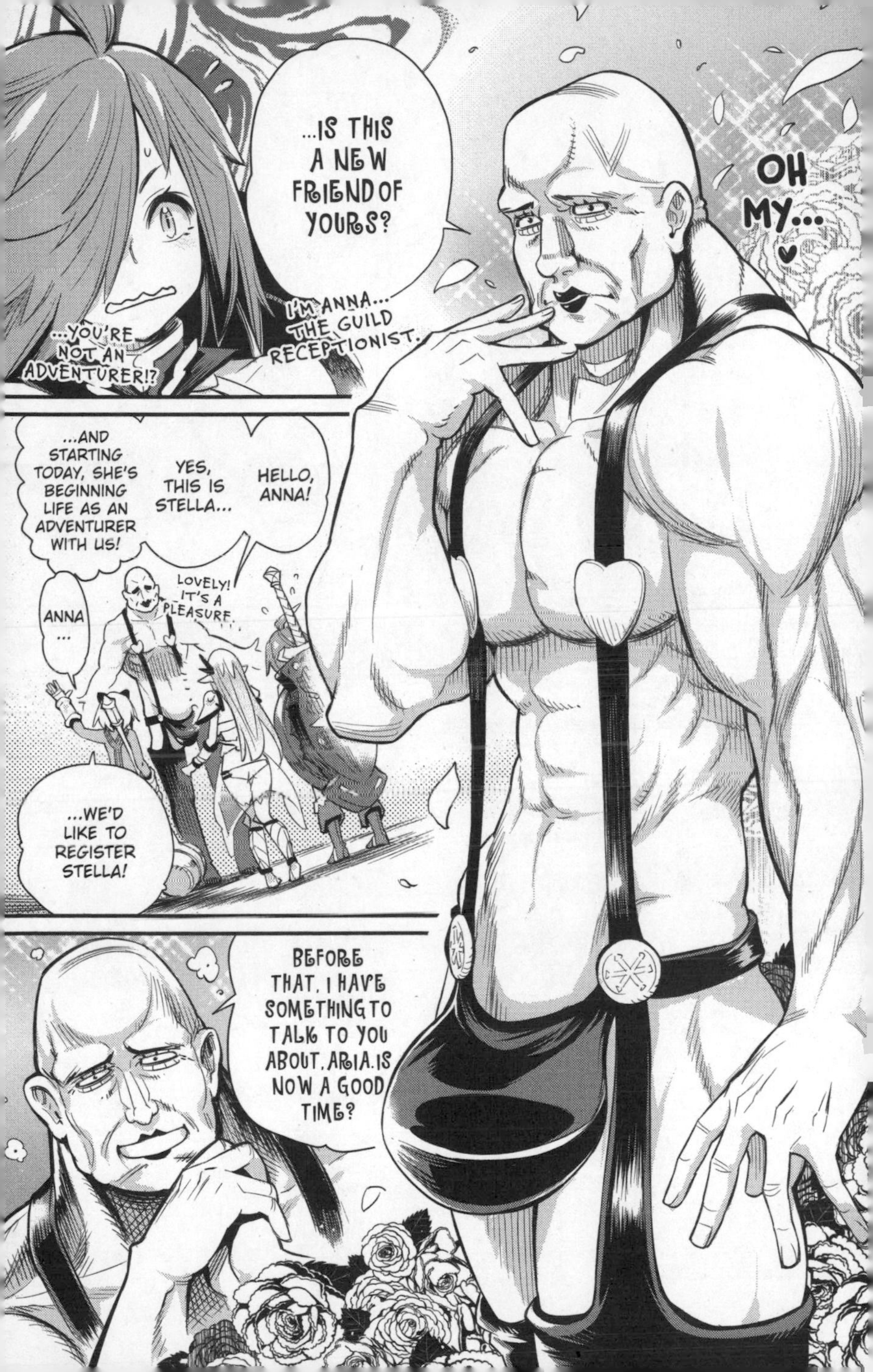
OH MY...♥
...IS THIS A NEW FRIEND OF YOURS?
I'M ANNA... THE GUILD RECEPTIONIST.
...YOU'RE NOT AN ADVENTURER!?
HELLO, ANNA!
YES, THIS IS STELLA...
...AND STARTING TODAY, SHE'S BEGINNING LIFE AS AN ADVENTURER WITH US!
LOVELY! IT'S A PLEASURE.
ANNA...
...WE'D LIKE TO REGISTER STELLA!
BEFORE THAT, I HAVE SOMETHING TO TALK TO YOU ABOUT, ARIA. IS NOW A GOOD TIME?

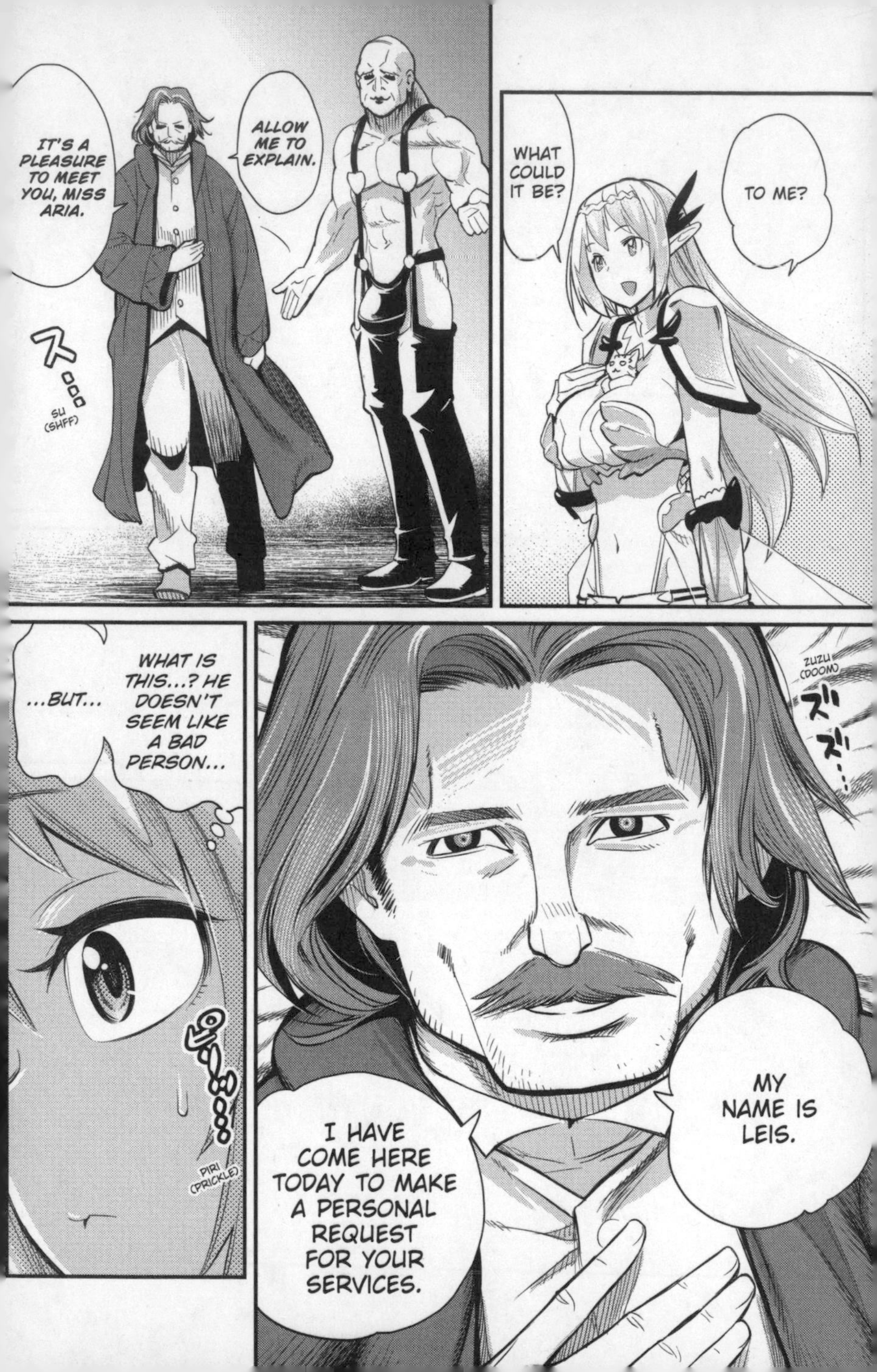

TO ME?
WHAT COULD IT BE?
ALLOW ME TO EXPLAIN.
IT'S A PLEASURE TO MEET YOU, MISS ARIA.
ス
SU (SHFF)
ズズ…
ZUZU (DOOM)
MY NAME IS LEIS.
I HAVE COME HERE TODAY TO MAKE A PERSONAL REQUEST FOR YOUR SERVICES.
WHAT IS THIS...? HE DOESN'T SEEM LIKE A BAD PERSON...
...BUT...
PIRI (PRICKLE)

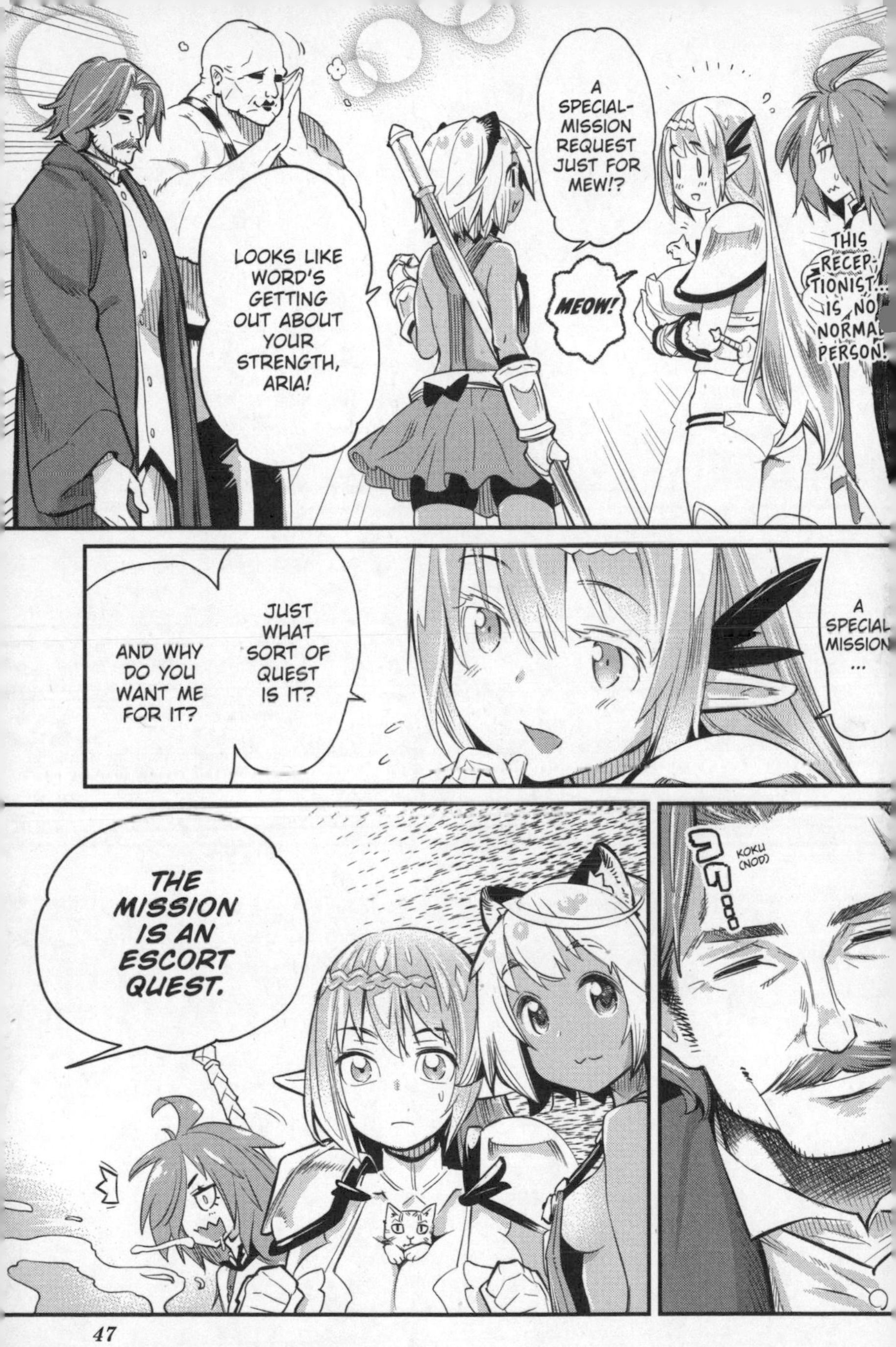
A SPECIAL-MISSION REQUEST JUST FOR MEW!?
THIS RECEPTIONIST... IS NO NORMAL PERSON!
MEOW!
LOOKS LIKE WORD'S GETTING OUT ABOUT YOUR STRENGTH, ARIA!
A SPECIAL MISSION...
JUST WHAT SORT OF QUEST IS IT?
AND WHY DO YOU WANT ME FOR IT?
KOKU (NOD)
THE MISSION IS AN ESCORT QUEST.

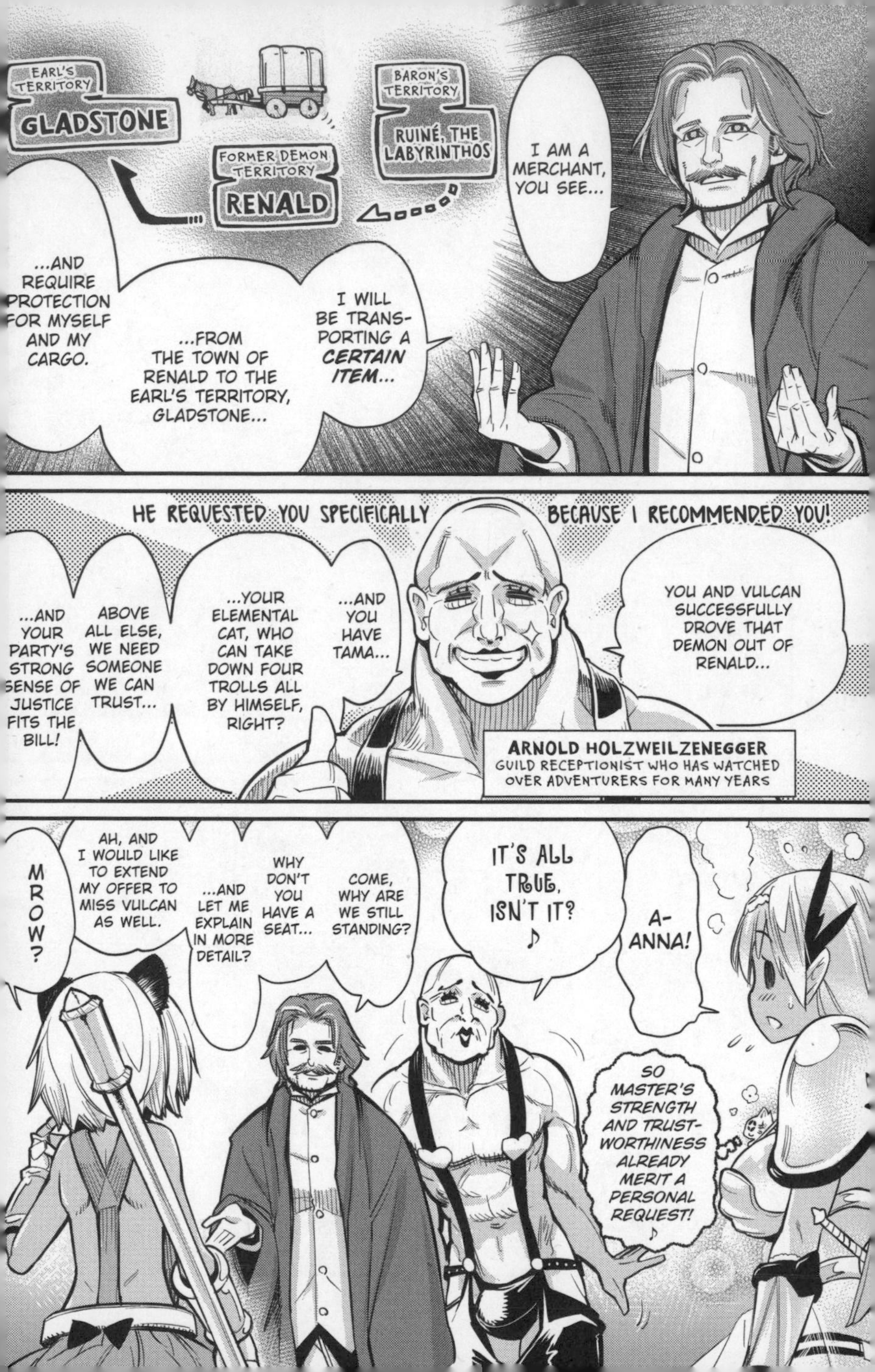
I AM A MERCHANT, YOU SEE...
BARON'S TERRITORY
RUINÉ, THE LABYRINTHOS
FORMER DEMON TERRITORY
RENALD
EARL'S TERRITORY
GLADSTONE
I WILL BE TRANSPORTING A *CERTAIN ITEM*...
...FROM THE TOWN OF RENALD TO THE EARL'S TERRITORY, GLADSTONE...
...AND REQUIRE PROTECTION FOR MYSELF AND MY CARGO.
HE REQUESTED YOU SPECIFICALLY BECAUSE I RECOMMENDED YOU!
YOU AND VULCAN SUCCESSFULLY DROVE THAT DEMON OUT OF RENALD...
ARNOLD HOLZWEILZENEGGER
GUILD RECEPTIONIST WHO HAS WATCHED OVER ADVENTURERS FOR MANY YEARS
...AND YOU HAVE TAMA...
...YOUR ELEMENTAL CAT, WHO CAN TAKE DOWN FOUR TROLLS ALL BY HIMSELF, RIGHT?
ABOVE ALL ELSE, WE NEED SOMEONE WE CAN TRUST...
...AND YOUR PARTY'S STRONG SENSE OF JUSTICE FITS THE BILL!
A-ANNA!
IT'S ALL TRUE, ISN'T IT? ♪
SO MASTER'S STRENGTH AND TRUSTWORTHINESS ALREADY MERIT A PERSONAL REQUEST! ♪
COME, WHY ARE WE STILL STANDING?
WHY DON'T YOU HAVE A SEAT...
...AND LET ME EXPLAIN IN MORE DETAIL?
AH, AND I WOULD LIKE TO EXTEND MY OFFER TO MISS VULCAN AS WELL.
MROW?

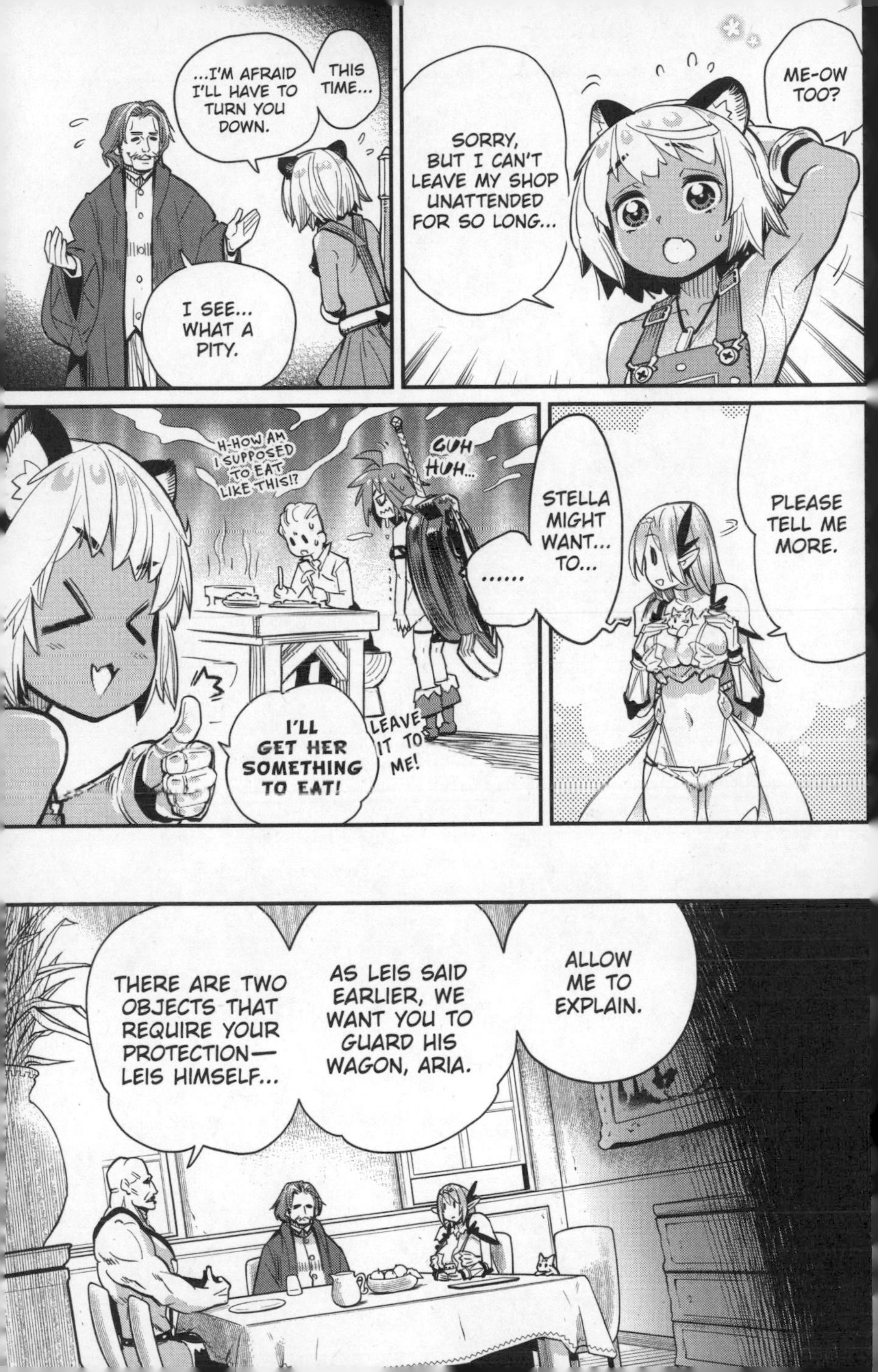
ME-OW TOO?
SORRY, BUT I CAN'T LEAVE MY SHOP UNATTENDED FOR SO LONG...
THIS TIME...
...I'M AFRAID I'LL HAVE TO TURN YOU DOWN.
I SEE... WHAT A PITY.
PLEASE TELL ME MORE.
STELLA MIGHT WANT... TO...
GUH HUH...
......
H-HOW AM I SUPPOSED TO EAT LIKE THIS!?
LEAVE IT TO ME!
I'LL GET HER SOMETHING TO EAT!
ALLOW ME TO EXPLAIN.
AS LEIS SAID EARLIER, WE WANT YOU TO GUARD HIS WAGON, ARIA.
THERE ARE TWO OBJECTS THAT REQUIRE YOUR PROTECTION—LEIS HIMSELF...

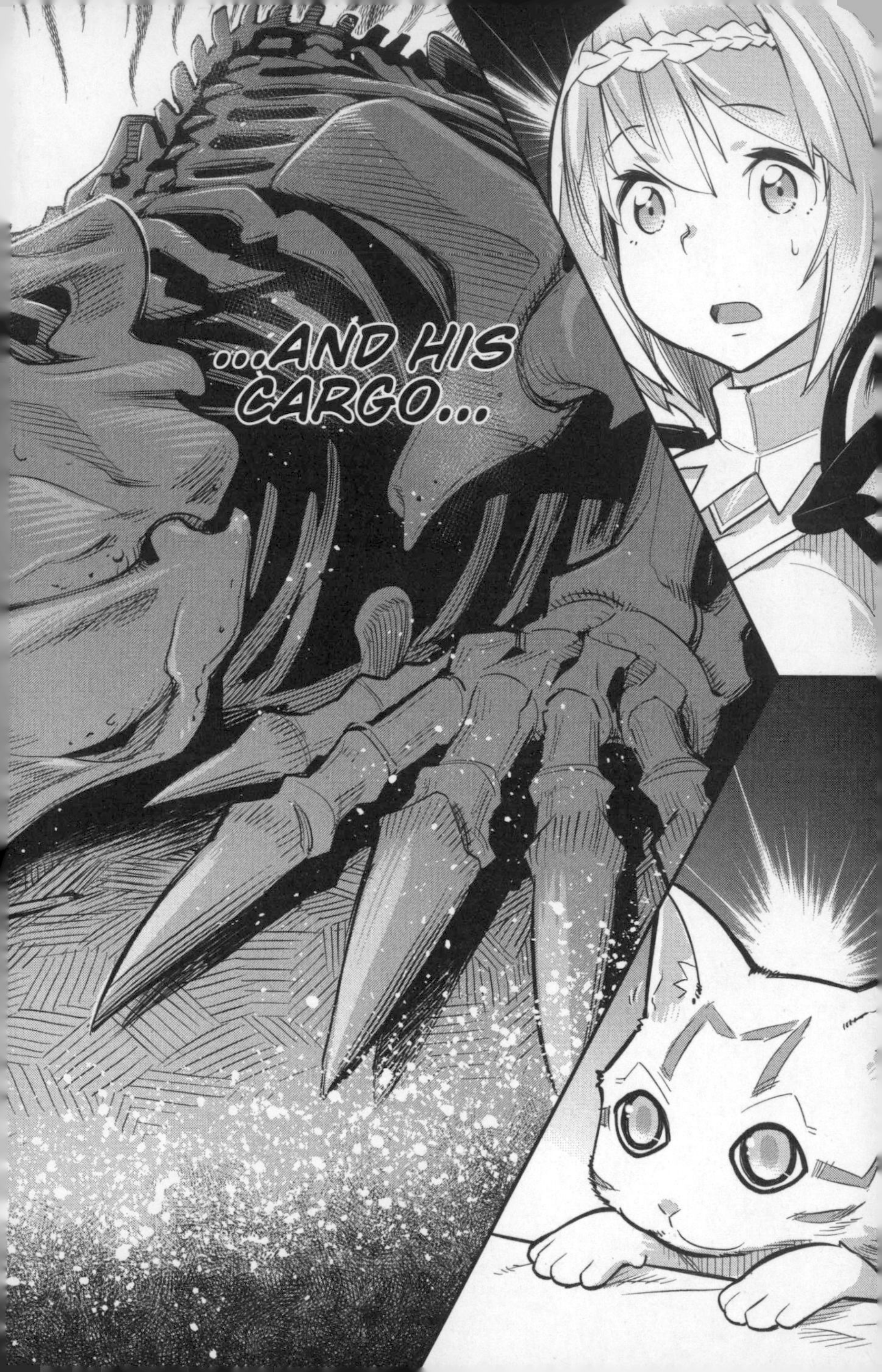
...AND HIS CARGO...

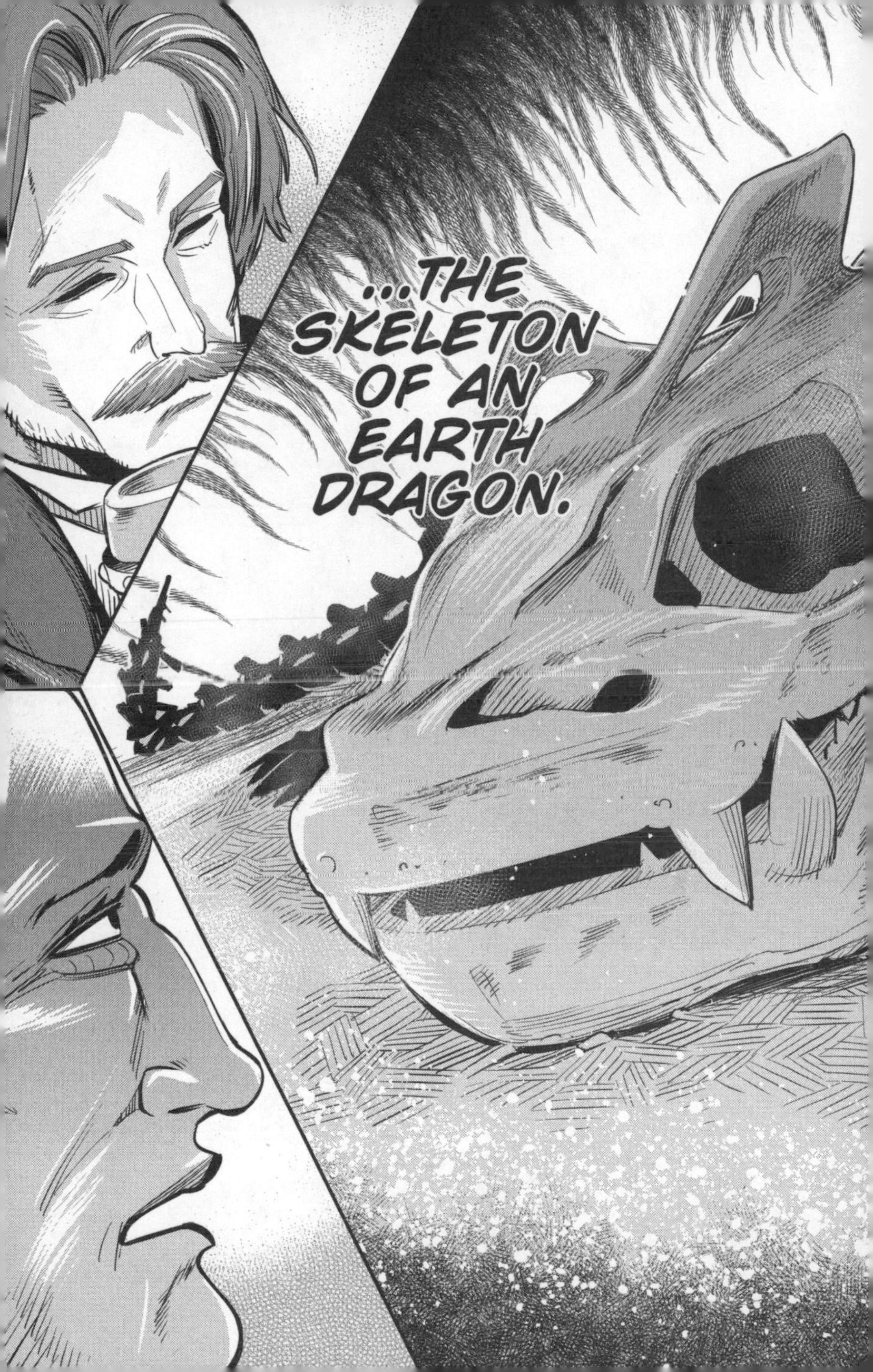
...THE SKELETON OF AN EARTH DRAGON.

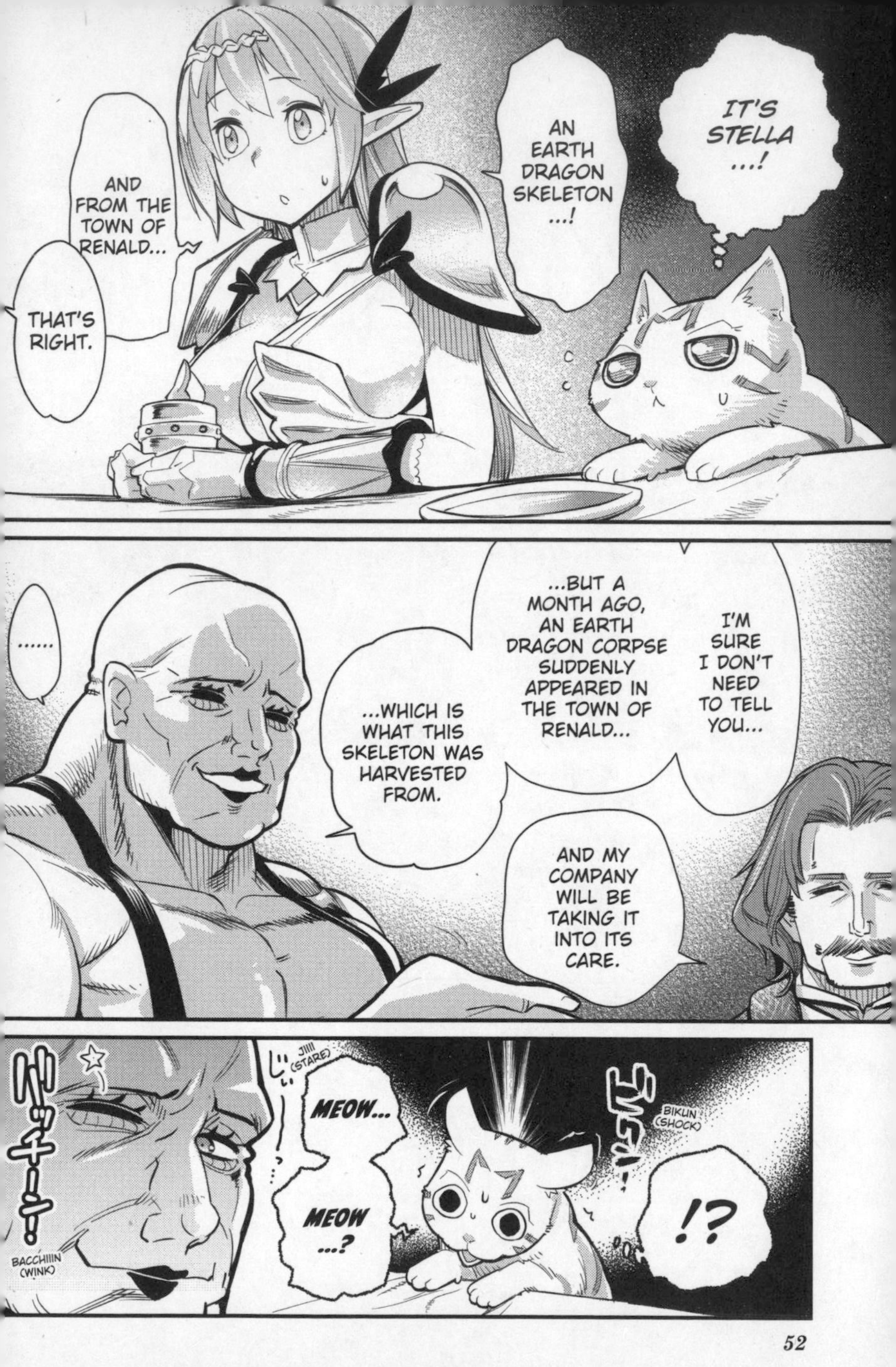
IT'S STELLA ...!
AN EARTH DRAGON SKELETON ...!
AND FROM THE TOWN OF RENALD...
THAT'S RIGHT.
I'M SURE I DON'T NEED TO TELL YOU...
...BUT A MONTH AGO, AN EARTH DRAGON CORPSE SUDDENLY APPEARED IN THE TOWN OF RENALD...
...WHICH IS WHAT THIS SKELETON WAS HARVESTED FROM.
AND MY COMPANY WILL BE TAKING IT INTO ITS CARE.
......
!?
BIKUN (SHOCK)
MEOW...
MEOW ...?
JIIII (STARE)
BACCHIIIN (WINK)

I'M A

BEHEMOTH,

an S-Ranked
MONSTER, but MISTAKEN for a CAT,

I Live
as an

ELF GIRL'S
PET

I'M A BEHEMOTH, an S-Ranked MONSTER, but MISTAKEN for a CAT, I Live as an ELF GIRL'S PET

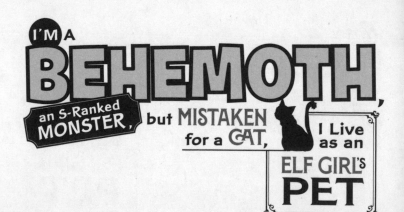

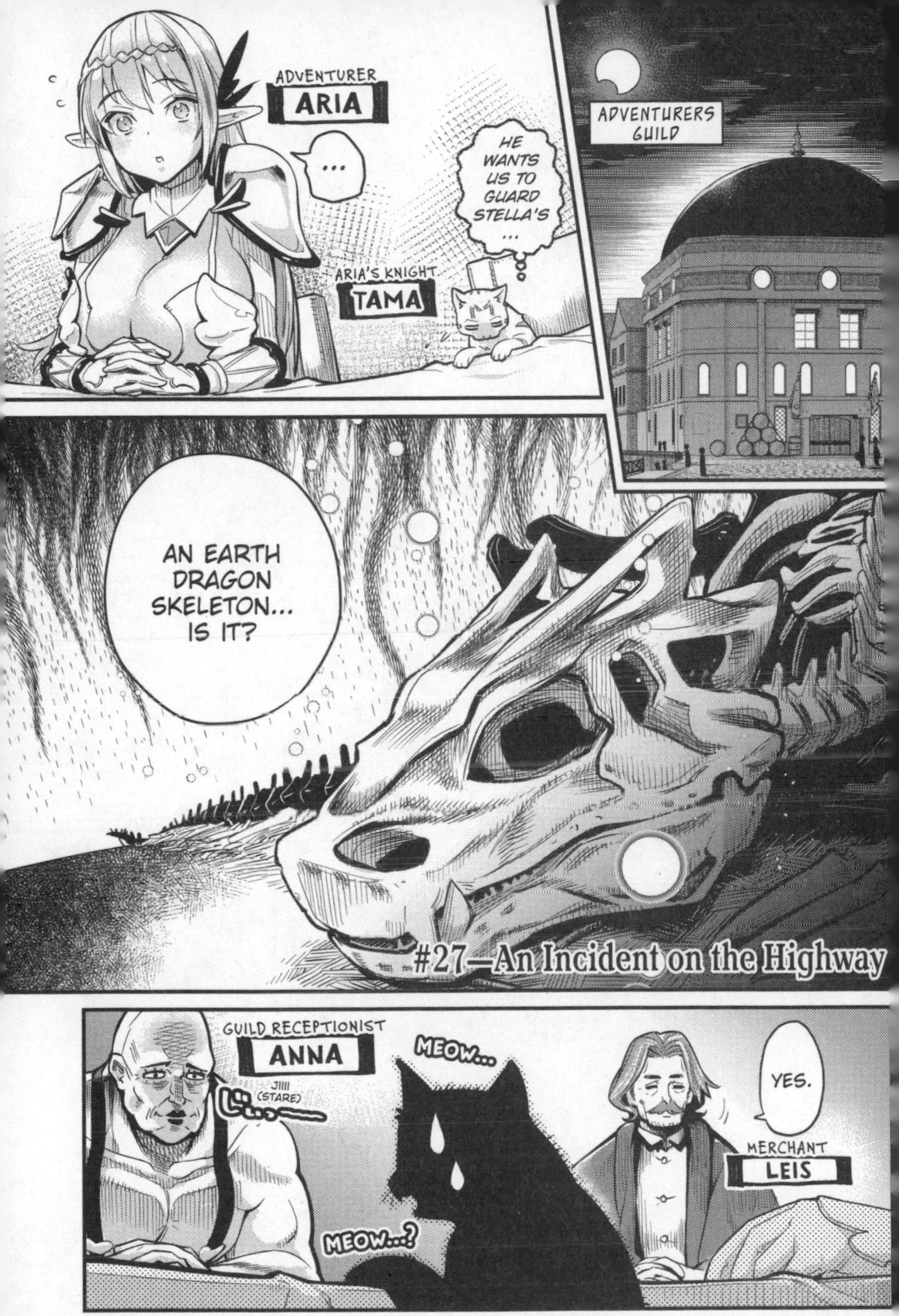
ADVENTURERS GUILD
ADVENTURER
ARIA
HE WANTS US TO GUARD STELLA'S ...
...
ARIA'S KNIGHT
TAMA
AN EARTH DRAGON SKELETON... IS IT?
#27—An Incident on the Highway
YES.
MERCHANT
LEIS
MEOW...
GUILD RECEPTIONIST
ANNA
JIIII (STARE)
MEOW...?

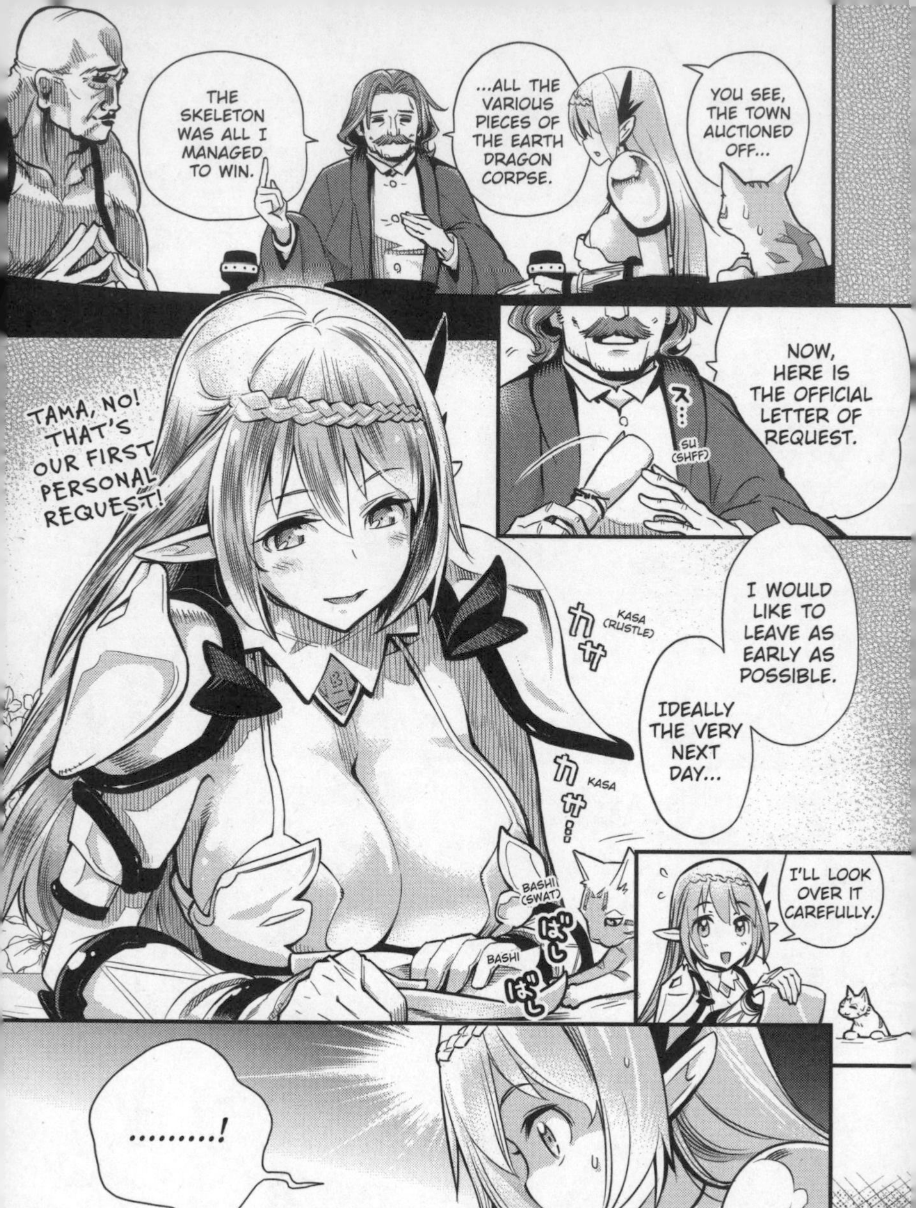
YOU SEE, THE TOWN AUCTIONED OFF...
...ALL THE VARIOUS PIECES OF THE EARTH DRAGON CORPSE.
THE SKELETON WAS ALL I MANAGED TO WIN.
NOW, HERE IS THE OFFICIAL LETTER OF REQUEST.
ス…
SU (SHFF)
I WOULD LIKE TO LEAVE AS EARLY AS POSSIBLE.
IDEALLY THE VERY NEXT DAY...
I'LL LOOK OVER IT CAREFULLY.
カサ
KASA (RUSTLE)
カサ…
KASA
ばし
BASHI (SWAT)
ばし
BASHI
TAMA, NO! THAT'S OUR FIRST PERSONAL REQUEST!
........!

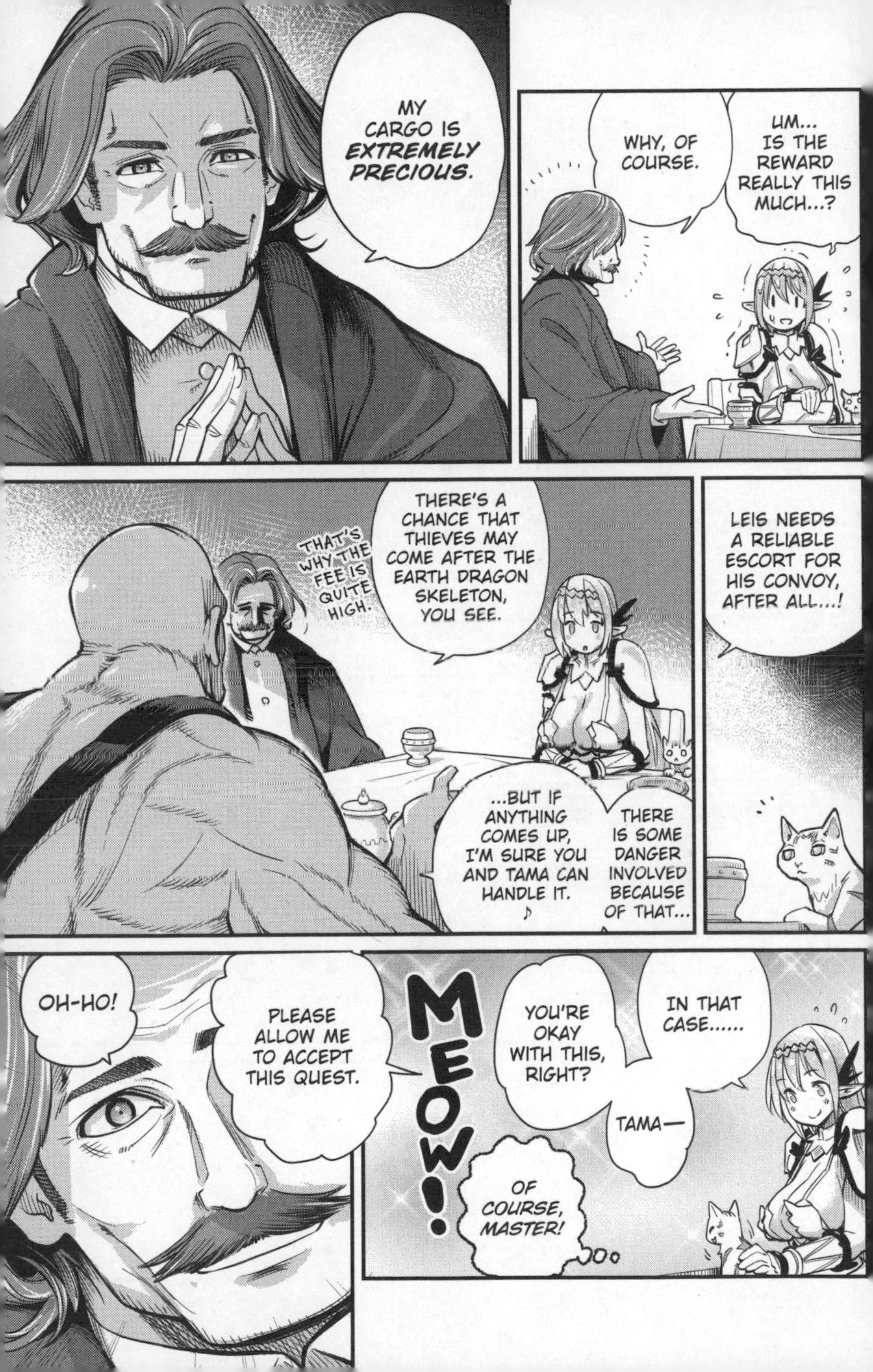
UM... IS THE REWARD REALLY THIS MUCH...?
WHY, OF COURSE.
MY CARGO IS EXTREMELY PRECIOUS.
LEIS NEEDS A RELIABLE ESCORT FOR HIS CONVOY, AFTER ALL...!
THERE'S A CHANCE THAT THIEVES MAY COME AFTER THE EARTH DRAGON SKELETON, YOU SEE.
THAT'S WHY THE FEE IS QUITE HIGH.
THERE IS SOME DANGER INVOLVED BECAUSE OF THAT...
...BUT IF ANYTHING COMES UP, I'M SURE YOU AND TAMA CAN HANDLE IT. ♪
IN THAT CASE......
YOU'RE OKAY WITH THIS, RIGHT?
TAMA—
MEOW!
OF COURSE, MASTER!
PLEASE ALLOW ME TO ACCEPT THIS QUEST.
OH-HO!

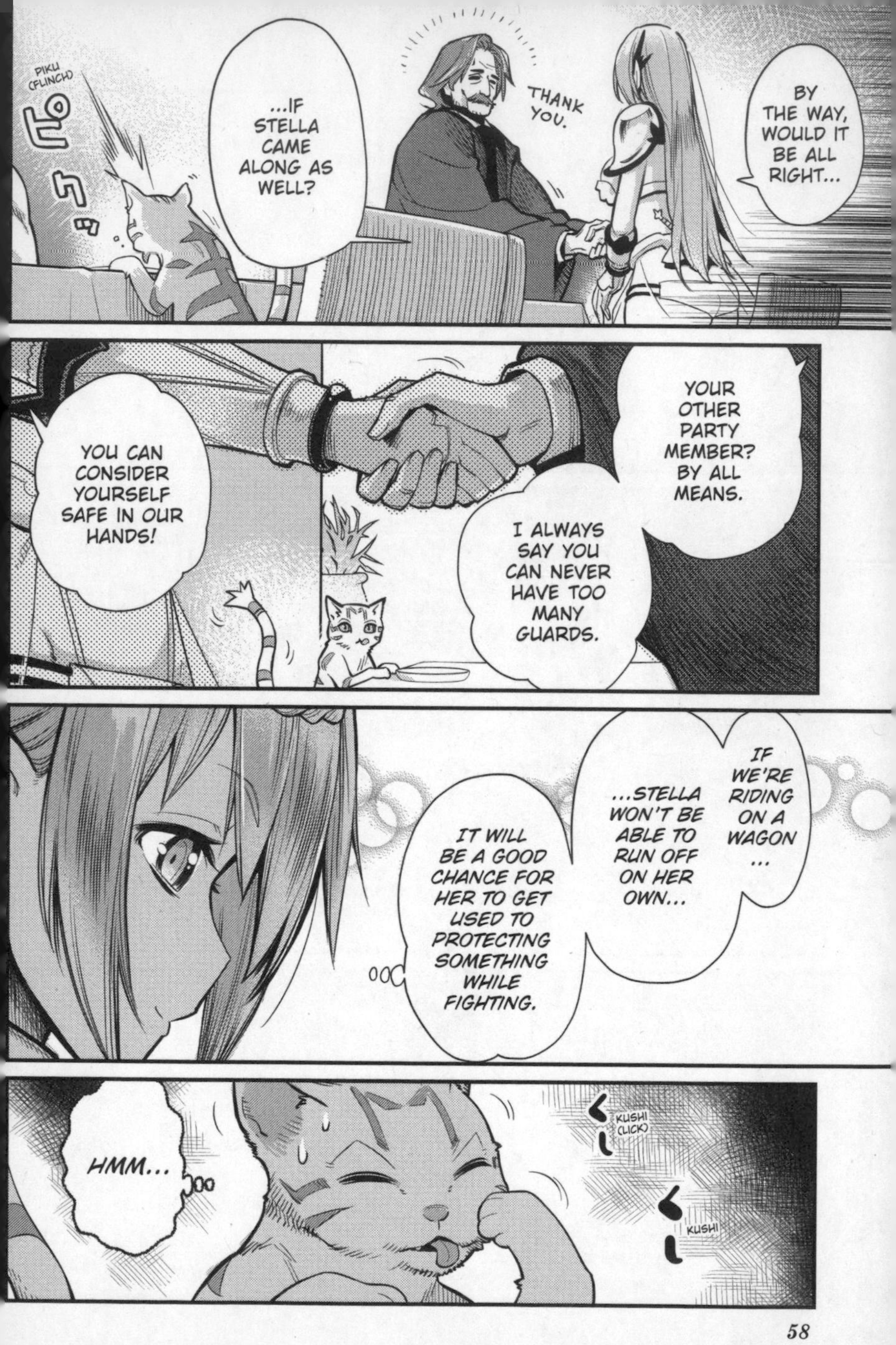
BY THE WAY, WOULD IT BE ALL RIGHT...
THANK YOU.
...IF STELLA CAME ALONG AS WELL?
PIKU (FLINCH)
YOUR OTHER PARTY MEMBER? BY ALL MEANS.
I ALWAYS SAY YOU CAN NEVER HAVE TOO MANY GUARDS.
YOU CAN CONSIDER YOURSELF SAFE IN OUR HANDS!
IF WE'RE RIDING ON A WAGON...
...STELLA WON'T BE ABLE TO RUN OFF ON HER OWN...
IT WILL BE A GOOD CHANCE FOR HER TO GET USED TO PROTECTING SOMETHING WHILE FIGHTING.
KUSHI (LICK)
KUSHI
HMM...

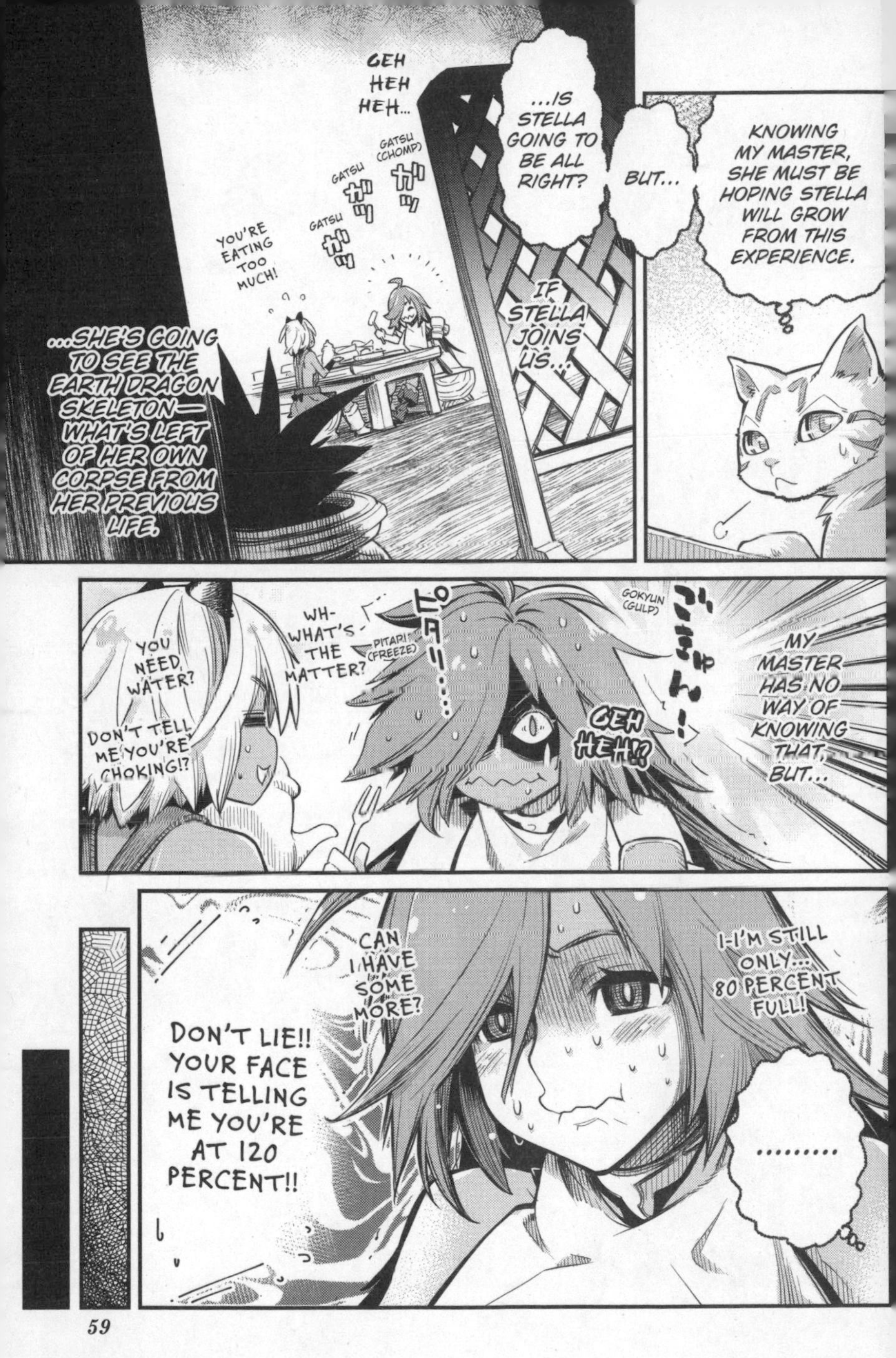
KNOWING MY MASTER, SHE MUST BE HOPING STELLA WILL GROW FROM THIS EXPERIENCE.
BUT...
...IS STELLA GOING TO BE ALL RIGHT?
GEH HEH HEH...
GATSU (CHOMP)
GATSU
GATSU
YOU'RE EATING TOO MUCH!
IF STELLA JOINS US...
...SHE'S GOING TO SEE THE EARTH DRAGON SKELETON—WHAT'S LEFT OF HER OWN CORPSE FROM HER PREVIOUS LIFE.
MY MASTER HAS NO WAY OF KNOWING THAT, BUT...
GOKYUN (GULP)
GEH HEH!?
PITARI (FREEZE)
WH-WHAT'S THE MATTER?
YOU NEED WATER?
DON'T TELL ME YOU'RE CHOKING!?
I-I'M STILL ONLY... 80 PERCENT FULL!
....
CAN I HAVE SOME MORE?
DON'T LIE!! YOUR FACE IS TELLING ME YOU'RE AT 120 PERCENT!!

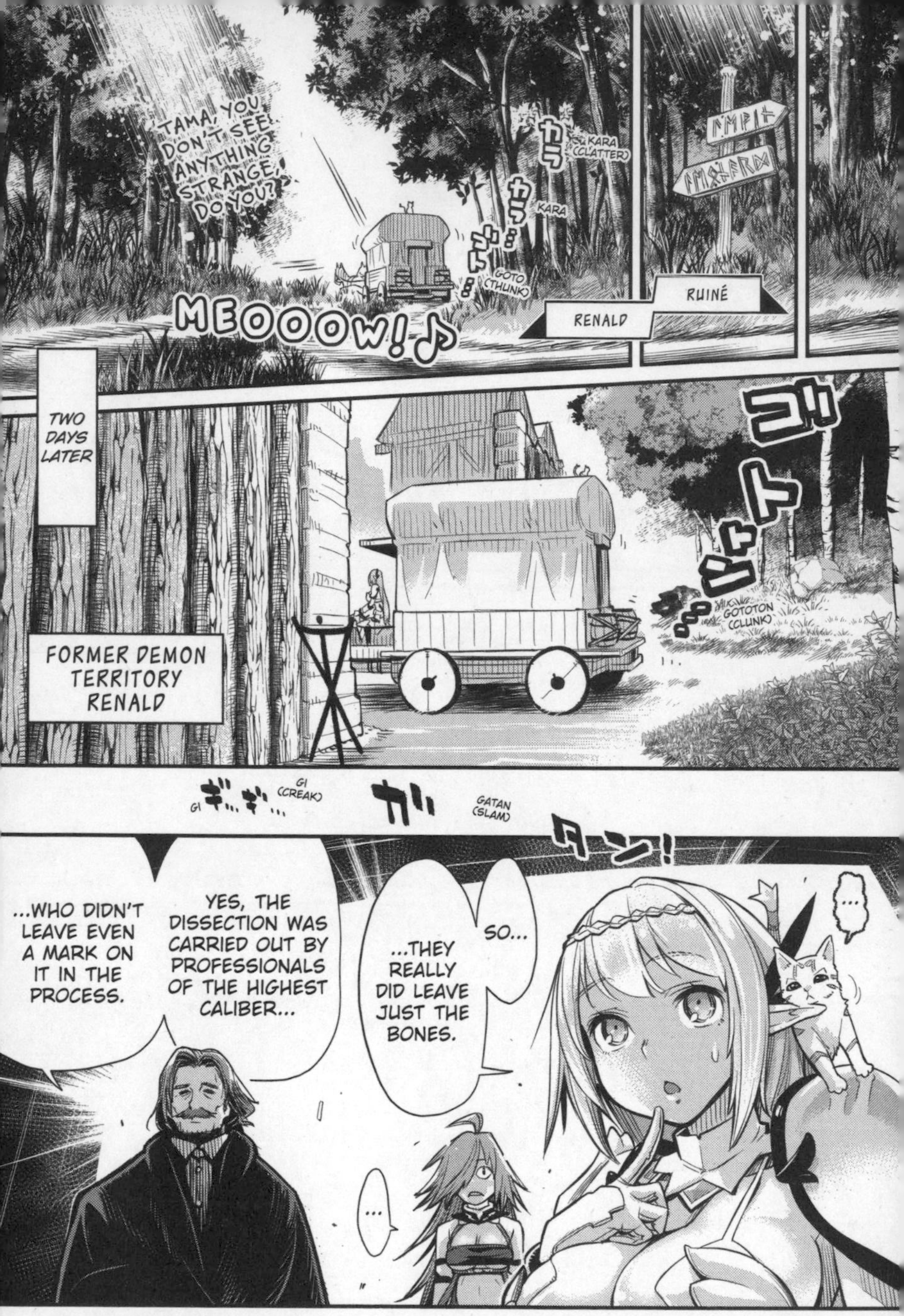
RUINÉ
RENALD
TAMA, YOU DON'T SEE ANYTHING STRANGE, DO YOU?
KARA (CLATTER)
KARA
GOTO (THUNK)
MEOOOW!♪
GOTOTON (CLUNK)
TWO DAYS LATER
FORMER DEMON TERRITORY RENALD
GATAN (SLAM)
GI (CREAK)
GI
...
SO...
...THEY REALLY DID LEAVE JUST THE BONES.
YES, THE DISSECTION WAS CARRIED OUT BY PROFESSIONALS OF THE HIGHEST CALIBER...
...WHO DIDN'T LEAVE EVEN A MARK ON IT IN THE PROCESS.
...

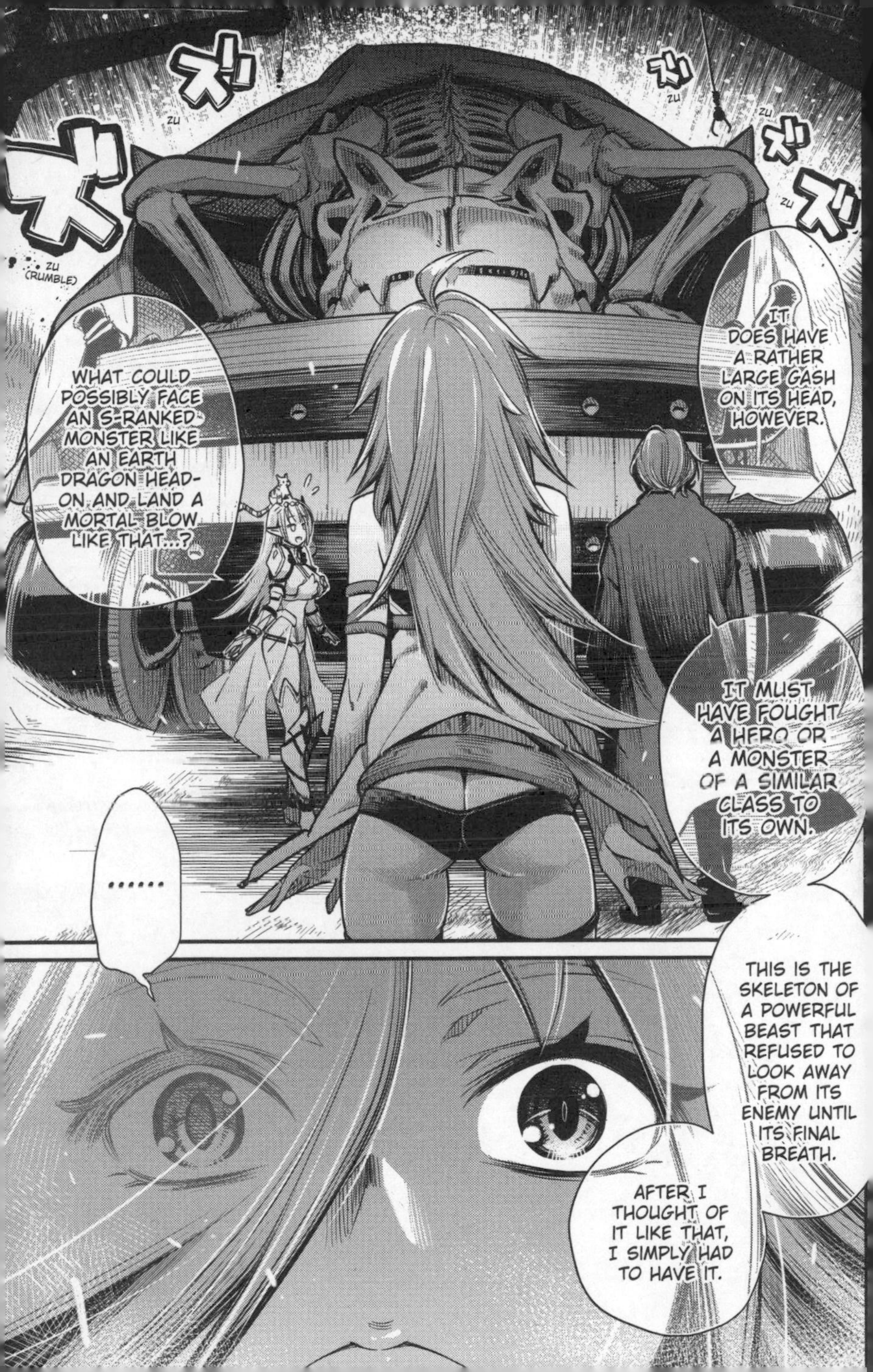
ZU
ZU
ZU
ZU
ZU (RUMBLE)
IT DOES HAVE A RATHER LARGE GASH ON ITS HEAD, HOWEVER.
WHAT COULD POSSIBLY FACE AN S-RANKED MONSTER LIKE AN EARTH DRAGON HEAD-ON AND LAND A MORTAL BLOW LIKE THAT...?
IT MUST HAVE FOUGHT A HERO OR A MONSTER OF A SIMILAR CLASS TO ITS OWN.
......
THIS IS THE SKELETON OF A POWERFUL BEAST THAT REFUSED TO LOOK AWAY FROM ITS ENEMY UNTIL ITS FINAL BREATH.
AFTER I THOUGHT OF IT LIKE THAT, I SIMPLY HAD TO HAVE IT.

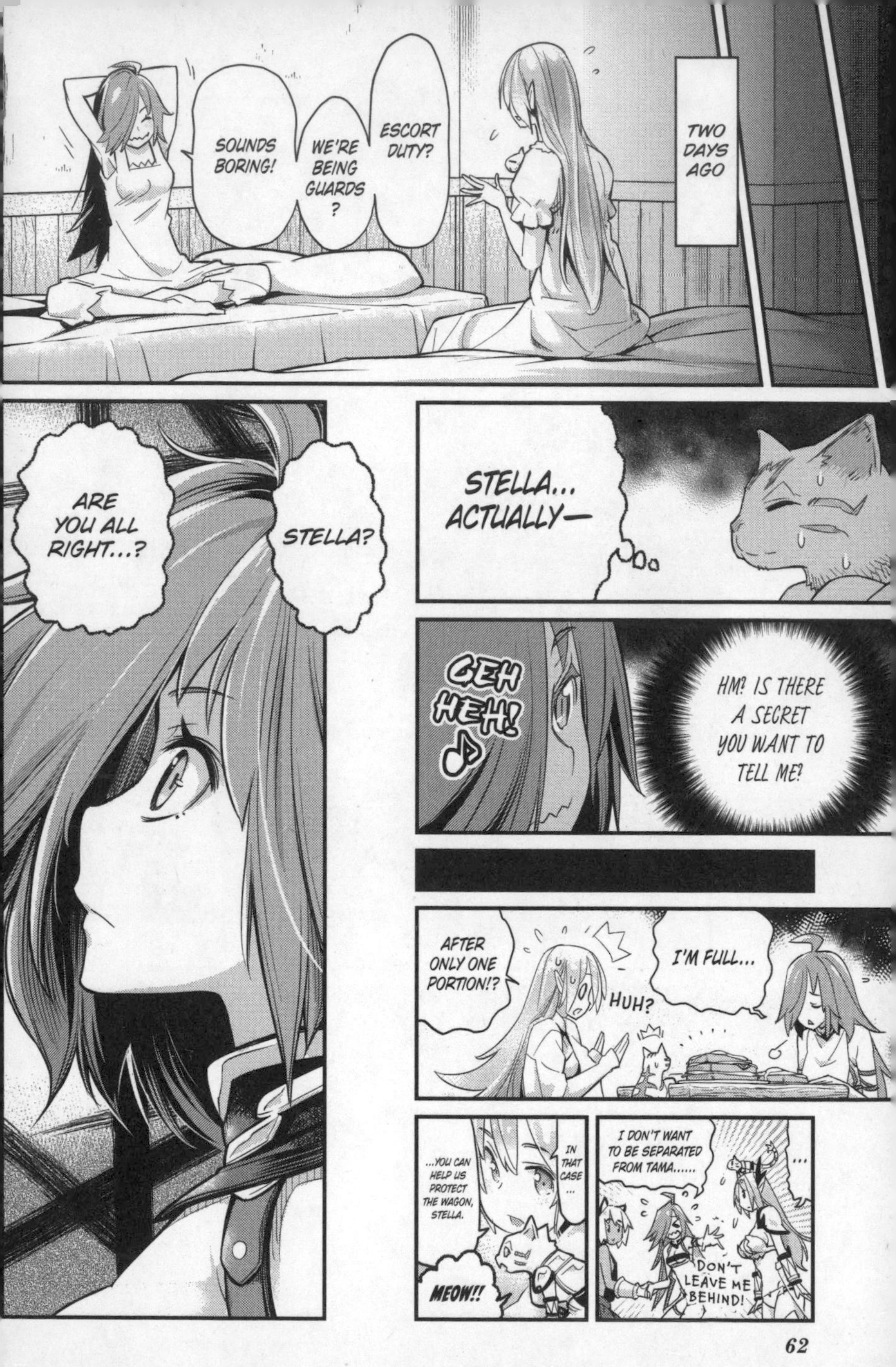
TWO DAYS AGO
ESCORT DUTY?
WE'RE BEING GUARDS?
SOUNDS BORING!
STELLA... ACTUALLY—
HM? IS THERE A SECRET YOU WANT TO TELL ME?
GEH HEH! ♪
I'M FULL...
HUH?
AFTER ONLY ONE PORTION!?
...
I DON'T WANT TO BE SEPARATED FROM TAMA......
DON'T LEAVE ME BEHIND!
IN THAT CASE...
...YOU CAN HELP US PROTECT THE WAGON, STELLA.
MEOW!!
STELLA?
ARE YOU ALL RIGHT...?

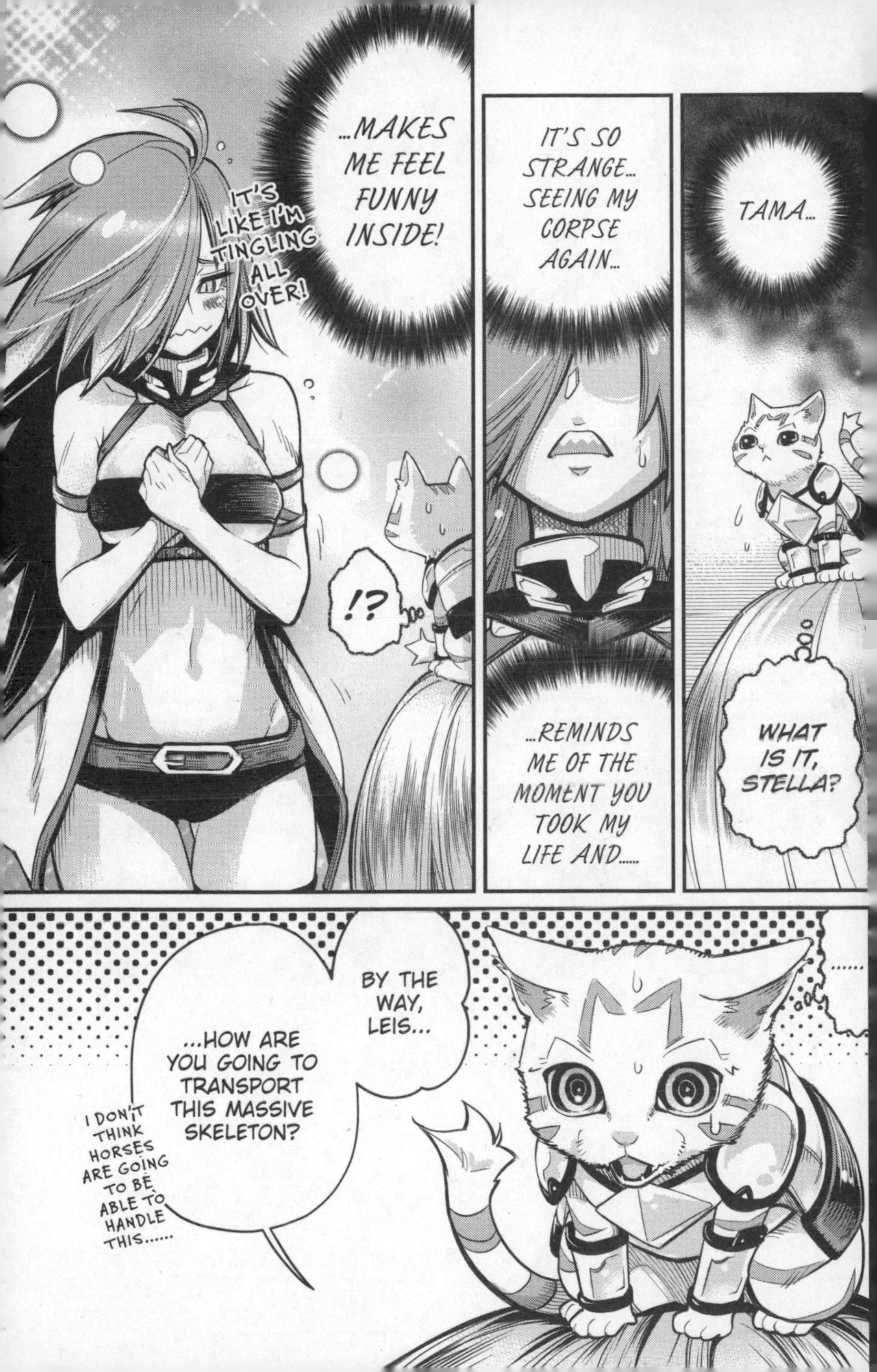
TAMA...
WHAT IS IT, STELLA?
IT'S SO STRANGE... SEEING MY CORPSE AGAIN...
...REMINDS ME OF THE MOMENT YOU TOOK MY LIFE AND......
...MAKES ME FEEL FUNNY INSIDE!
IT'S LIKE I'M TINGLING ALL OVER!
!?
......
BY THE WAY, LEIS...
...HOW ARE YOU GOING TO TRANSPORT THIS MASSIVE SKELETON?
I DON'T THINK HORSES ARE GOING TO BE ABLE TO HANDLE THIS......

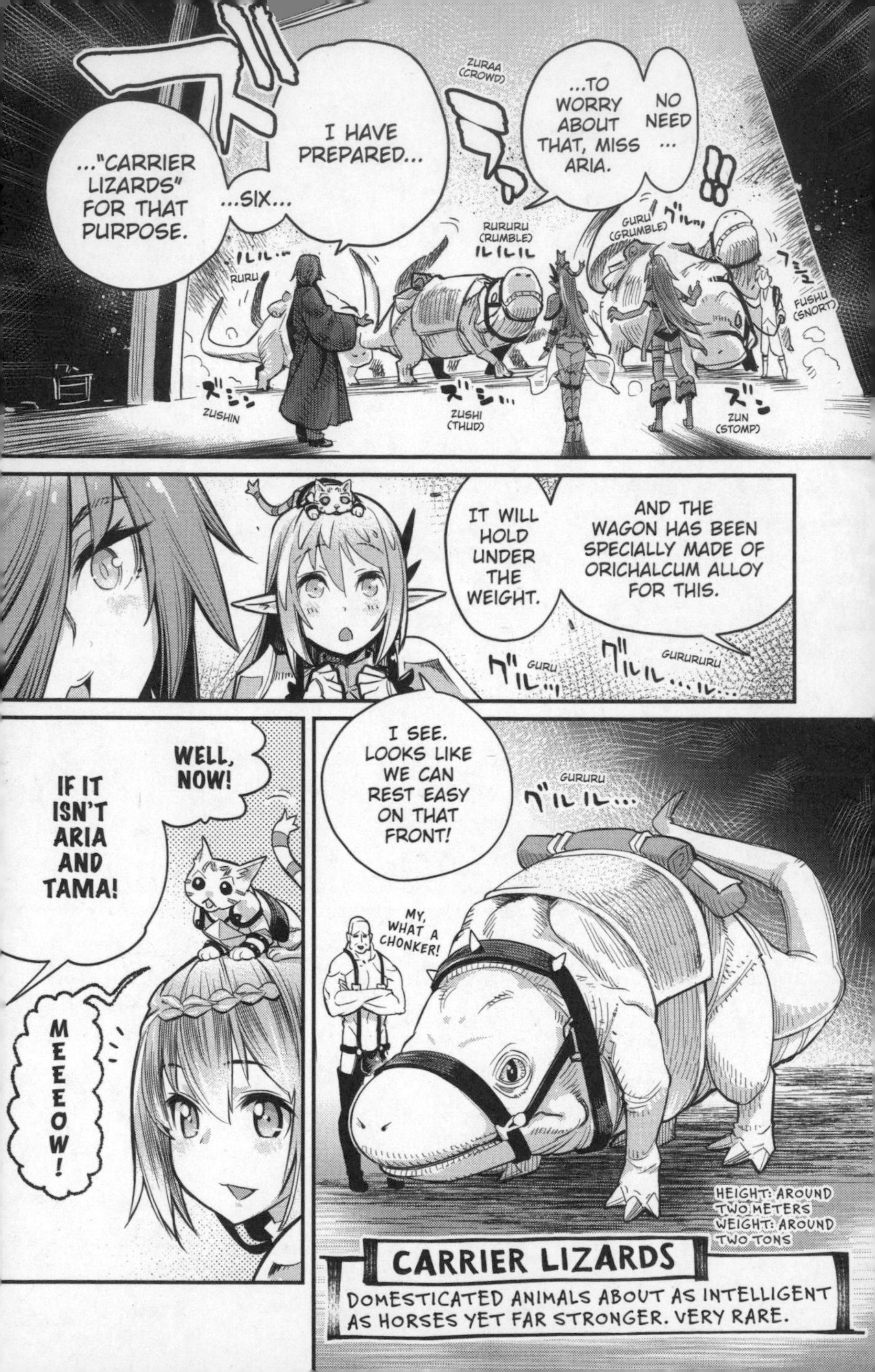
NO NEED...
...TO WORRY ABOUT THAT, MISS ARIA.
ZURAA (CROWD)
I HAVE PREPARED...
...SIX...
..."CARRIER LIZARDS" FOR THAT PURPOSE.
GURU (GRUMBLE)
FUSHU (SNORT)
RURURU (RUMBLE)
RURU
ZUN (STOMP)
ZUSHI (THUD)
ZUSHIN
AND THE WAGON HAS BEEN SPECIALLY MADE OF ORICHALCUM ALLOY FOR THIS.
IT WILL HOLD UNDER THE WEIGHT.
GURURURU
GURU
I SEE. LOOKS LIKE WE CAN REST EASY ON THAT FRONT!
GURURU
MY, WHAT A CHONKER!
HEIGHT: AROUND TWO METERS
WEIGHT: AROUND TWO TONS
CARRIER LIZARDS
DOMESTICATED ANIMALS ABOUT AS INTELLIGENT AS HORSES YET FAR STRONGER. VERY RARE.
WELL, NOW!
IF IT ISN'T ARIA AND TAMA!
MEEEOW!

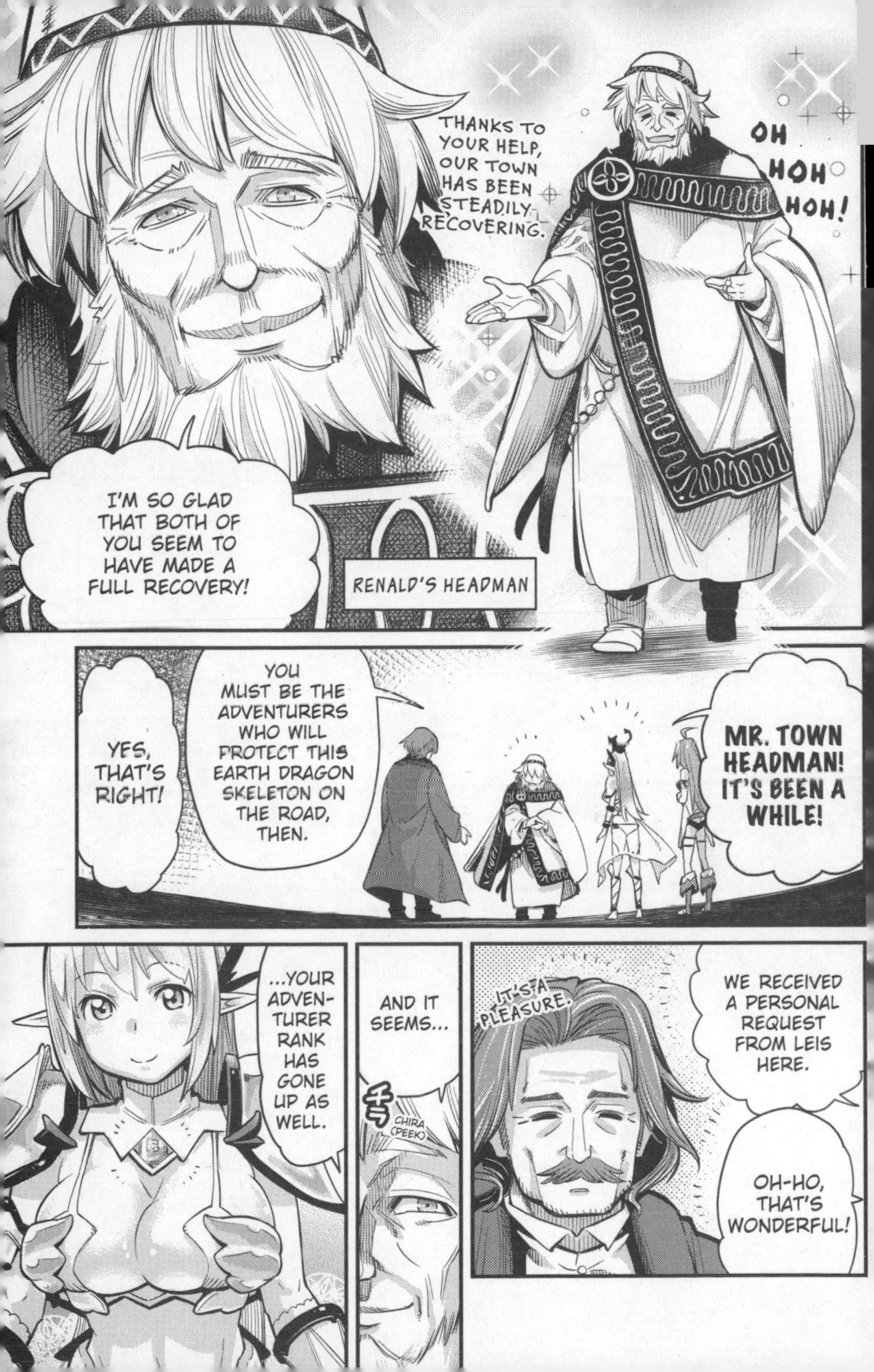
OH HOH HOH!
THANKS TO YOUR HELP, OUR TOWN HAS BEEN STEADILY RECOVERING.
I'M SO GLAD THAT BOTH OF YOU SEEM TO HAVE MADE A FULL RECOVERY!
RENALD'S HEADMAN
MR. TOWN HEADMAN! IT'S BEEN A WHILE!
YOU MUST BE THE ADVENTURERS WHO WILL PROTECT THIS EARTH DRAGON SKELETON ON THE ROAD, THEN.
YES, THAT'S RIGHT!
WE RECEIVED A PERSONAL REQUEST FROM LEIS HERE.
IT'S A PLEASURE.
OH-HO, THAT'S WONDERFUL!
AND IT SEEMS...
チラ
CHIRA (PEEK)
...YOUR ADVENTURER RANK HAS GONE UP AS WELL.

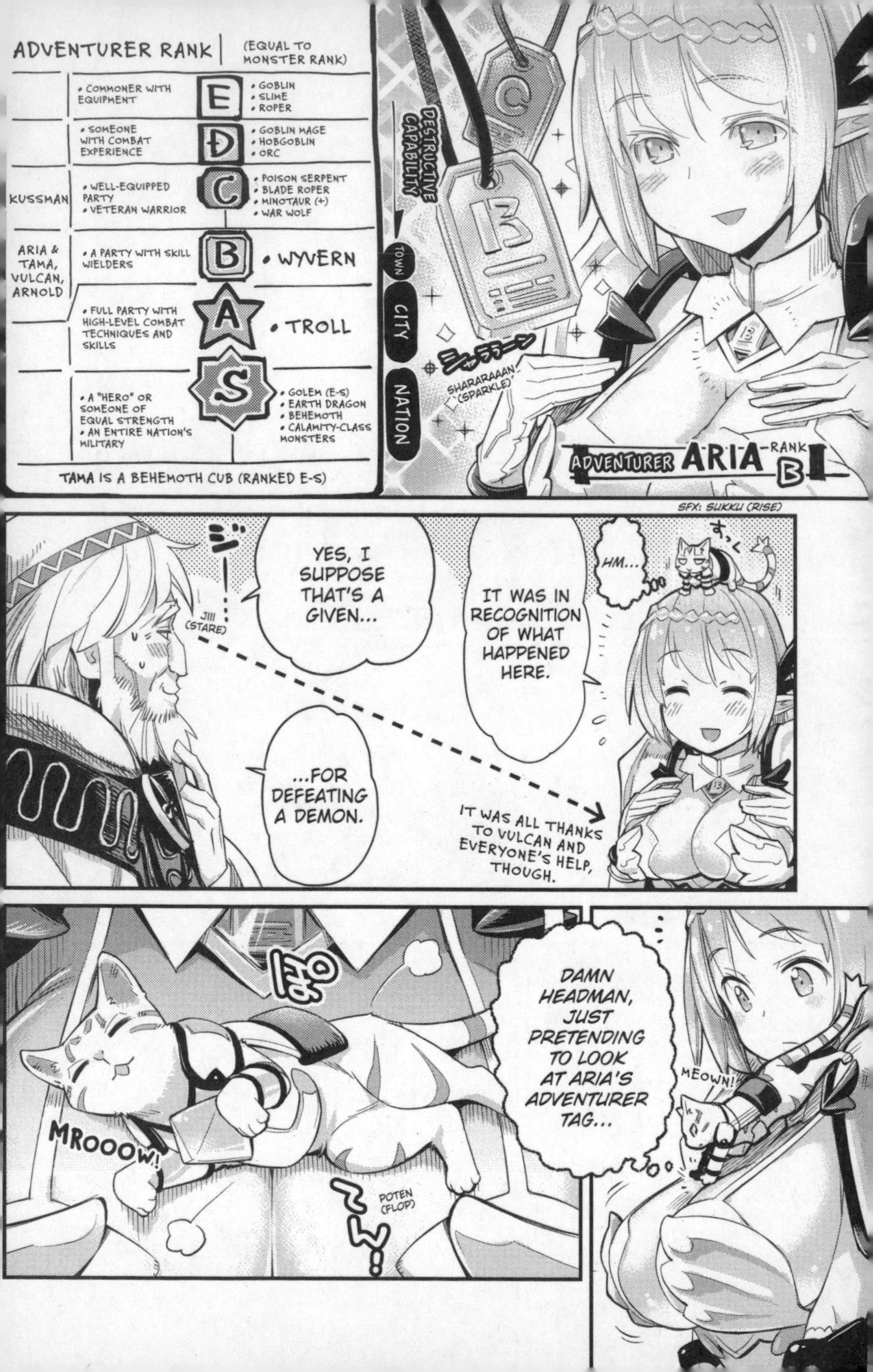
DESTRUCTIVE CAPABILITY
TOWN
CITY
NATION
シャラララーン
SHARARAAAN (SPARKLE)
ADVENTURER ARIA RANK B
ADVENTURER RANK (EQUAL TO MONSTER RANK)
E
• COMMONER WITH EQUIPMENT
• GOBLIN • SLIME • ROPER
D
• SOMEONE WITH COMBAT EXPERIENCE
• GOBLIN MAGE • HOBGOBLIN • ORC
C
KUSSMAN
• WELL-EQUIPPED PARTY • VETERAN WARRIOR
• POISON SERPENT • BLADE ROPER • MINOTAUR (+) • WAR WOLF
B
ARIA & TAMA, VULCAN, ARNOLD
• A PARTY WITH SKILL WIELDERS
• WYVERN
A
• FULL PARTY WITH HIGH-LEVEL COMBAT TECHNIQUES AND SKILLS
• TROLL
S
• A "HERO" OR SOMEONE OF EQUAL STRENGTH • AN ENTIRE NATION'S MILITARY
• GOLEM (E-S) • EARTH DRAGON • BEHEMOTH • CALAMITY-CLASS MONSTERS
TAMA IS A BEHEMOTH CUB (RANKED E-S)
SFX: SUKKU (RISE)
すっく
HM...
IT WAS IN RECOGNITION OF WHAT HAPPENED HERE.
IT WAS ALL THANKS TO VULCAN AND EVERYONE'S HELP, THOUGH.
YES, I SUPPOSE THAT'S A GIVEN...
...FOR DEFEATING A DEMON.
JIII (STARE)
MEOWN!
DAMN HEADMAN, JUST PRETENDING TO LOOK AT ARIA'S ADVENTURER TAG...
POTEN (FLOP)
MROOOW!

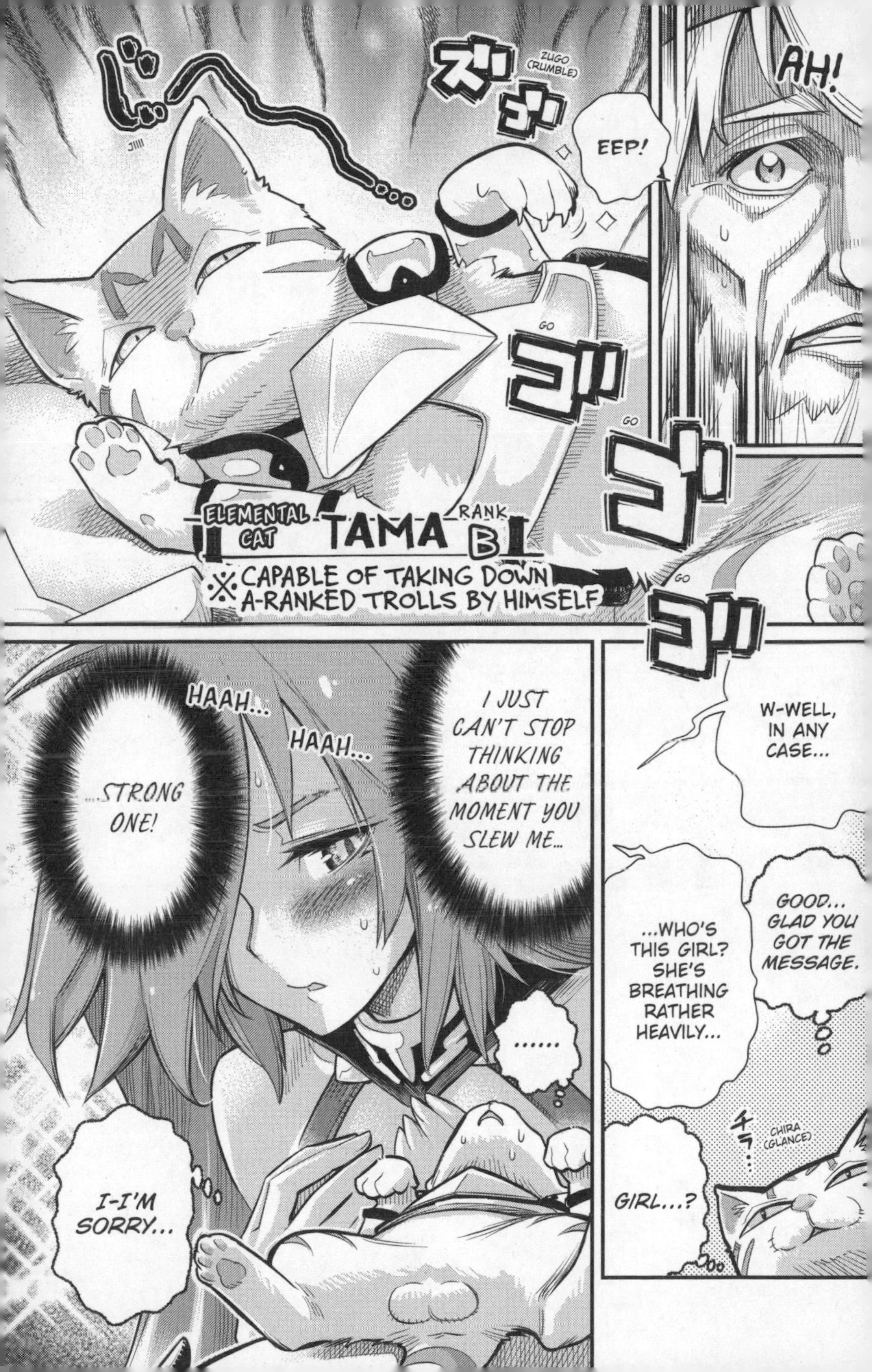
AH!
ズゴ
ZUGO (RUMBLE)
EEP!
じ〜…
JI~
ELEMENTAL CAT TAMA RANK B
※CAPABLE OF TAKING DOWN A-RANKED TROLLS BY HIMSELF
ゴ GO
ゴ GO
ゴ GO
W-WELL, IN ANY CASE...
GOOD... GLAD YOU GOT THE MESSAGE.
...WHO'S THIS GIRL? SHE'S BREATHING RATHER HEAVILY...
チラ…
CHIRA (GLANCE)
GIRL...?
I JUST CAN'T STOP THINKING ABOUT THE MOMENT YOU SLEW ME...
HAAH...
HAAH...
...STRONG ONE!
......
I-I'M SORRY...

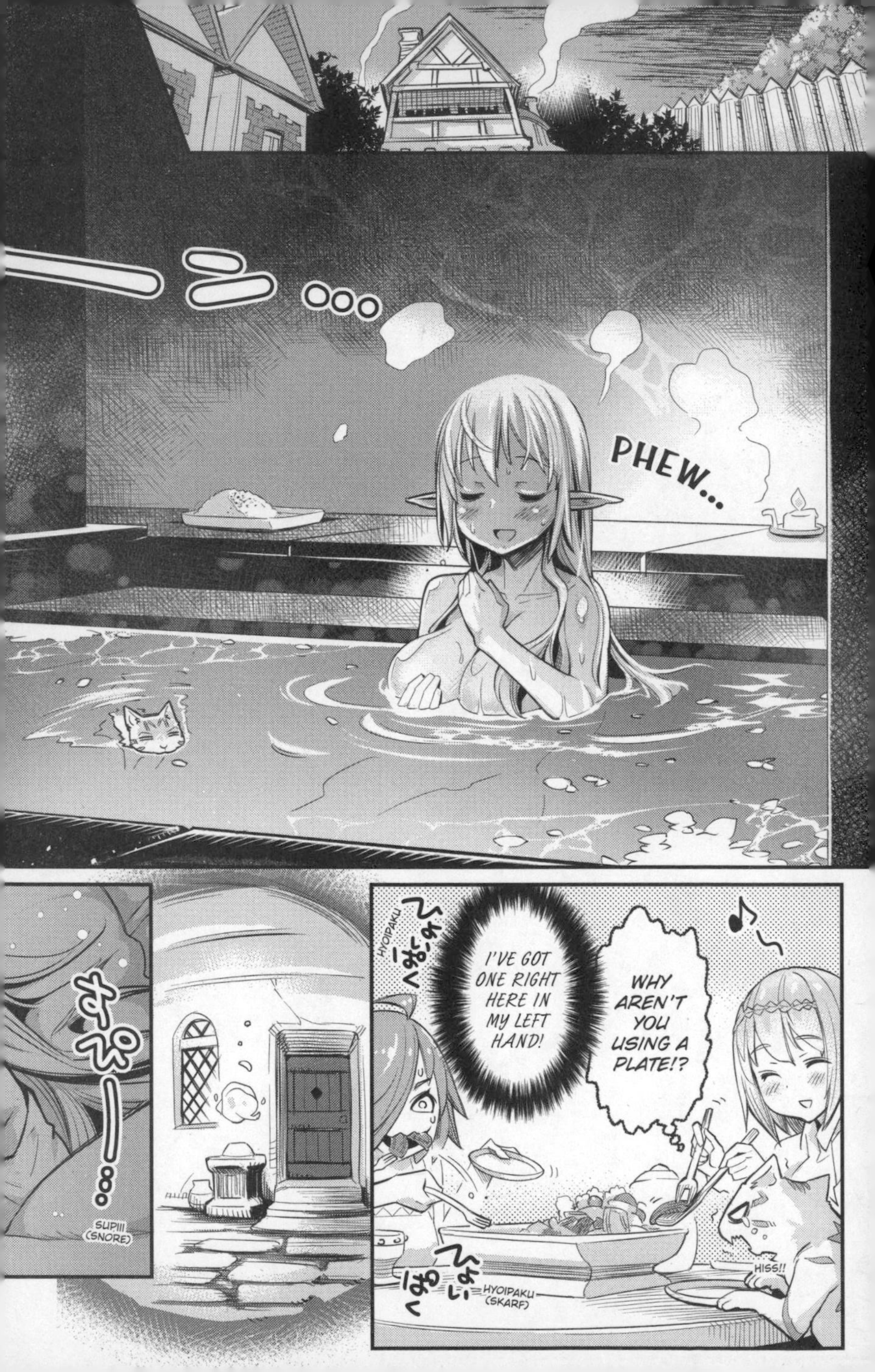
PHEW...
♪〜
WHY AREN'T YOU USING A PLATE!?
I'VE GOT ONE RIGHT HERE IN MY LEFT HAND!
ひょいぱく
HYOIPAKU
HISS!!
ひょいぱく
HYOIPAKU (SKARF)
すぴー…
SUPIII (SNORE)

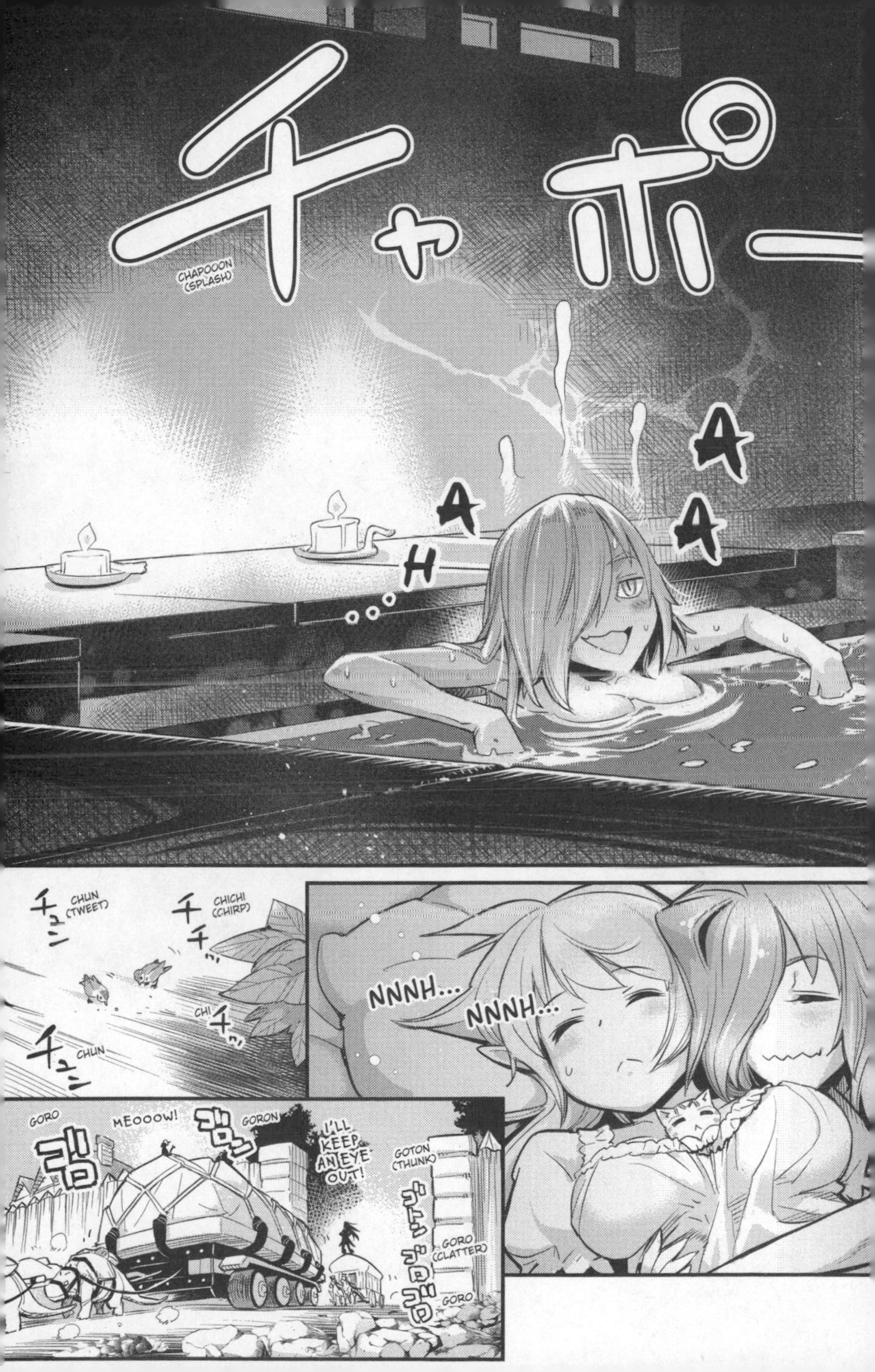

チャポーン
CHAPOOON (SPLASH)
...HAAA
NNNH...
NNNH...
チチ
CHICHI (CHIRP)
チュン
CHUN (TWEET)
チ
CHI
チュン
CHUN
ゴトン
GOTON (THUNK)
ゴロゴロ
GORO (CLATTER)
GORO
I'LL KEEP AN EYE OUT!
ゴロン
GORON
MEOOOW!
GORO

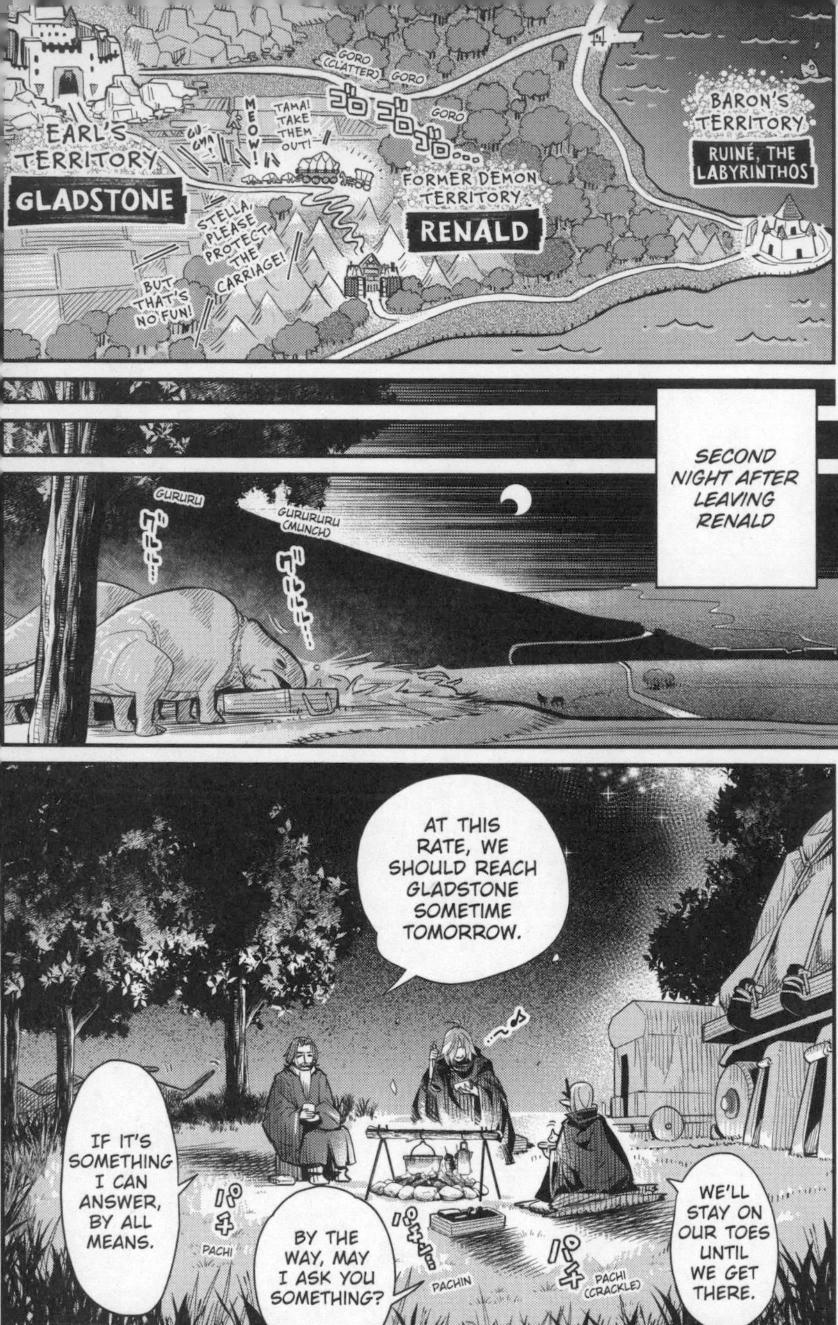
BARON'S TERRITORY
RUINÉ, THE LABYRINTHOS
GORO (CLATTER)
GORO
GORO
ゴロゴロゴロ...
FORMER DEMON TERRITORY
RENALD
TAMA! TAKE THEM OUT!
MEOW!
GU GYA!
EARL'S TERRITORY
GLADSTONE
STELLA, PLEASE PROTECT THE CARRIAGE!
BUT THAT'S NO FUN!
SECOND NIGHT AFTER LEAVING RENALD
GURURURU (MUNCH)
GURURU
AT THIS RATE, WE SHOULD REACH GLADSTONE SOMETIME TOMORROW.
WE'LL STAY ON OUR TOES UNTIL WE GET THERE.
PACHI (CRACKLE)
PACHIN
BY THE WAY, MAY I ASK YOU SOMETHING?
PACHI
IF IT'S SOMETHING I CAN ANSWER, BY ALL MEANS.

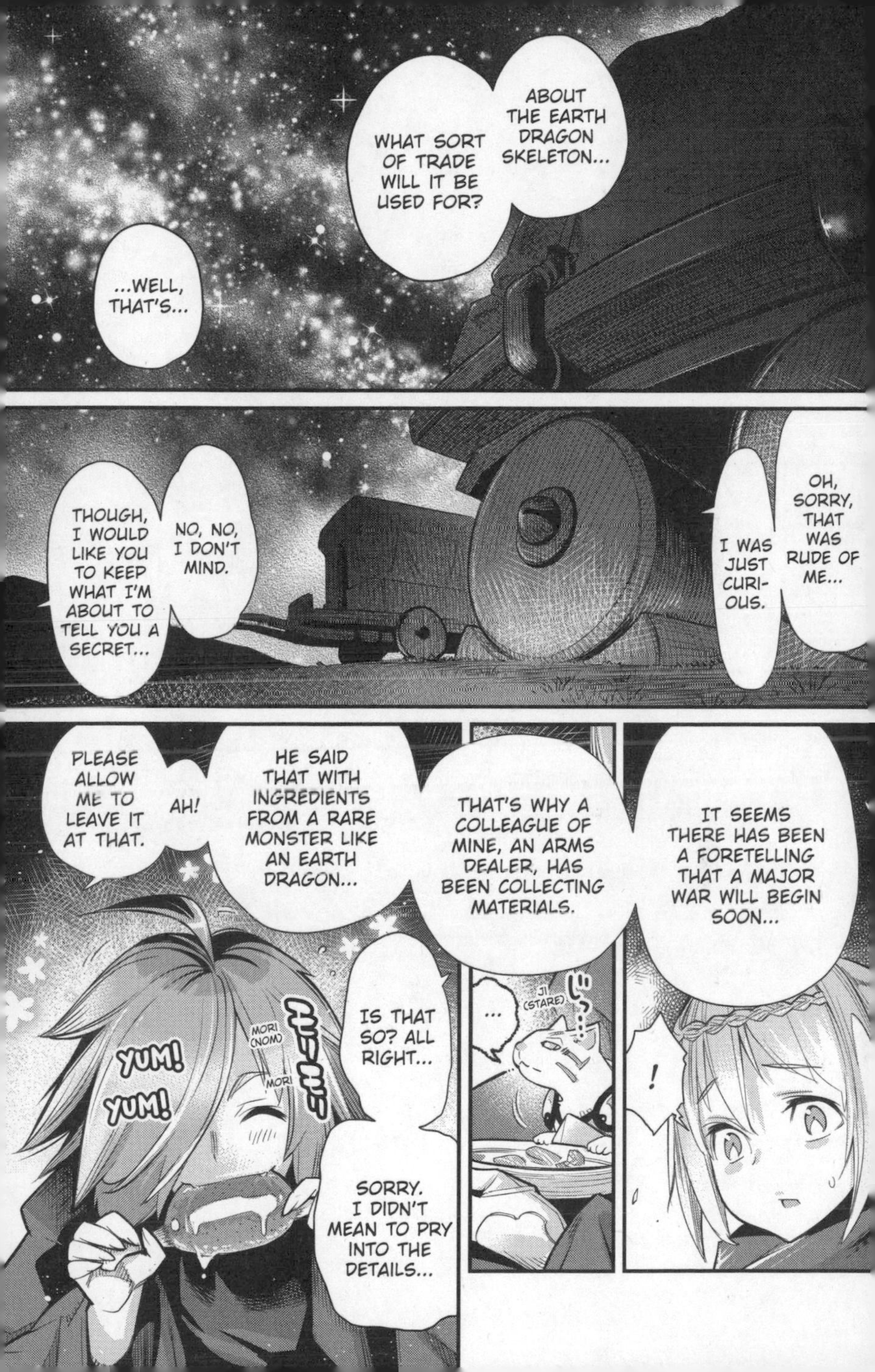
ABOUT THE EARTH DRAGON SKELETON...
WHAT SORT OF TRADE WILL IT BE USED FOR?
...WELL, THAT'S...
OH, SORRY, THAT WAS RUDE OF ME...
I WAS JUST CURI-OUS.
NO, NO, I DON'T MIND.
THOUGH, I WOULD LIKE YOU TO KEEP WHAT I'M ABOUT TO TELL YOU A SECRET...
IT SEEMS THERE HAS BEEN A FORETELLING THAT A MAJOR WAR WILL BEGIN SOON...
!
THAT'S WHY A COLLEAGUE OF MINE, AN ARMS DEALER, HAS BEEN COLLECTING MATERIALS.
JI (STARE)
...
HE SAID THAT WITH INGREDIENTS FROM A RARE MONSTER LIKE AN EARTH DRAGON...
AH!
PLEASE ALLOW ME TO LEAVE IT AT THAT.
IS THAT SO? ALL RIGHT...
MORI (NOM) MORI
YUM! YUM!
SORRY. I DIDN'T MEAN TO PRY INTO THE DETAILS...

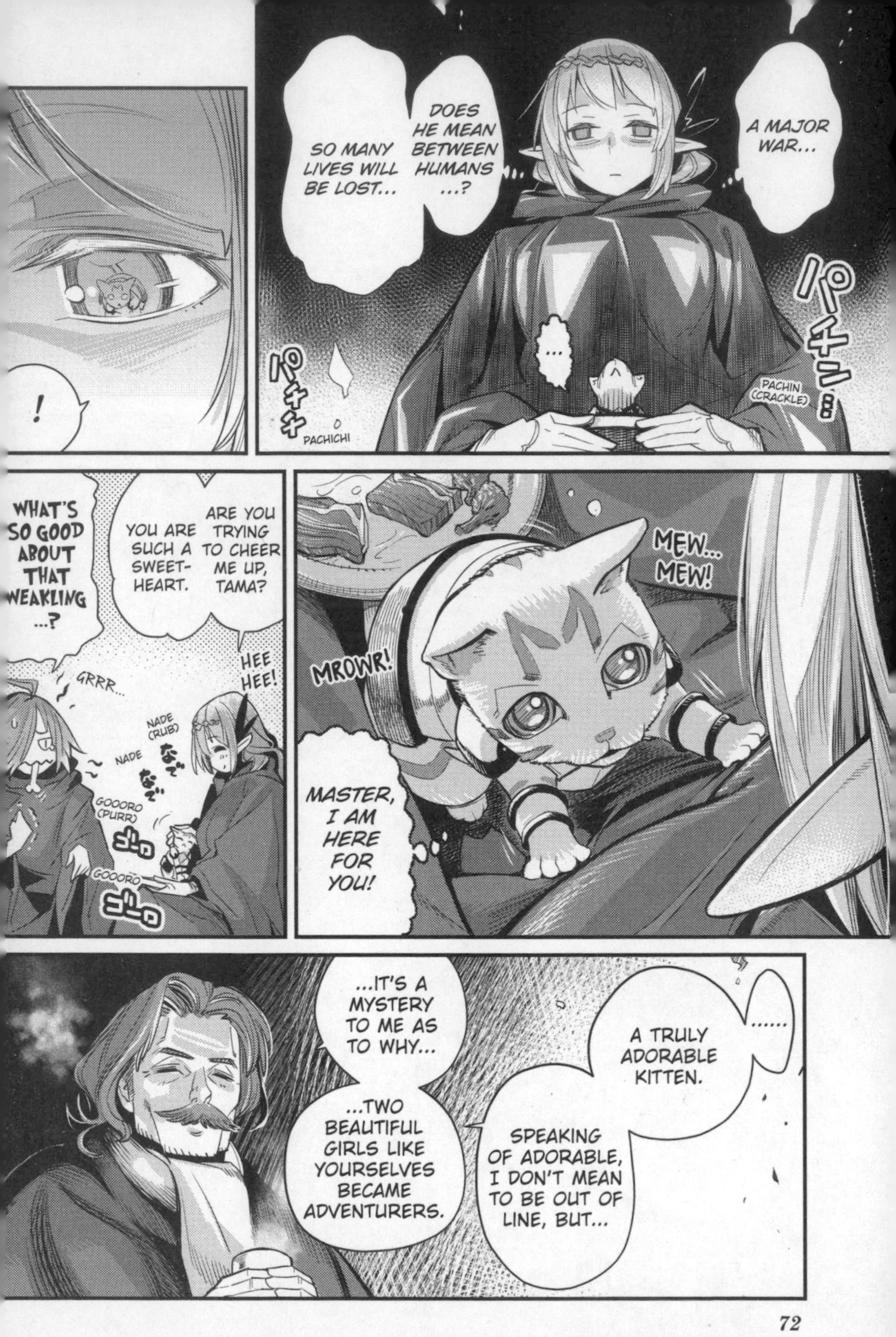
A MAJOR WAR...
DOES HE MEAN BETWEEN HUMANS ...?
SO MANY LIVES WILL BE LOST...
パチン!!
PACHIN (CRACKLE)
...
パチチ
PACHICHI
!
MEW... MEW!
MROWR!
MASTER, I AM HERE FOR YOU!
ARE YOU TRYING TO CHEER ME UP, TAMA?
YOU ARE SUCH A SWEET-HEART.
WHAT'S SO GOOD ABOUT THAT WEAKLING ...?
HEE HEE!
NADE (RUB)
なで
NADE
なで
GRRR...
GOOORO (PURR)
ゴロ
GOOORO
ゴロ
......
A TRULY ADORABLE KITTEN.
SPEAKING OF ADORABLE, I DON'T MEAN TO BE OUT OF LINE, BUT...
...IT'S A MYSTERY TO ME AS TO WHY...
...TWO BEAUTIFUL GIRLS LIKE YOURSELVES BECAME ADVENTURERS.

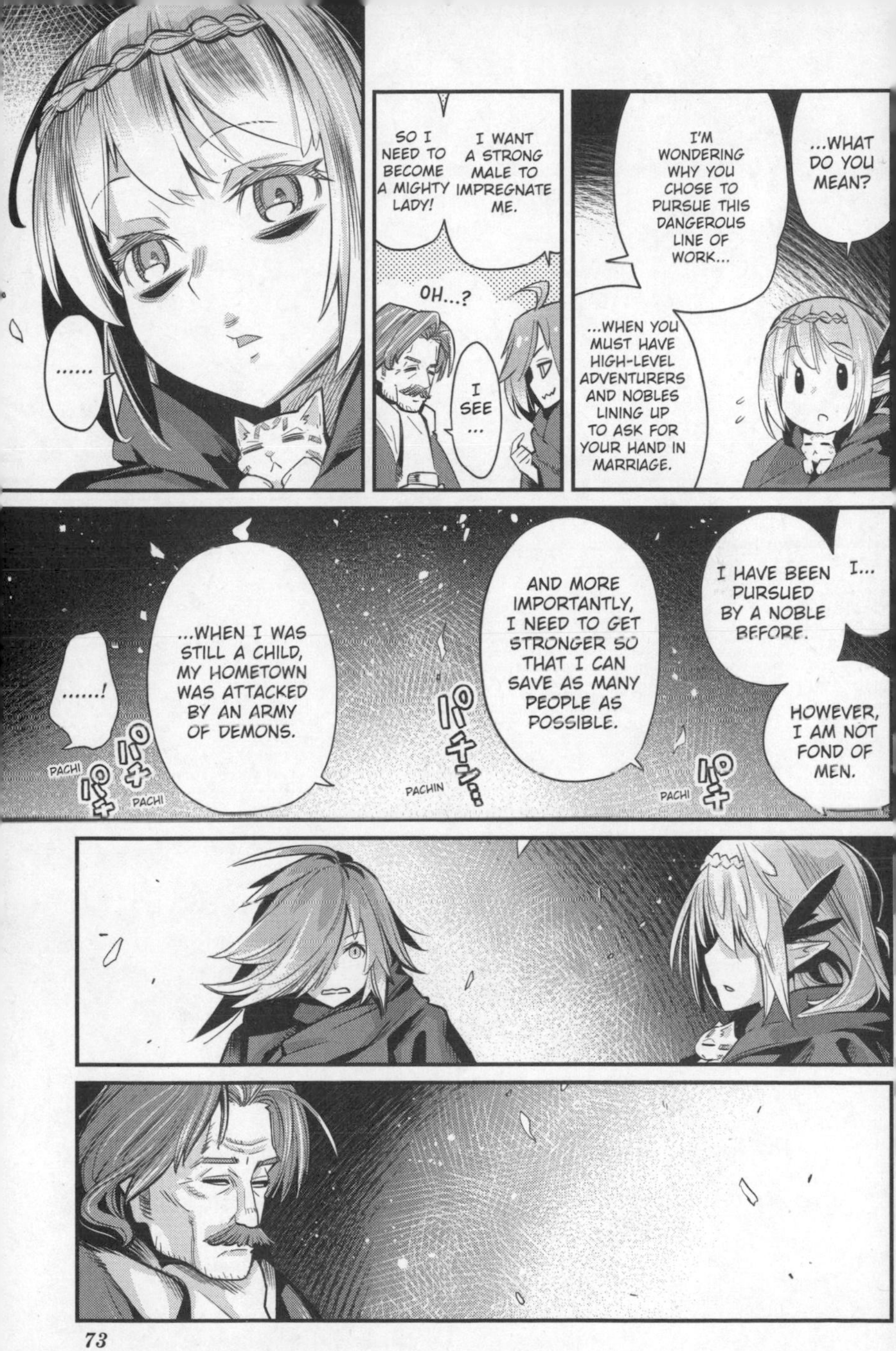
...WHAT DO YOU MEAN?
I'M WONDERING WHY YOU CHOSE TO PURSUE THIS DANGEROUS LINE OF WORK...
...WHEN YOU MUST HAVE HIGH-LEVEL ADVENTURERS AND NOBLES LINING UP TO ASK FOR YOUR HAND IN MARRIAGE.
I WANT A STRONG MALE TO IMPREGNATE ME.
SO I NEED TO BECOME A MIGHTY LADY!
OH...?
I SEE ...
......
I...
I HAVE BEEN PURSUED BY A NOBLE BEFORE.
HOWEVER, I AM NOT FOND OF MEN.
パチ
PACHI
AND MORE IMPORTANTLY, I NEED TO GET STRONGER SO THAT I CAN SAVE AS MANY PEOPLE AS POSSIBLE.
パチン…
PACHIN
...WHEN I WAS STILL A CHILD, MY HOMETOWN WAS ATTACKED BY AN ARMY OF DEMONS.
パチ パチ
PACHI PACHI
.......!

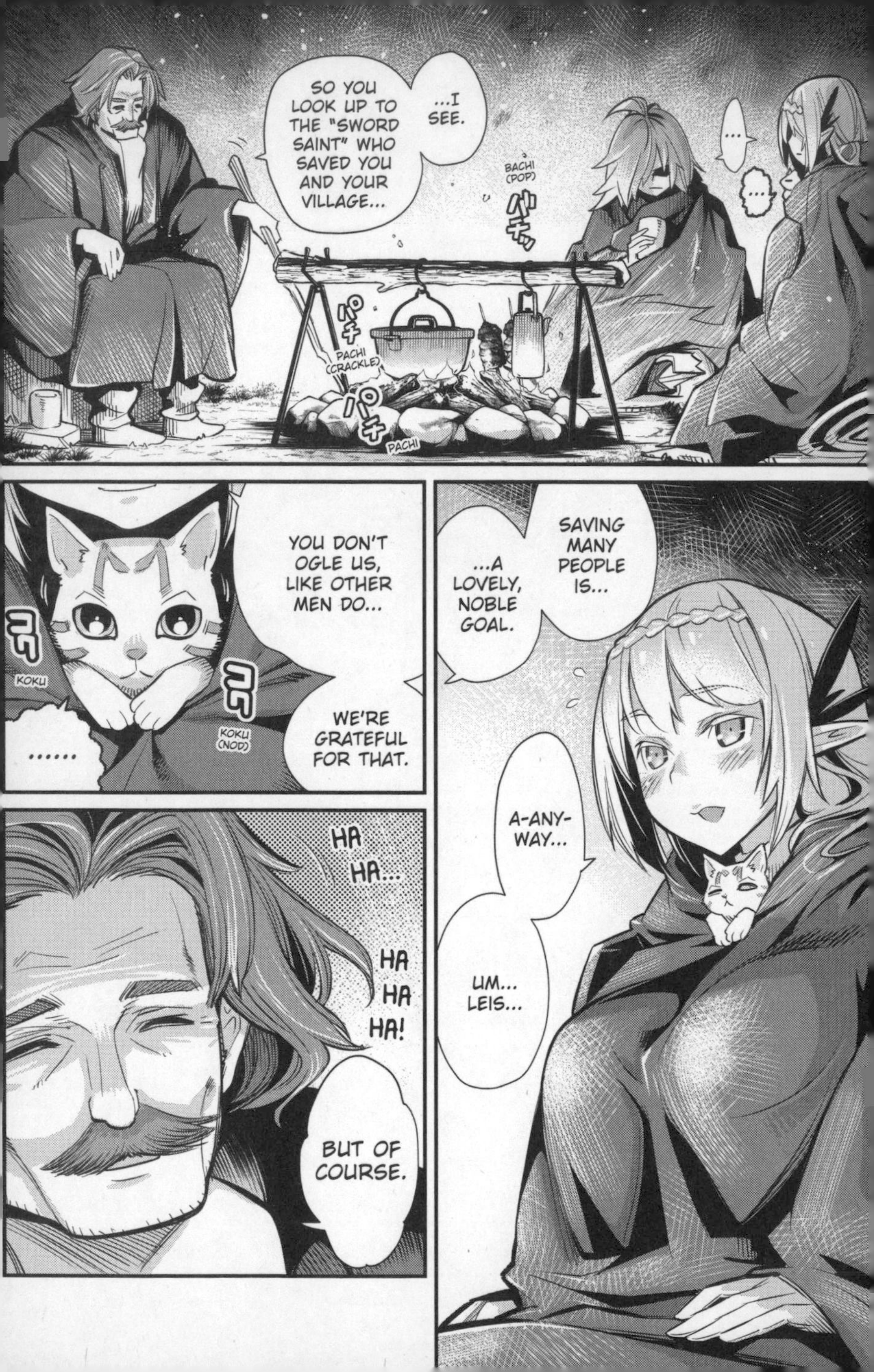
...
.....
...I SEE.
SO YOU LOOK UP TO THE "SWORD SAINT" WHO SAVED YOU AND YOUR VILLAGE...
BACHI (POP)
PACHI (CRACKLE)
PACHI
SAVING MANY PEOPLE IS...
...A LOVELY, NOBLE GOAL.
A-ANY-WAY...
UM... LEIS...
YOU DON'T OGLE US, LIKE OTHER MEN DO...
WE'RE GRATEFUL FOR THAT.
KOKU (NOD)
KOKU
......
HA HA...
HA HA HA!
BUT OF COURSE.

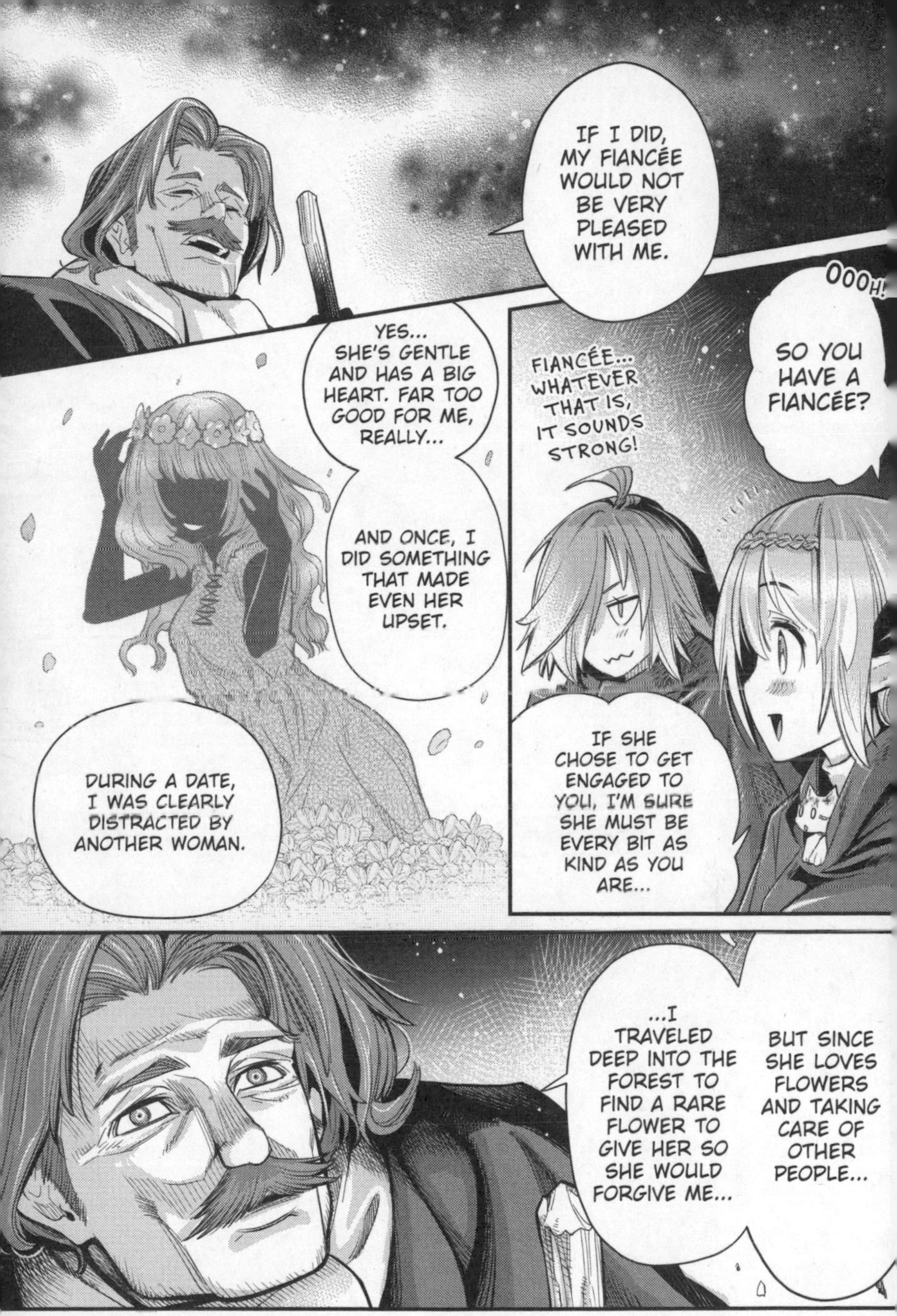
IF I DID, MY FIANCÉE WOULD NOT BE VERY PLEASED WITH ME.
OOOH!
SO YOU HAVE A FIANCÉE?
FIANCÉE... WHATEVER THAT IS, IT SOUNDS STRONG!
IF SHE CHOSE TO GET ENGAGED TO YOU, I'M SURE SHE MUST BE EVERY BIT AS KIND AS YOU ARE...
YES... SHE'S GENTLE AND HAS A BIG HEART. FAR TOO GOOD FOR ME, REALLY...
AND ONCE, I DID SOMETHING THAT MADE EVEN HER UPSET.
DURING A DATE, I WAS CLEARLY DISTRACTED BY ANOTHER WOMAN.
BUT SINCE SHE LOVES FLOWERS AND TAKING CARE OF OTHER PEOPLE...
...I TRAVELED DEEP INTO THE FOREST TO FIND A RARE FLOWER TO GIVE HER SO SHE WOULD FORGIVE ME...

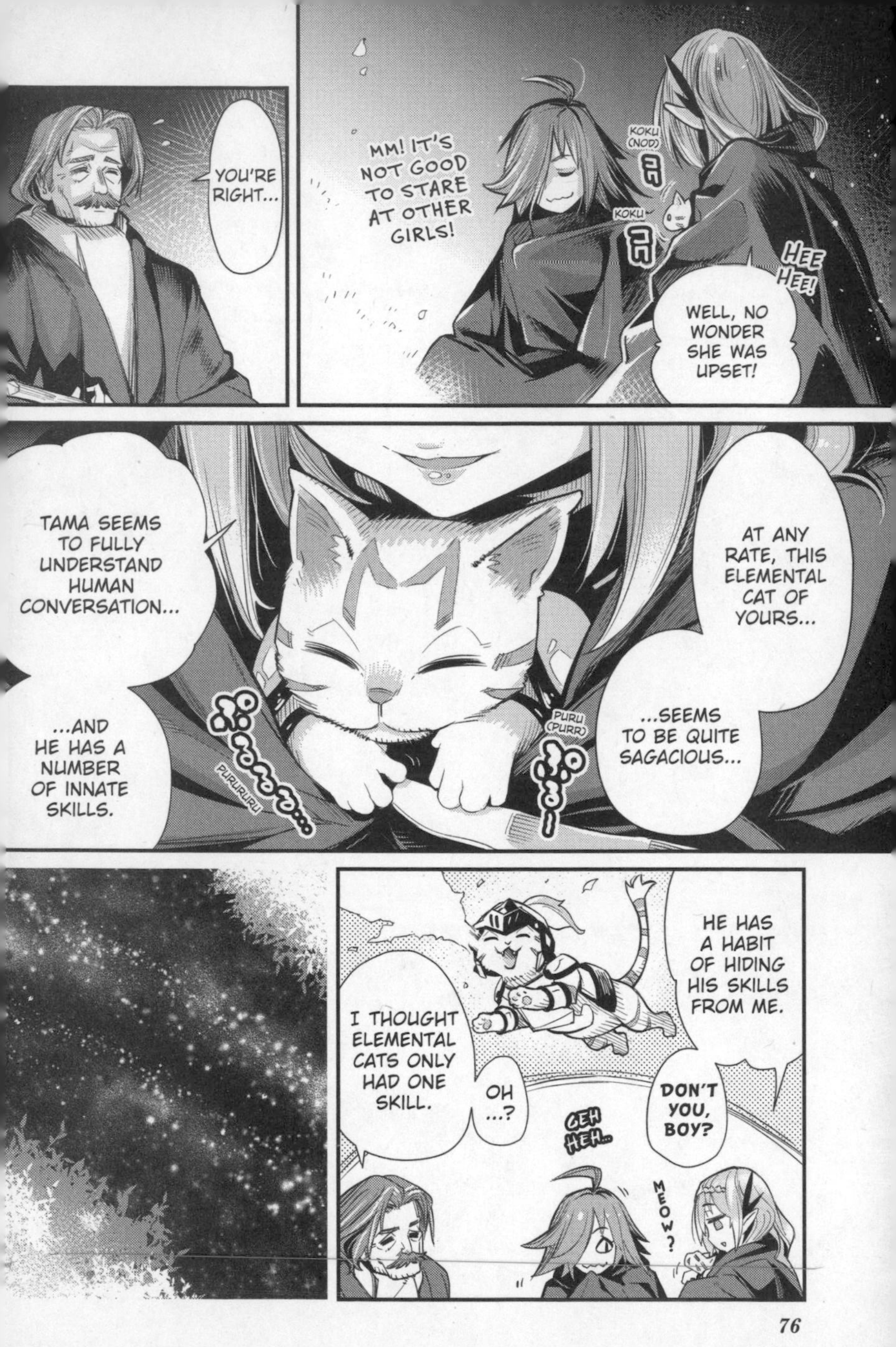
MM! IT'S NOT GOOD TO STARE AT OTHER GIRLS!
KOKU (NOD)
KOKU
HEE HEE!
WELL, NO WONDER SHE WAS UPSET!
YOU'RE RIGHT...
AT ANY RATE, THIS ELEMENTAL CAT OF YOURS...
...SEEMS TO BE QUITE SAGACIOUS...
PURU (PURR)
TAMA SEEMS TO FULLY UNDERSTAND HUMAN CONVERSATION...
...AND HE HAS A NUMBER OF INNATE SKILLS.
PURURURU
HE HAS A HABIT OF HIDING HIS SKILLS FROM ME.
DON'T YOU, BOY?
GEH HEH...
MEOW?
OH ...?
I THOUGHT ELEMENTAL CATS ONLY HAD ONE SKILL.

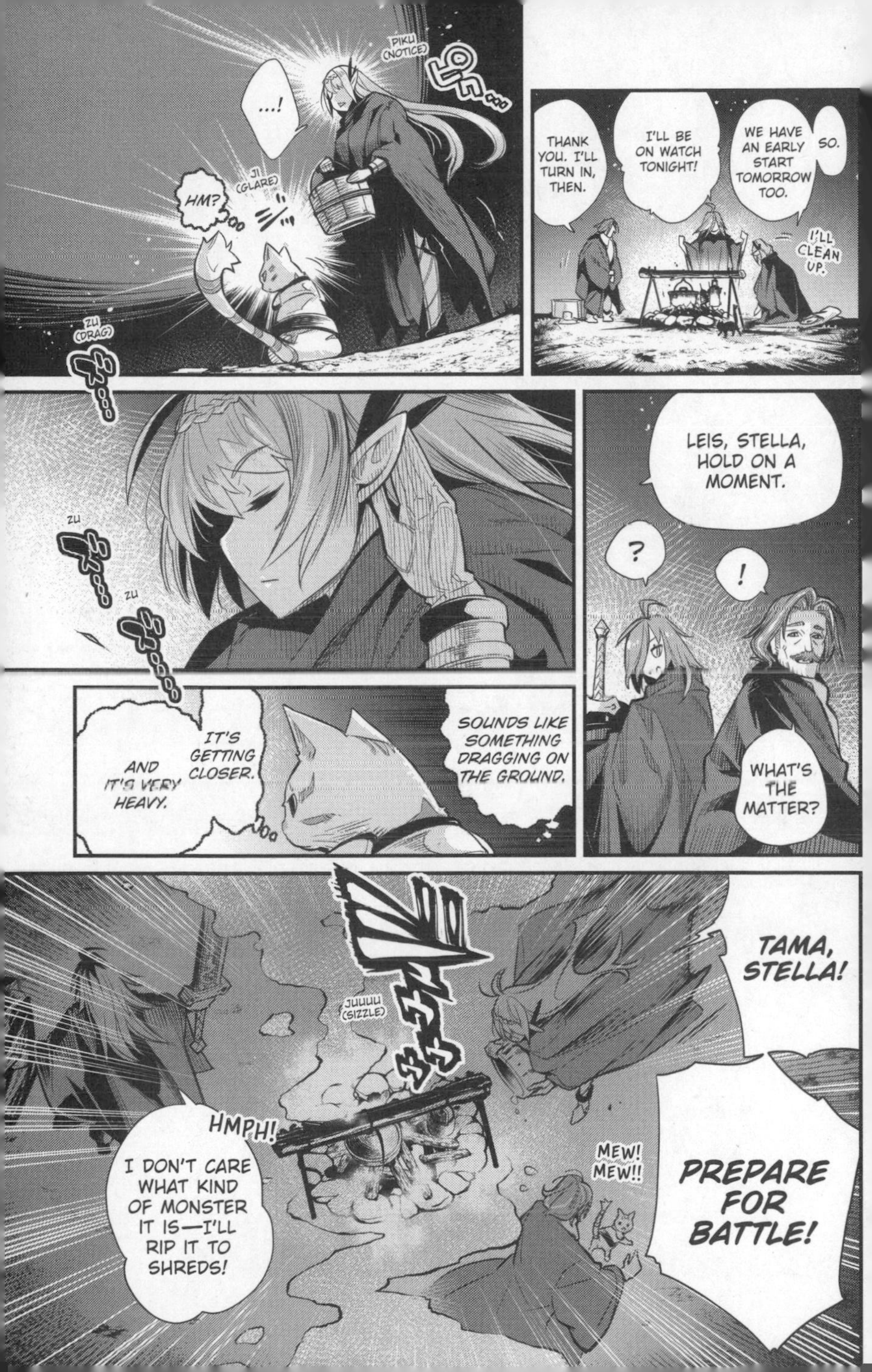
SO.
WE HAVE AN EARLY START TOMORROW TOO.
I'LL CLEAN UP.
I'LL BE ON WATCH TONIGHT!
THANK YOU. I'LL TURN IN, THEN.
PIKU (NOTICE)
...!
JI (GLARE)
HM?
ZU (DRAG)
LEIS, STELLA, HOLD ON A MOMENT.
!
?
WHAT'S THE MATTER?
ZU
ZU
SOUNDS LIKE SOMETHING DRAGGING ON THE GROUND.
IT'S GETTING CLOSER.
AND IT'S VERY HEAVY.
TAMA, STELLA!
PREPARE FOR BATTLE!
JUUUU (SIZZLE)
MEW! MEW!!
HMPH!
I DON'T CARE WHAT KIND OF MONSTER IT IS—I'LL RIP IT TO SHREDS!

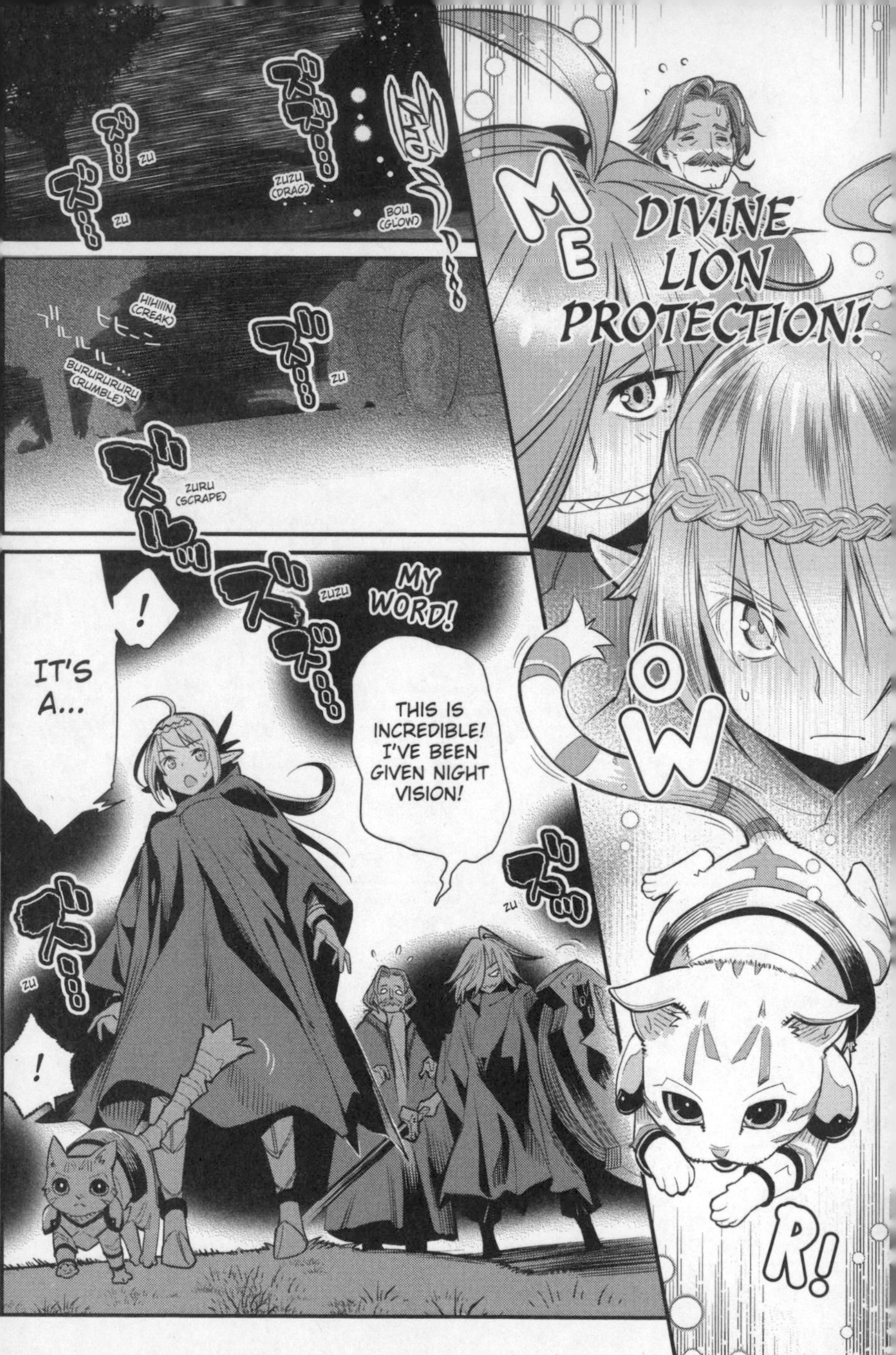
DIVINE LION PROTECTION!
ME
OW
R!
ZU
ZUZU (DRAG)
BOU (GLOW)
ZU
HIHIIIN (CREAK)
BURURURURU (RUMBLE)
ZU
ZURU (SCRAPE)
ZUZU
MY WORD!
!
IT'S A...
THIS IS INCREDIBLE! I'VE BEEN GIVEN NIGHT VISION!
ZU
ZU
!

#28 — An Unsullied Labyrinth

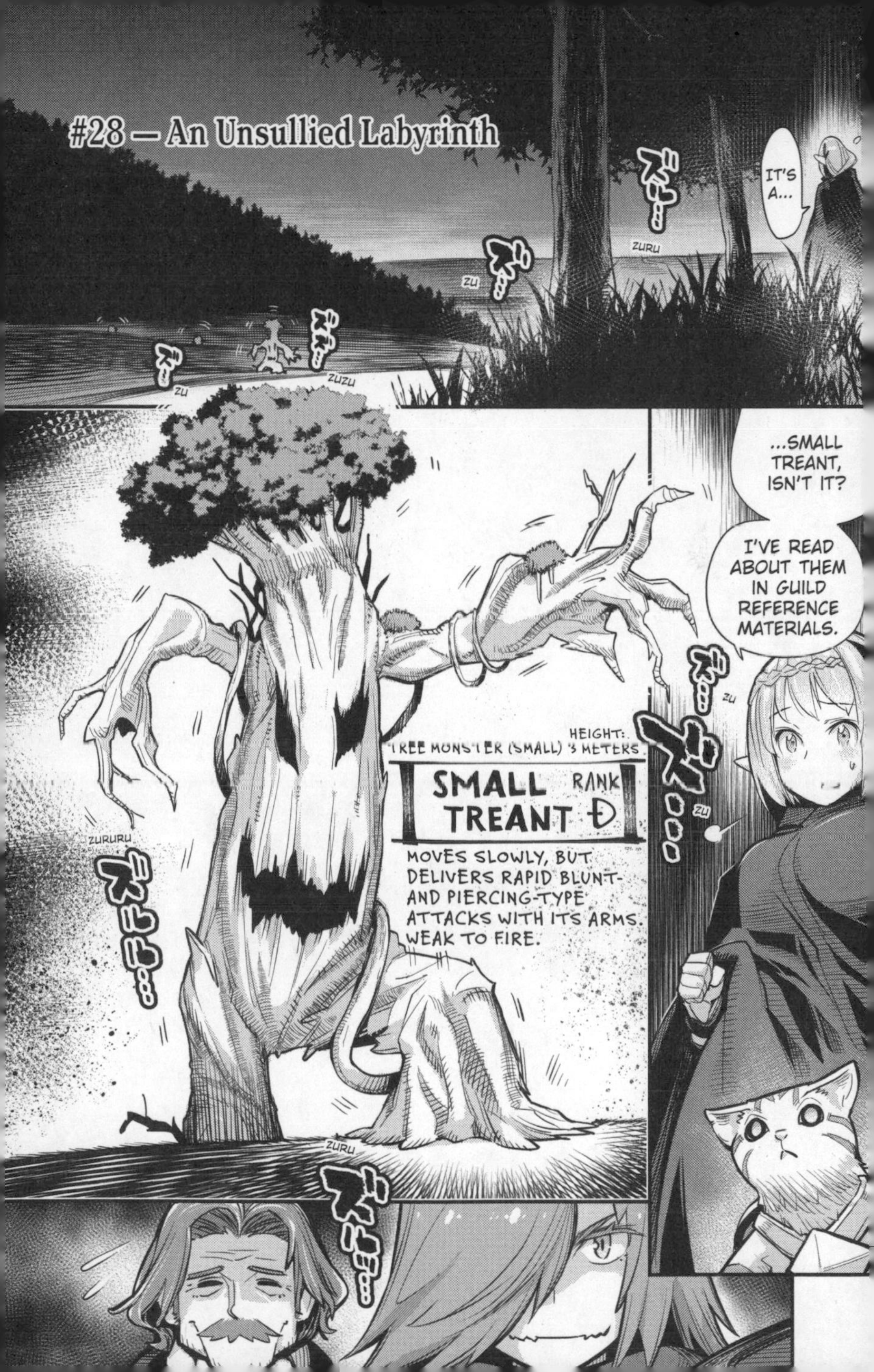
IT'S A...
ZURU
ZU
ZUZU
ZU
...SMALL TREANT, ISN'T IT?
I'VE READ ABOUT THEM IN GUILD REFERENCE MATERIALS.
ZU
ZU
TREE MONSTER (SMALL) HEIGHT: 3 METERS
SMALL TREANT RANK D
MOVES SLOWLY, BUT DELIVERS RAPID BLUNT- AND PIERCING-TYPE ATTACKS WITH ITS ARMS. WEAK TO FIRE.
ZURURU
ZURU

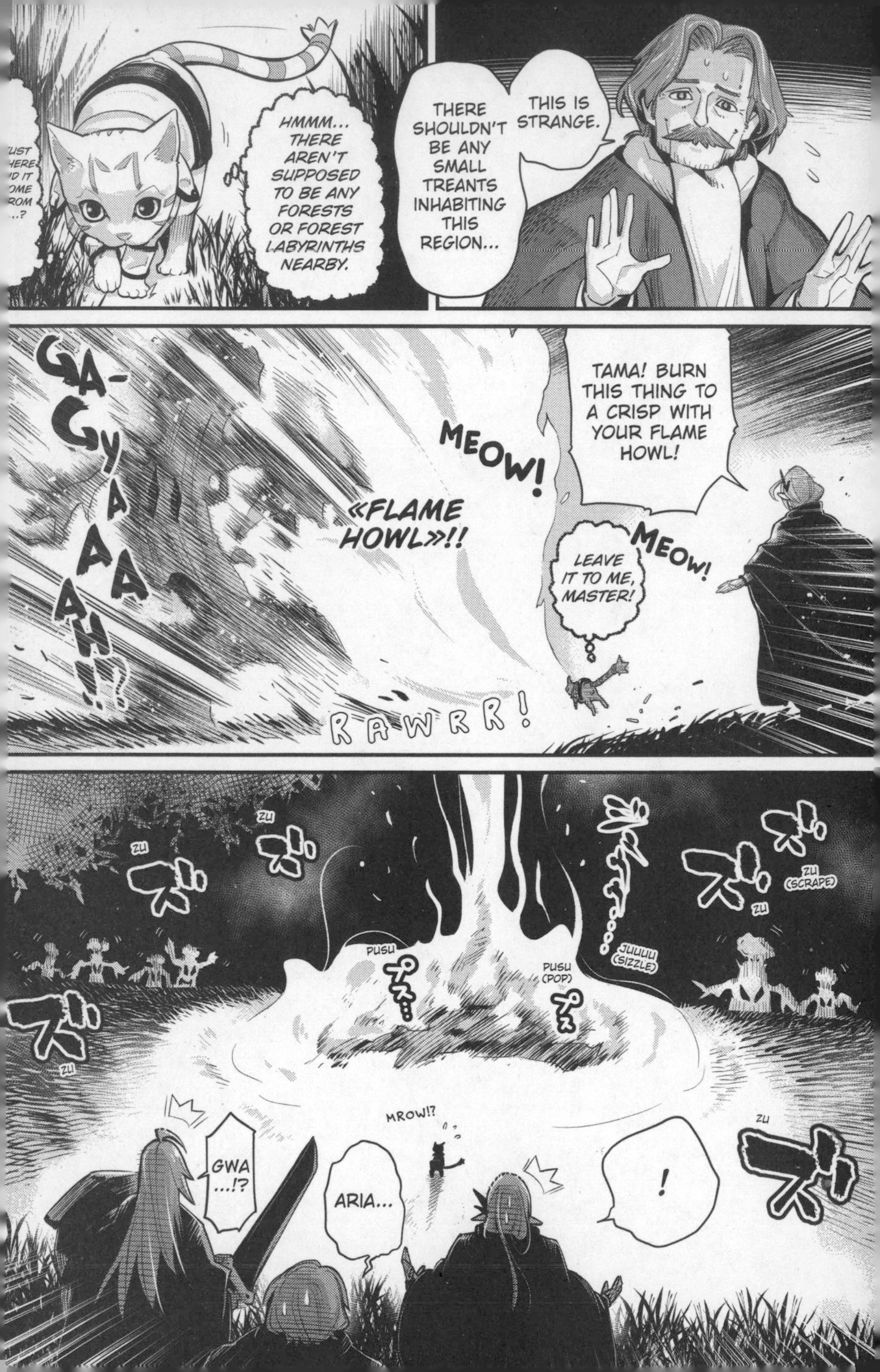
THIS IS STRANGE.
THERE SHOULDN'T BE ANY SMALL TREANTS INHABITING THIS REGION...
HMMM... THERE AREN'T SUPPOSED TO BE ANY FORESTS OR FOREST LABYRINTHS NEARBY.
TAMA! BURN THIS THING TO A CRISP WITH YOUR FLAME HOWL!
MEOW!
MEOW!
LEAVE IT TO ME, MASTER!
«FLAME HOWL»!!
GA-GYAAPPAAH!!?
RAWRR!
ZU (SCRAPE)
ZU
JUUUU (SIZZLE)
PUSU (POP)
PUSU
ZU
ZU
ZU
ZU
!
MROW!?
ARIA...
GWA...!?

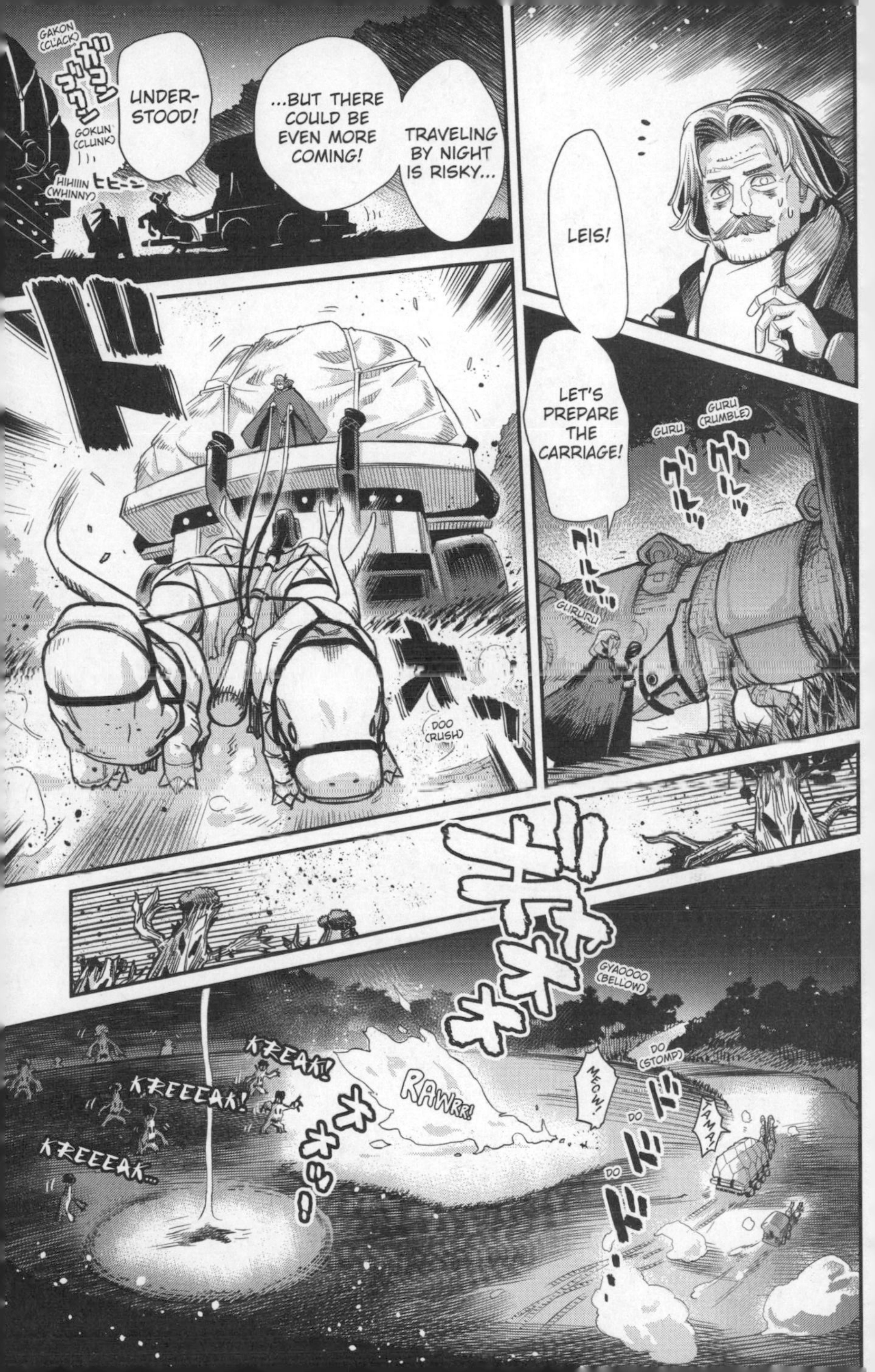
...
LEIS!
TRAVELING BY NIGHT IS RISKY...
...BUT THERE COULD BE EVEN MORE COMING!
UNDER-STOOD!
GAKON (CLACK)
GOKUN (CLUNK)
HIHIIIN (WHINNY)
LET'S PREPARE THE CARRIAGE!
GURU (RUMBLE)
GURU
GURURU
DOO (RUSH)
GYAOOOO (BELLOW)
DO (STOMP)
DO
DO
TAMA!
MEOW!
RAWRR!
KREAK!!
KREEEAK!
KREEEAK...

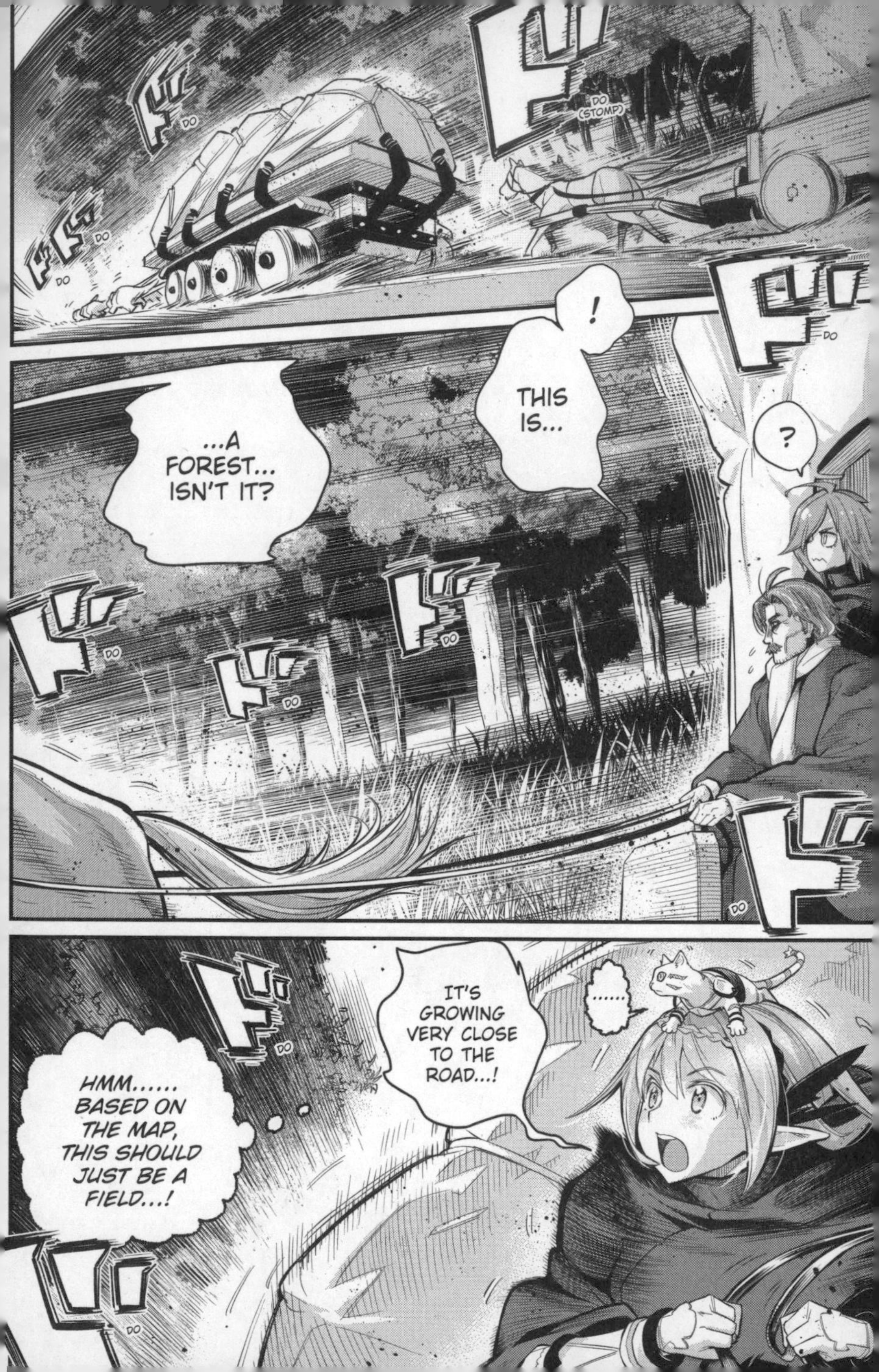
DO
(STOMP)
DO
DO
DO
DO
!
?
THIS IS...
...A FOREST... ISN'T IT?
DO
DO
DO
DO
......
IT'S GROWING VERY CLOSE TO THE ROAD...!
HMM...... BASED ON THE MAP, THIS SHOULD JUST BE A FIELD...!
DO
DO

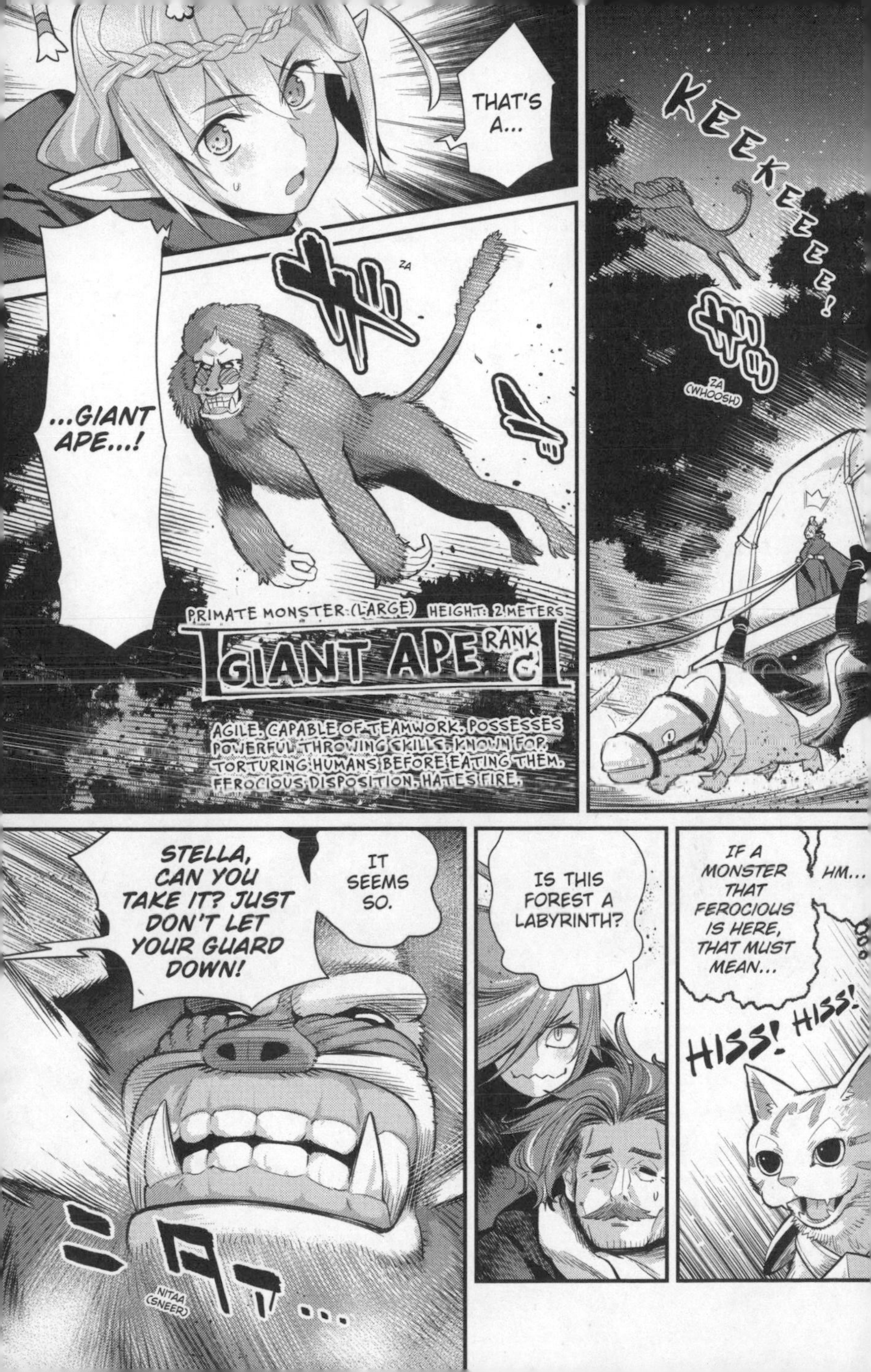
KEEKEEEE!
ZA (WHOOSH)
THAT'S A...
ZA
...GIANT APE...!
PRIMATE MONSTER (LARGE) HEIGHT: 2 METERS
GIANT APE RANK C
AGILE. CAPABLE OF TEAMWORK. POSSESSES POWERFUL THROWING SKILLS. KNOWN FOR TORTURING HUMANS BEFORE EATING THEM. FEROCIOUS DISPOSITION. HATES FIRE.
HM...
IF A MONSTER THAT FEROCIOUS IS HERE, THAT MUST MEAN...
HISS! HISS!
IS THIS FOREST A LABYRINTH?
IT SEEMS SO.
STELLA, CAN YOU TAKE IT? JUST DON'T LET YOUR GUARD DOWN!
NITAA (SNEER)

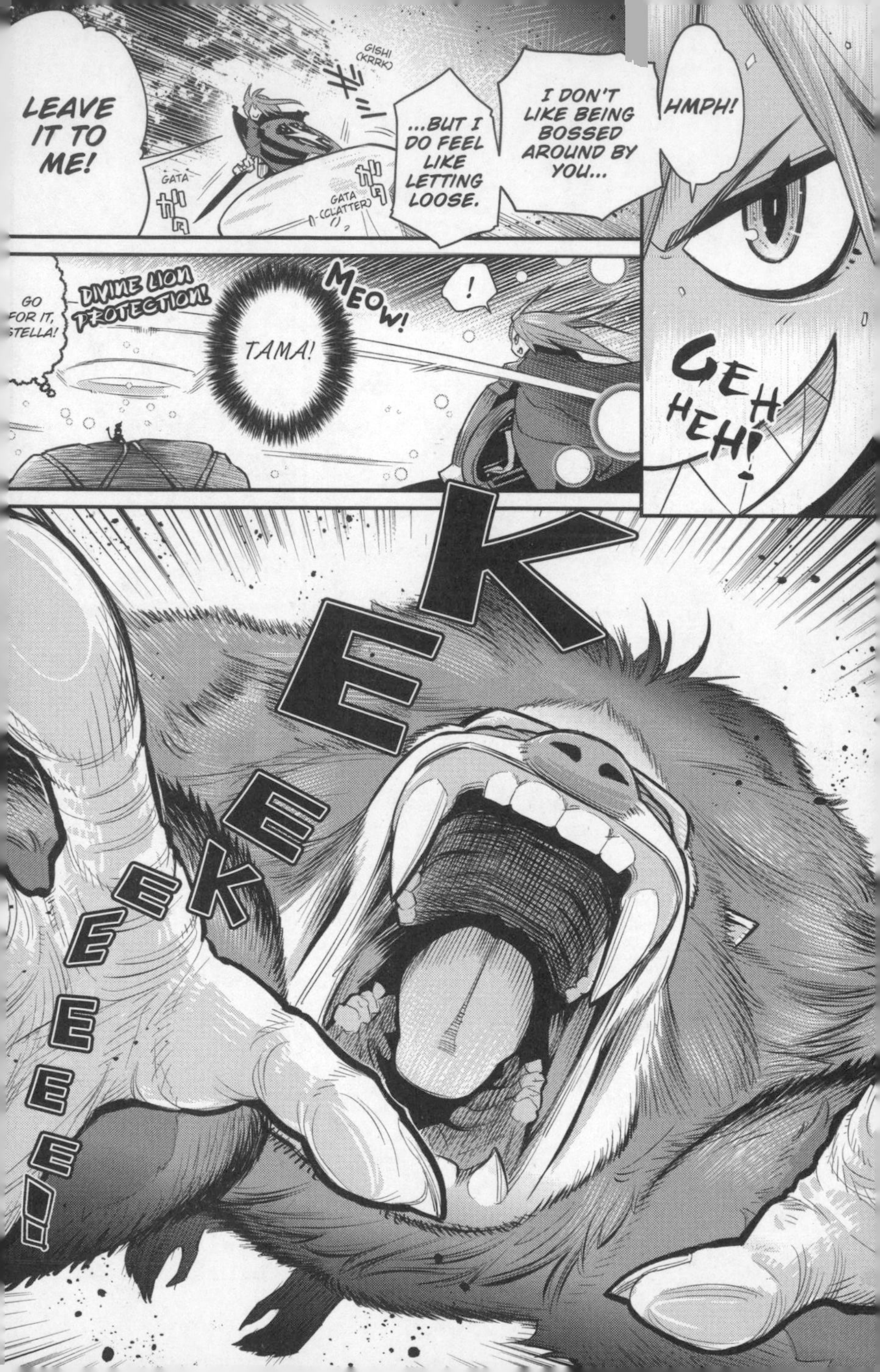
HMPH!
GEH HEH!
I DON'T LIKE BEING BOSSED AROUND BY YOU...
...BUT I DO FEEL LIKE LETTING LOOSE.
GISHI (KRRK)
GATA (CLATTER)
GATA
LEAVE IT TO ME!
!
MEOW!
TAMA!
DIVINE LION PROTECTION!
GO FOR IT, STELLA!
EEK
EEKEEEEEE!!

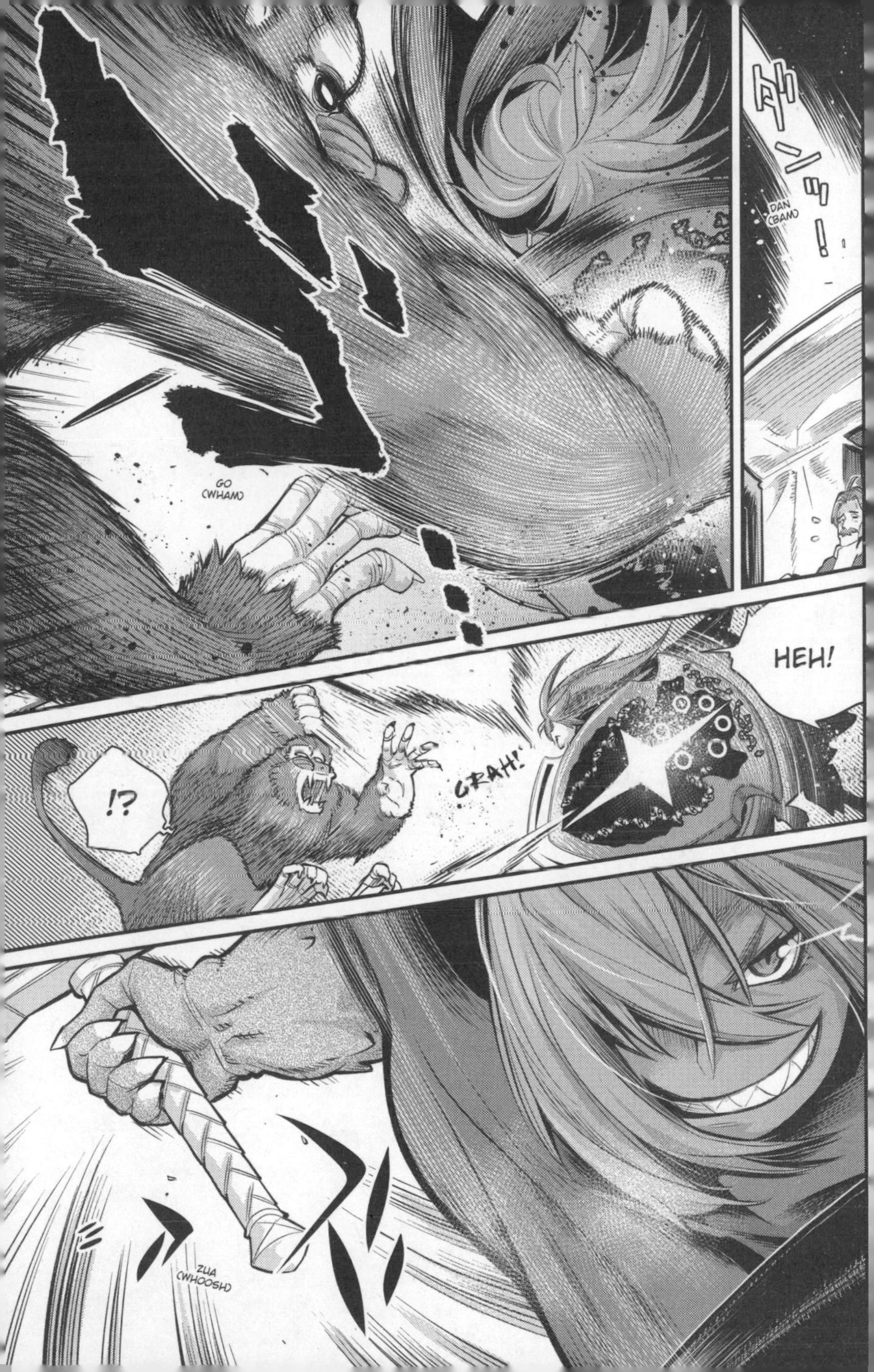
DAN (BAM)
GO (WHAM)
HEH!
GRAH!
!?
ZUA (WHOOSH)

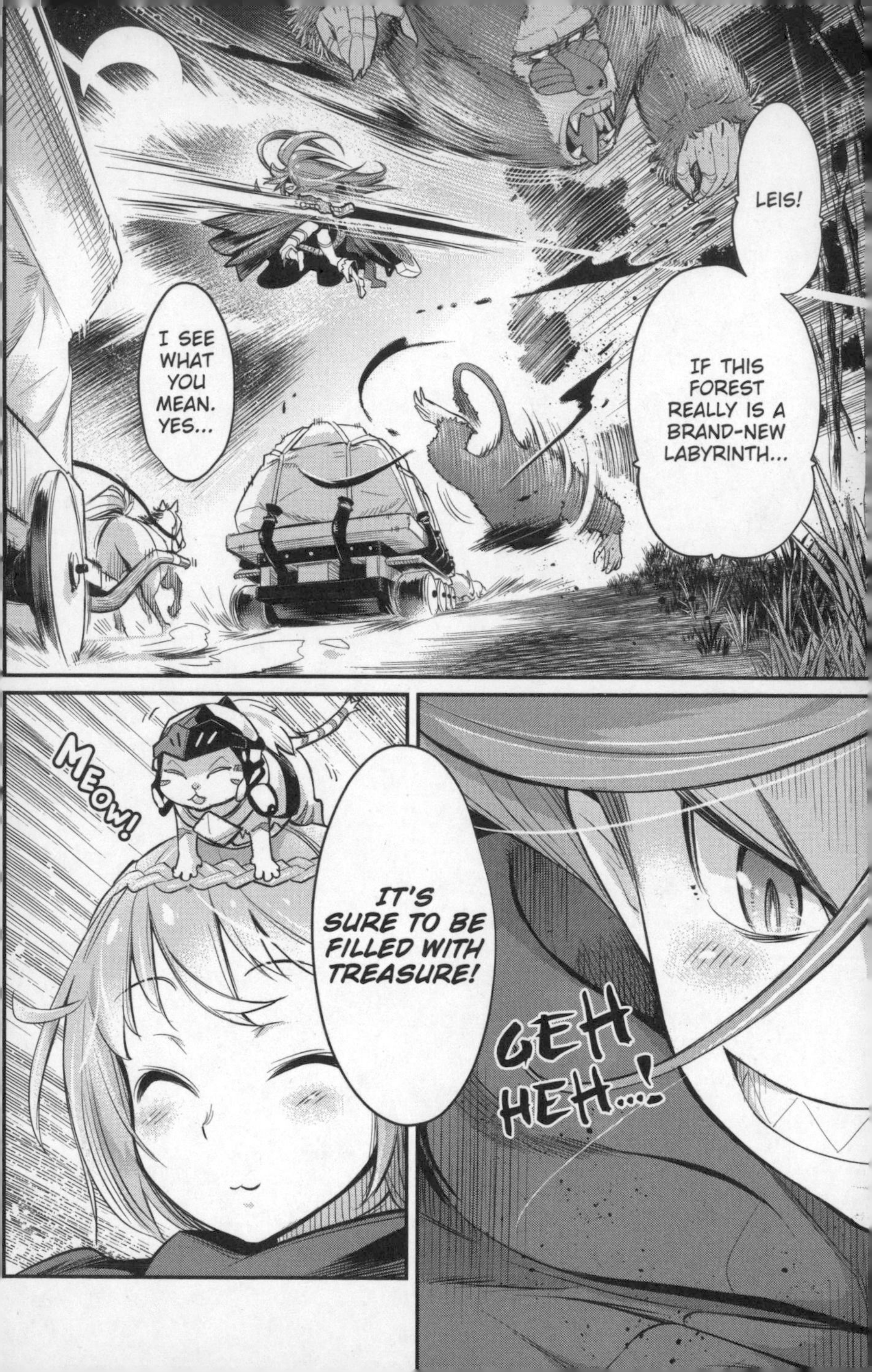
LEIS!
IF THIS FOREST REALLY IS A BRAND-NEW LABYRINTH...
I SEE WHAT YOU MEAN. YES...
GEH HEH...!
IT'S SURE TO BE FILLED WITH TREASURE!
MEOW!

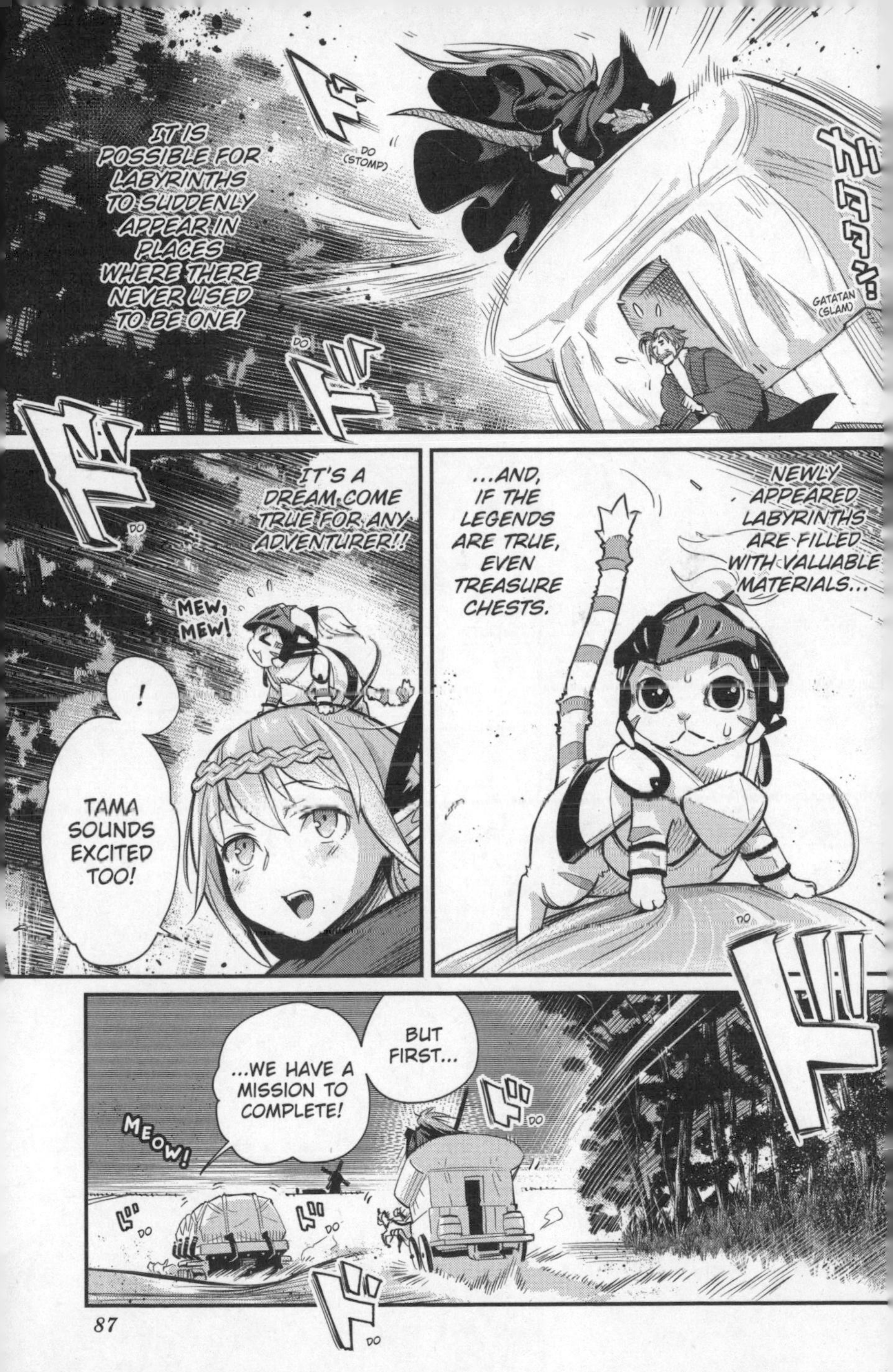
GATATAN (SLAM)
DO (STOMP)
IT IS POSSIBLE FOR LABYRINTHS TO SUDDENLY APPEAR IN PLACES WHERE THERE NEVER USED TO BE ONE!
DO
NEWLY APPEARED LABYRINTHS ARE FILLED WITH VALUABLE MATERIALS...
...AND, IF THE LEGENDS ARE TRUE, EVEN TREASURE CHESTS.
DO
IT'S A DREAM COME TRUE FOR ANY ADVENTURER!!
DO
MEW, MEW!
!
TAMA SOUNDS EXCITED TOO!
BUT FIRST...
...WE HAVE A MISSION TO COMPLETE!
DO
MEOW!
DO
DO
DO

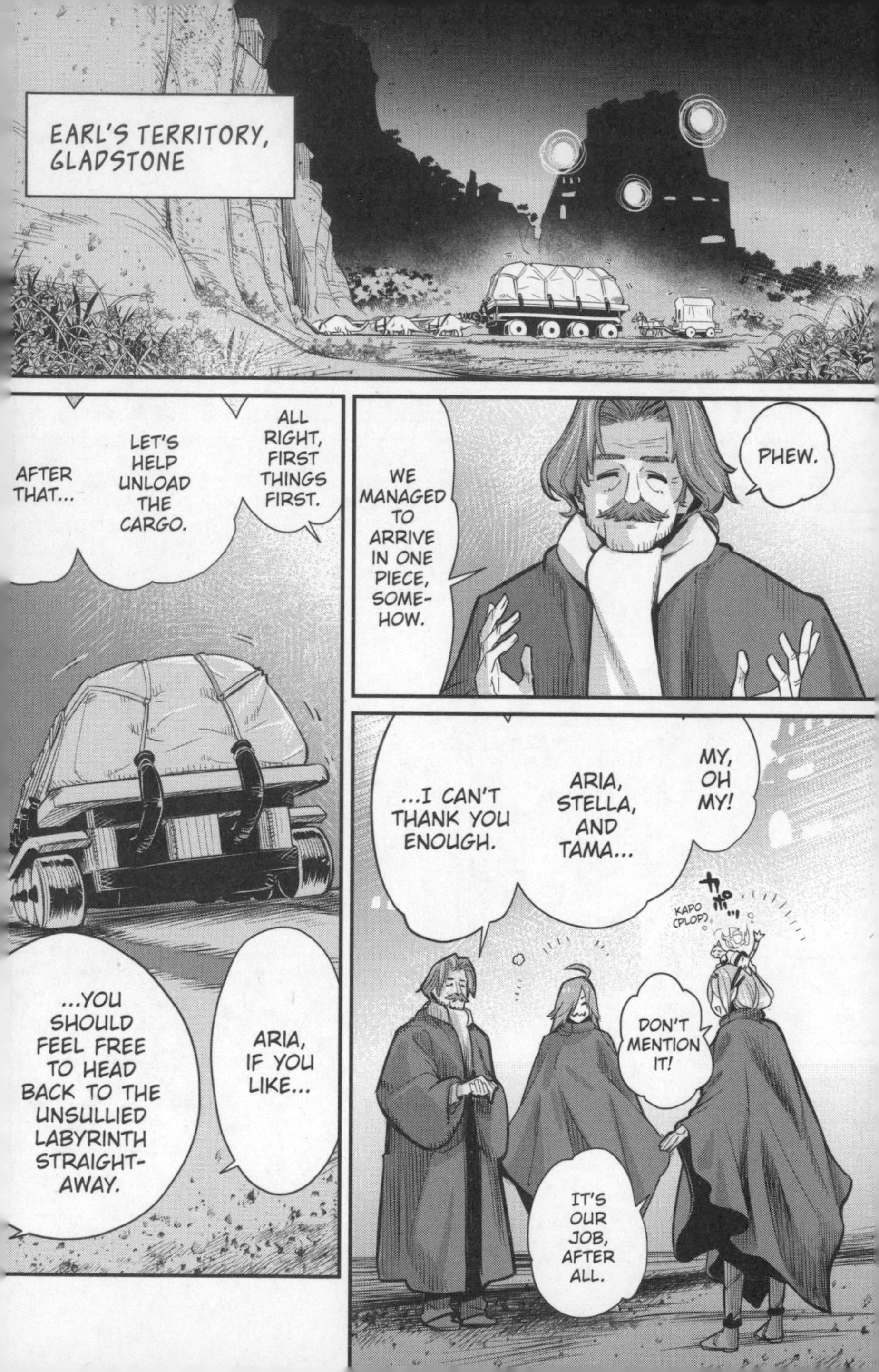
EARL'S TERRITORY, GLADSTONE
PHEW.
WE MANAGED TO ARRIVE IN ONE PIECE, SOMEHOW.
MY, OH MY!
ARIA, STELLA, AND TAMA...
...I CAN'T THANK YOU ENOUGH.
KAPO (PLOP)
DON'T MENTION IT!
IT'S OUR JOB, AFTER ALL.
ALL RIGHT, FIRST THINGS FIRST.
LET'S HELP UNLOAD THE CARGO.
AFTER THAT...
ARIA, IF YOU LIKE...
...YOU SHOULD FEEL FREE TO HEAD BACK TO THE UNSULLIED LABYRINTH STRAIGHTAWAY.

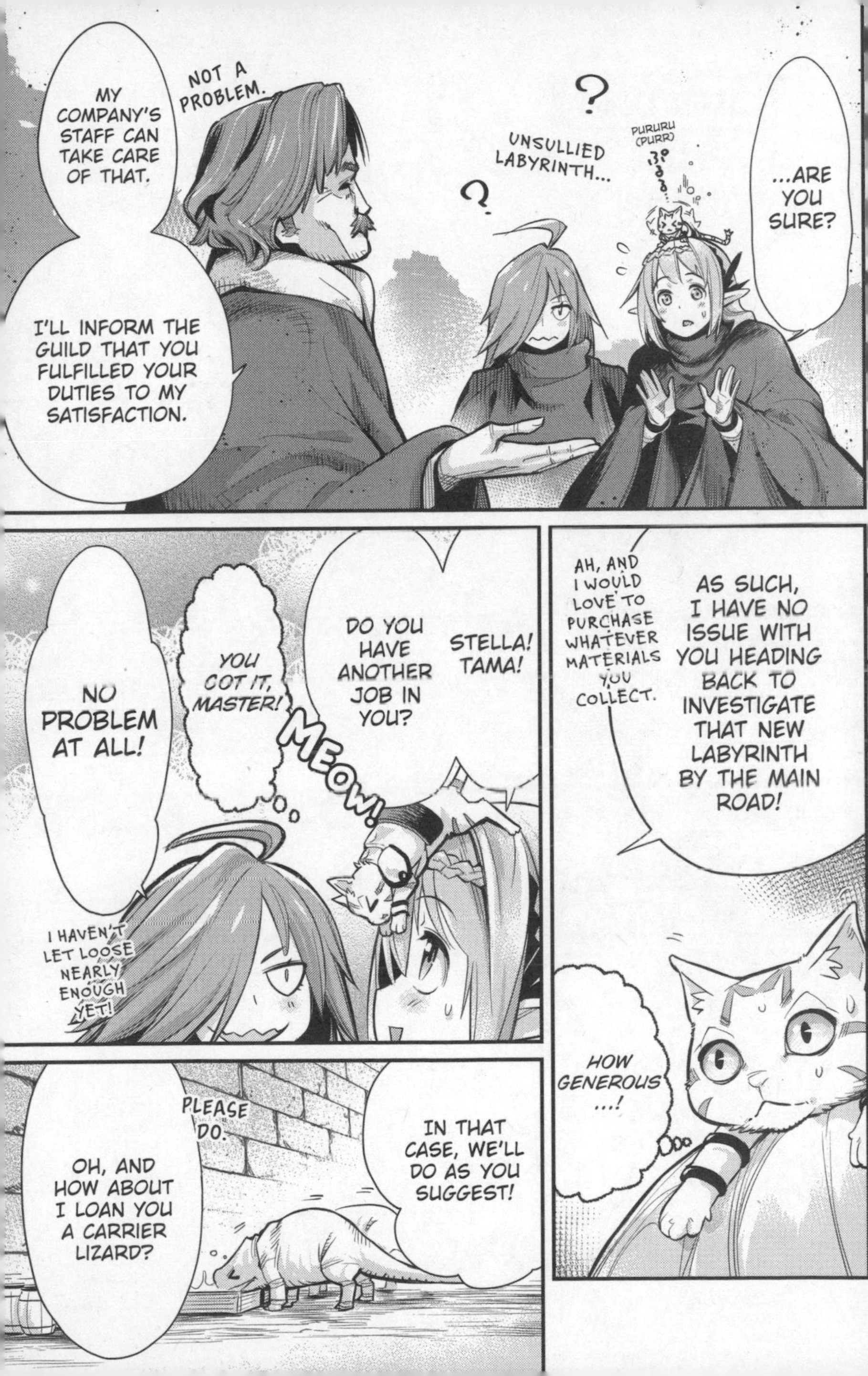
...ARE YOU SURE?
PURURU (PURR)
UNSULLIED LABYRINTH...
NOT A PROBLEM.
MY COMPANY'S STAFF CAN TAKE CARE OF THAT.
I'LL INFORM THE GUILD THAT YOU FULFILLED YOUR DUTIES TO MY SATISFACTION.
AS SUCH, I HAVE NO ISSUE WITH YOU HEADING BACK TO INVESTIGATE THAT NEW LABYRINTH BY THE MAIN ROAD!
AH, AND I WOULD LOVE TO PURCHASE WHATEVER MATERIALS YOU COLLECT.
HOW GENEROUS...!
STELLA! TAMA!
DO YOU HAVE ANOTHER JOB IN YOU?
MEOW!
YOU GOT IT, MASTER!
NO PROBLEM AT ALL!
I HAVEN'T LET LOOSE NEARLY ENOUGH YET!
IN THAT CASE, WE'LL DO AS YOU SUGGEST!
PLEASE DO.
OH, AND HOW ABOUT I LOAN YOU A CARRIER LIZARD?

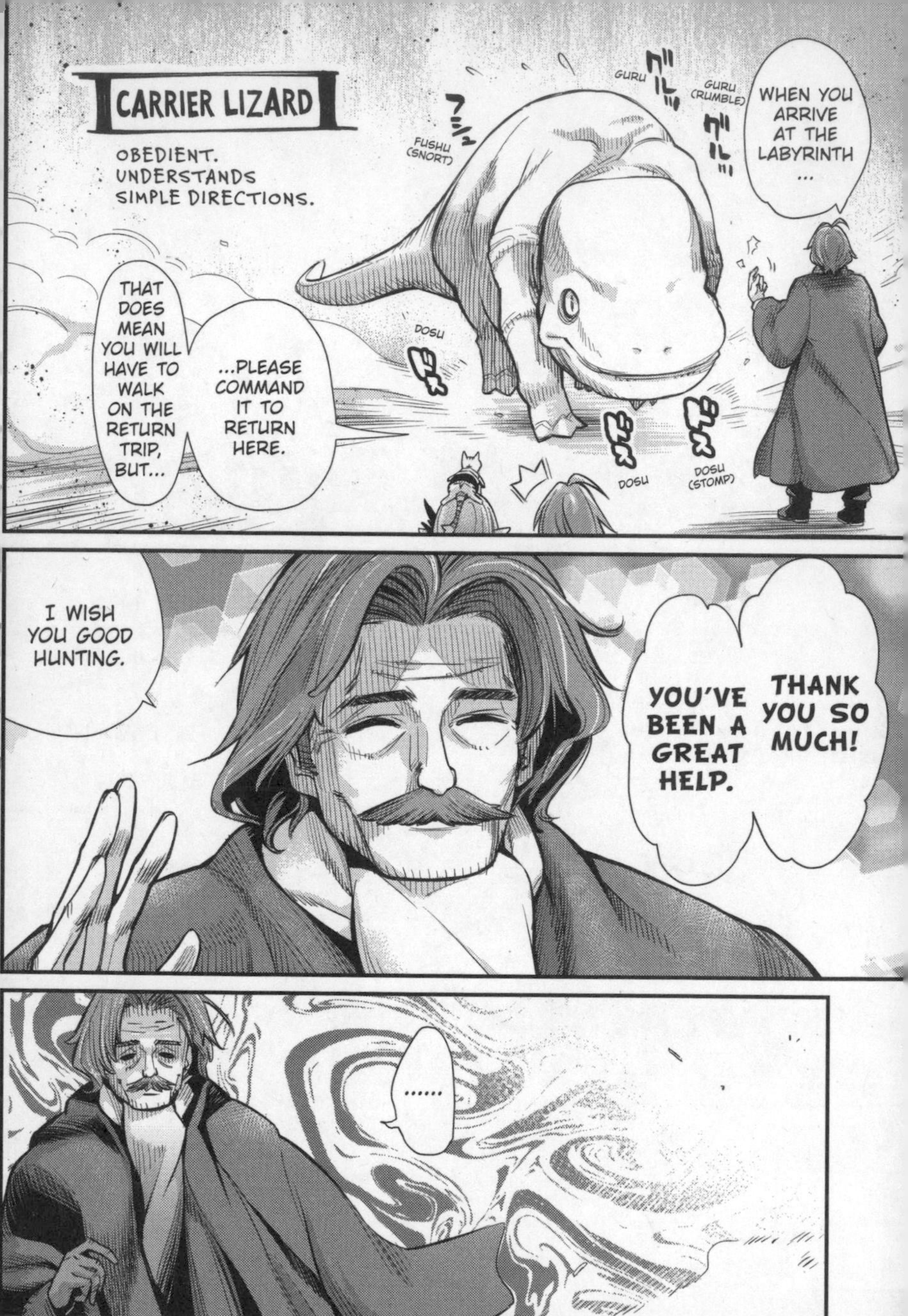
WHEN YOU ARRIVE AT THE LABYRINTH ...
GURU GURU (RUMBLE)
GURU
FUSHU (SNORT)
CARRIER LIZARD
OBEDIENT. UNDERSTANDS SIMPLE DIRECTIONS.
DOSU (STOMP)
DOSU
DOSU
...PLEASE COMMAND IT TO RETURN HERE.
THAT DOES MEAN YOU WILL HAVE TO WALK ON THE RETURN TRIP, BUT...
THANK YOU SO MUCH!
YOU'VE BEEN A GREAT HELP.
I WISH YOU GOOD HUNTING.
......

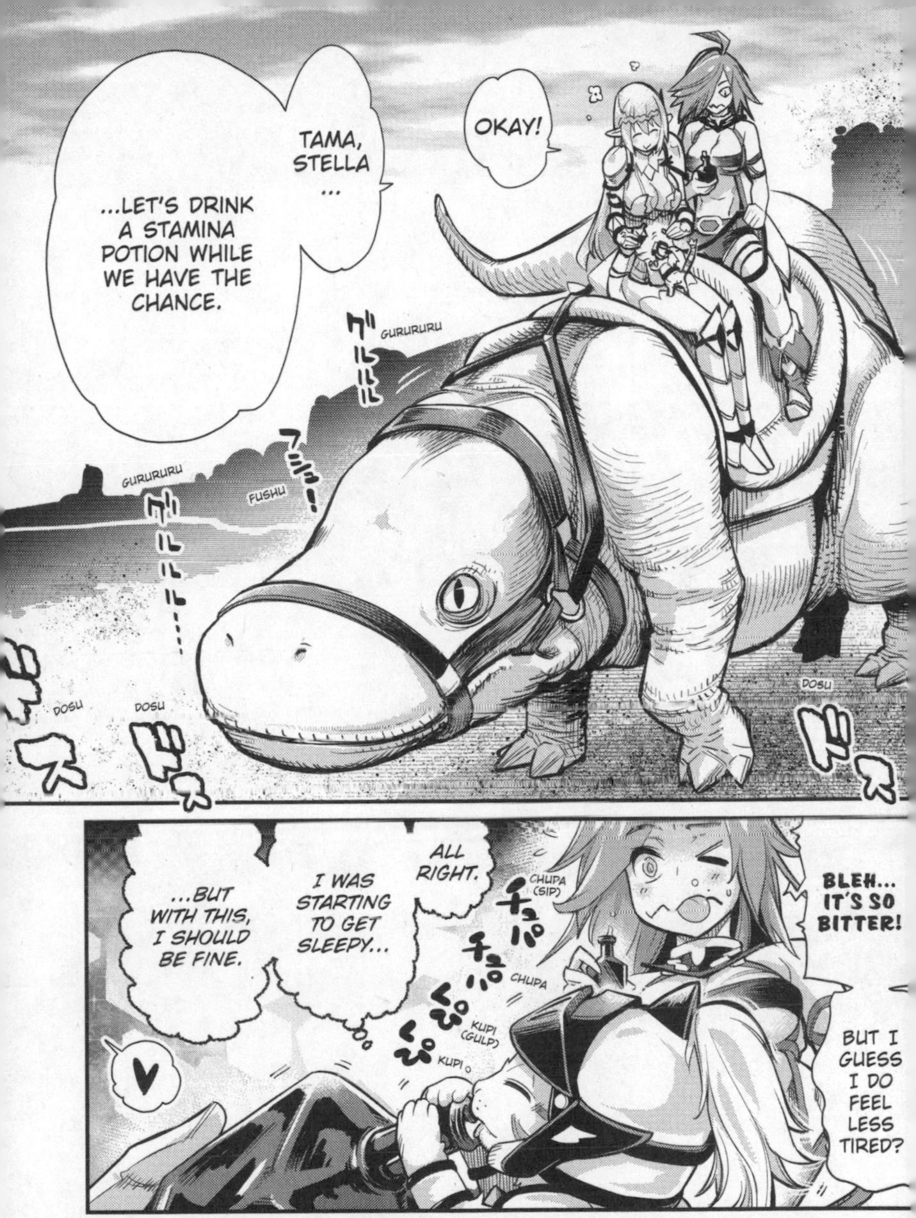
OKAY!
TAMA, STELLA ...
...LET'S DRINK A STAMINA POTION WHILE WE HAVE THE CHANCE.
GURURURU
FUSHU
GURURURU
DOSU
DOSU
DOSU
BLEH... IT'S SO BITTER!
BUT I GUESS I DO FEEL LESS TIRED?
CHUPA (SIP)
CHUPA
KUPI (GULP)
KUPI
ALL RIGHT.
I WAS STARTING TO GET SLEEPY...
...BUT WITH THIS, I SHOULD BE FINE.
♥

[redacted]

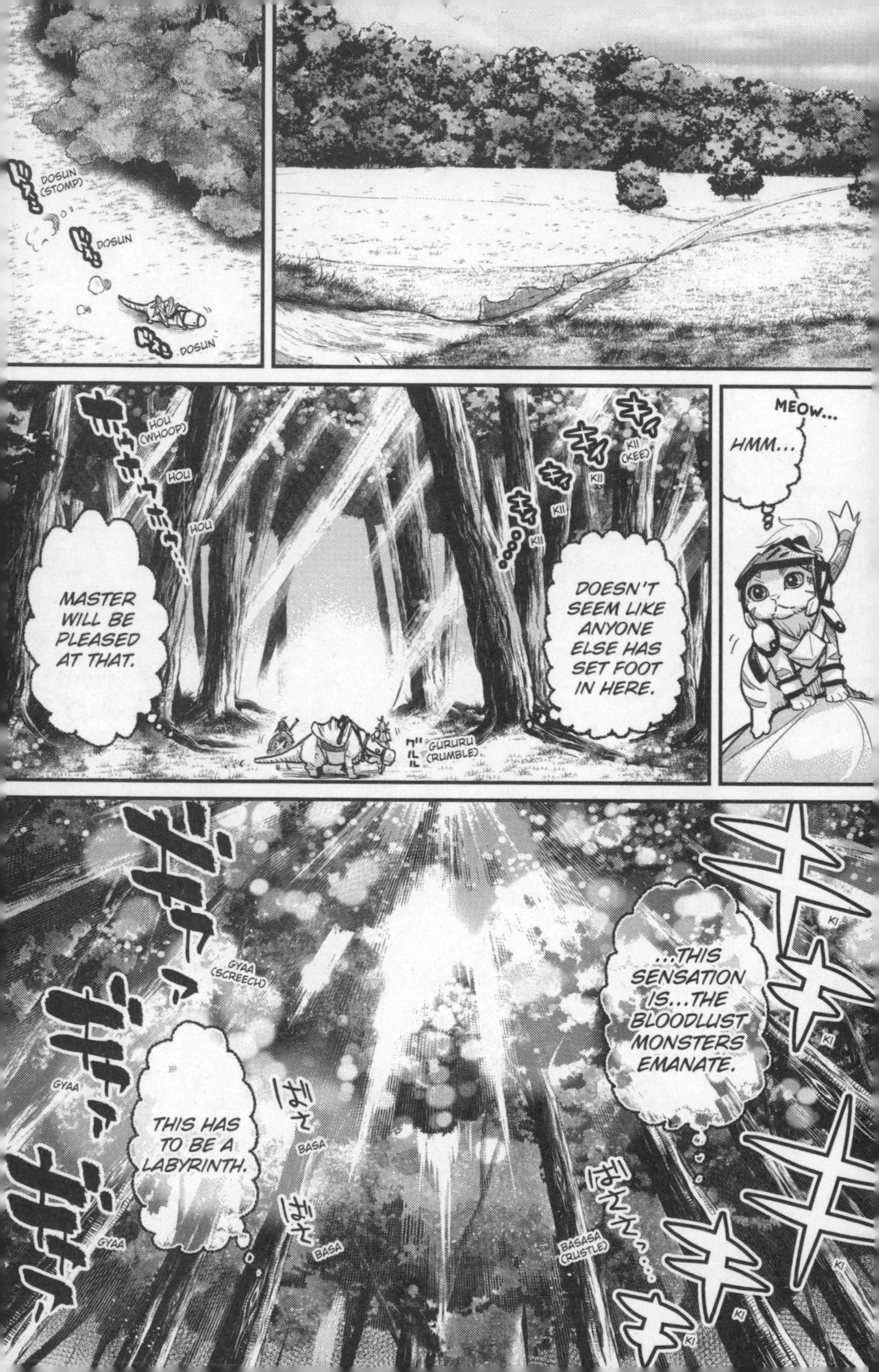
DOSUN (STOMP)
DOSUN
DOSUN
MEOW...
HMM...
KII (KEE)
KII
KII
KII
DOESN'T SEEM LIKE ANYONE ELSE HAS SET FOOT IN HERE.
GURURU (RUMBLE)
HOU (WHOOP)
HOU
HOU
MASTER WILL BE PLEASED AT THAT.
KI
KI
...THIS SENSATION IS...THE BLOODLUST MONSTERS EMANATE.
KI
KI
KI
BASASA (RUSTLE)
BASA
BASA
THIS HAS TO BE A LABYRINTH.
GYAA (SCREECH)
GYAA
GYAA

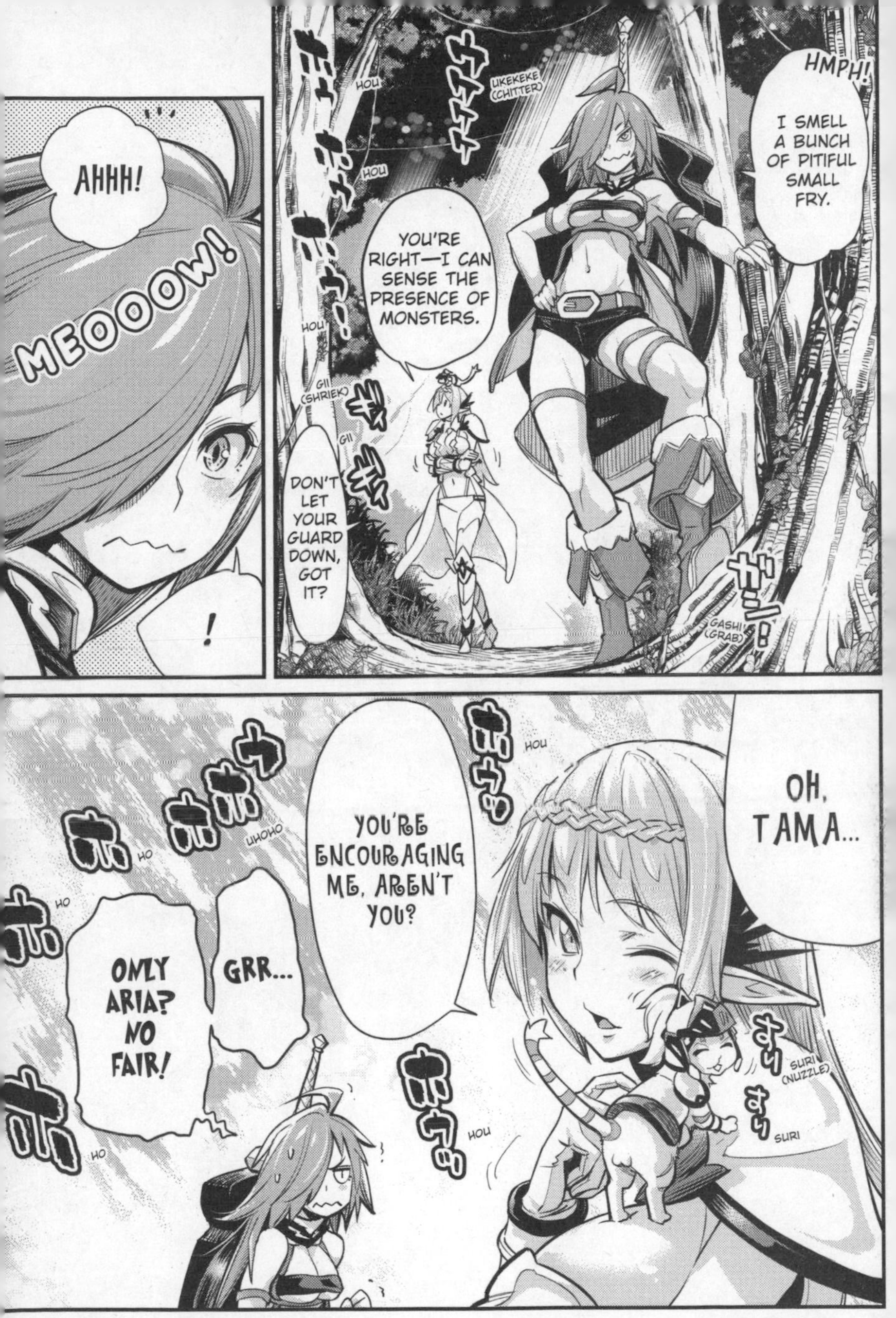
HMPH!
I SMELL A BUNCH OF PITIFUL SMALL FRY.
UKEKEKE (CHITTER)
HOU
HOU
YOU'RE RIGHT—I CAN SENSE THE PRESENCE OF MONSTERS.
HOU
GII (SHRIEK)
GII
DON'T LET YOUR GUARD DOWN, GOT IT?
GASHI (GRAB)
...
AHHH!
MEOOOW!
!
OH, TAMA...
SURI (NUZZLE)
SURI
HOU
YOU'RE ENCOURAGING ME, AREN'T YOU?
HOU
UHOHO
HO
GRR...
HO
ONLY ARIA? NO FAIR!
HO

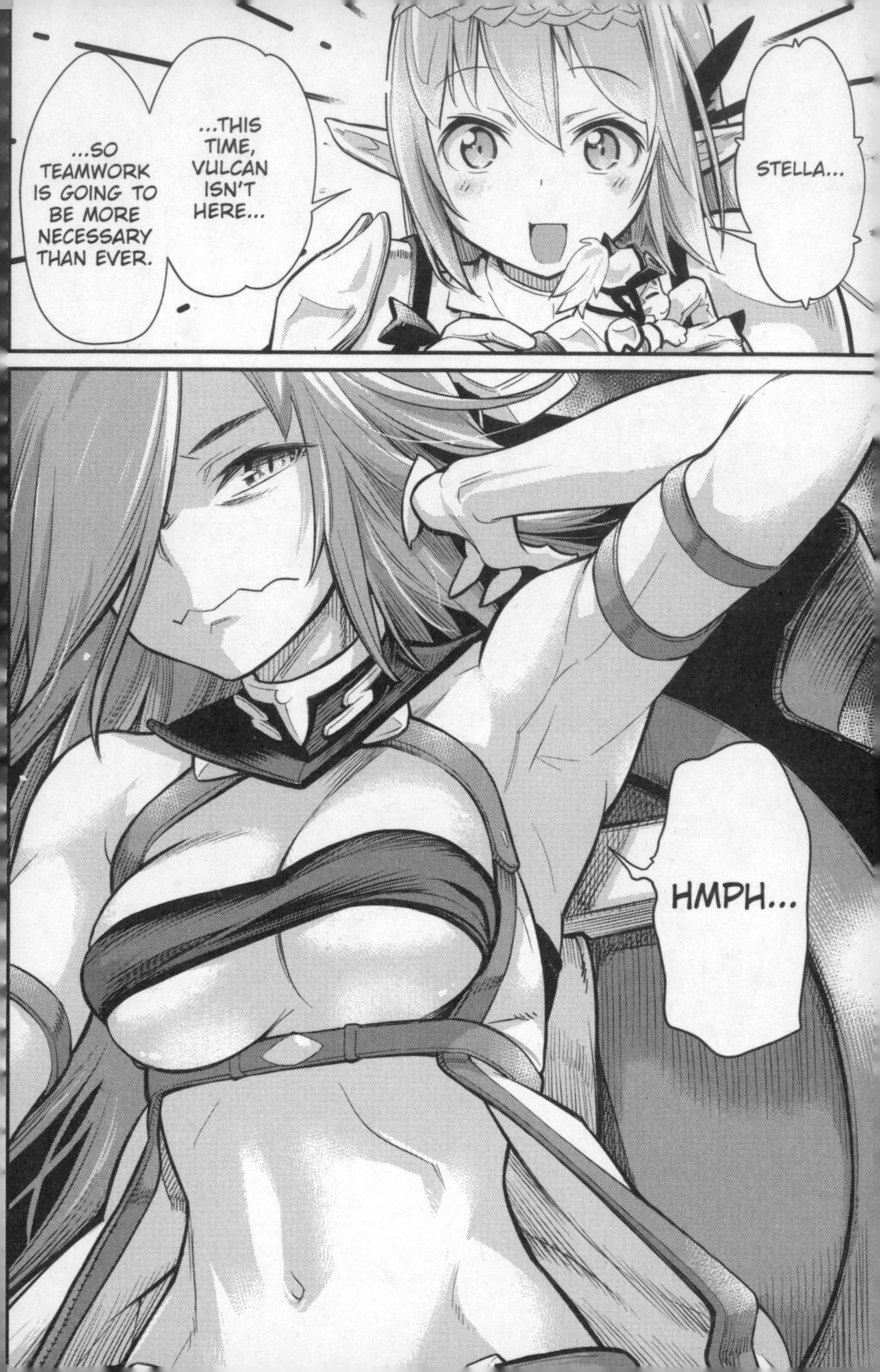
STELLA...
...THIS TIME, VULCAN ISN'T HERE...
...SO TEAMWORK IS GOING TO BE MORE NECESSARY THAN EVER.
HMPH...

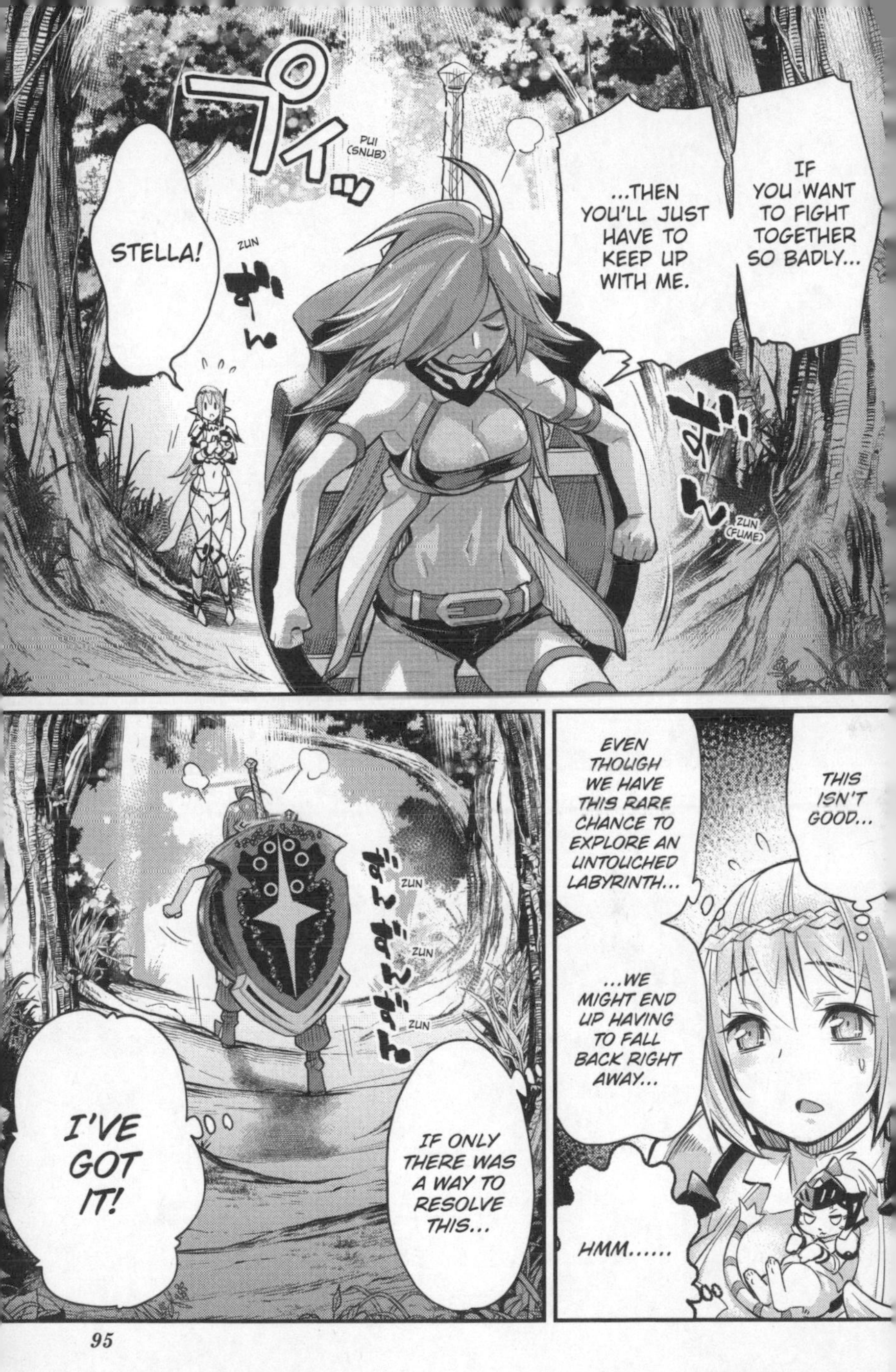
IF YOU WANT TO FIGHT TOGETHER SO BADLY...
...THEN YOU'LL JUST HAVE TO KEEP UP WITH ME.
ZUN (FUME)
PUI (SNUB)
ZUN
STELLA!
THIS ISN'T GOOD...
EVEN THOUGH WE HAVE THIS RARE CHANCE TO EXPLORE AN UNTOUCHED LABYRINTH...
...WE MIGHT END UP HAVING TO FALL BACK RIGHT AWAY...
HMM......
ZUN
ZUN
ZUN
IF ONLY THERE WAS A WAY TO RESOLVE THIS...
I'VE GOT IT!

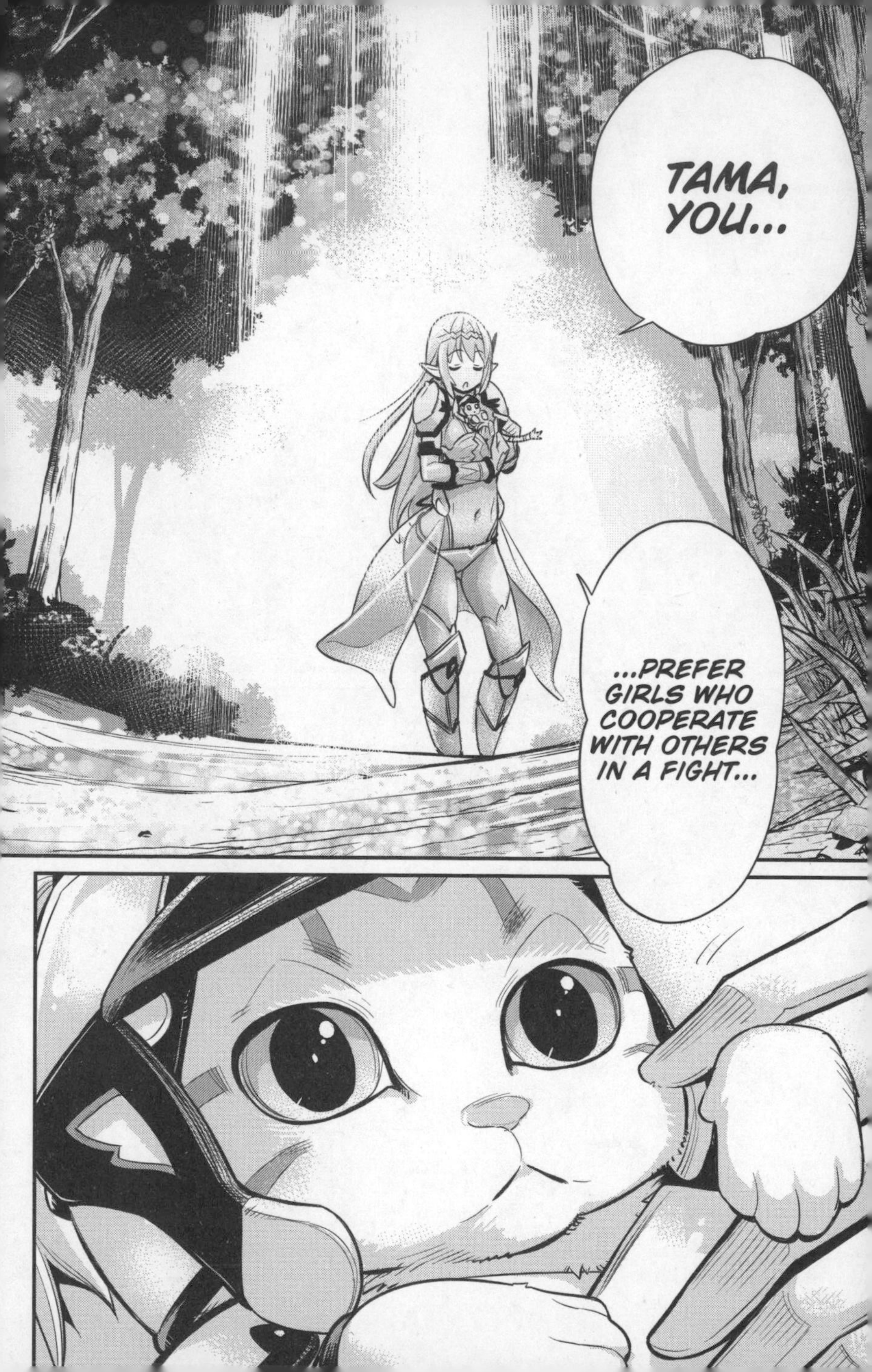
TAMA, YOU...
...PREFER GIRLS WHO COOPERATE WITH OTHERS IN A FIGHT...

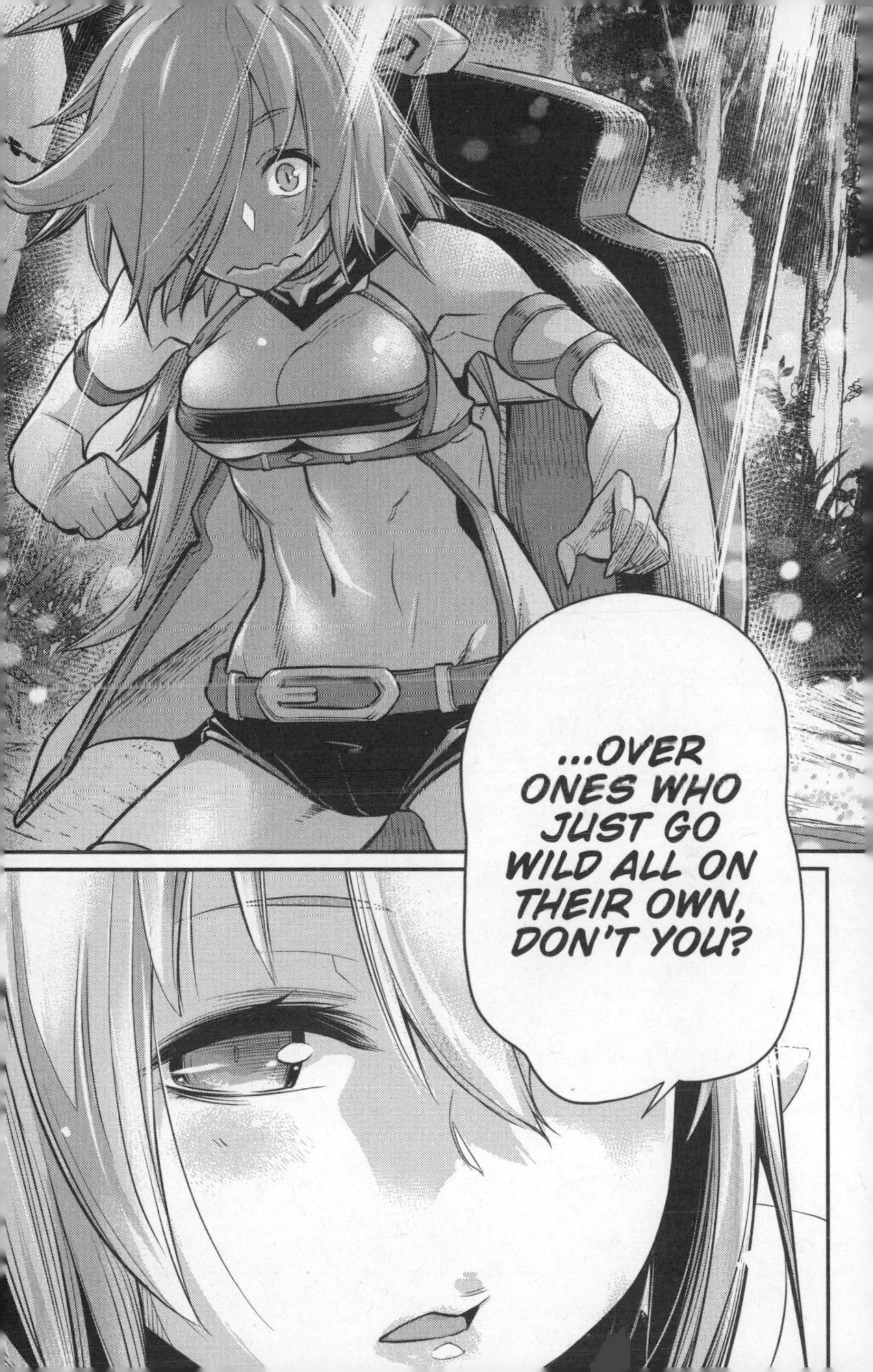
...OVER ONES WHO JUST GO WILD ALL ON THEIR OWN, DON'T YOU?

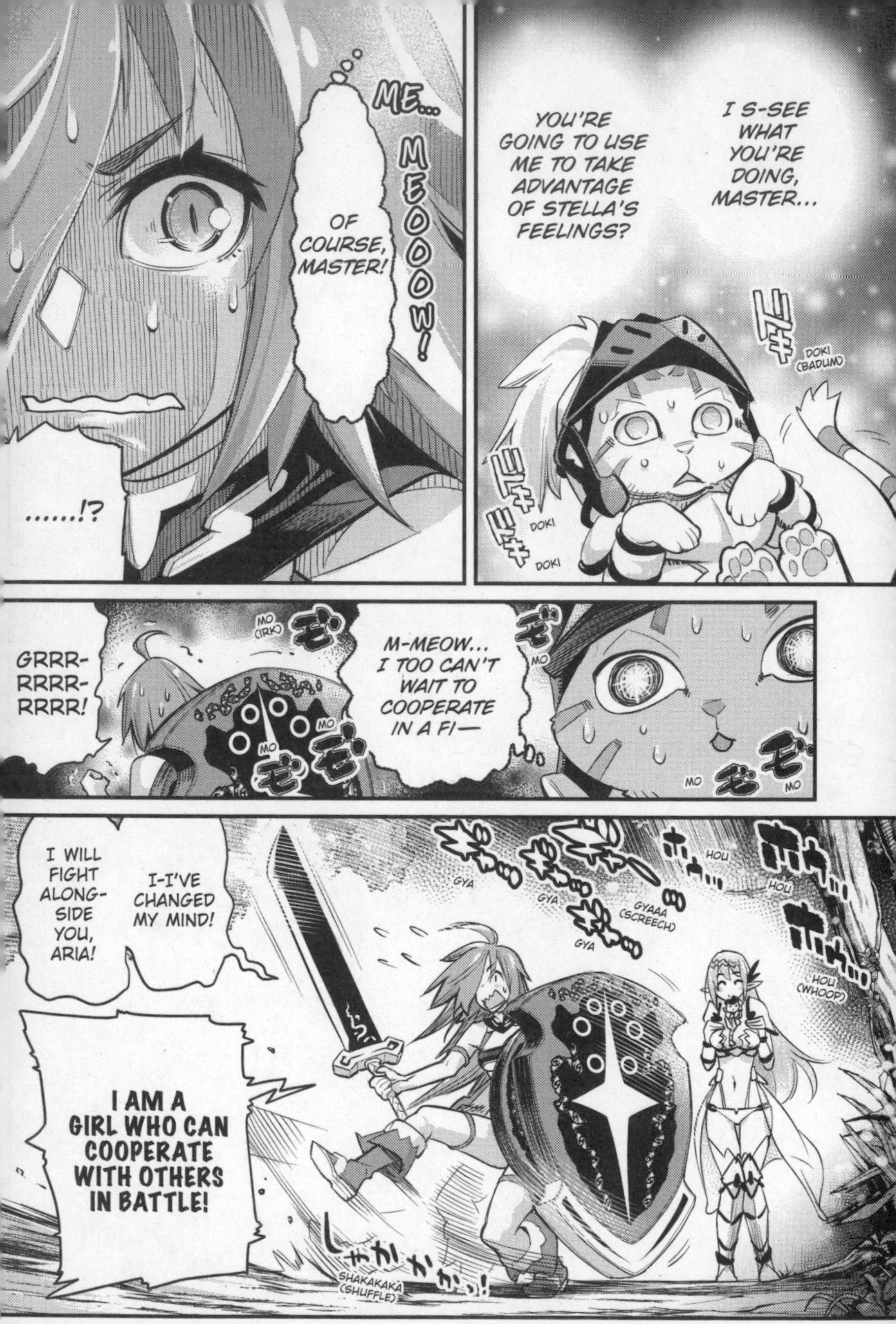
I S-SEE WHAT YOU'RE DOING, MASTER...
YOU'RE GOING TO USE ME TO TAKE ADVANTAGE OF STELLA'S FEELINGS?
DOKI (BADUM)
DOKI
DOKI
ME... MEOOOOW!
OF COURSE, MASTER!
......!?
MO
M-MEOW... I TOO CAN'T WAIT TO COOPERATE IN A FI—
MO
MO
MO (IRK)
MO
MO
GRRR-RRRR-RRRR!
HOU
HOU
HOU (WHOOP)
GYA
GYA
GYAAA (SCREECH)
GYA
I-I'VE CHANGED MY MIND!
I WILL FIGHT ALONG-SIDE YOU, ARIA!
I AM A GIRL WHO CAN COOPERATE WITH OTHERS IN BATTLE!
SHAKAKAKA (SHUFFLE)

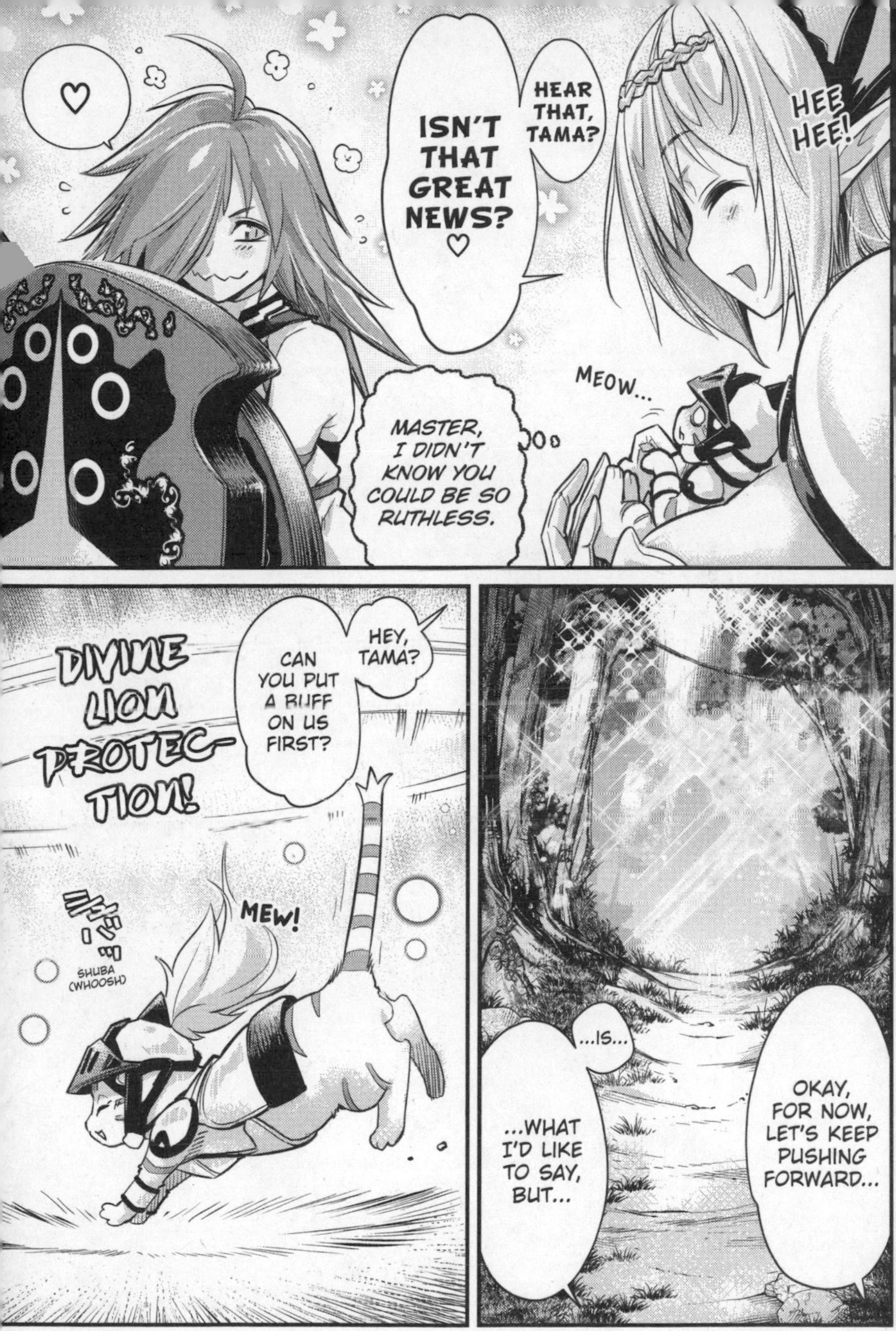
HEE HEE!
HEAR THAT, TAMA?
ISN'T THAT GREAT NEWS? ♡
♡
MEOW...
MASTER, I DIDN'T KNOW YOU COULD BE SO RUTHLESS.
OKAY, FOR NOW, LET'S KEEP PUSHING FORWARD...
...IS...
...WHAT I'D LIKE TO SAY, BUT...
HEY, TAMA?
CAN YOU PUT A BUFF ON US FIRST?
DIVINE LION PROTECTION!
MEW!
SHUBA (WHOOSH)

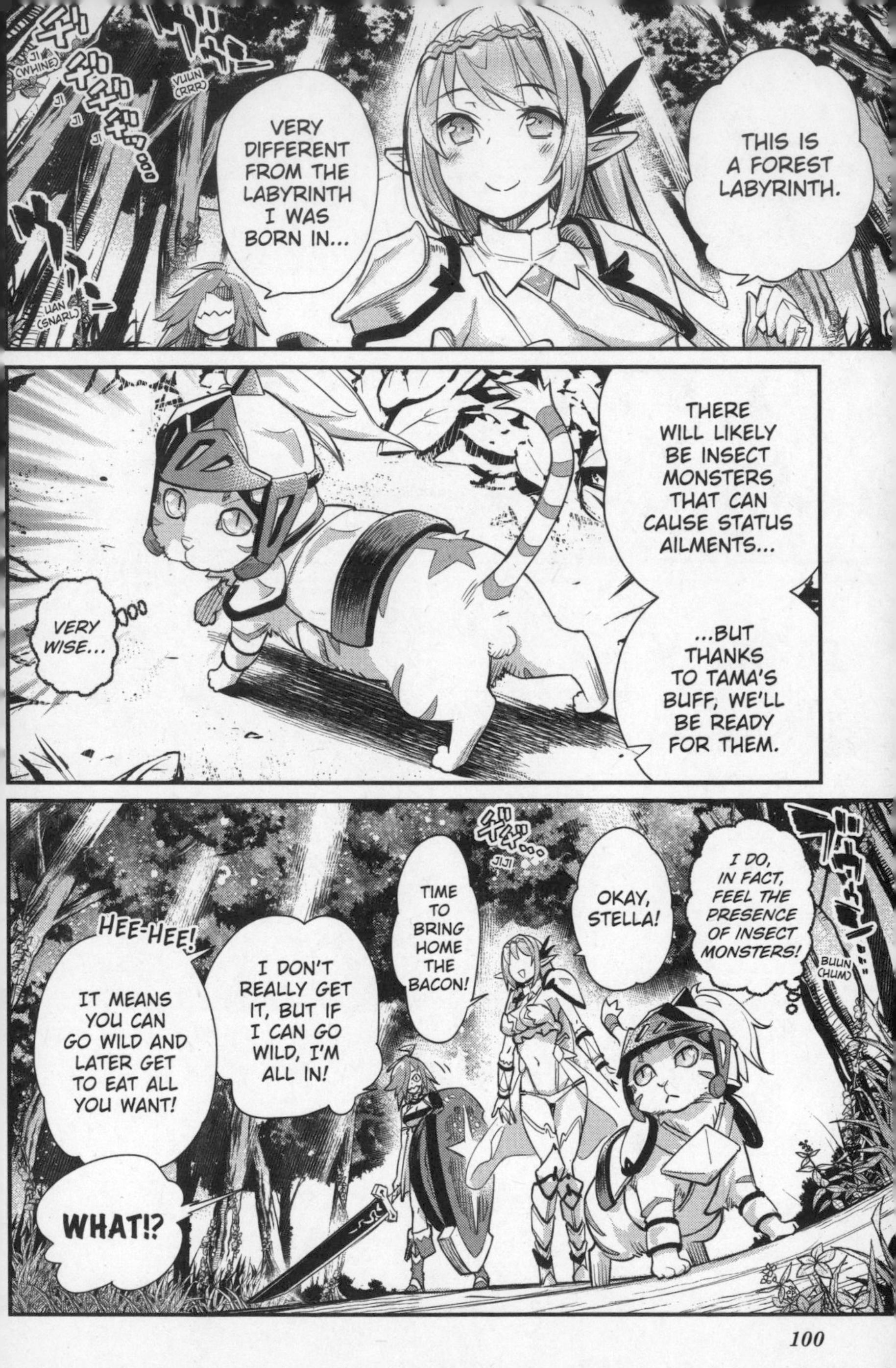
THIS IS A FOREST LABYRINTH.
VERY DIFFERENT FROM THE LABYRINTH I WAS BORN IN...
VUUN (RRR)
JI (WHINE)
JI
JI
UAN (SNARL)
THERE WILL LIKELY BE INSECT MONSTERS THAT CAN CAUSE STATUS AILMENTS...
...BUT THANKS TO TAMA'S BUFF, WE'LL BE READY FOR THEM.
VERY WISE...
I DO, IN FACT, FEEL THE PRESENCE OF INSECT MONSTERS!
BULIN (HUM)
OKAY, STELLA!
JIJI
TIME TO BRING HOME THE BACON!
I DON'T REALLY GET IT, BUT IF I CAN GO WILD, I'M ALL IN!
HEE-HEE!
IT MEANS YOU CAN GO WILD AND LATER GET TO EAT ALL YOU WANT!
WHAT!?

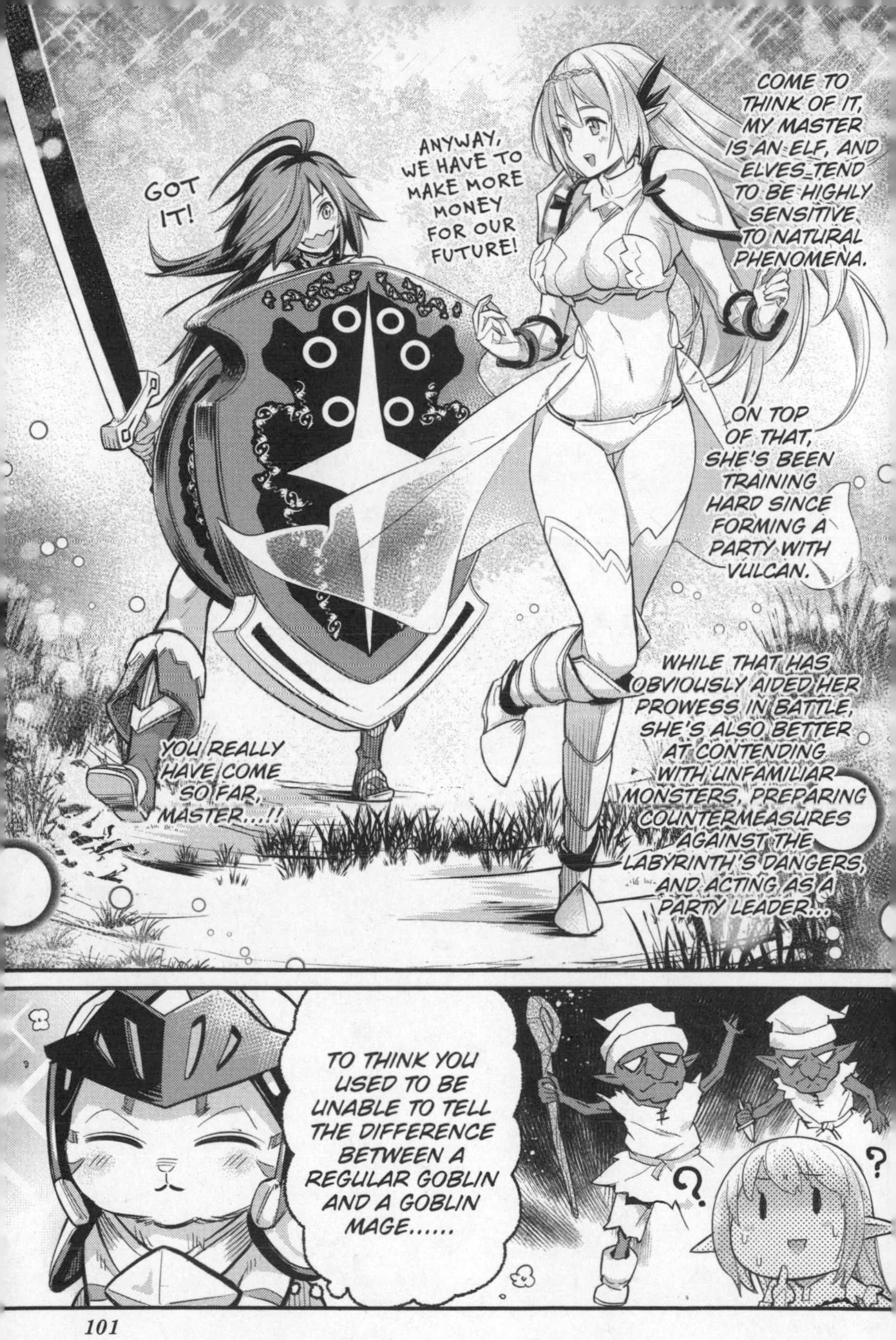
COME TO THINK OF IT, MY MASTER IS AN ELF, AND ELVES TEND TO BE HIGHLY SENSITIVE TO NATURAL PHENOMENA.
ANYWAY, WE HAVE TO MAKE MORE MONEY FOR OUR FUTURE!
GOT IT!
ON TOP OF THAT, SHE'S BEEN TRAINING HARD SINCE FORMING A PARTY WITH VULCAN.
WHILE THAT HAS OBVIOUSLY AIDED HER PROWESS IN BATTLE, SHE'S ALSO BETTER AT CONTENDING WITH UNFAMILIAR MONSTERS, PREPARING COUNTERMEASURES AGAINST THE LABYRINTH'S DANGERS, AND ACTING AS A PARTY LEADER...
YOU REALLY HAVE COME SO FAR, MASTER...!!
?
?
TO THINK YOU USED TO BE UNABLE TO TELL THE DIFFERENCE BETWEEN A REGULAR GOBLIN AND A GOBLIN MAGE......

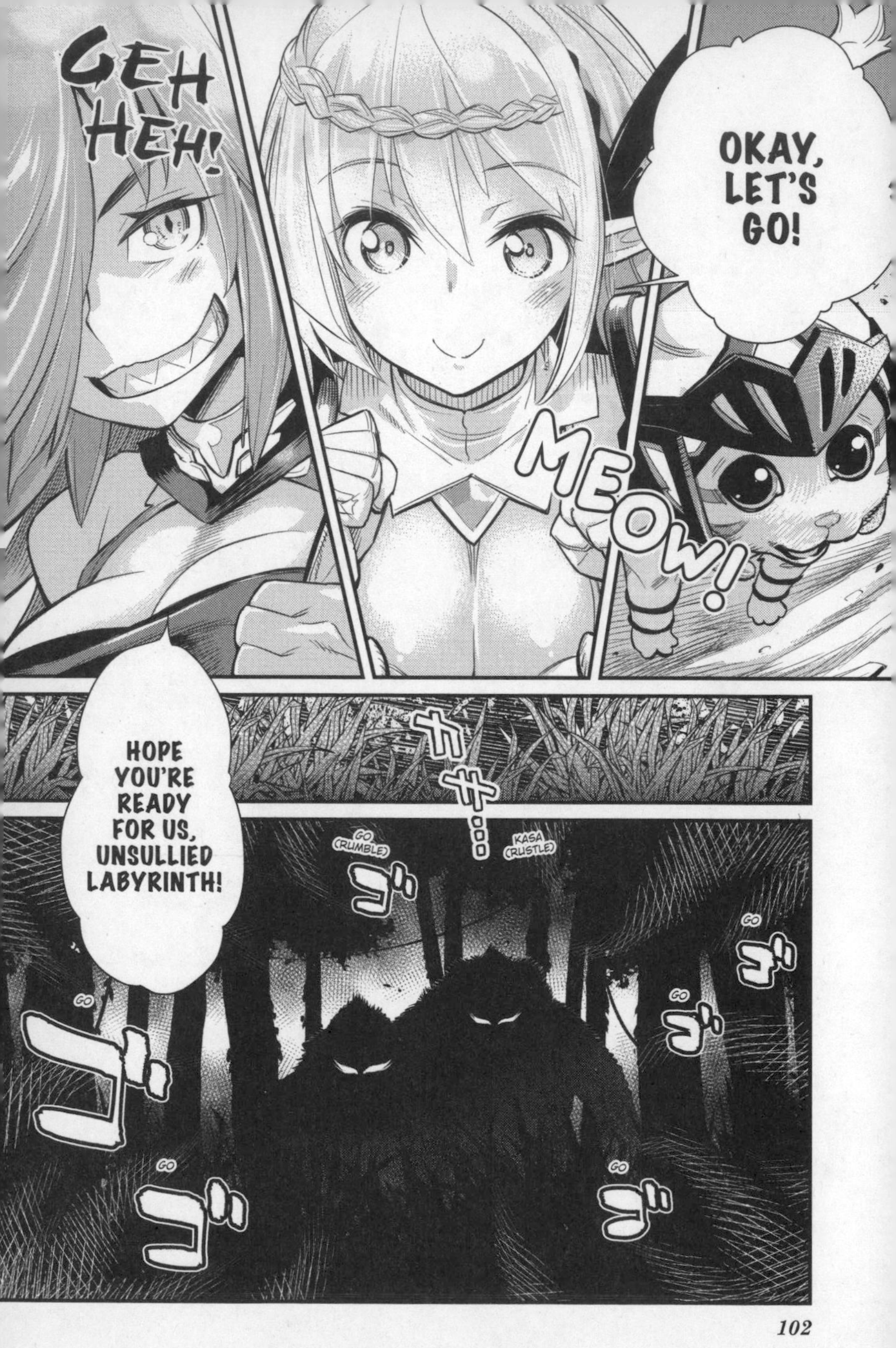
OKAY, LET'S GO!
MEOW!
GEH HEH!
HOPE YOU'RE READY FOR US, UNSULLIED LABYRINTH!
KASA (RUSTLE)
GO (RUMBLE)
GO
GO
GO
GO
GO

I'M A BEHEMOTH,

an S-Ranked MONSTER, but MISTAKEN for a CAT, I Live as an ELF GIRL'S PET

I'M A **BEHEMOTH,** an S-Ranked **MONSTER,** but **MISTAKEN** for a **CAT,** I Live as an **ELF GIRL'S PET**

#29 — Fairies of the Forest

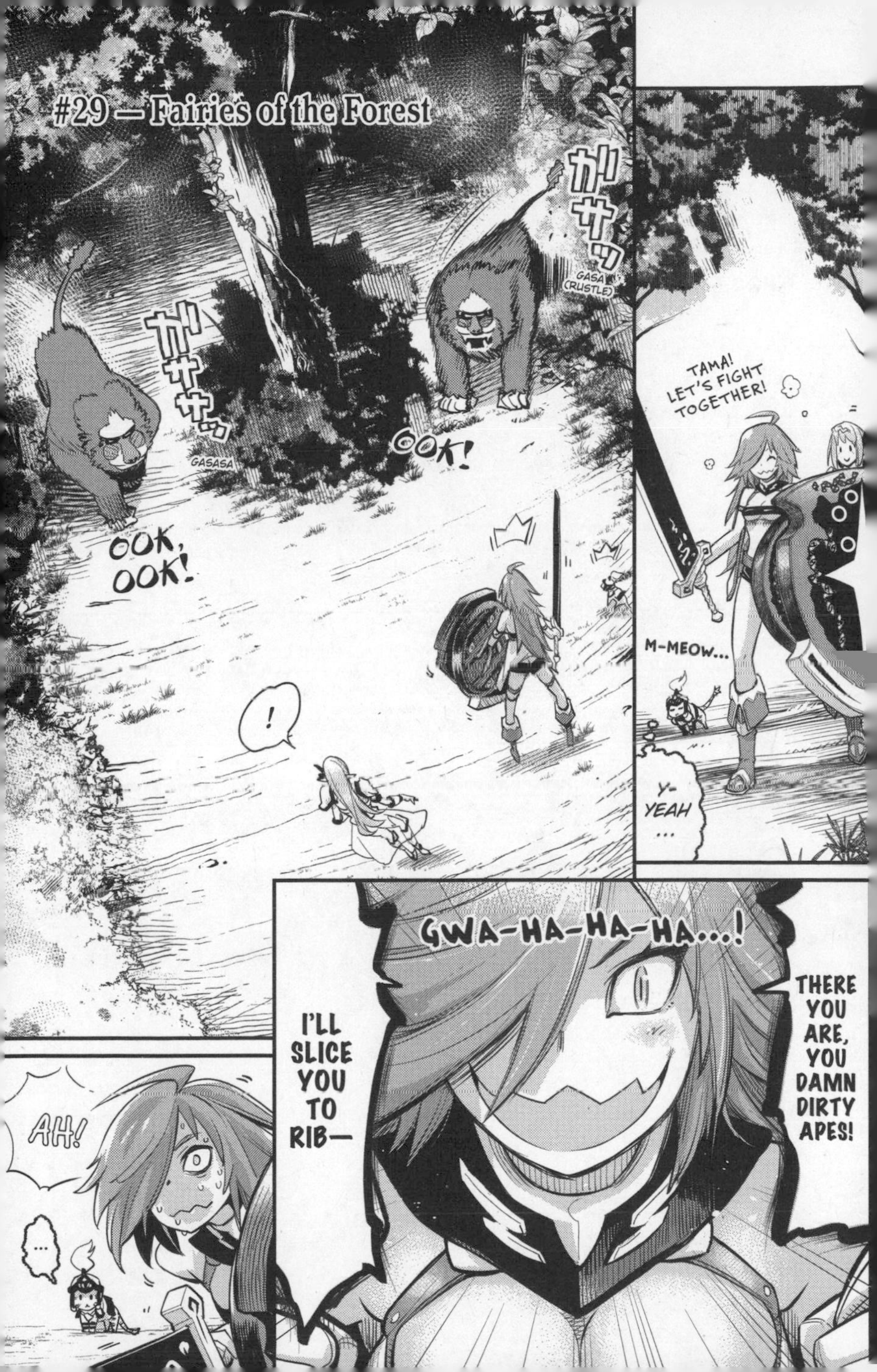

TAMA! LET'S FIGHT TOGETHER!
M-MEOW...
Y-YEAH...
カリサッ
GASA (RUSTLE)
カサササッ
GASASA
OOK!
OOK, OOK!
!
GWA-HA-HA-HA...!
THERE YOU ARE, YOU DAMN DIRTY APES!
I'LL SLICE YOU TO RIB—
AH!
...

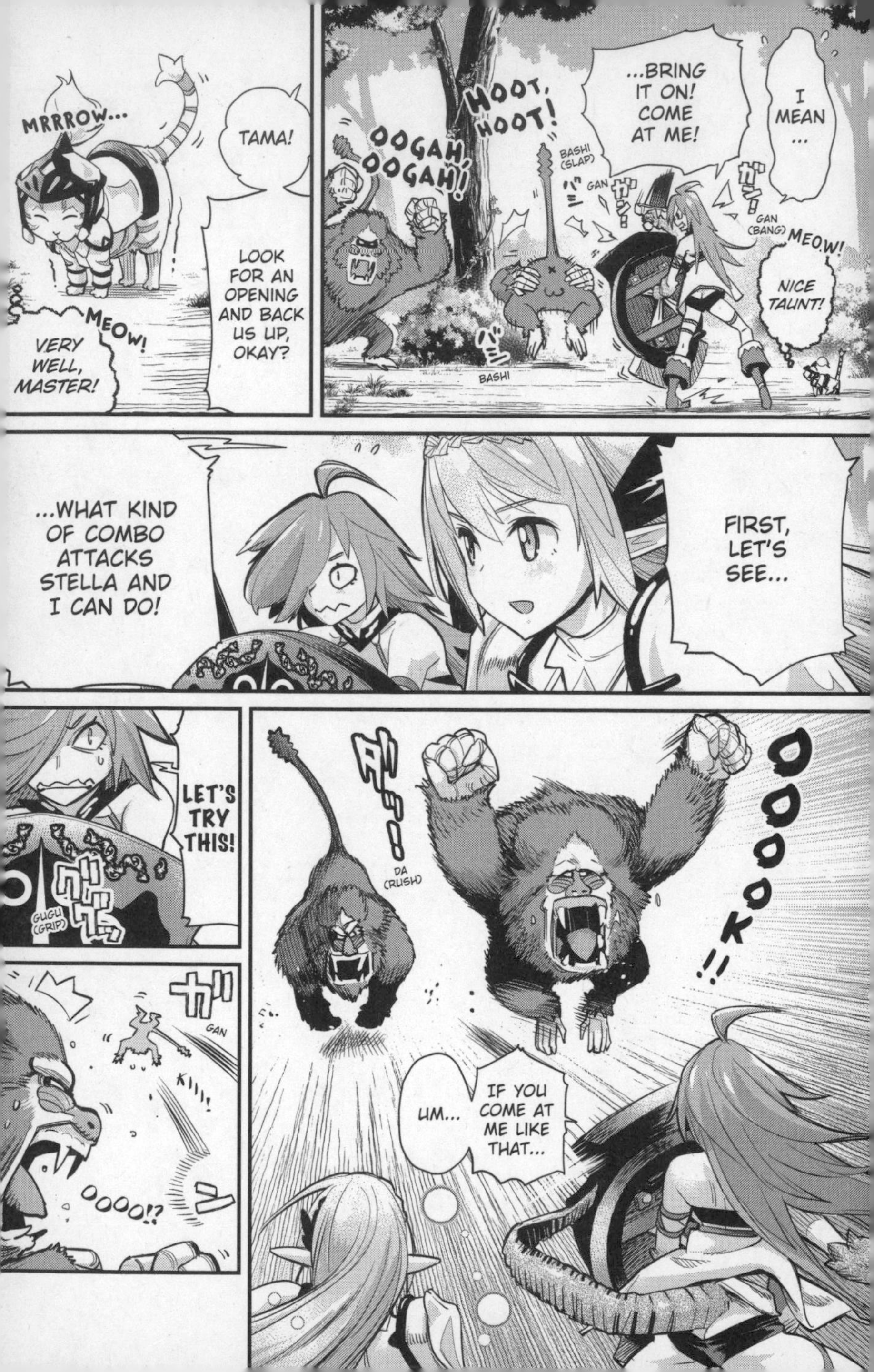
I MEAN...
...BRING IT ON! COME AT ME!
HOOT, HOOT!
BASHI (SLAP)
GAN
GAN (BANG)
MEOW!
NICE TAUNT!
OOGAH OOGAH!
BASHI
TAMA!
LOOK FOR AN OPENING AND BACK US UP, OKAY?
MRRROW...
MEOW!
VERY WELL, MASTER!
FIRST, LET'S SEE...
...WHAT KIND OF COMBO ATTACKS STELLA AND I CAN DO!
OOOOOK!!
DA (RUSH)
IF YOU COME AT ME LIKE THAT...
UM...
LET'S TRY THIS!
GUGU (GRIP)
GAN
KIII!
OOOO!?

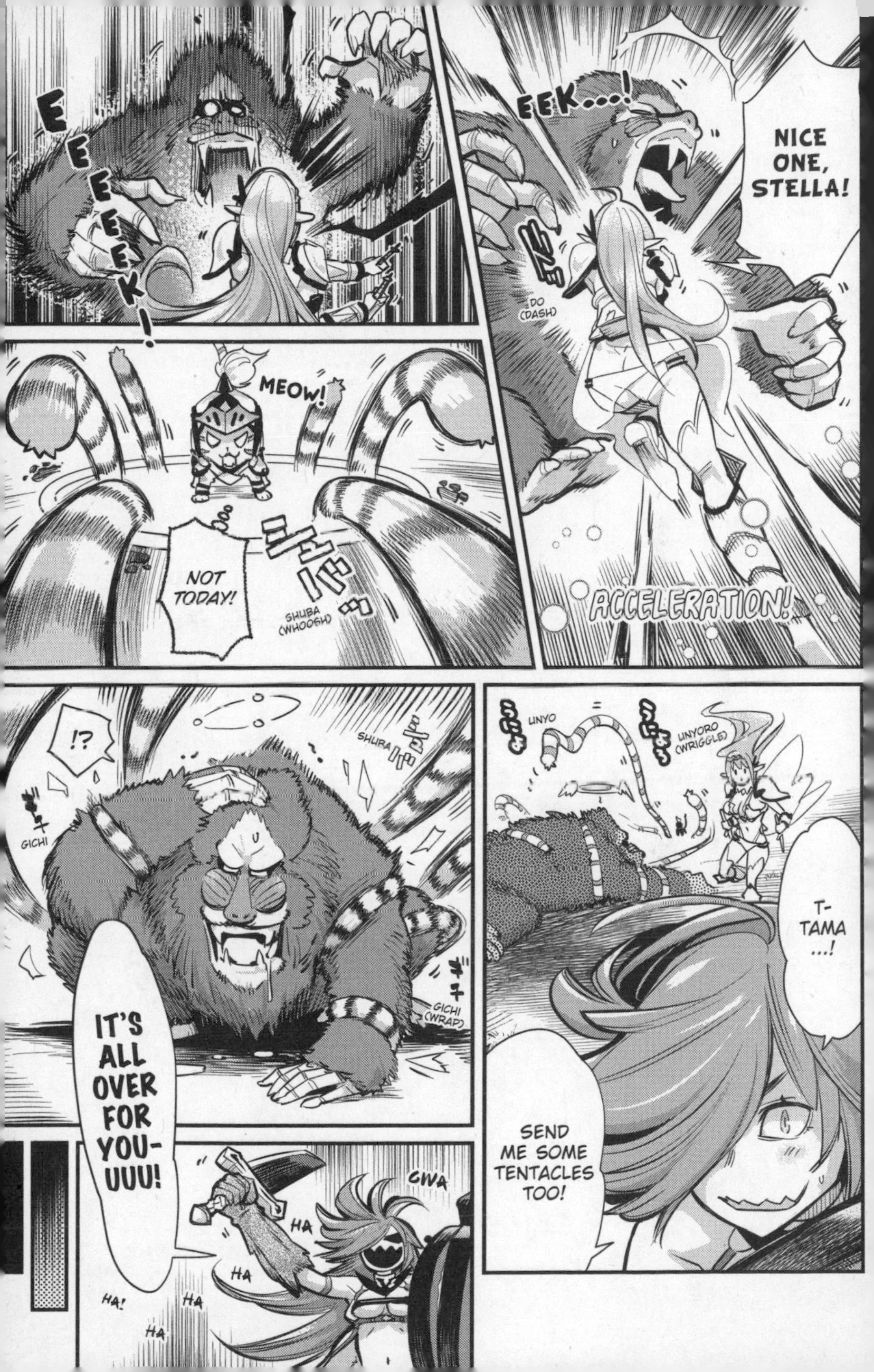
EEK...!
NICE ONE, STELLA!
DO (DASH)
ACCELERATION!
EEEEEEK!
MEOW!
NOT TODAY!
SHUBA (WHOOSH)
UNYO
UNYORO (WRIGGLE)
T-TAMA...!
SEND ME SOME TENTACLES TOO!
!?
SHURA
GICHI
GICHI (WRAP)
IT'S ALL OVER FOR YOU-UUU!
GWA
HA
HA
HA!
HA
HA

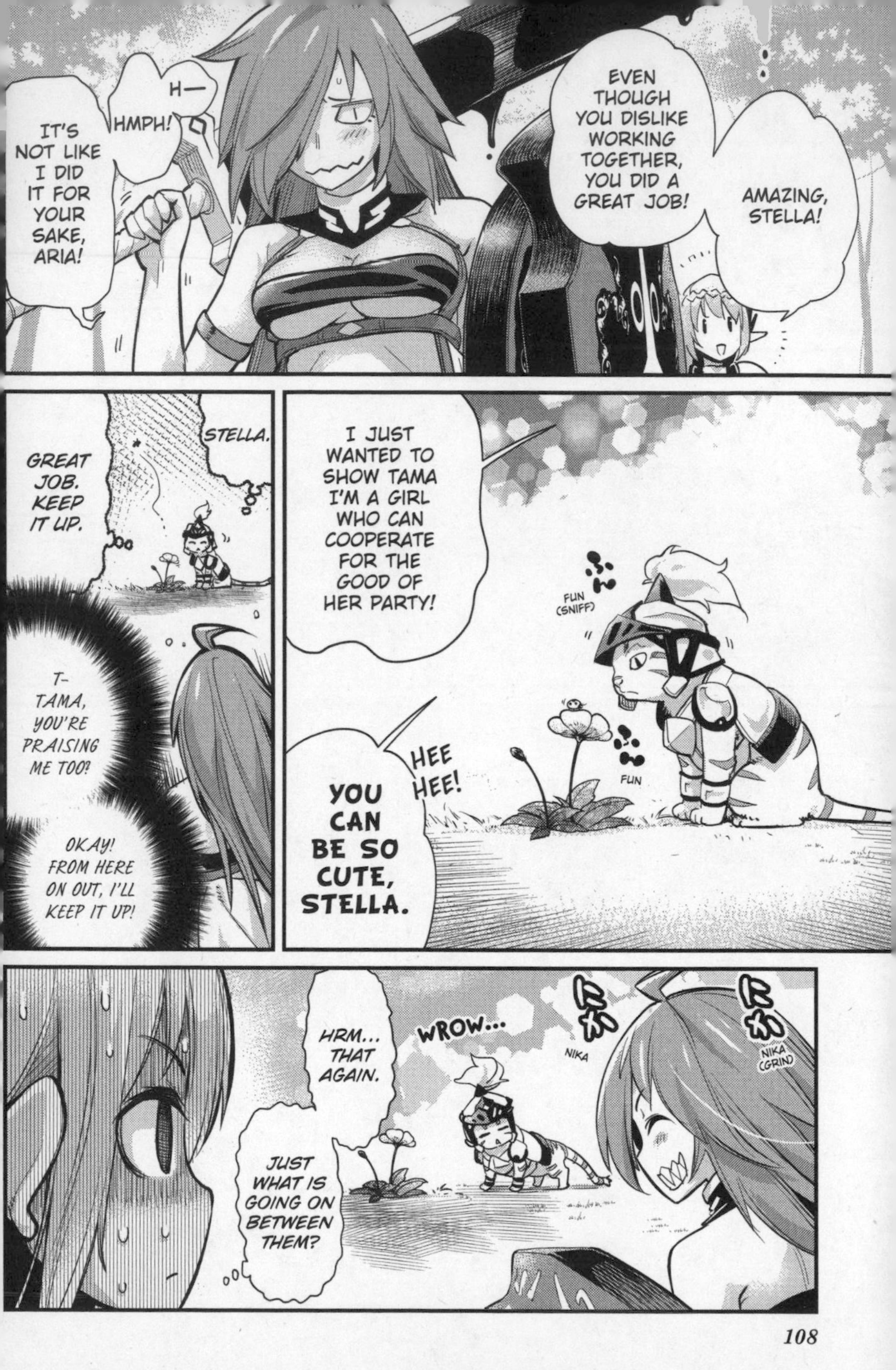
AMAZING, STELLA!
EVEN THOUGH YOU DISLIKE WORKING TOGETHER, YOU DID A GREAT JOB!
H— HMPH!
IT'S NOT LIKE I DID IT FOR YOUR SAKE, ARIA!
I JUST WANTED TO SHOW TAMA I'M A GIRL WHO CAN COOPERATE FOR THE GOOD OF HER PARTY!
FUN (SNIFF)
FUN
HEE HEE!
YOU CAN BE SO CUTE, STELLA.
STELLA.
GREAT JOB. KEEP IT UP.
T-TAMA, YOU'RE PRAISING ME TOO?
OKAY! FROM HERE ON OUT, I'LL KEEP IT UP!
NIKA (GRIN)
NIKA
WROW...
HRM... THAT AGAIN.
JUST WHAT IS GOING ON BETWEEN THEM?

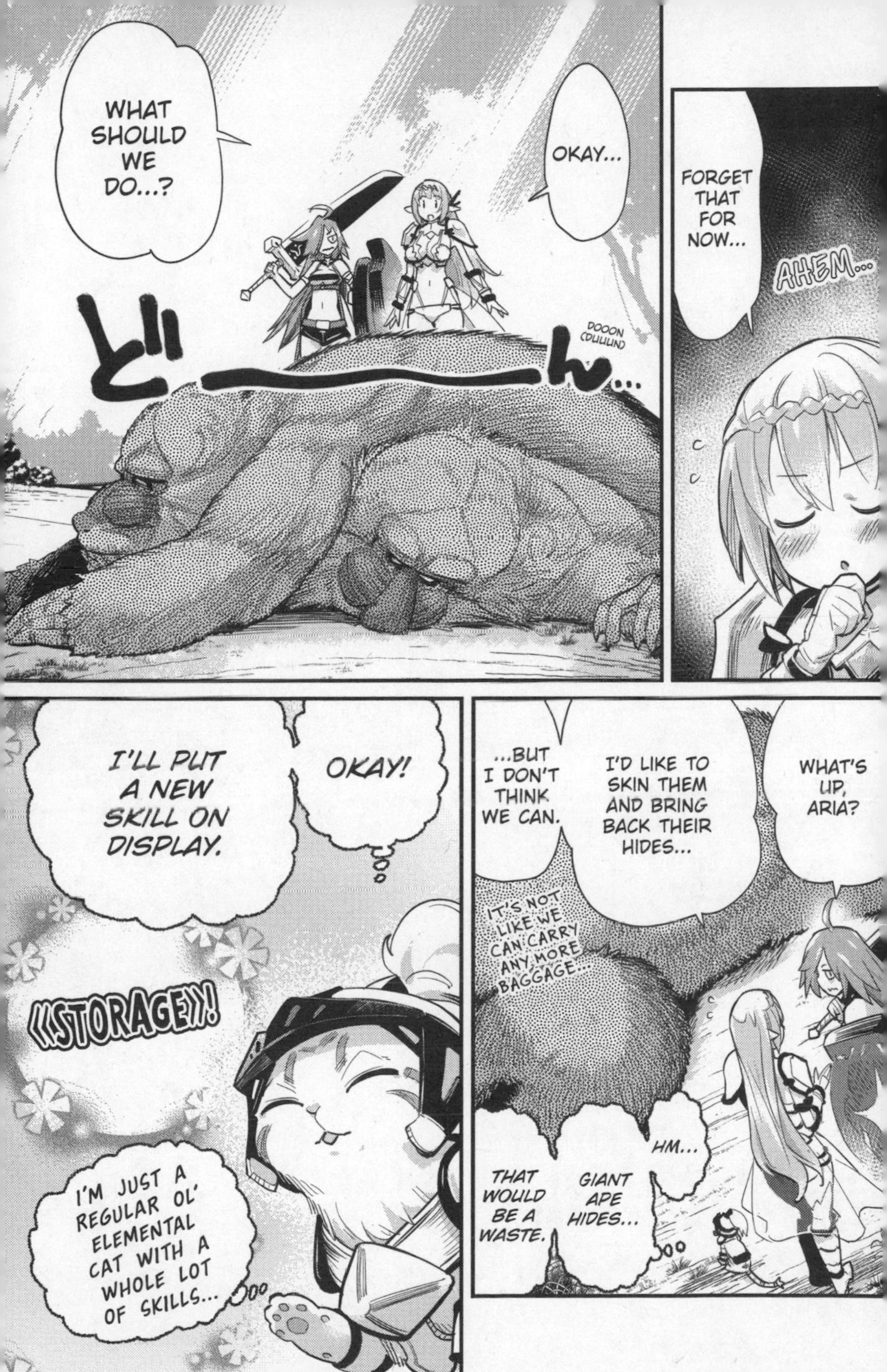
FORGET THAT FOR NOW...
AHEM...
OKAY...
WHAT SHOULD WE DO...?
DOOON (DUUUN)
WHAT'S UP, ARIA?
I'D LIKE TO SKIN THEM AND BRING BACK THEIR HIDES...
...BUT I DON'T THINK WE CAN.
IT'S NOT LIKE WE CAN CARRY ANY MORE BAGGAGE...
HM...
GIANT APE HIDES...
THAT WOULD BE A WASTE.
OKAY!
I'LL PUT A NEW SKILL ON DISPLAY.
《STORAGE》!
I'M JUST A REGULAR OL' ELEMENTAL CAT WITH A WHOLE LOT OF SKILLS...

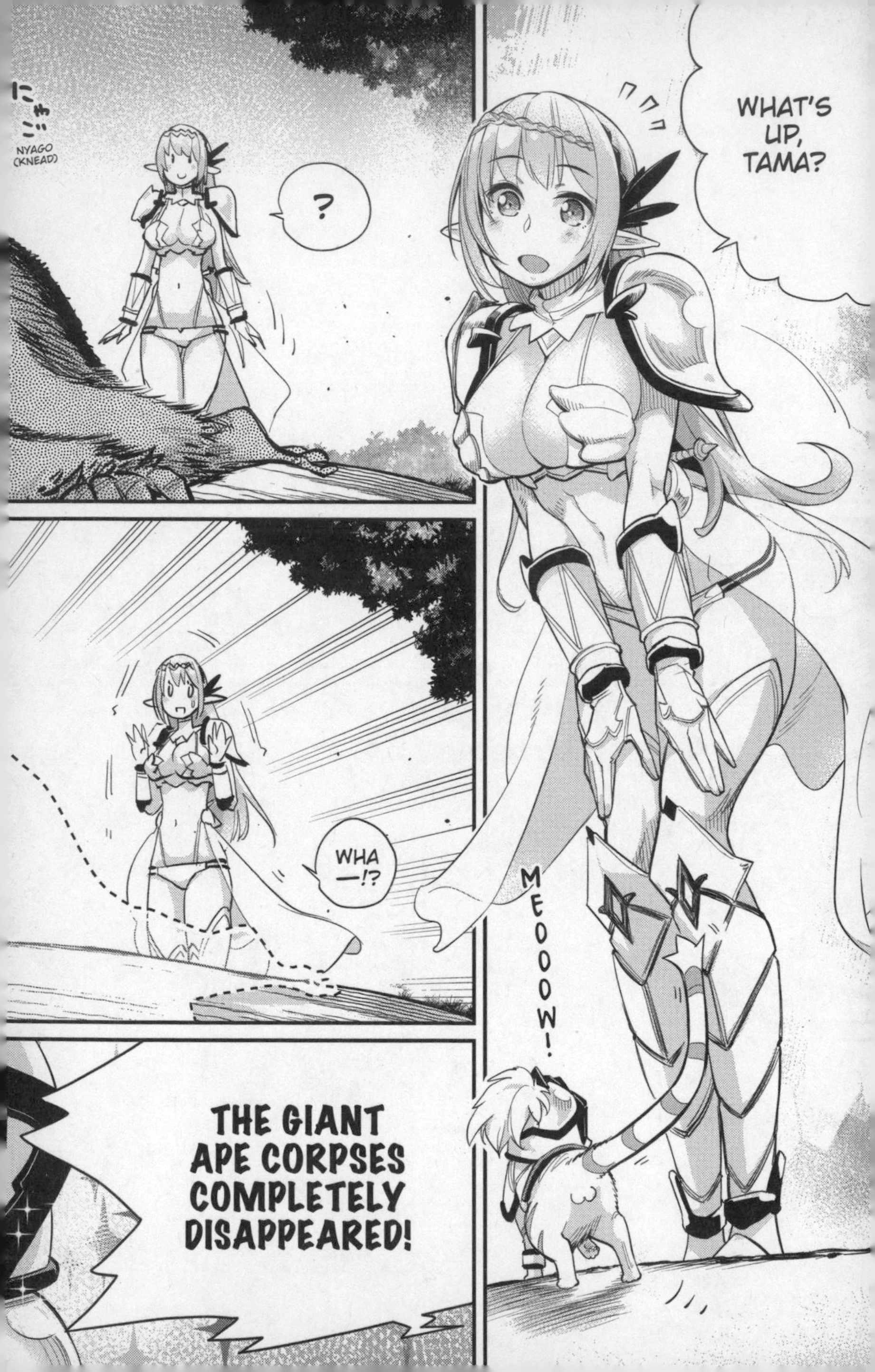
WHAT'S UP, TAMA?
MEOOOOW!
にゃご
NYAGO (KNEAD)
?
WHA—!?
THE GIANT APE CORPSES COMPLETELY DISAPPEARED!

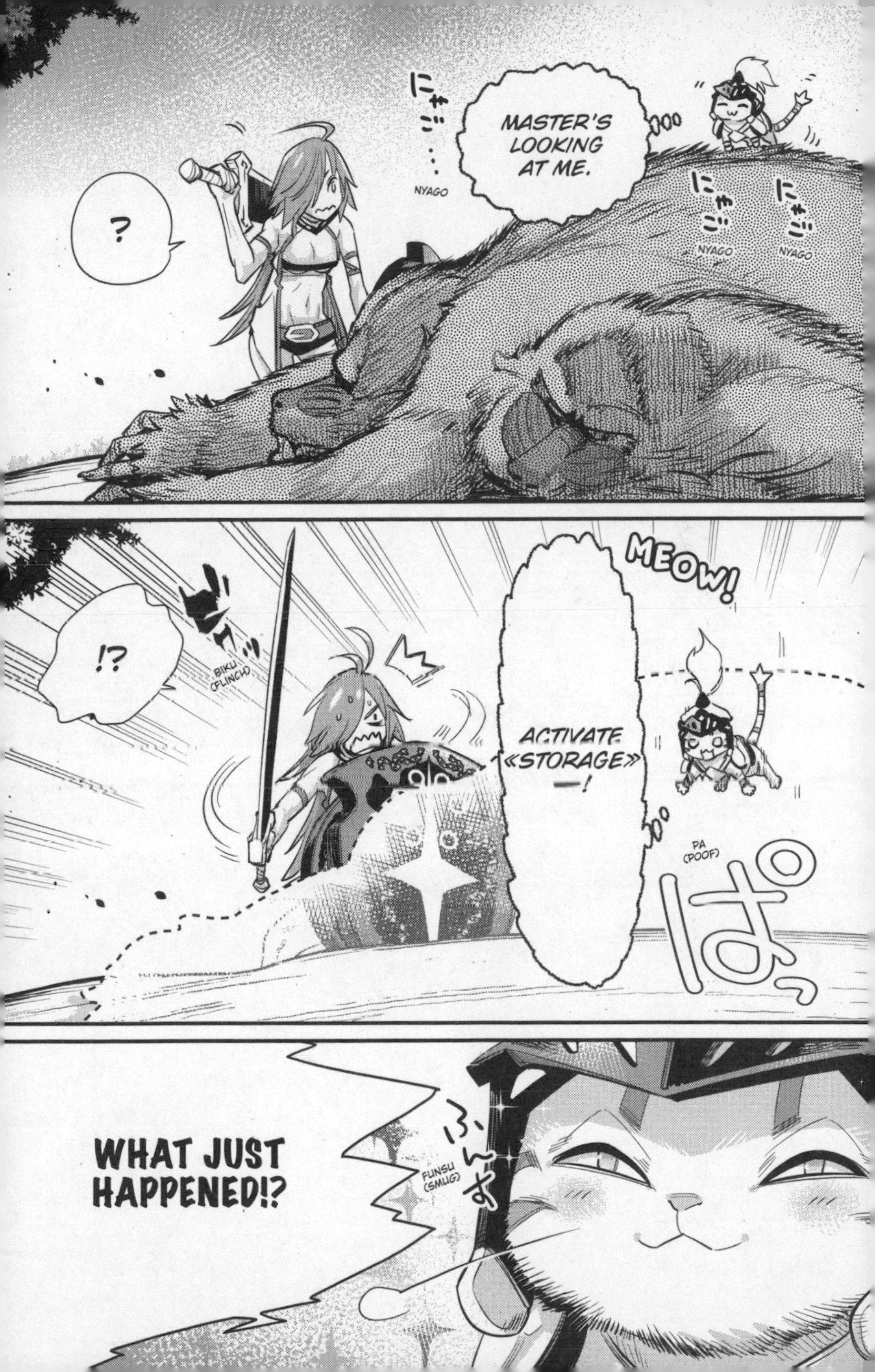
にゃご
NYAGO
にゃご
NYAGO
MASTER'S LOOKING AT ME.
にゃご…
NYAGO
?
MEOW!
ACTIVATE «STORAGE» —!
ぱっ
PA (POOF)
!?
BIKU (FLINCH)
ふんす
FUNSU (SMUG)
WHAT JUST HAPPENED!?

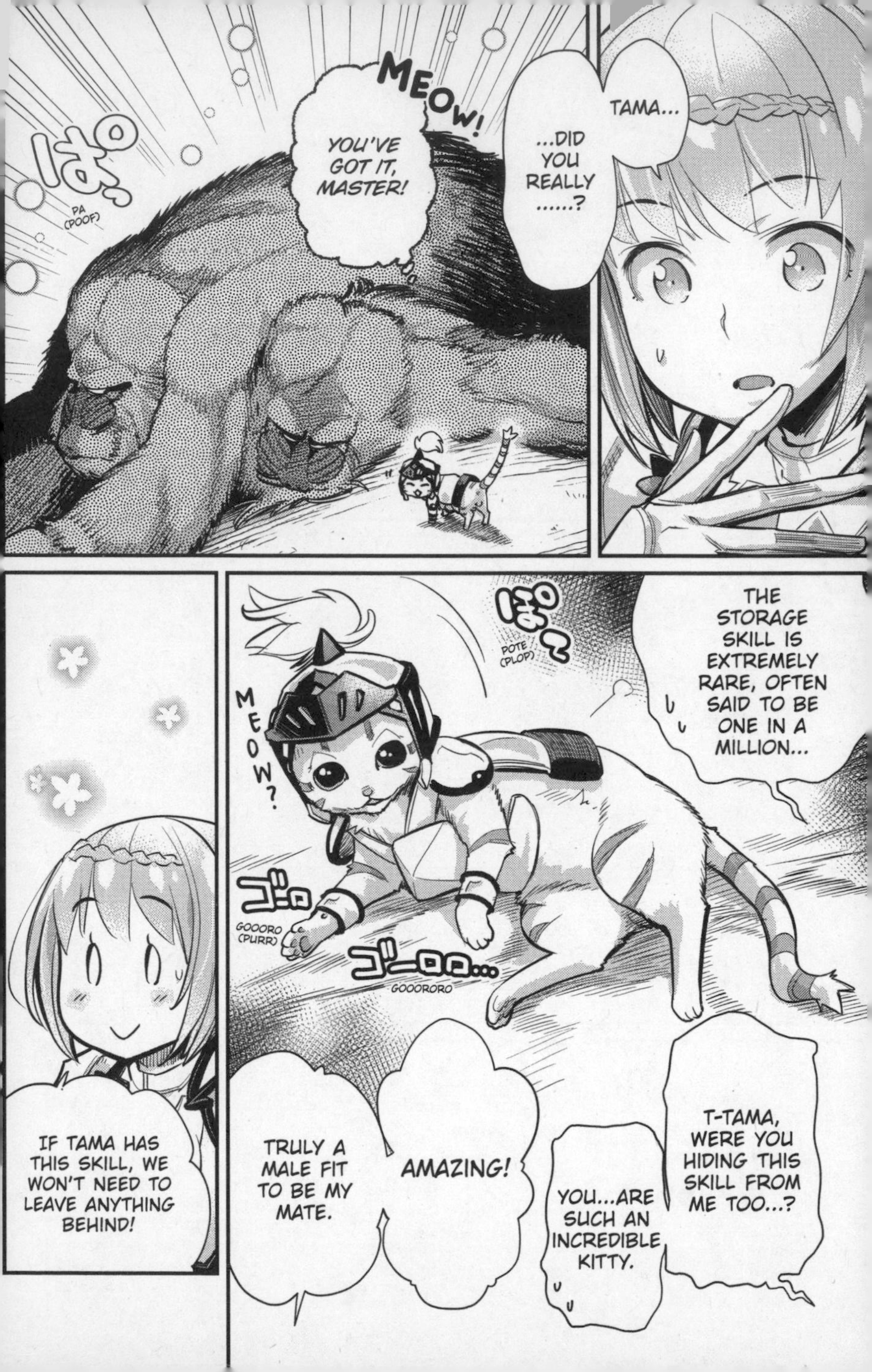
TAMA...
...DID YOU REALLY ......?
MEOW!
YOU'VE GOT IT, MASTER!
ぱっ
PA (POOF)
ぽてっ
POTE (PLOP)
THE STORAGE SKILL IS EXTREMELY RARE, OFTEN SAID TO BE ONE IN A MILLION...
MEOW?
ゴロ
GOOORO (PURR)
ゴーロロ...
GOOORORO
T-TAMA, WERE YOU HIDING THIS SKILL FROM ME TOO...?
YOU...ARE SUCH AN INCREDIBLE KITTY.
AMAZING!
TRULY A MALE FIT TO BE MY MATE.
IF TAMA HAS THIS SKILL, WE WON'T NEED TO LEAVE ANYTHING BEHIND!

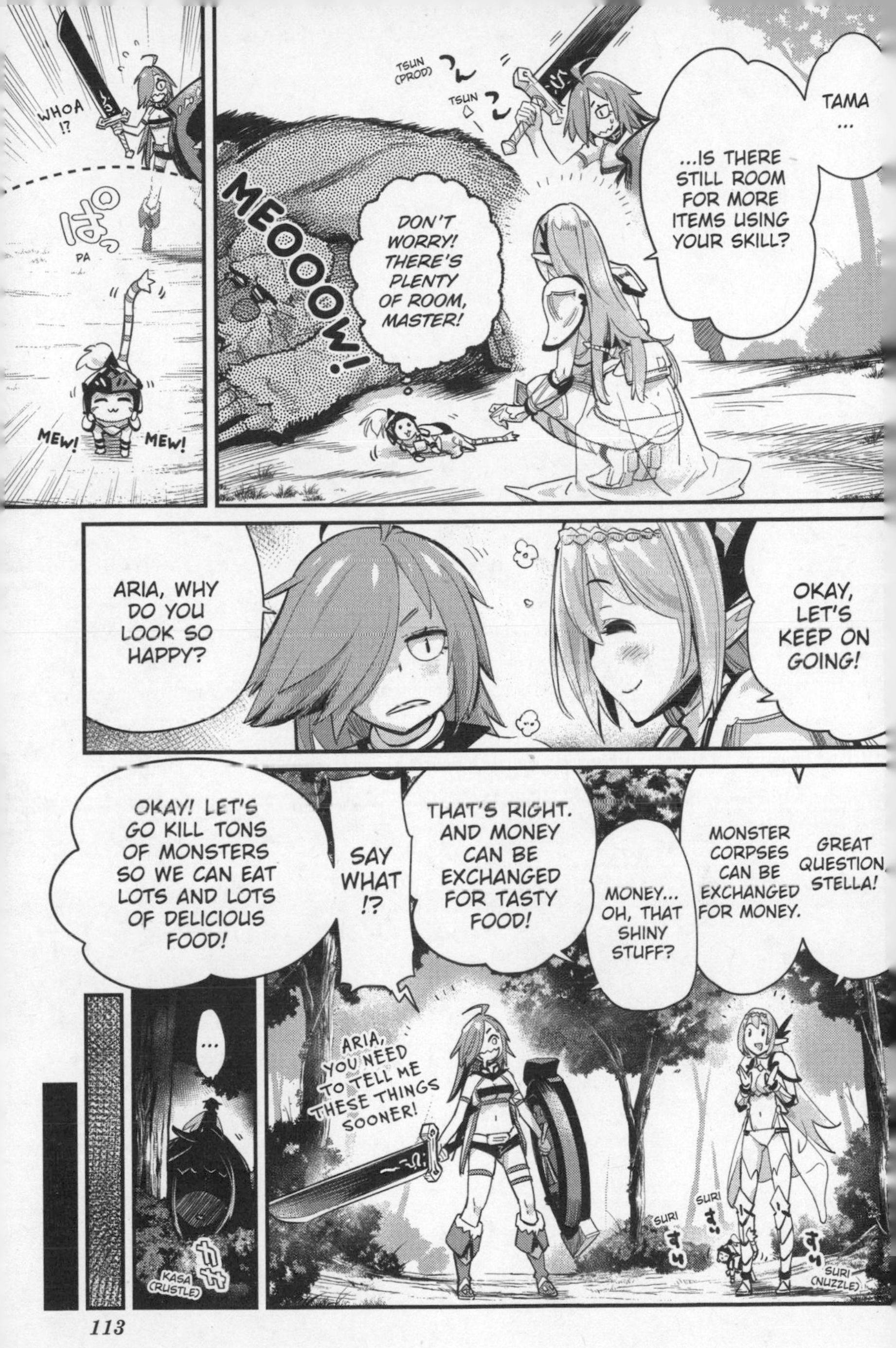
TAMA ...
...IS THERE STILL ROOM FOR MORE ITEMS USING YOUR SKILL?
TSUN (PROD)
TSUN
DON'T WORRY! THERE'S PLENTY OF ROOM, MASTER!
MEOOOW!
WHOA !?
PA
MEW!
MEW!
OKAY, LET'S KEEP ON GOING!
ARIA, WHY DO YOU LOOK SO HAPPY?
GREAT QUESTION, STELLA!
MONSTER CORPSES CAN BE EXCHANGED FOR MONEY.
MONEY... OH, THAT SHINY STUFF?
THAT'S RIGHT. AND MONEY CAN BE EXCHANGED FOR TASTY FOOD!
SAY WHAT !?
OKAY! LET'S GO KILL TONS OF MONSTERS SO WE CAN EAT LOTS AND LOTS OF DELICIOUS FOOD!
ARIA, YOU NEED TO TELL ME THESE THINGS SOONER!
SURI (NUZZLE)
SURI
SURI
...
KASA (RUSTLE)

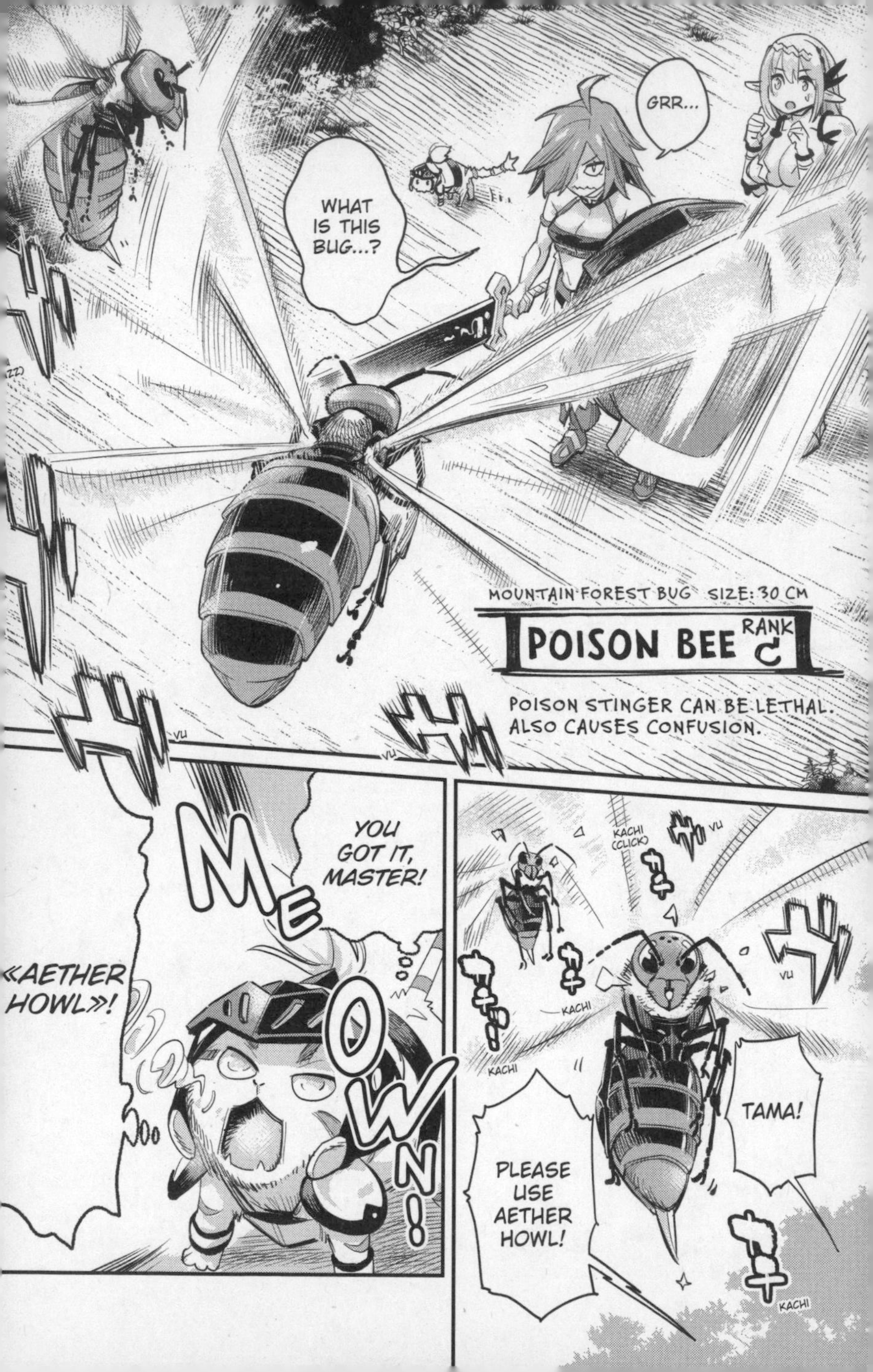
GRR...
WHAT IS THIS BUG...?
MOUNTAIN FOREST BUG SIZE: 30 CM
POISON BEE RANK C
POISON STINGER CAN BE LETHAL. ALSO CAUSES CONFUSION.
VU
VU
KACHI (CLICK)
VU
VU
KACHI
KACHI
TAMA!
PLEASE USE AETHER HOWL!
KACHI
YOU GOT IT, MASTER!
«AETHER HOWL»!
MEOOWN!

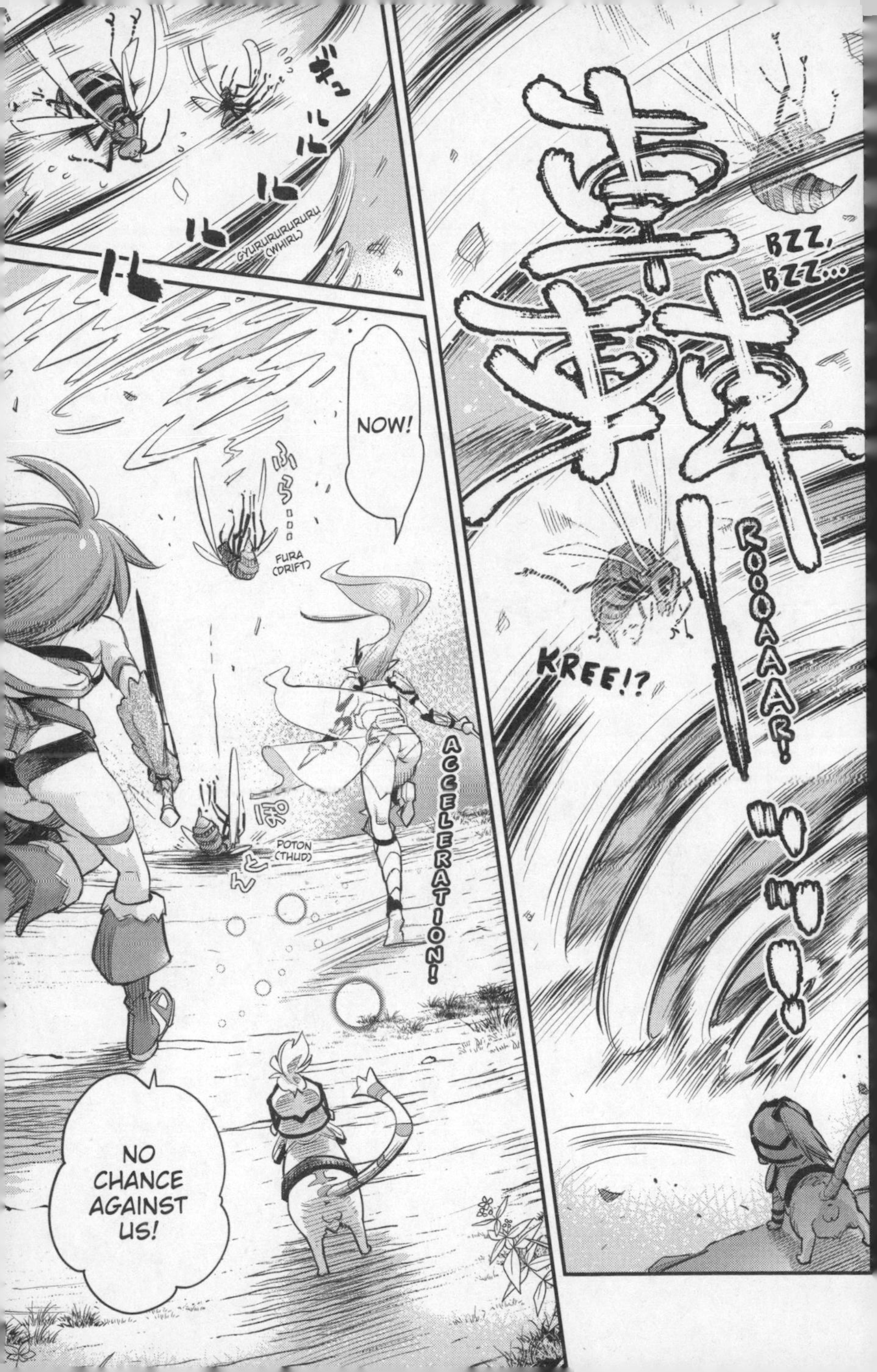
BZZ, BZZ...
ROOOAAAAR!
KREE!?
ギュルルルルル
GYURURURURURU (WHIRL)
NOW!
ふら…
FURA (DRIFT)
ぽとん
POTON (THUD)
ACCELERATION!
NO CHANCE AGAINST US!

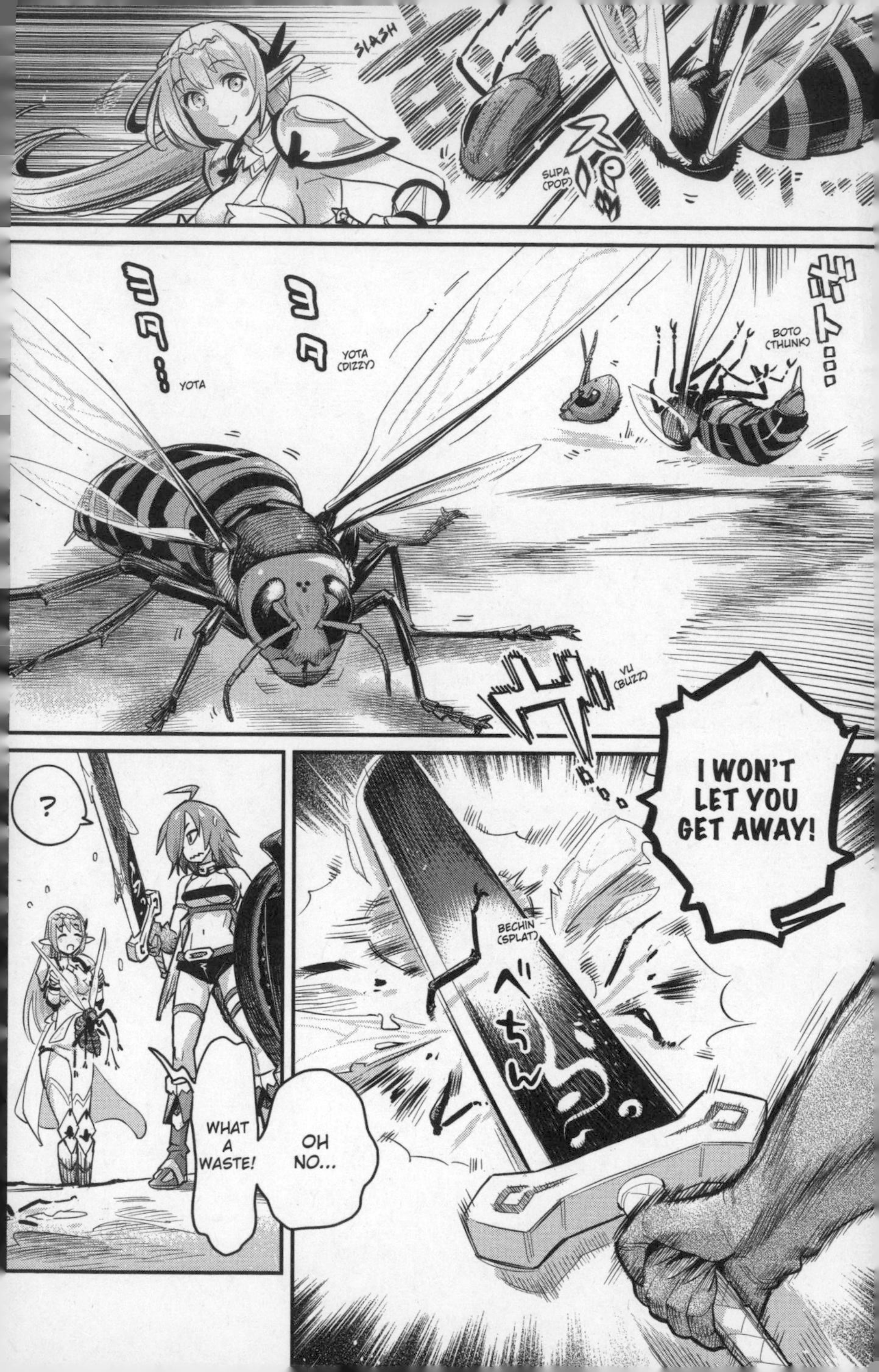
SLASH
SUPA (POP)
BOTO (THUNK)
YOTA (DIZZY)
YOTA
VU (BUZZ)
I WON'T LET YOU GET AWAY!
BECHIN (SPLAT)
?
OH NO...
WHAT A WASTE!

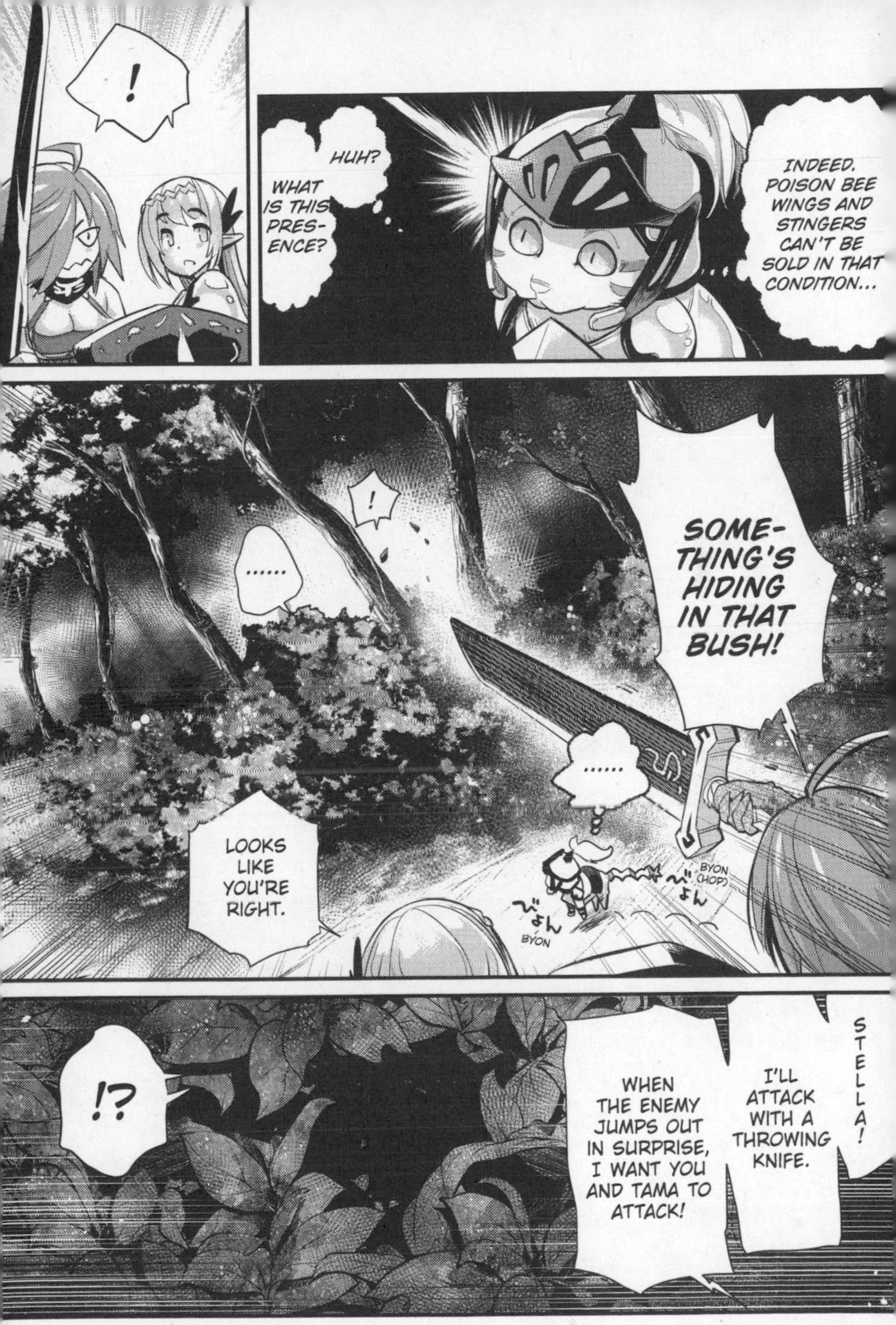
INDEED. POISON BEE WINGS AND STINGERS CAN'T BE SOLD IN THAT CONDITION...
HUH? WHAT IS THIS PRESENCE?
!
SOMETHING'S HIDING IN THAT BUSH!
!
......
......
BYON (HOP)
LOOKS LIKE YOU'RE RIGHT.
BYON
STELLA!
I'LL ATTACK WITH A THROWING KNIFE.
WHEN THE ENEMY JUMPS OUT IN SURPRISE, I WANT YOU AND TAMA TO ATTACK!
!?

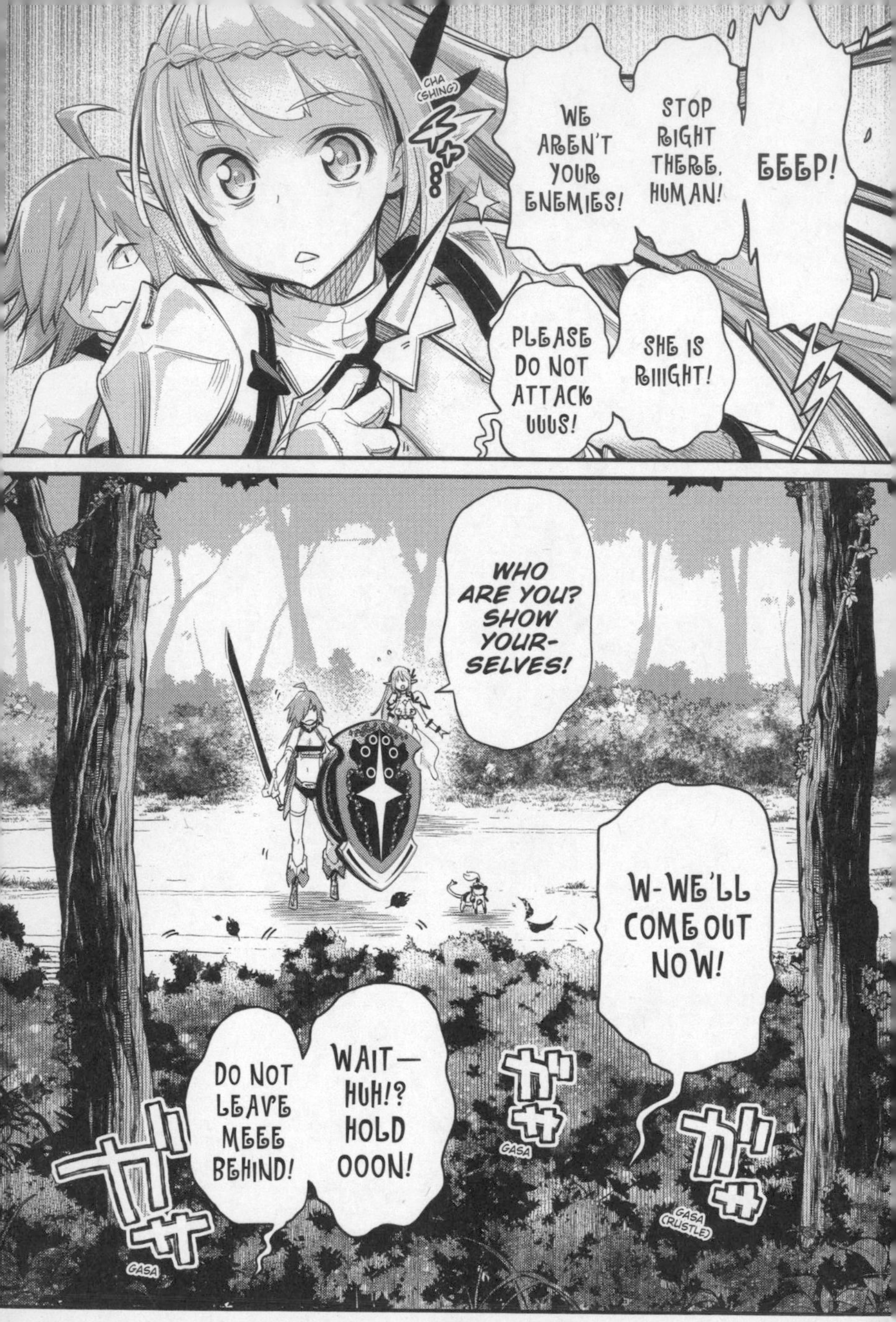
EEEP!
STOP RIGHT THERE, HUMAN!
WE AREN'T YOUR ENEMIES!
CHA (SHING)
SHE IS RIIIGHT!
PLEASE DO NOT ATTACK UUUS!
WHO ARE YOU? SHOW YOUR-SELVES!
W-WE'LL COME OUT NOW!
GASA (RUSTLE)
GASA
WAIT— HUH!? HOLD OOON!
DO NOT LEAVE MEEE BEHIND!
GASA

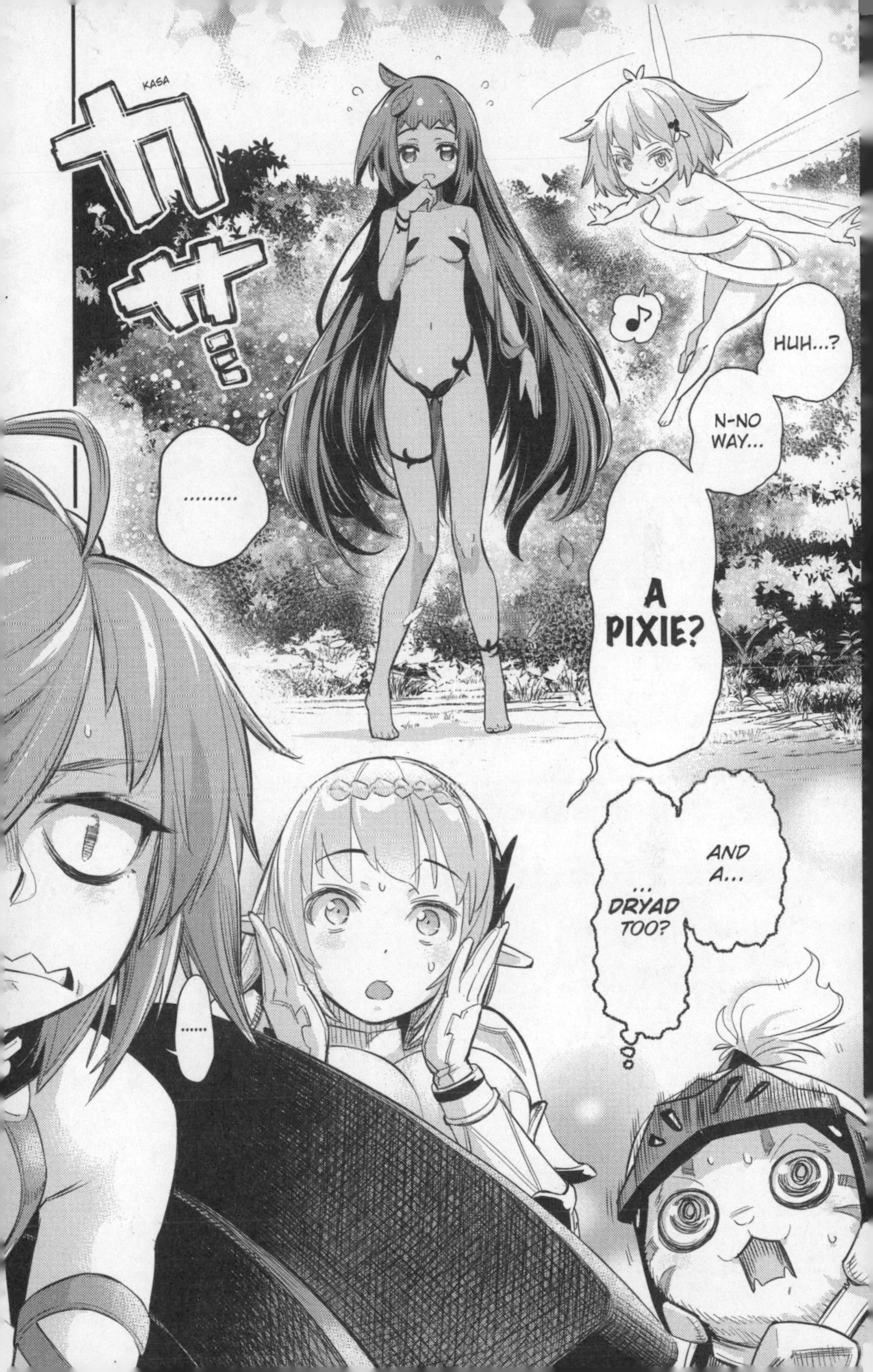
カサッ
KASA
HUH...?
N-NO WAY...
A PIXIE?
....
AND A...
...DRYAD TOO?
......

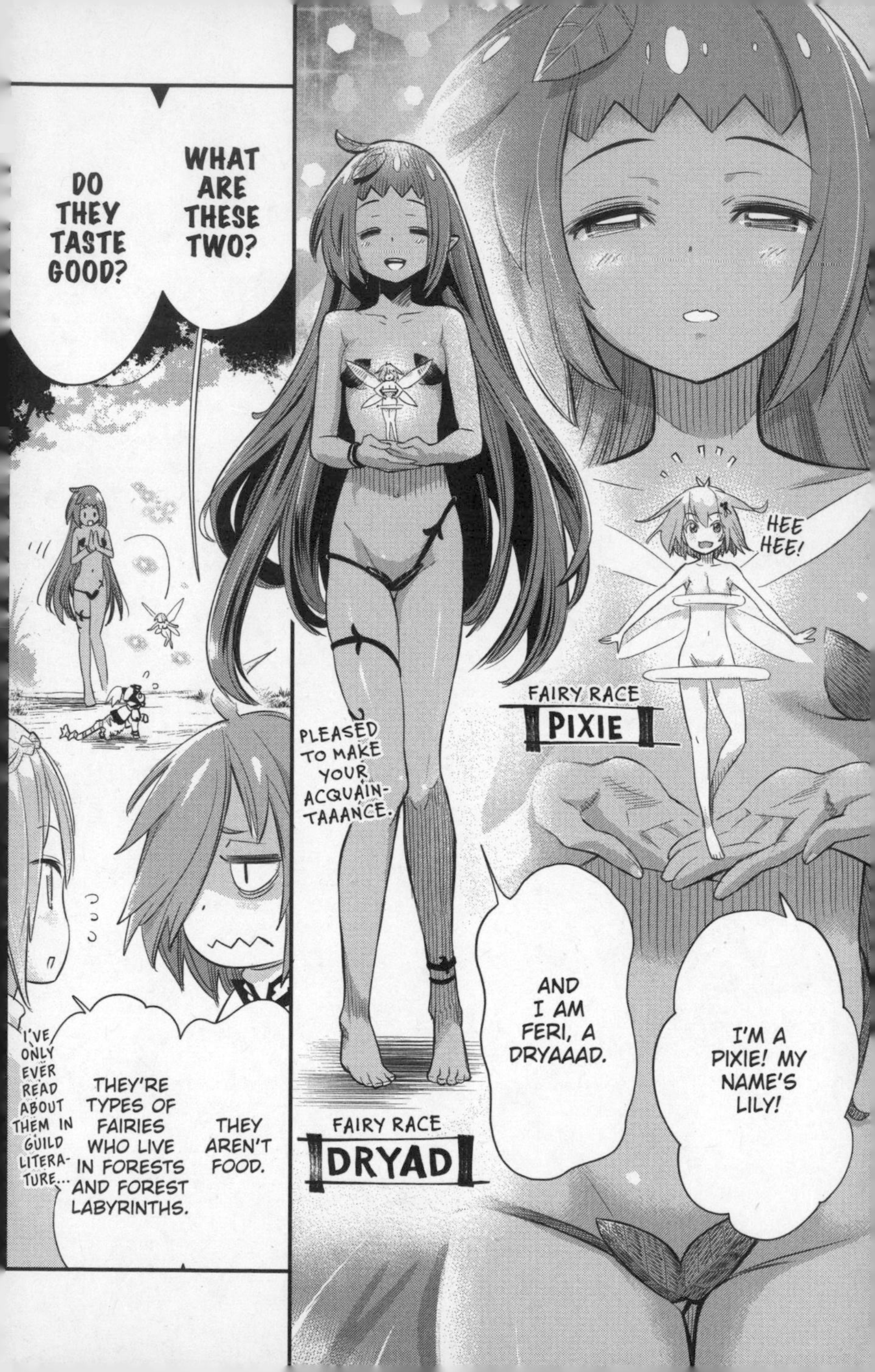
HEE HEE!
FAIRY RACE PIXIE
I'M A PIXIE! MY NAME'S LILY!
AND I AM FERI, A DRYAAAD.
PLEASED TO MAKE YOUR ACQUAIN-TAAANCE.
FAIRY RACE DRYAD
WHAT ARE THESE TWO?
DO THEY TASTE GOOD?
THEY AREN'T FOOD.
THEY'RE TYPES OF FAIRIES WHO LIVE IN FORESTS AND FOREST LABYRINTHS.
I'VE ONLY EVER READ ABOUT THEM IN GUILD LITERA-TURE...

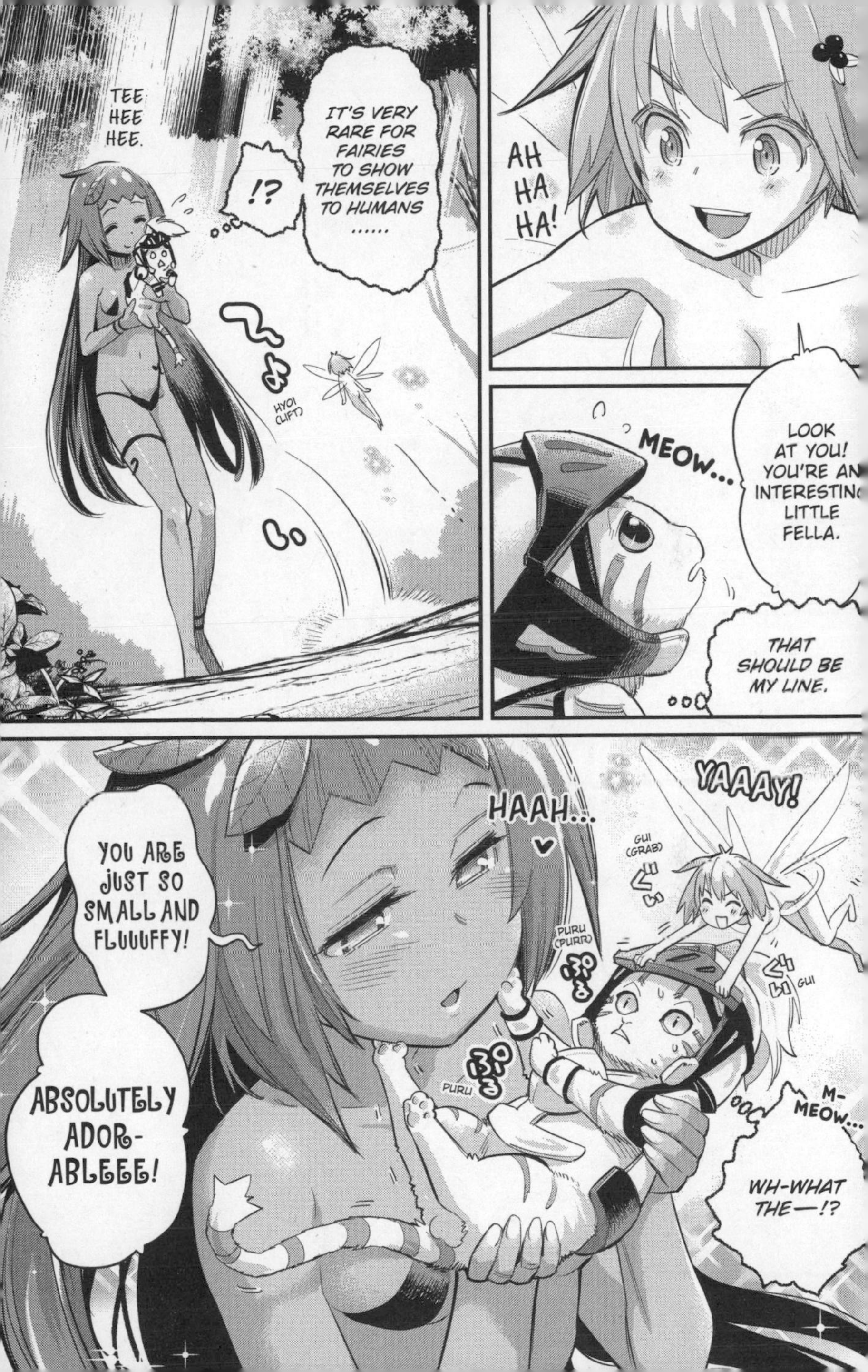
AH HA HA!
LOOK AT YOU! YOU'RE AN INTERESTING LITTLE FELLA.
MEOW...
THAT SHOULD BE MY LINE.
IT'S VERY RARE FOR FAIRIES TO SHOW THEMSELVES TO HUMANS......
!?
TEE HEE HEE.
HYOI (LIFT)
YAAAY!
GUI (GRAB)
GUI
HAAAH...
PURU (PURR)
PURU
M-MEOW...
WH-WHAT THE—!?
YOU ARE JUST SO SMALL AND FLUUUFFY!
ABSOLUTELY ADOR-ABLEEE!

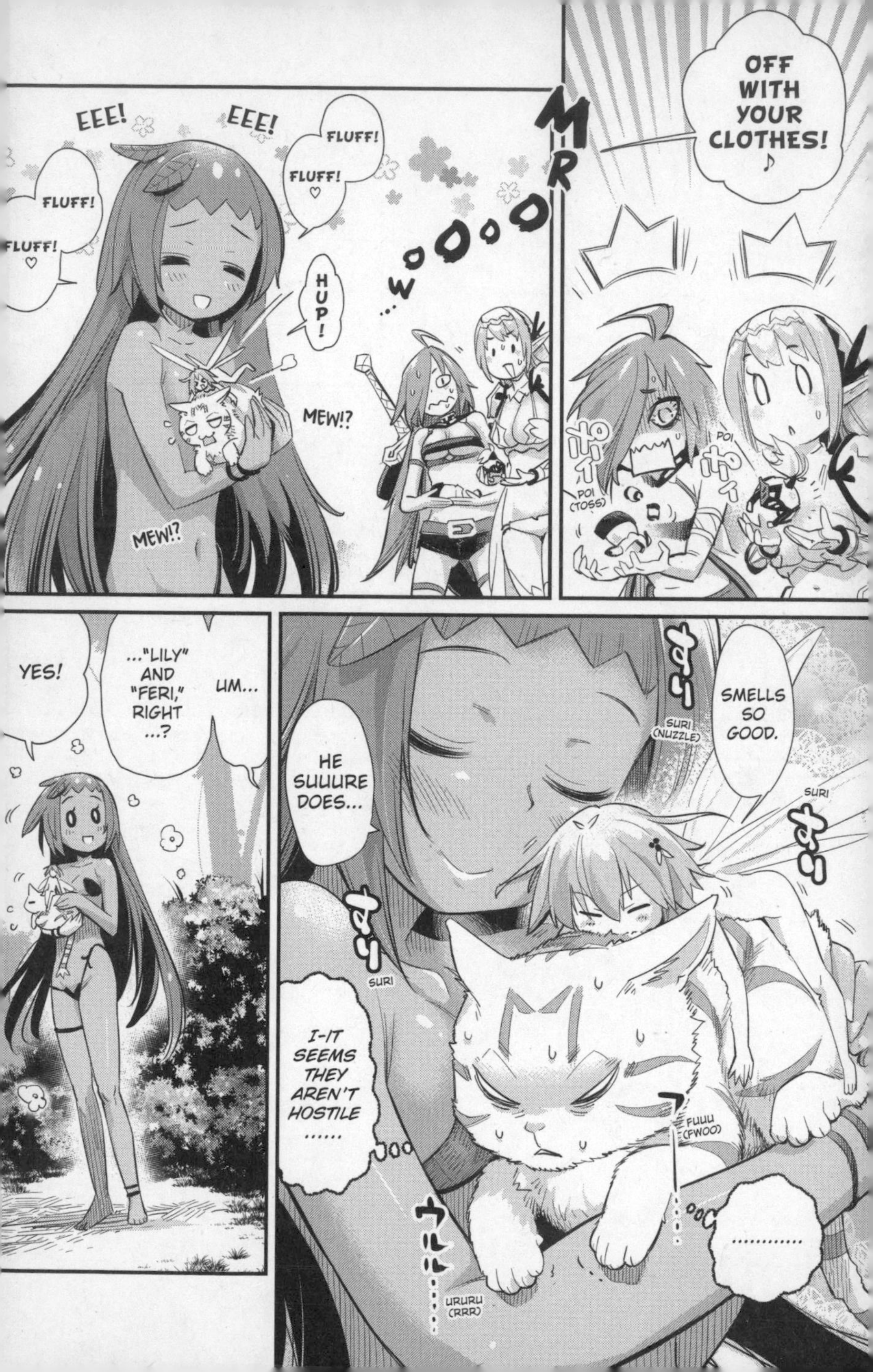
OFF WITH YOUR CLOTHES! ♪
POI
POI (TOSS)
MROOOOOW...
EEE!
EEE!
FLUFF! FLUFF! ♡
FLUFF! FLUFF! ♡
HUP!
MEW!?
MEW!?
SMELLS SO GOOD.
SURI (NUZZLE)
SURI
HE SUUURE DOES...
SURI
I-IT SEEMS THEY AREN'T HOSTILE ......
FUUU (FWOO)
URURU (RRR)
....
UM...
..."LILY" AND "FERI," RIGHT ...?
YES!

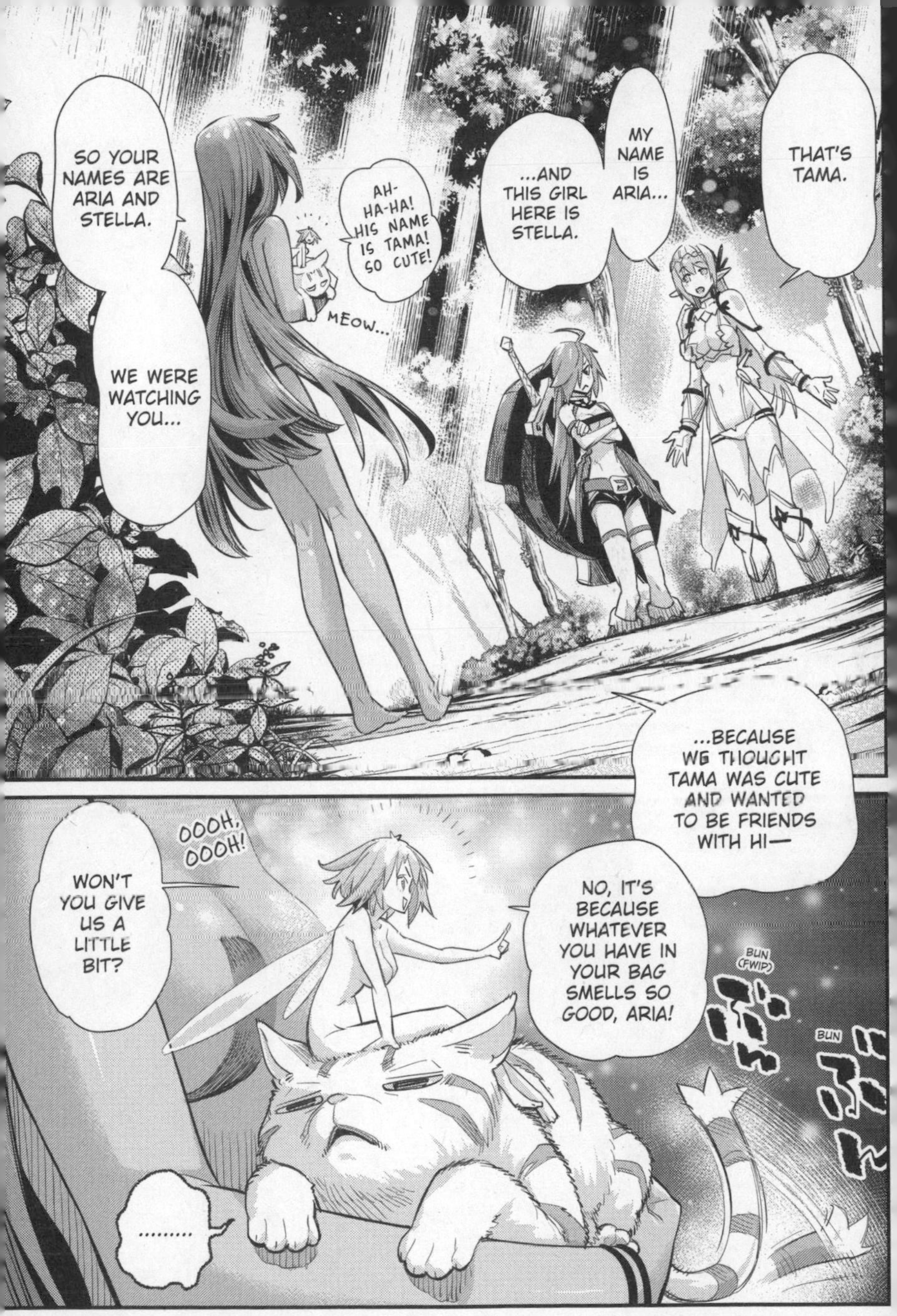
THAT'S TAMA.
MY NAME IS ARIA...
...AND THIS GIRL HERE IS STELLA.
AH-HA-HA! HIS NAME IS TAMA! SO CUTE!
MEOW...
SO YOUR NAMES ARE ARIA AND STELLA.
WE WERE WATCHING YOU...
...BECAUSE WE THOUGHT TAMA WAS CUTE AND WANTED TO BE FRIENDS WITH HI—
BUN
BUN (FWIP)
NO, IT'S BECAUSE WHATEVER YOU HAVE IN YOUR BAG SMELLS SO GOOD, ARIA!
OOOH, OOOH!
WON'T YOU GIVE US A LITTLE BIT?
....

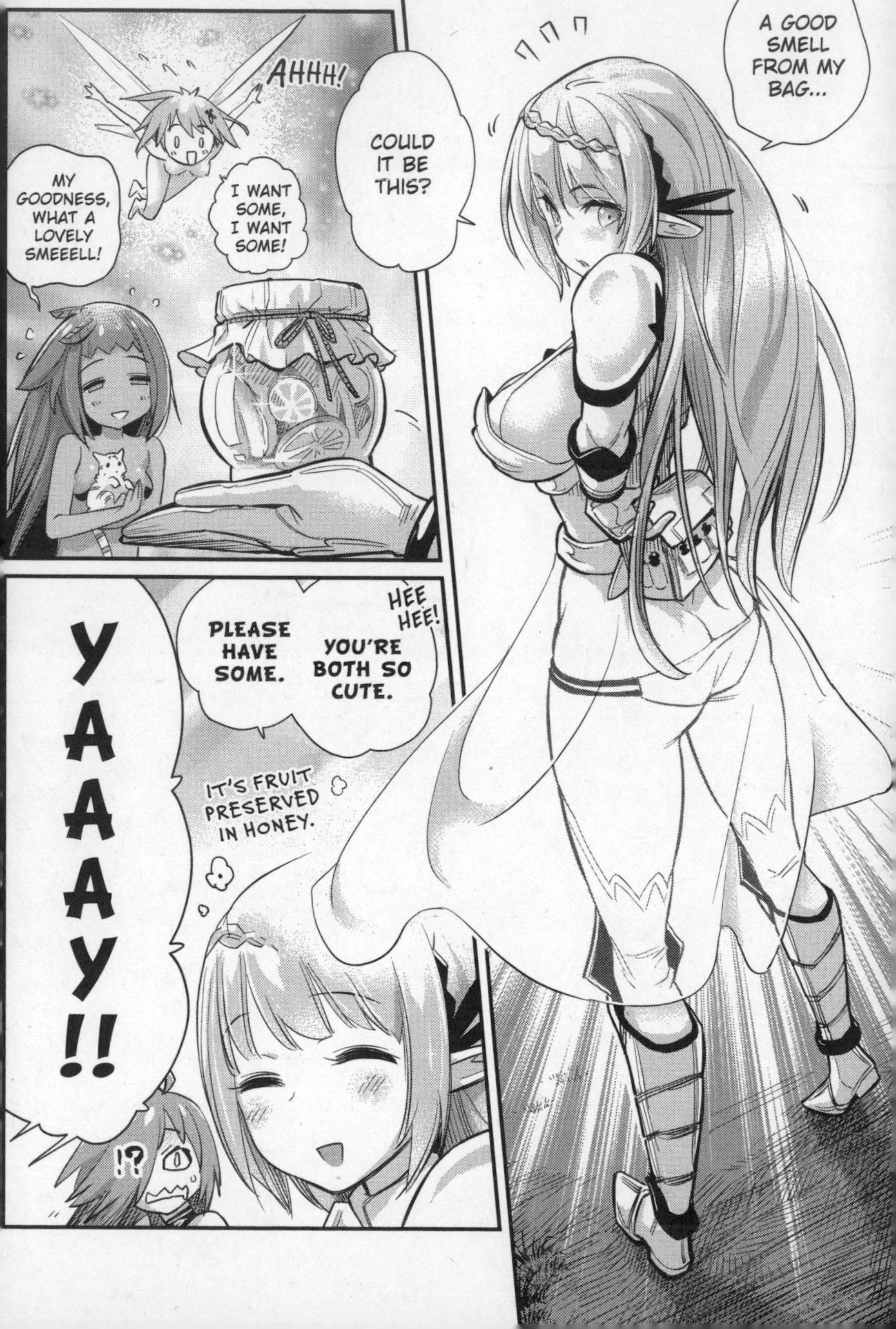
A GOOD SMELL FROM MY BAG...
COULD IT BE THIS?
AHHH!
I WANT SOME, I WANT SOME!
MY GOODNESS, WHAT A LOVELY SMEEELL!
HEE HEE!
YOU'RE BOTH SO CUTE.
PLEASE HAVE SOME.
IT'S FRUIT PRESERVED IN HONEY.
YAAAAY!!
!?

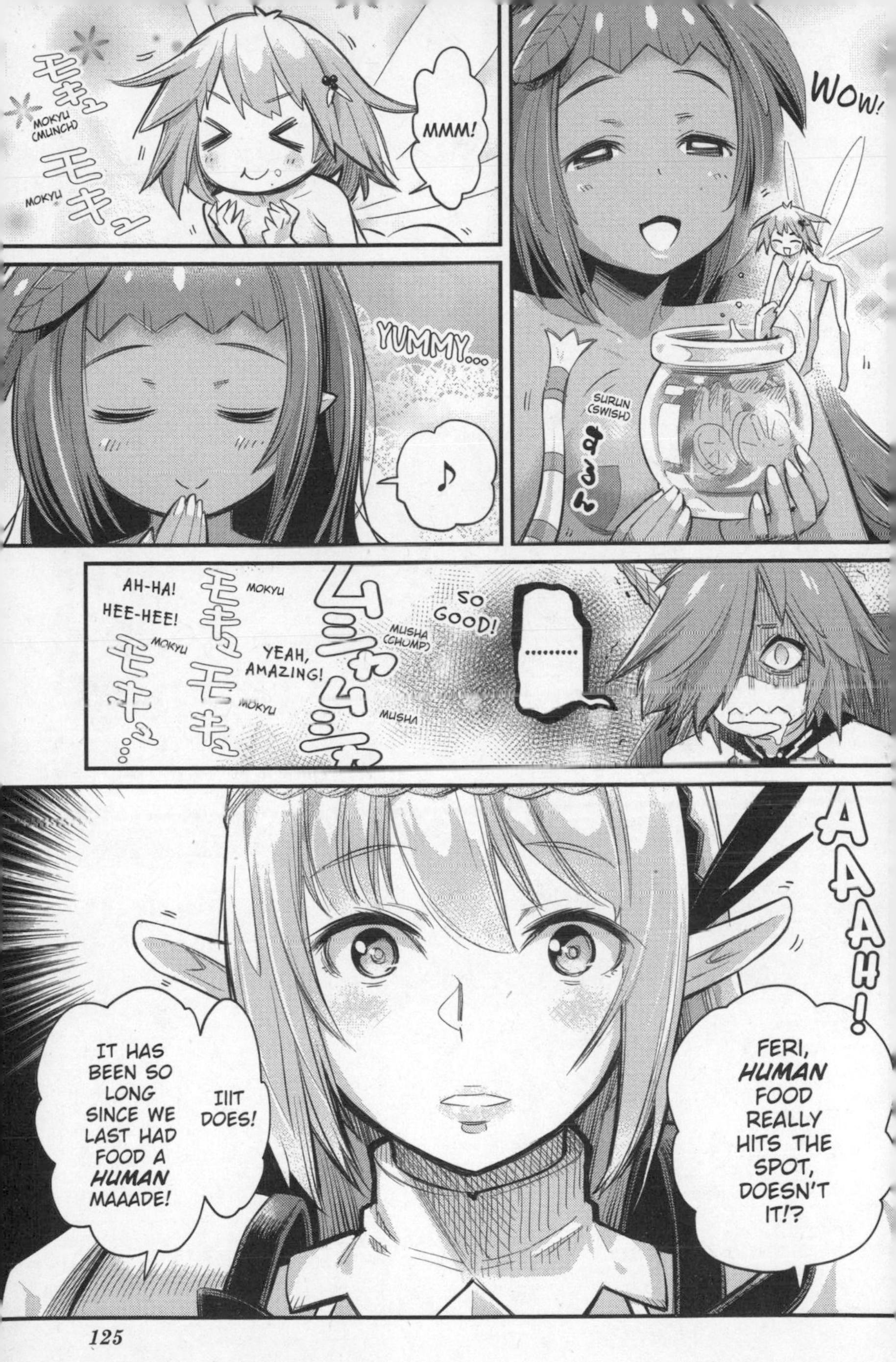
WOW!
SURUN (SWISH)
するん
MMM!
モキュ
MOKYU (MUNCH)
モキュ
MOKYU
YUMMY...
♪
....
SO GOOD!
MUSHA (CHUMP)
MUSHA
YEAH, AMAZING!
MOKYU
MOKYU
MOKYU
AH-HA! HEE-HEE!
AAAAH!
FERI, HUMAN FOOD REALLY HITS THE SPOT, DOESN'T IT!?
IIIT DOES!
IT HAS BEEN SO LONG SINCE WE LAST HAD FOOD A HUMAN MAAADE!

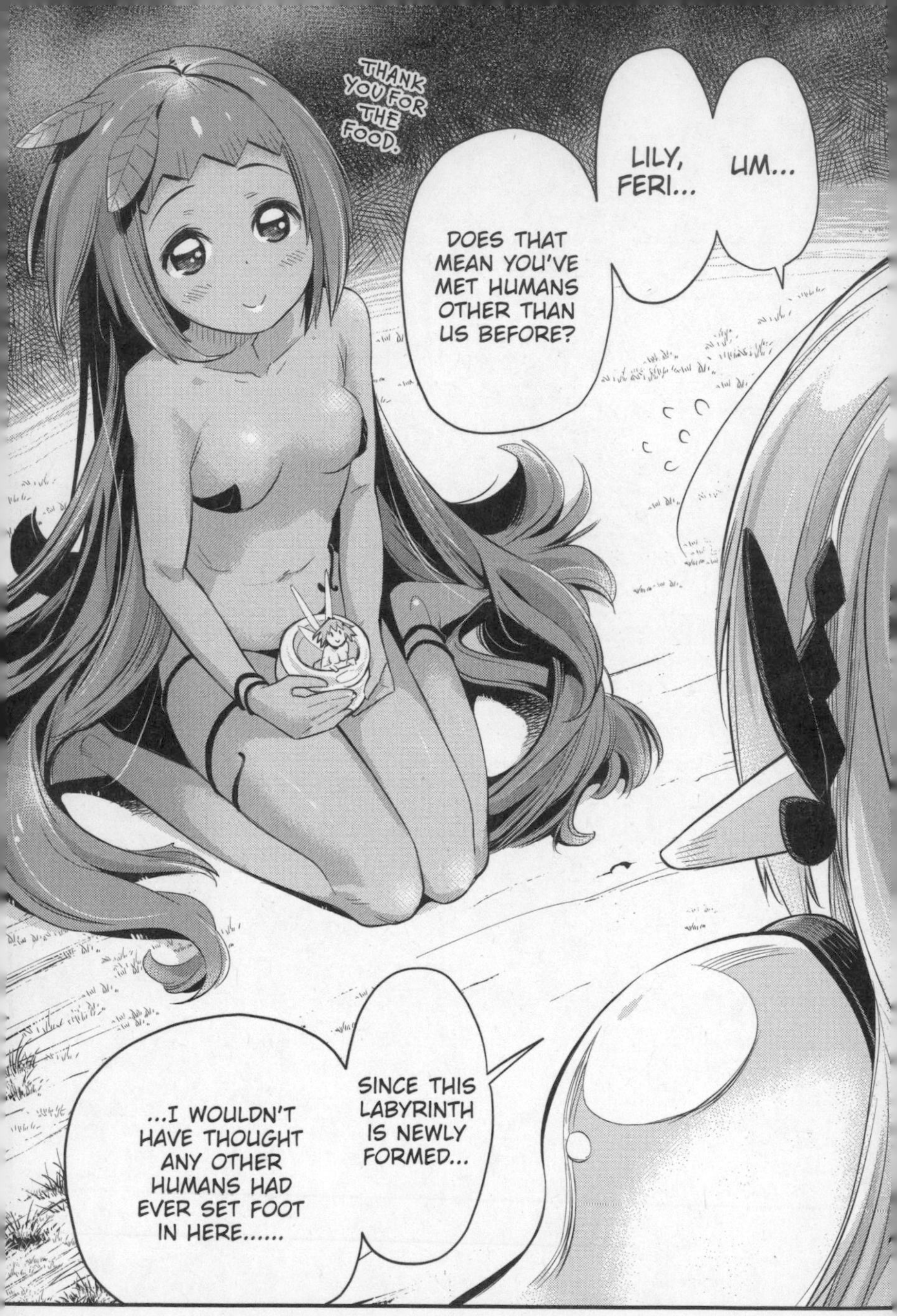
UM...
LILY, FERI...
THANK YOU FOR THE FOOD.
DOES THAT MEAN YOU'VE MET HUMANS OTHER THAN US BEFORE?
SINCE THIS LABYRINTH IS NEWLY FORMED...
...I WOULDN'T HAVE THOUGHT ANY OTHER HUMANS HAD EVER SET FOOT IN HERE......

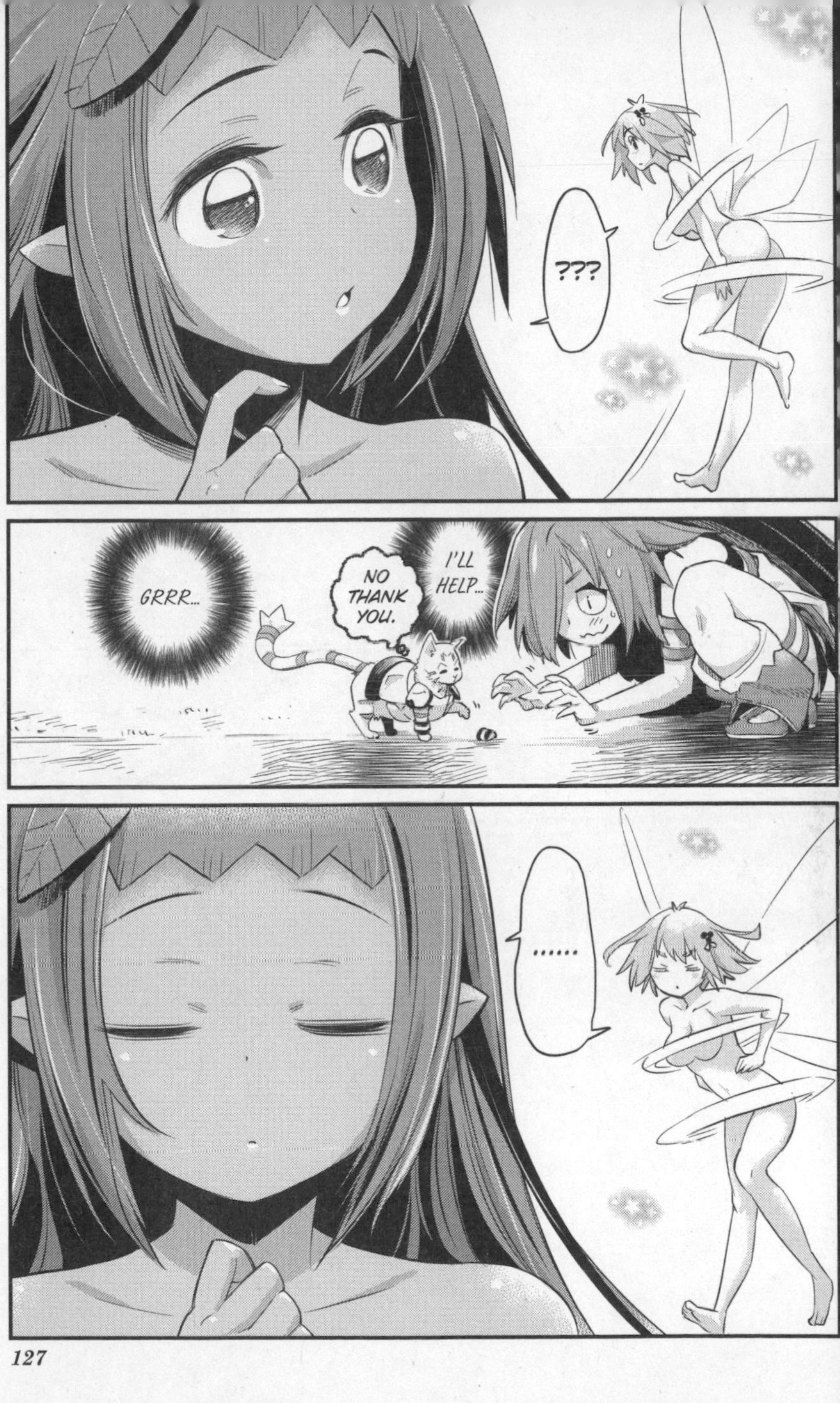
???
I'LL HELP...
NO THANK YOU.
GRRR...
......

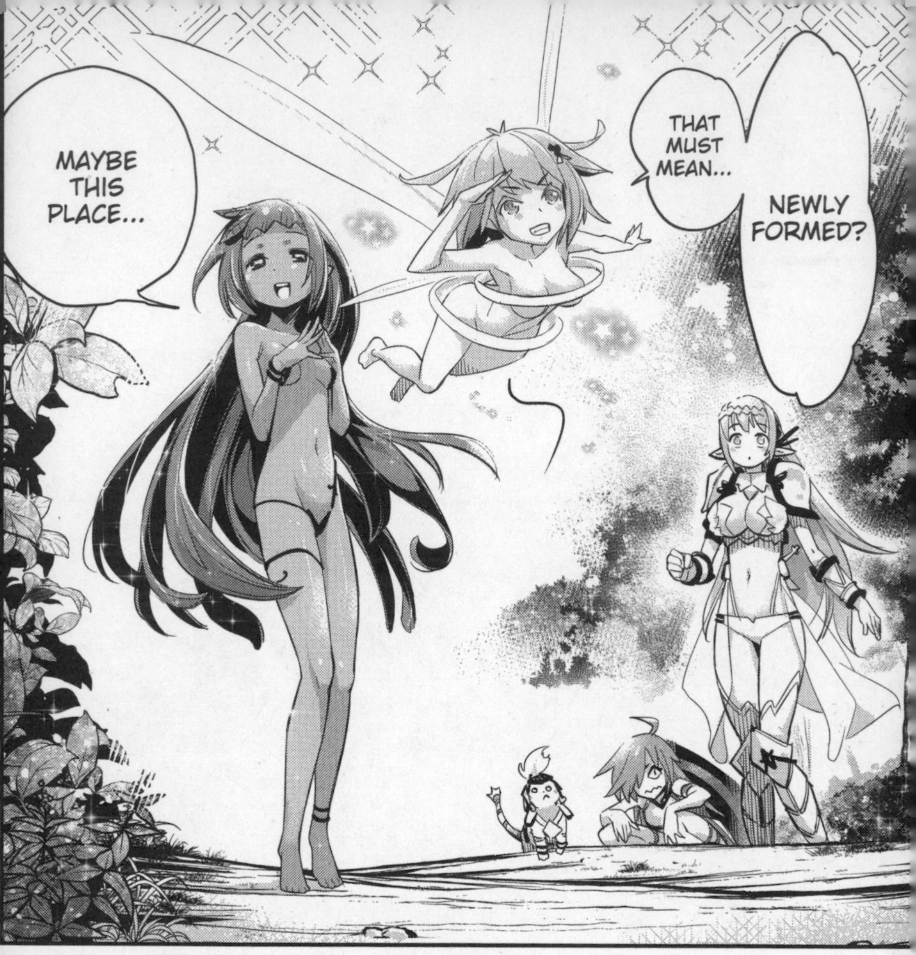
THAT MUST MEAN...
NEWLY FORMED?
MAYBE THIS PLACE...

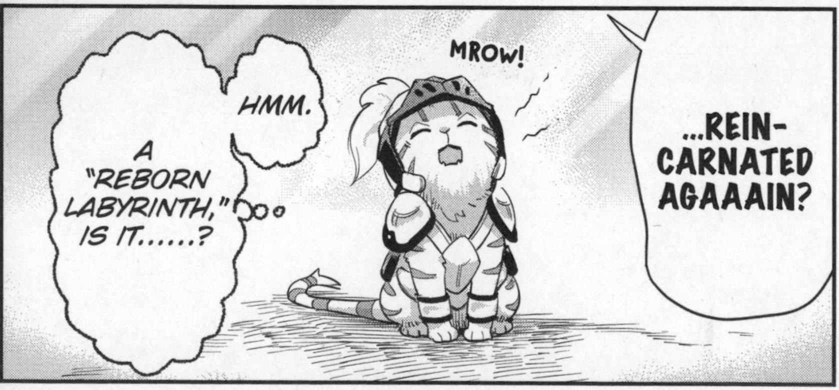
...REIN-CARNATED AGAAAIN?
MROW!
HMM.
A "REBORN LABYRINTH," IS IT......?

#30 — Teardrops of Truth

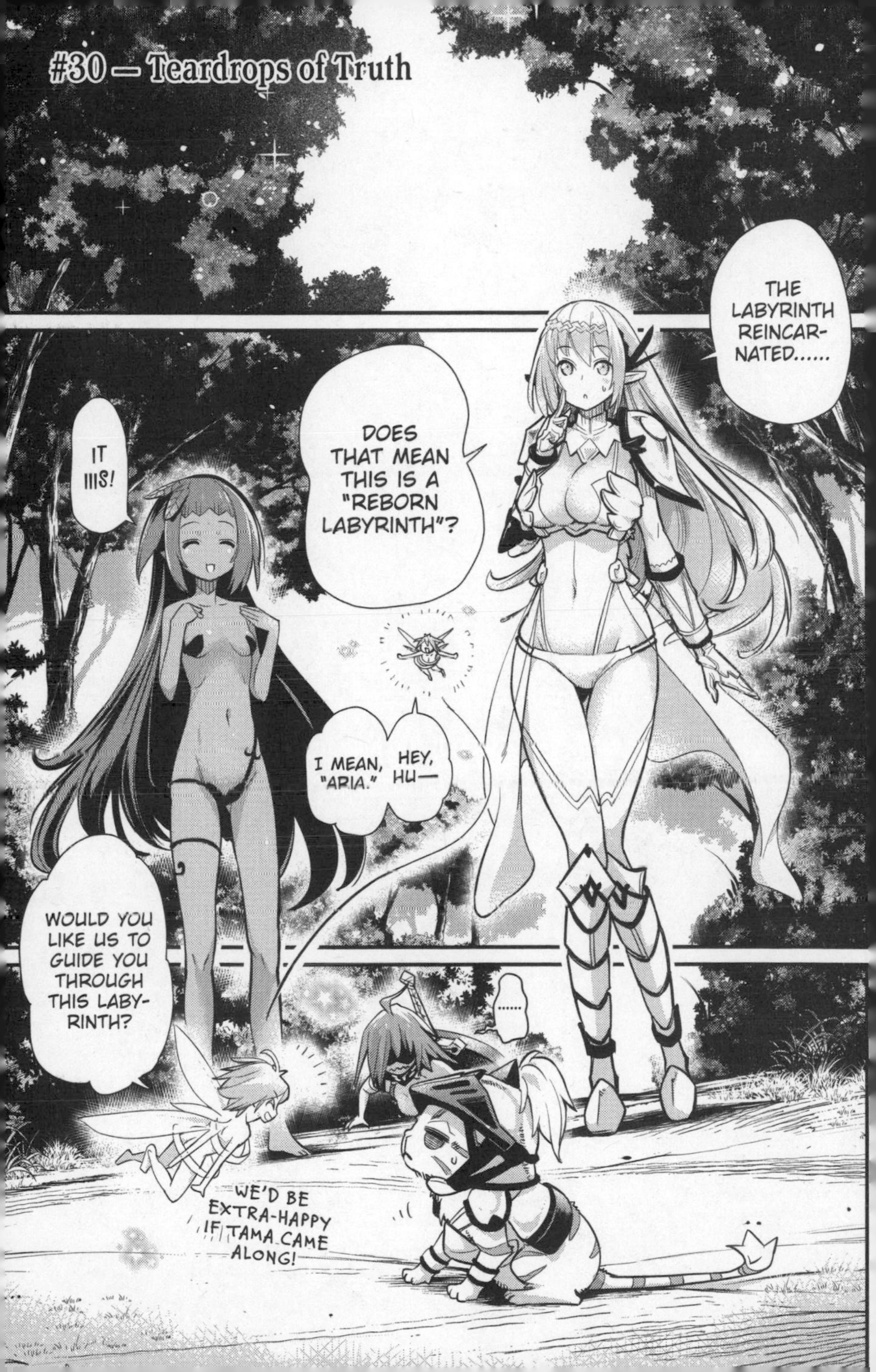
THE LABYRINTH REINCAR-NATED......
DOES THAT MEAN THIS IS A "REBORN LABYRINTH"?
IT IIIS!
HEY, HU—
I MEAN, "ARIA."
......
WOULD YOU LIKE US TO GUIDE YOU THROUGH THIS LABY-RINTH?
WE'D BE EXTRA-HAPPY IF TAMA CAME ALONG!

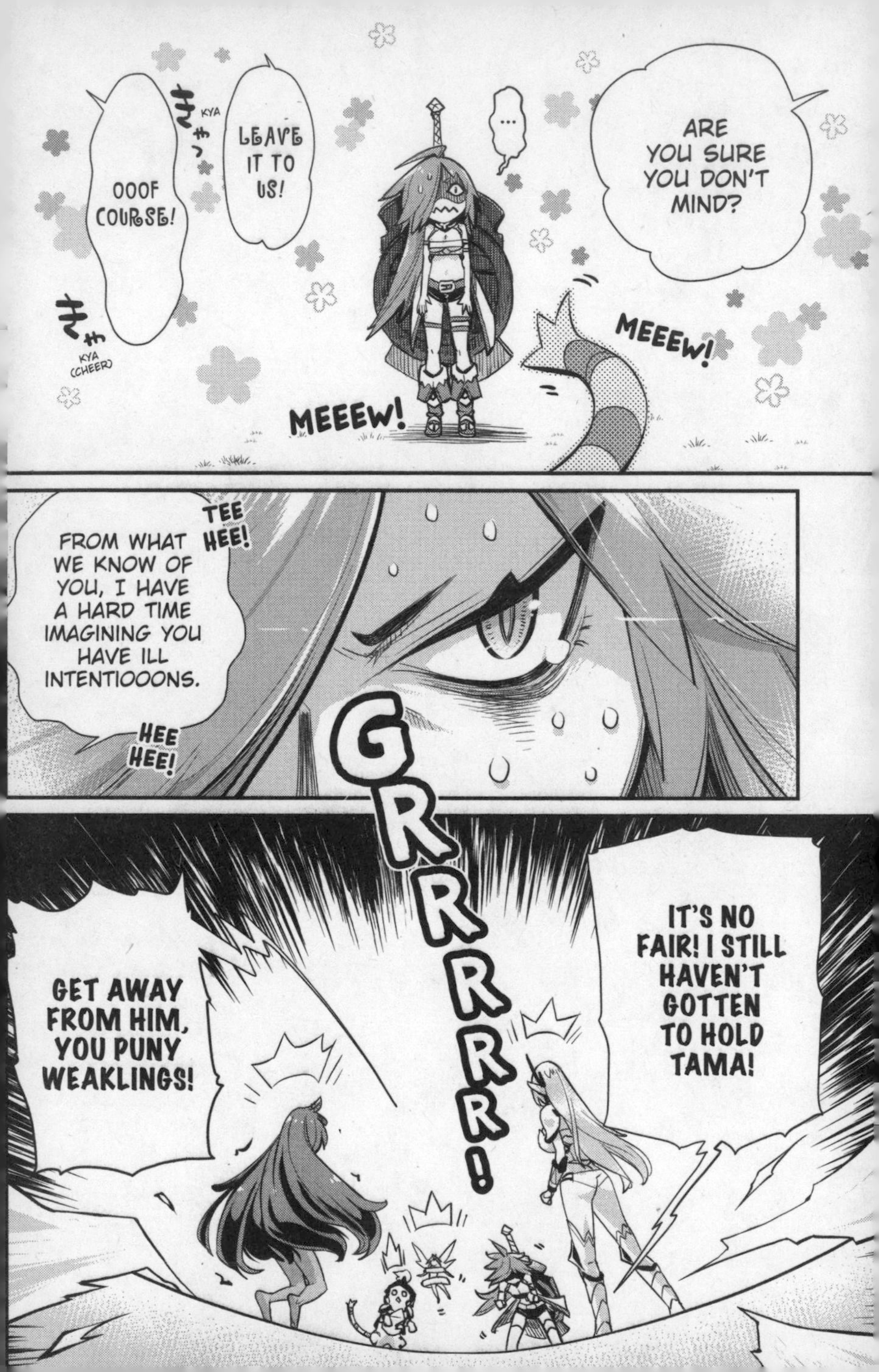
ARE YOU SURE YOU DON'T MIND?
MEEEW!
...
MEEEW!
LEAVE IT TO US!
きゃっ
KYA
OOOF COURSE!
きゃ
KYA (CHEER)
TEE HEE!
FROM WHAT WE KNOW OF YOU, I HAVE A HARD TIME IMAGINING YOU HAVE ILL INTENTIOOONS.
HEE HEE!
GRRRRR!
IT'S NO FAIR! I STILL HAVEN'T GOTTEN TO HOLD TAMA!
GET AWAY FROM HIM, YOU PUNY WEAKLINGS!

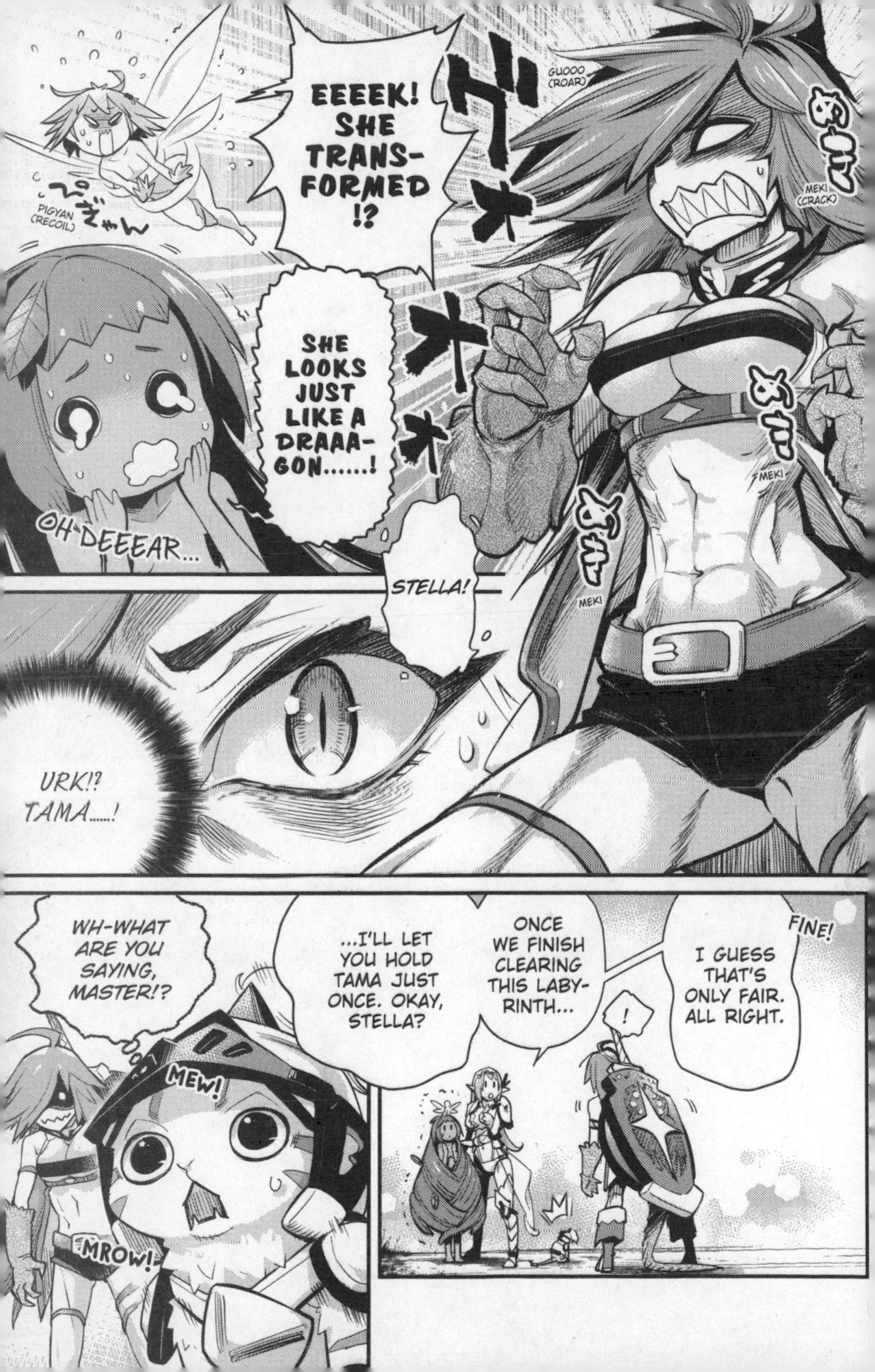
GUOOO (ROAR)
MEKI (CRACK)
MEKI
MEKI
EEEEK! SHE TRANS-FORMED!?
PIGYAN (RECOIL)
SHE LOOKS JUST LIKE A DRAAA-GON......!
OH DEEEAR...
STELLA!
URK!? TAMA......!
FINE!
I GUESS THAT'S ONLY FAIR. ALL RIGHT.
!
ONCE WE FINISH CLEARING THIS LABY-RINTH...
...I'LL LET YOU HOLD TAMA JUST ONCE. OKAY, STELLA?
WH-WHAT ARE YOU SAYING, MASTER!?
MEW!
MROW!

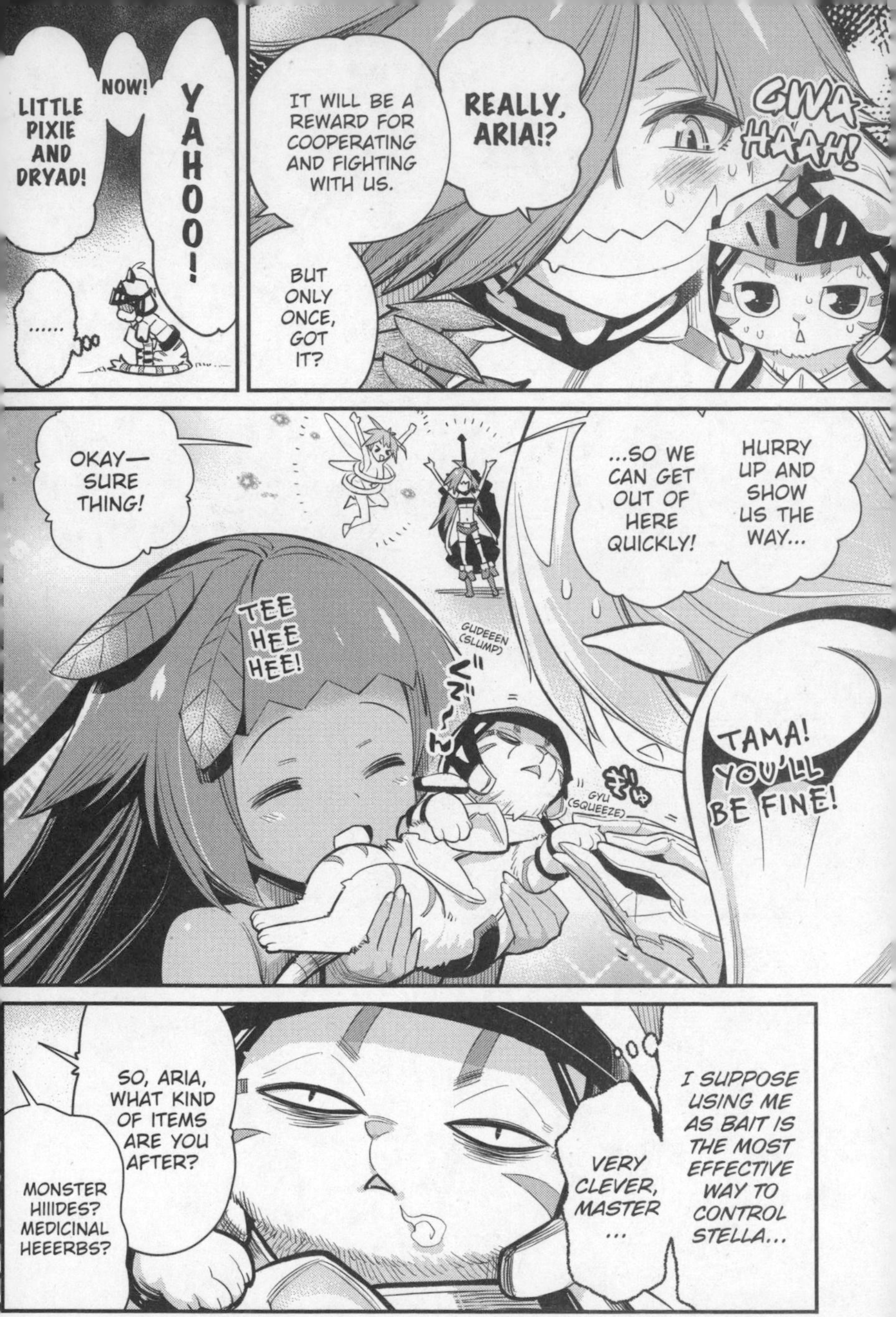
GWA HAAH!
REALLY, ARIA!?
IT WILL BE A REWARD FOR COOPERATING AND FIGHTING WITH US.
BUT ONLY ONCE, GOT IT?
YAHOOO!
NOW!
LITTLE PIXIE AND DRYAD!
......
HURRY UP AND SHOW US THE WAY...
...SO WE CAN GET OUT OF HERE QUICKLY!
OKAY— SURE THING!
TEE HEE HEE!
GUDEEEN (SLUMP)
TAMA! YOU'LL BE FINE!
GYU (SQUEEZE)
I SUPPOSE USING ME AS BAIT IS THE MOST EFFECTIVE WAY TO CONTROL STELLA...
VERY CLEVER, MASTER ...
SO, ARIA, WHAT KIND OF ITEMS ARE YOU AFTER?
MONSTER HIIIDES? MEDICINAL HEEERBS?

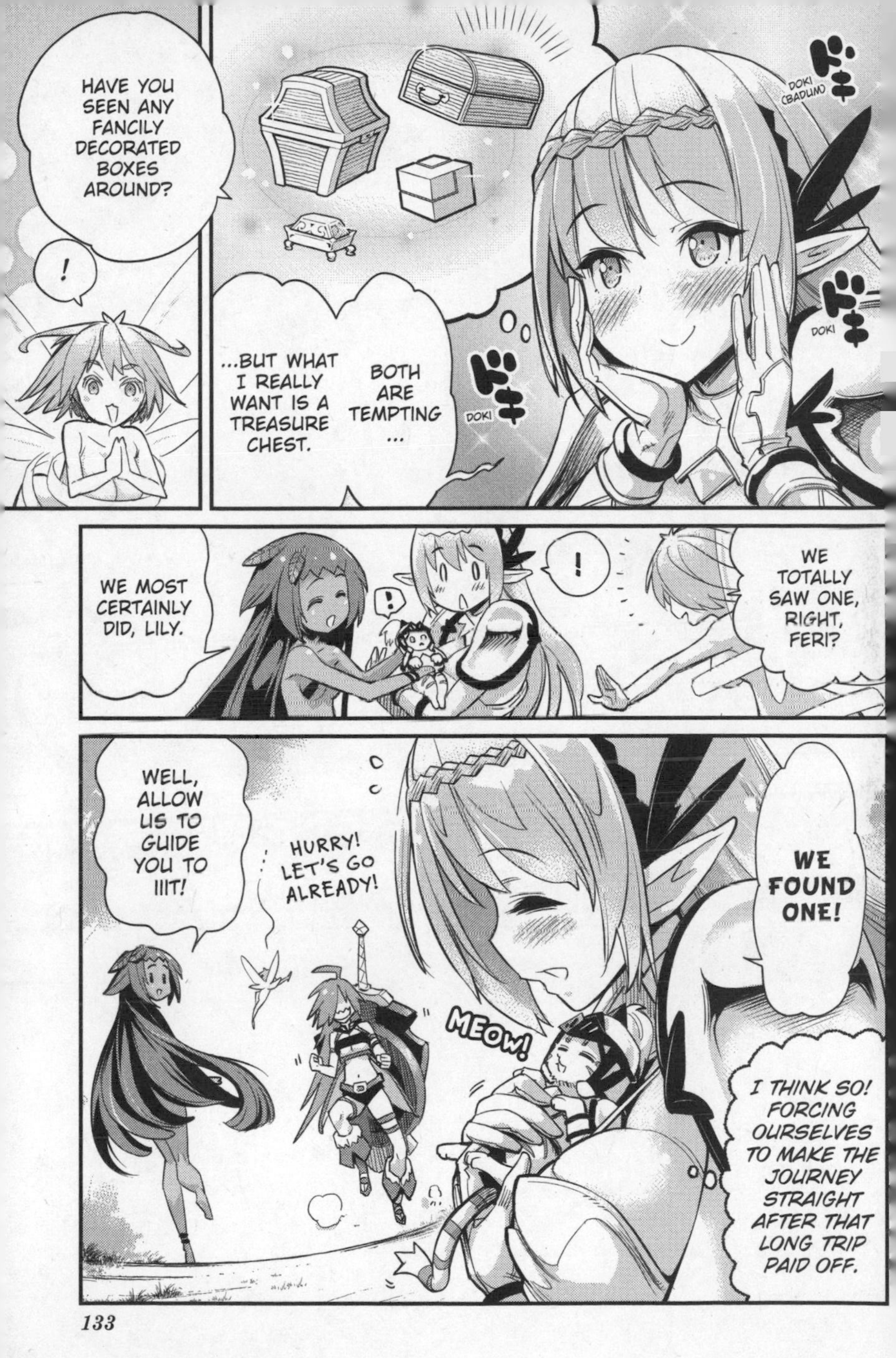
ドキ
DOKI (BADUM)
ドキ
DOKI
BOTH ARE TEMPTING ...
...BUT WHAT I REALLY WANT IS A TREASURE CHEST.
ドキ
DOKI
HAVE YOU SEEN ANY FANCILY DECORATED BOXES AROUND?
!
WE TOTALLY SAW ONE, RIGHT, FERI?
!
!
WE MOST CERTAINLY DID, LILY.
WE FOUND ONE!
I THINK SO! FORCING OURSELVES TO MAKE THE JOURNEY STRAIGHT AFTER THAT LONG TRIP PAID OFF.
MEOW!
HURRY! LET'S GO ALREADY!
WELL, ALLOW US TO GUIDE YOU TO IIIT!

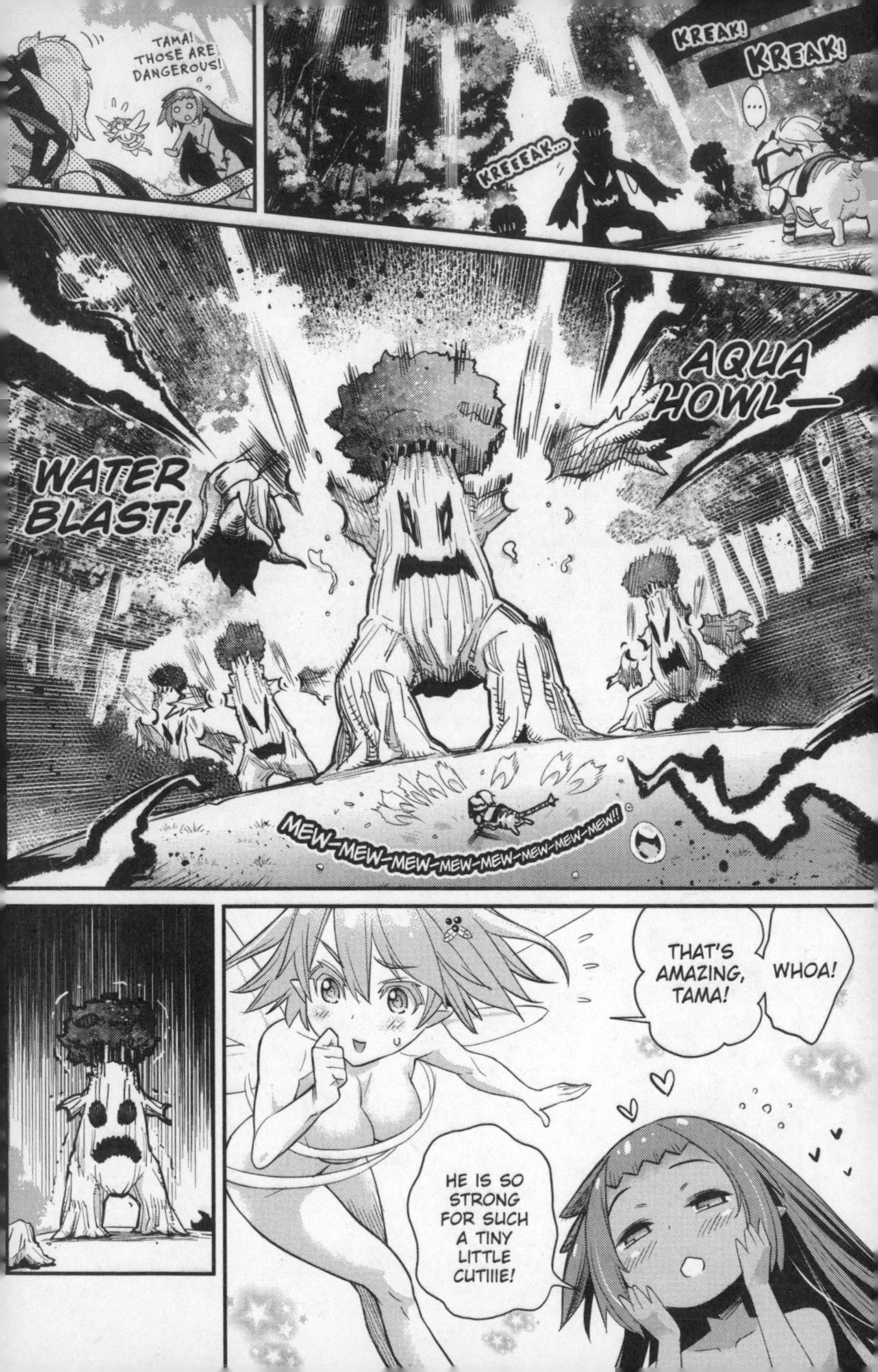
KREAK!
KREAK!
...
KREEEAK...
TAMA! THOSE ARE DANGEROUS!
AQUA HOWL—
WATER BLAST!
MEW-MEW-MEW-MEW-MEW-MEW-MEW-MEW!!
WHOA!
THAT'S AMAZING, TAMA!
HE IS SO STRONG FOR SUCH A TINY LITTLE CUTIIIE!

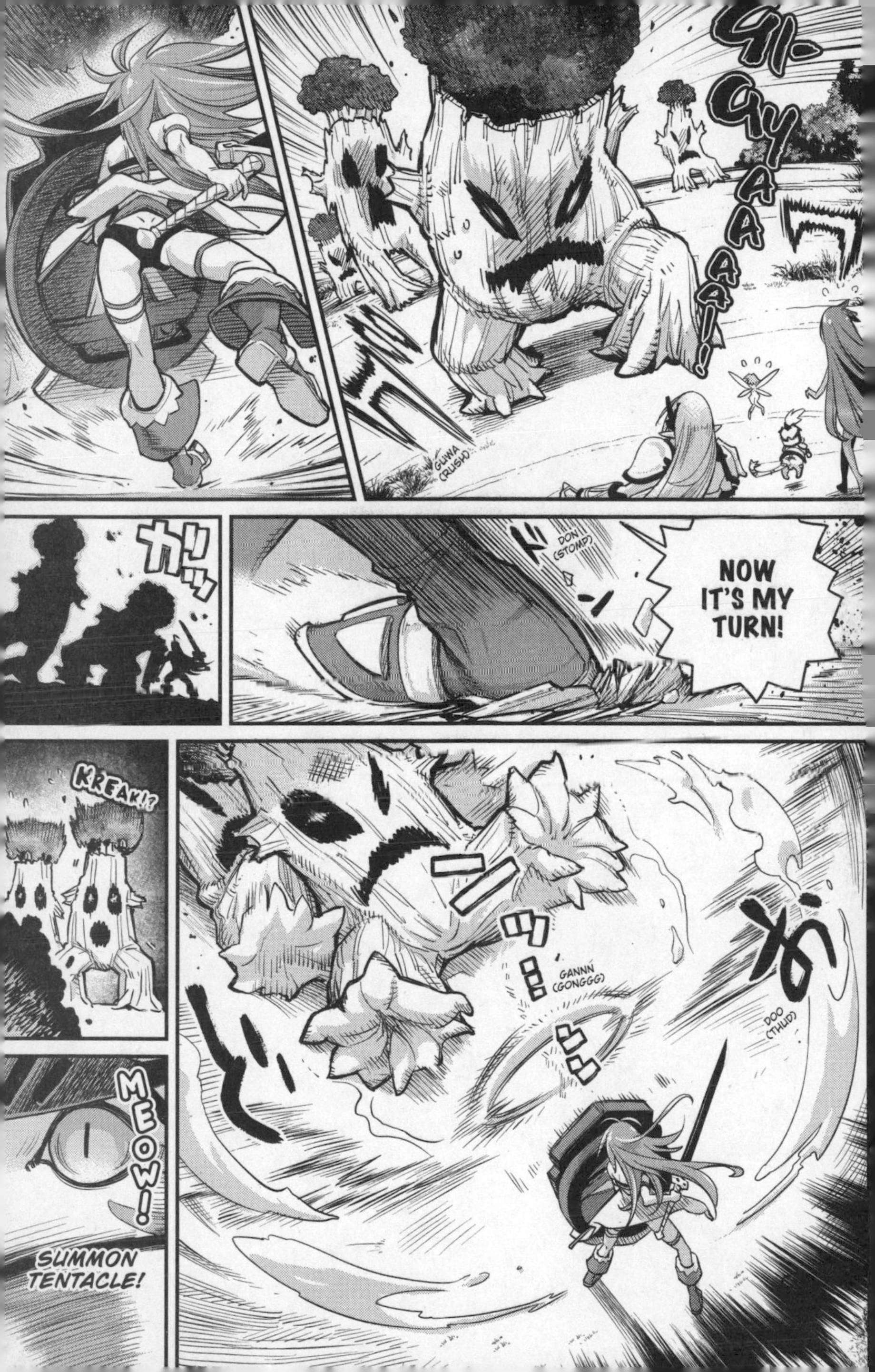
GYAAAA!!
GUWA (RUSH)
DON (STOMP)
NOW IT'S MY TURN!
GANNN (GONGGG)
DOO (THUD)
KREAK!?
MEOW!
SUMMON TENTACLE!

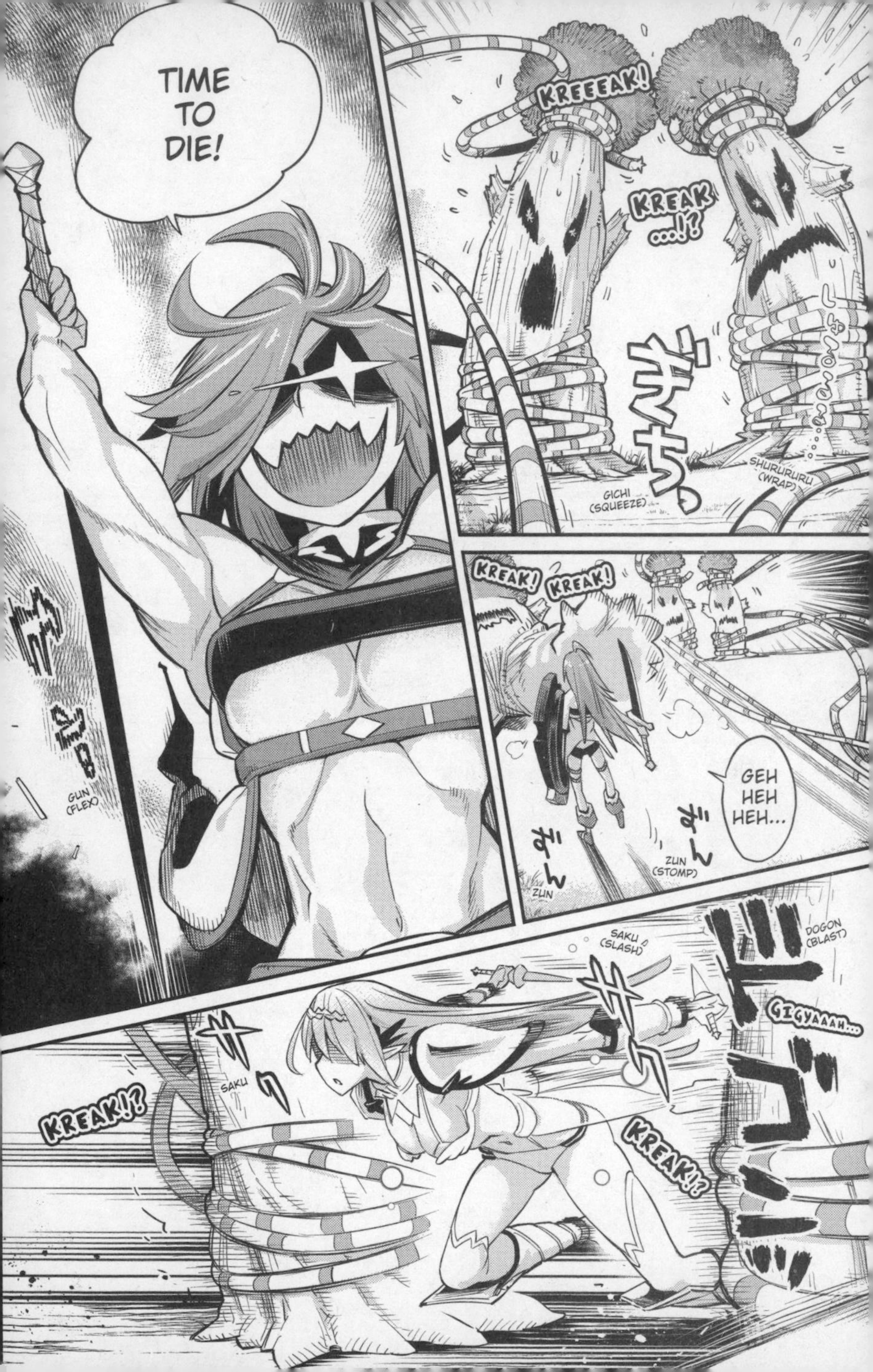
KREEEAK!
KREAK ...!?
SHURURURU (WRAP)
GICHI (SQUEEZE)
KREAK! KREAK!
GEH HEH HEH...
ZUN (STOMP)
ZUN
TIME TO DIE!
GUN (FLEX)
DOGON (BLAST)
GIGYAAAH...
SAKU (SLASH)
KREAK!!?
SAKU
KREAK!!?

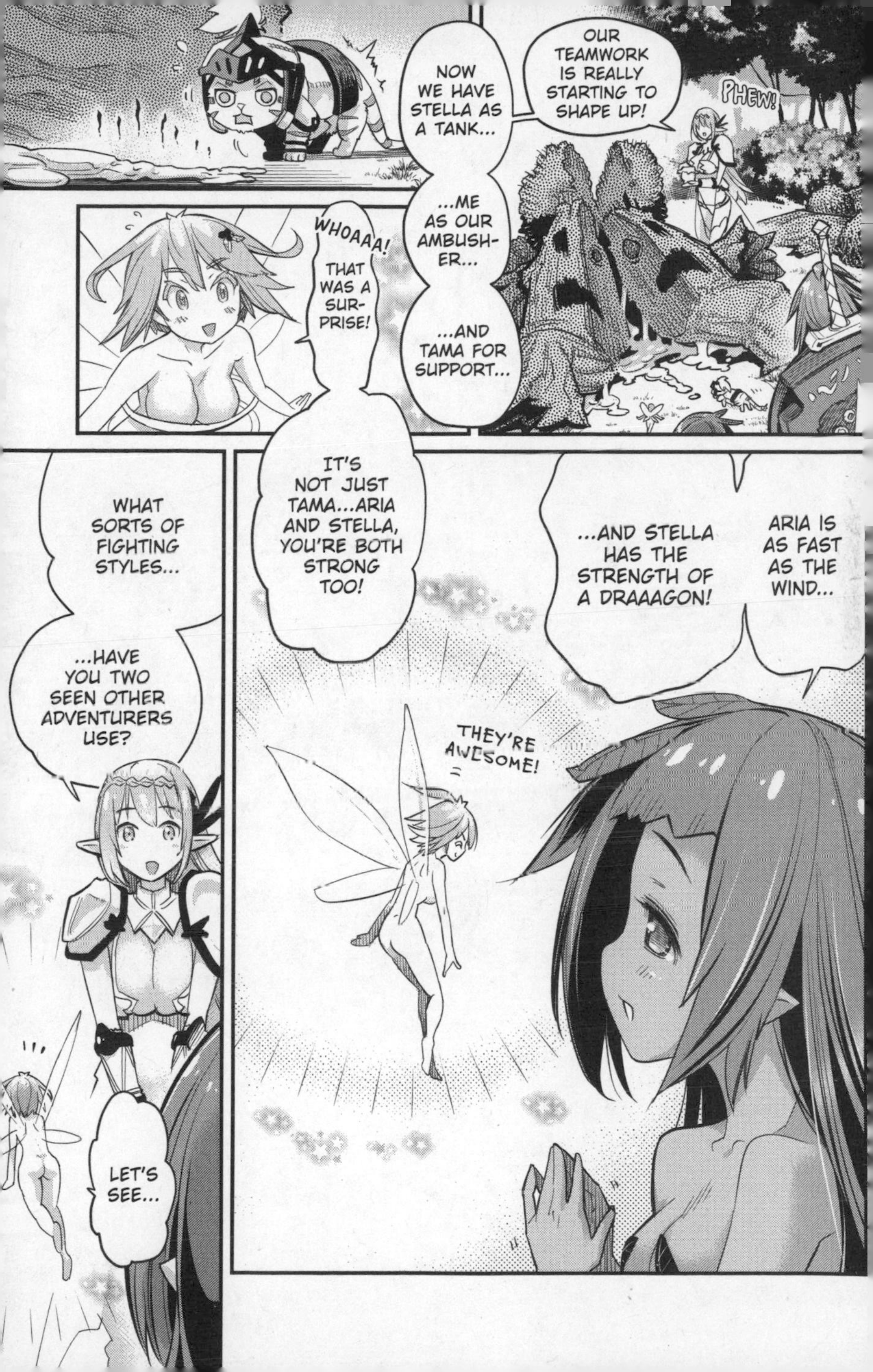
OUR TEAMWORK IS REALLY STARTING TO SHAPE UP!
PHEW!
NOW WE HAVE STELLA AS A TANK...
...ME AS OUR AMBUSHER...
...AND TAMA FOR SUPPORT...
WHOAAA!
THAT WAS A SURPRISE!
ARIA IS AS FAST AS THE WIND...
...AND STELLA HAS THE STRENGTH OF A DRAAAGON!
IT'S NOT JUST TAMA...ARIA AND STELLA, YOU'RE BOTH STRONG TOO!
THEY'RE AWESOME!
WHAT SORTS OF FIGHTING STYLES...
...HAVE YOU TWO SEEN OTHER ADVENTURERS USE?
LET'S SEE...

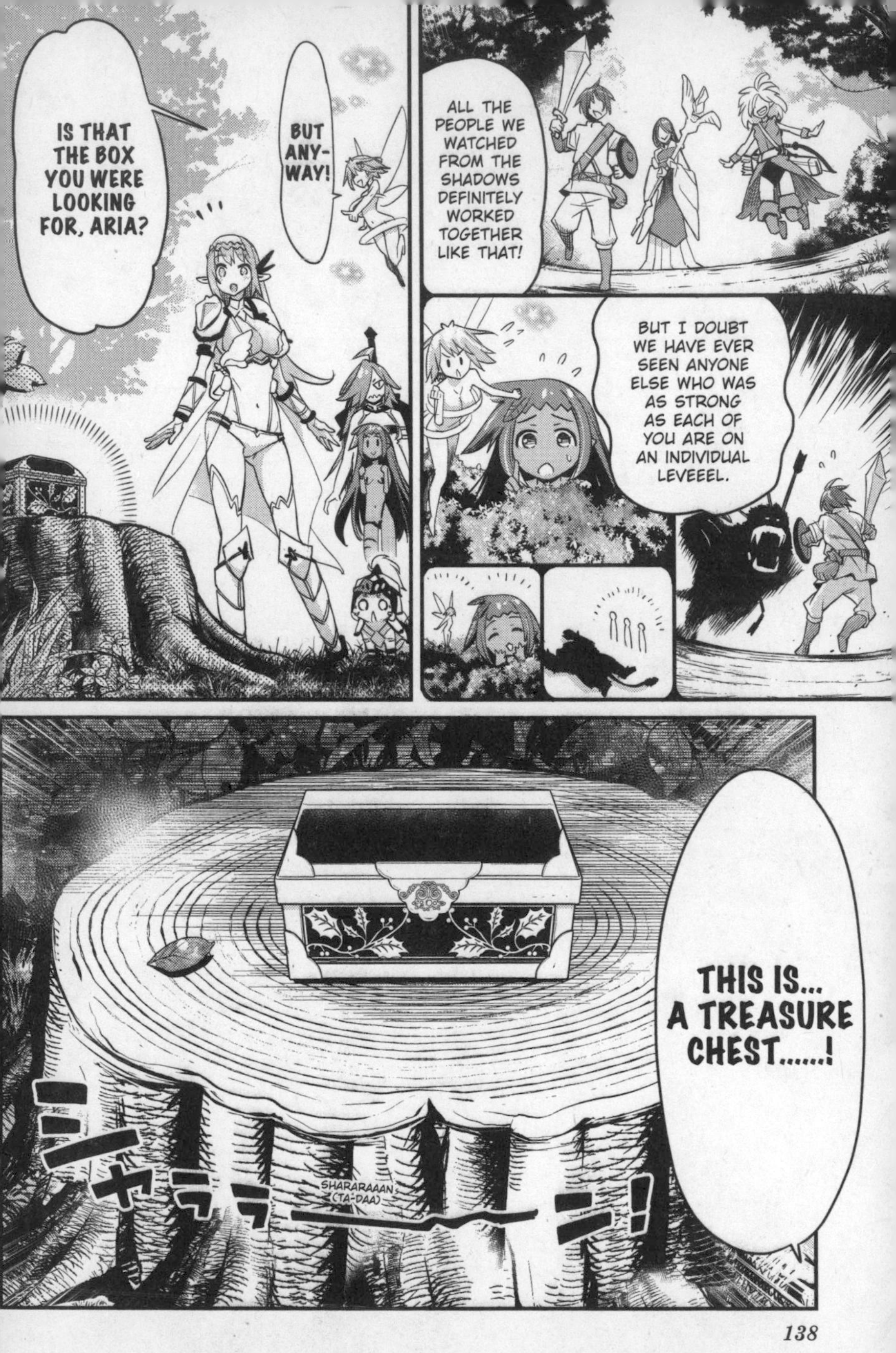

ALL THE PEOPLE WE WATCHED FROM THE SHADOWS DEFINITELY WORKED TOGETHER LIKE THAT!
BUT I DOUBT WE HAVE EVER SEEN ANYONE ELSE WHO WAS AS STRONG AS EACH OF YOU ARE ON AN INDIVIDUAL LEVEEEL.
BUT ANYWAY!
IS THAT THE BOX YOU WERE LOOKING FOR, ARIA?
THIS IS... A TREASURE CHEST......!
シャラララーーーン!
SHARARAAAN (TA-DAA)

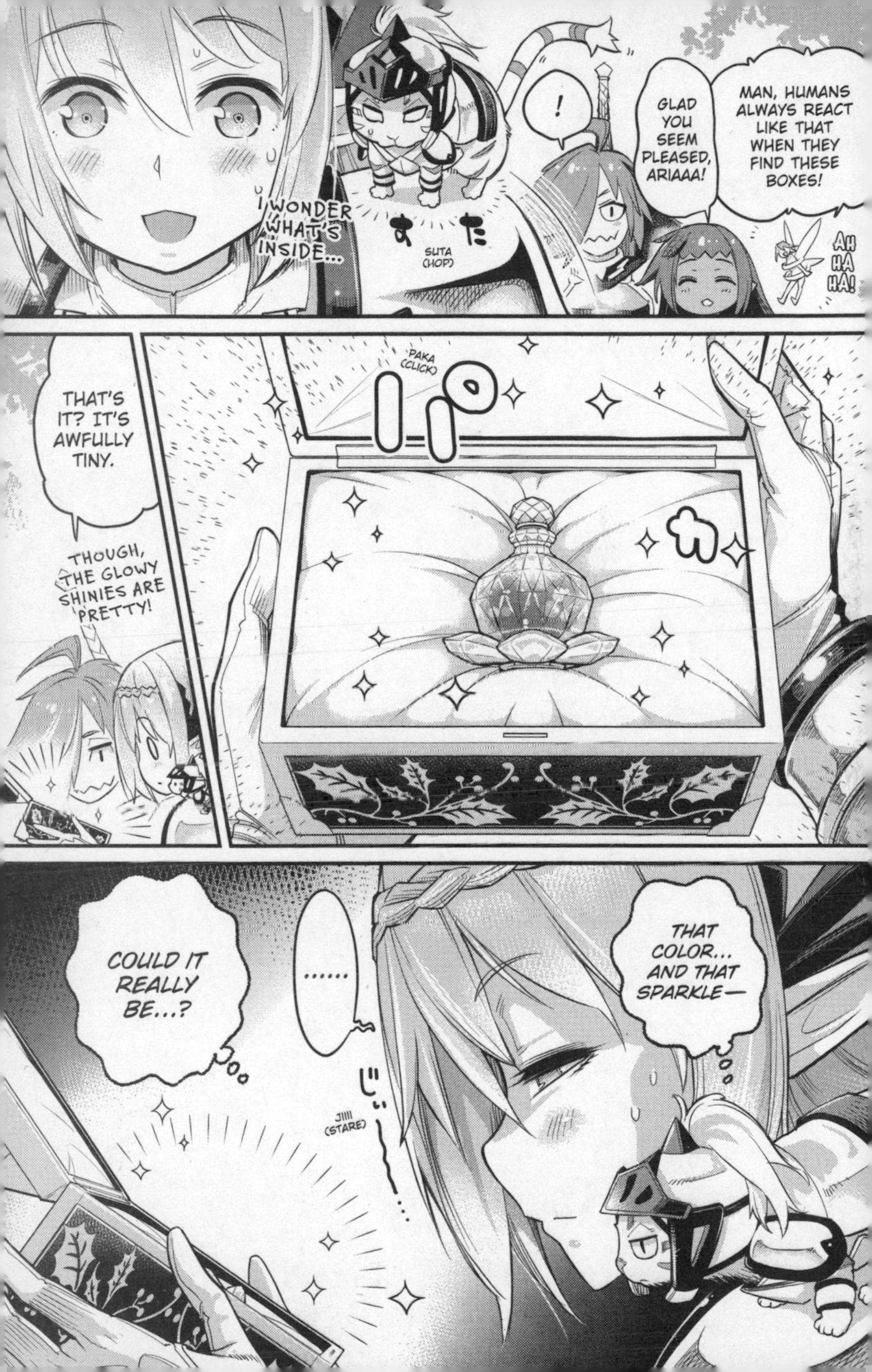
MAN, HUMANS ALWAYS REACT LIKE THAT WHEN THEY FIND THESE BOXES!
AH HA HA!
GLAD YOU SEEM PLEASED, ARIAAA!
!
I WONDER WHAT'S INSIDE...
SUTA (HOP)
PAKA (CLICK)
THAT'S IT? IT'S AWFULLY TINY.
THOUGH, THE GLOWY SHINIES ARE PRETTY!
THAT COLOR... AND THAT SPARKLE—
......
JIIII (STARE)
COULD IT REALLY BE...?

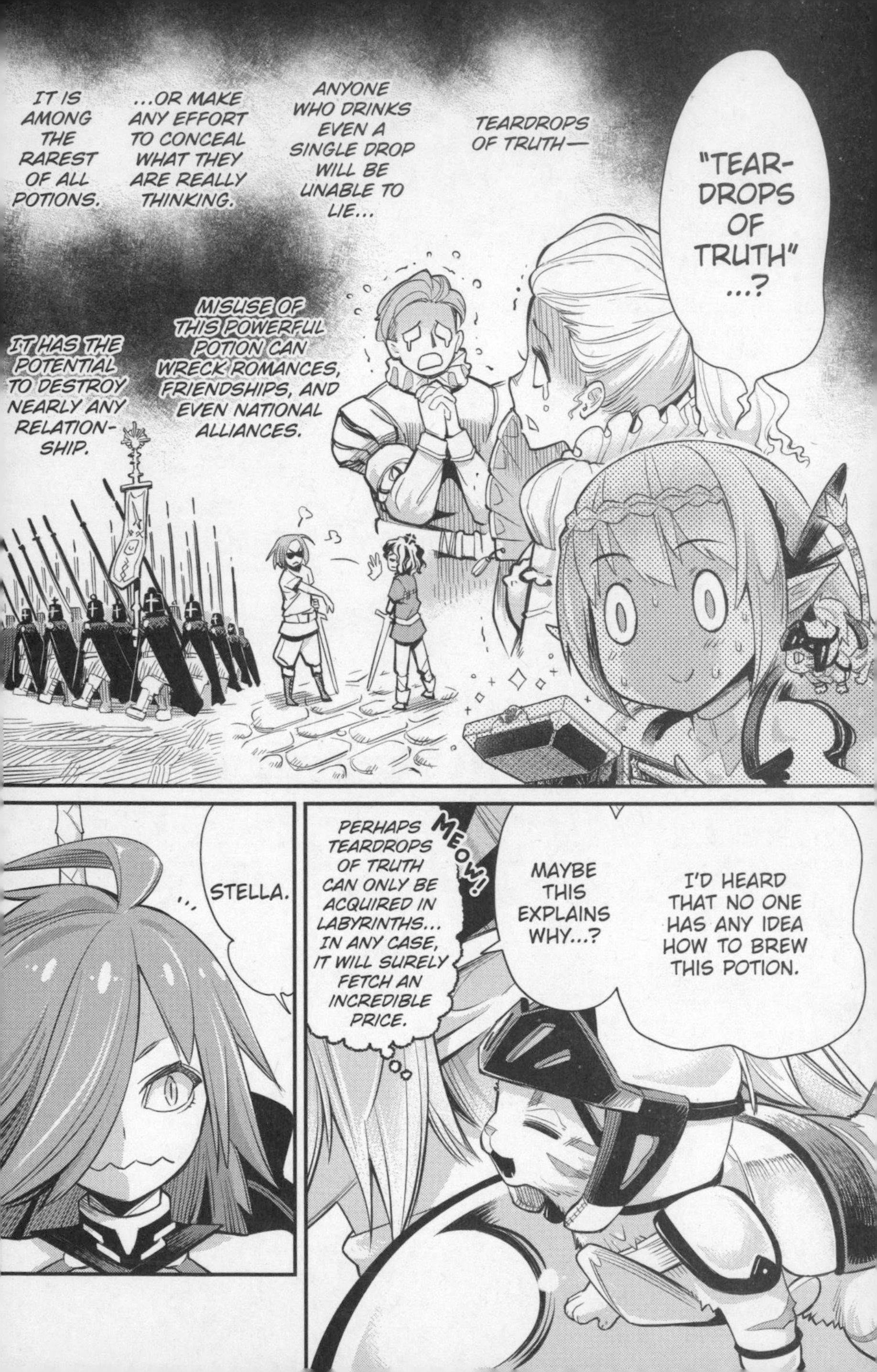
"TEAR-DROPS OF TRUTH" ...?
TEARDROPS OF TRUTH—
ANYONE WHO DRINKS EVEN A SINGLE DROP WILL BE UNABLE TO LIE...
...OR MAKE ANY EFFORT TO CONCEAL WHAT THEY ARE REALLY THINKING.
IT IS AMONG THE RAREST OF ALL POTIONS.
MISUSE OF THIS POWERFUL POTION CAN WRECK ROMANCES, FRIENDSHIPS, AND EVEN NATIONAL ALLIANCES.
IT HAS THE POTENTIAL TO DESTROY NEARLY ANY RELATION-SHIP.
I'D HEARD THAT NO ONE HAS ANY IDEA HOW TO BREW THIS POTION.
MAYBE THIS EXPLAINS WHY...?
MEOW!
PERHAPS TEARDROPS OF TRUTH CAN ONLY BE ACQUIRED IN LABYRINTHS... IN ANY CASE, IT WILL SURELY FETCH AN INCREDIBLE PRICE.
STELLA.

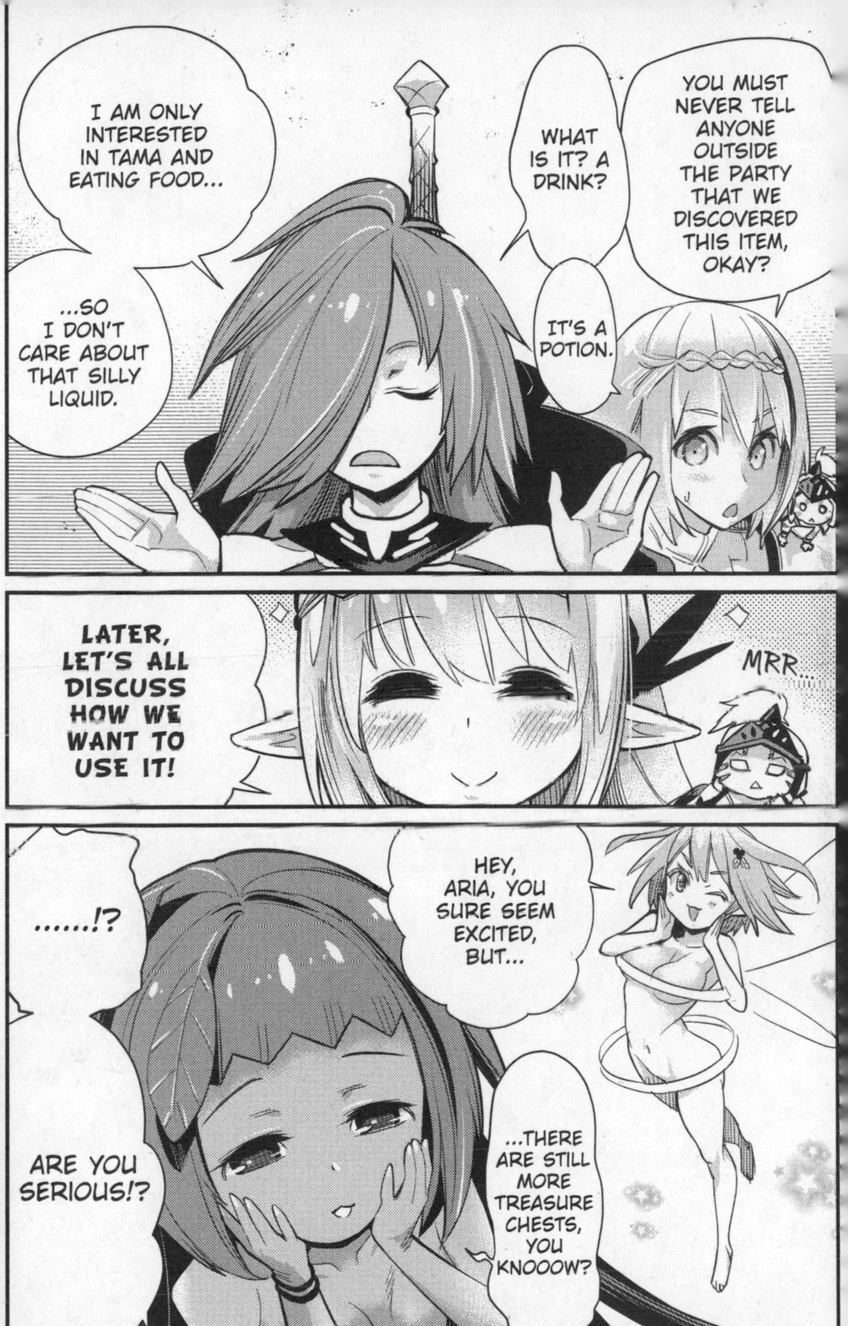
YOU MUST NEVER TELL ANYONE OUTSIDE THE PARTY THAT WE DISCOVERED THIS ITEM, OKAY?
WHAT IS IT? A DRINK?
IT'S A POTION.
I AM ONLY INTERESTED IN TAMA AND EATING FOOD...
...SO I DON'T CARE ABOUT THAT SILLY LIQUID.
MRR...
LATER, LET'S ALL DISCUSS HOW WE WANT TO USE IT!
HEY, ARIA, YOU SURE SEEM EXCITED, BUT...
...THERE ARE STILL MORE TREASURE CHESTS, YOU KNOOOW?
......!?
ARE YOU SERIOUS!?

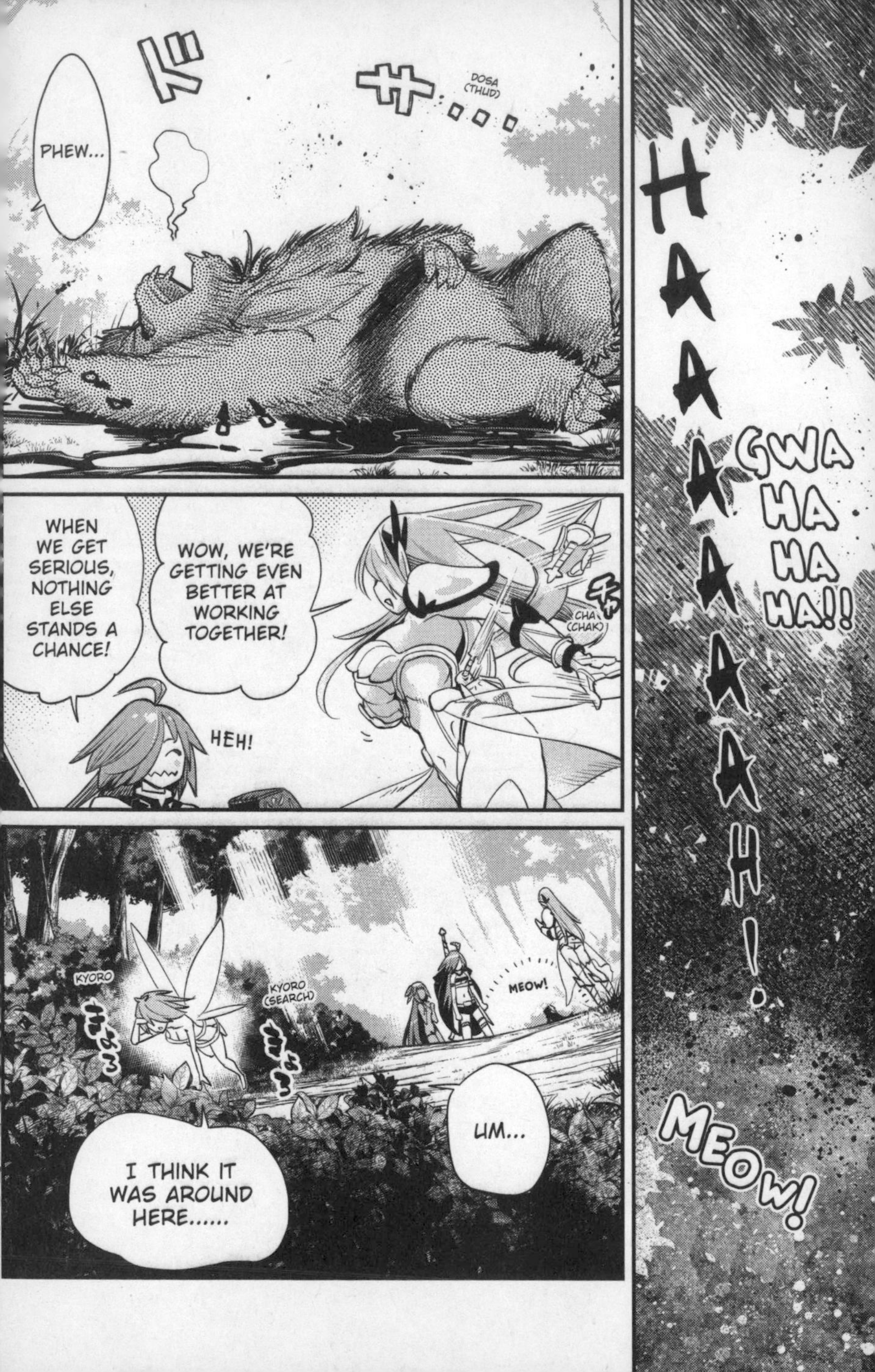
HAAAAAAAH!
GWAHAHAHAHA!!
MEOW!
PHEW...
DOSA (THUD)
WOW, WE'RE GETTING EVEN BETTER AT WORKING TOGETHER!
CHA (CHAK)
WHEN WE GET SERIOUS, NOTHING ELSE STANDS A CHANCE!
HEH!
MEOW!
KYORO (SEARCH)
KYORO
UM...
I THINK IT WAS AROUND HERE......

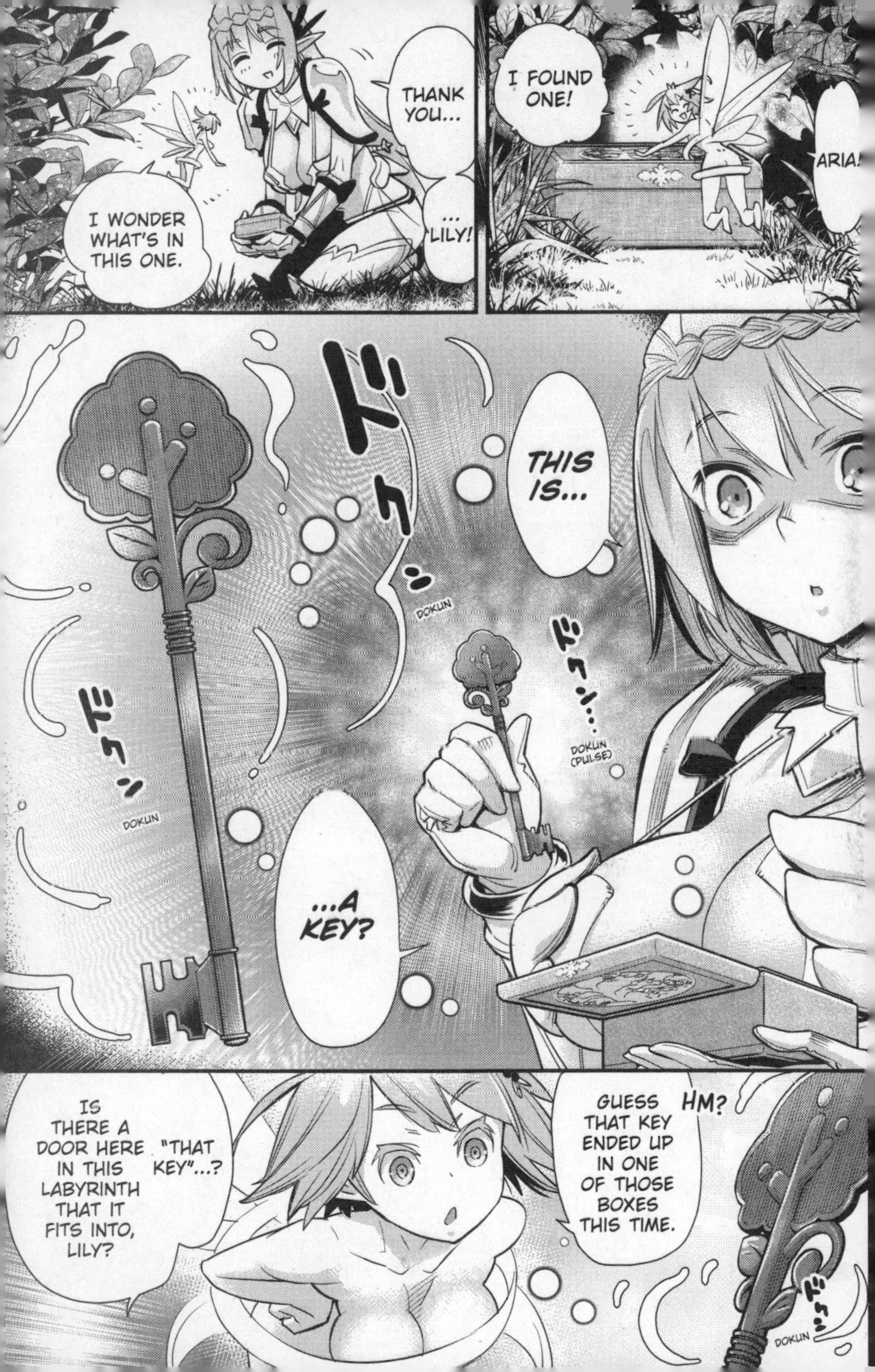
ARIA!
I FOUND ONE!
THANK YOU...
...LILY!
I WONDER WHAT'S IN THIS ONE.
DOKUN (PULSE)
THIS IS...
DOKUN
DOKUN
...A KEY?
HM?
GUESS THAT KEY ENDED UP IN ONE OF THOSE BOXES THIS TIME.
"THAT KEY"...?
IS THERE A DOOR HERE IN THIS LABYRINTH THAT IT FITS INTO, LILY?
DOKUN

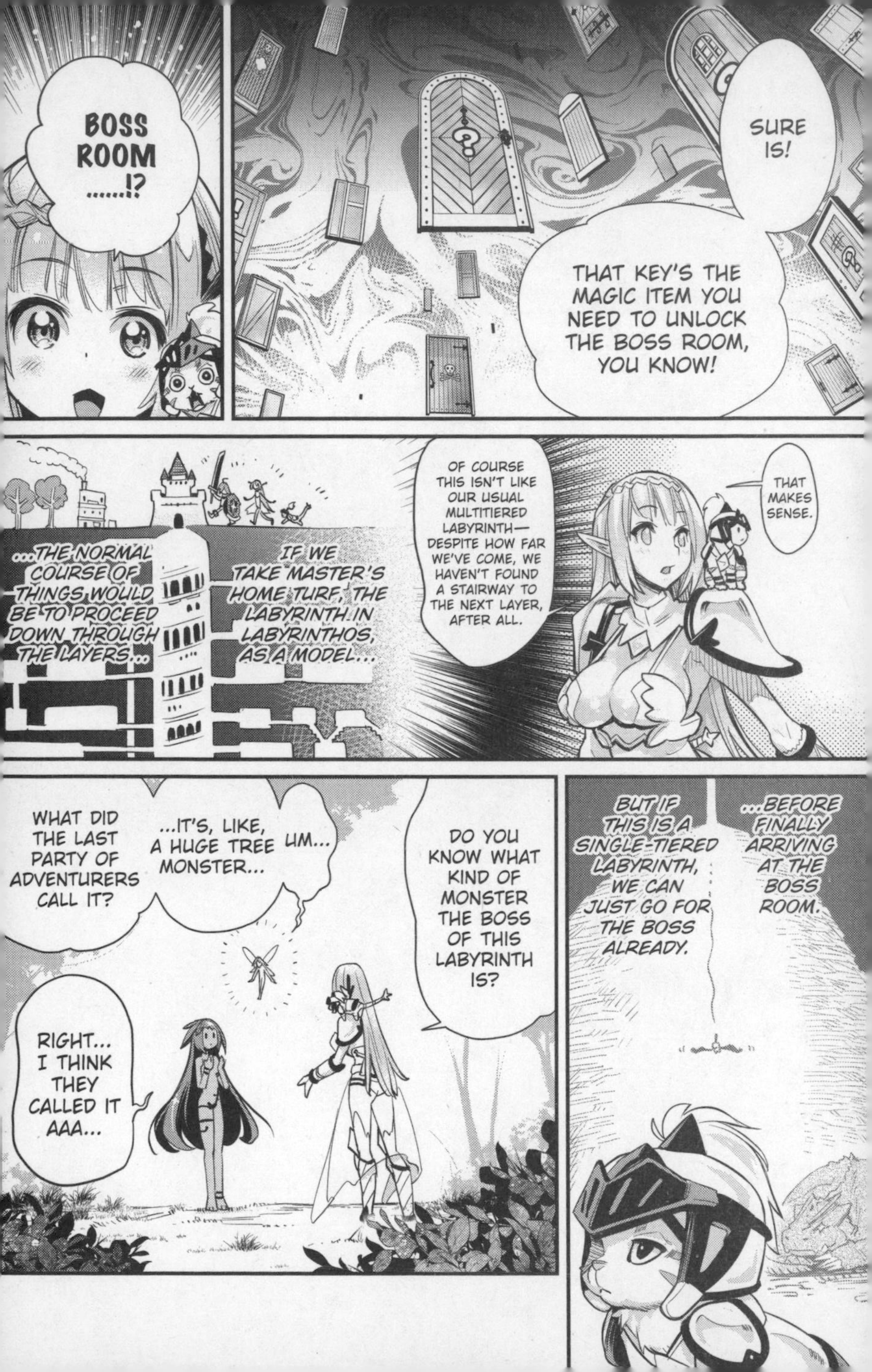
SURE IS!
THAT KEY'S THE MAGIC ITEM YOU NEED TO UNLOCK THE BOSS ROOM, YOU KNOW!
BOSS ROOM ......!?
THAT MAKES SENSE.
OF COURSE THIS ISN'T LIKE OUR USUAL MULTITIERED LABYRINTH— DESPITE HOW FAR WE'VE COME, WE HAVEN'T FOUND A STAIRWAY TO THE NEXT LAYER, AFTER ALL.
IF WE TAKE MASTER'S HOME TURF, THE LABYRINTH IN LABYRINTHOS, AS A MODEL...
...THE NORMAL COURSE OF THINGS WOULD BE TO PROCEED DOWN THROUGH THE LAYERS...
...BEFORE FINALLY ARRIVING AT THE BOSS ROOM.
BUT IF THIS IS A SINGLE-TIERED LABYRINTH, WE CAN JUST GO FOR THE BOSS ALREADY.
DO YOU KNOW WHAT KIND OF MONSTER THE BOSS OF THIS LABYRINTH IS?
UM...
...IT'S, LIKE, A HUGE TREE MONSTER...
WHAT DID THE LAST PARTY OF ADVENTURERS CALL IT?
RIGHT... I THINK THEY CALLED IT AAA...

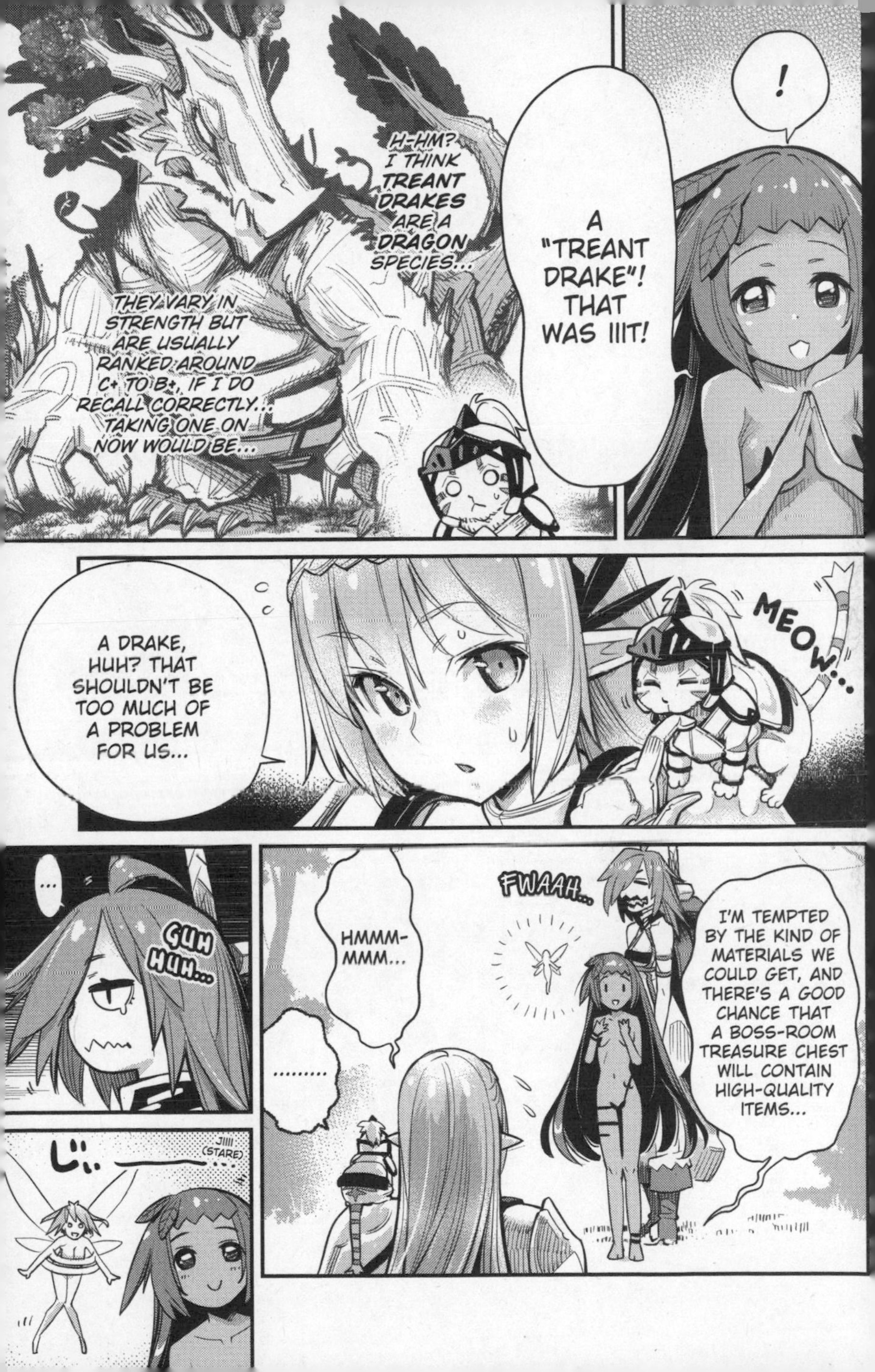
!
A "TREANT DRAKE"! THAT WAS IIIT!
H-HM? I THINK TREANT DRAKES ARE A DRAGON SPECIES...
THEY VARY IN STRENGTH BUT ARE USUALLY RANKED AROUND C+ TO B+, IF I DO RECALL CORRECTLY... TAKING ONE ON NOW WOULD BE...
MEOW...
A DRAKE, HUH? THAT SHOULDN'T BE TOO MUCH OF A PROBLEM FOR US...
FWAAH...
I'M TEMPTED BY THE KIND OF MATERIALS WE COULD GET, AND THERE'S A GOOD CHANCE THAT A BOSS-ROOM TREASURE CHEST WILL CONTAIN HIGH-QUALITY ITEMS...
HMMM-MMM...
....
...
GUH HUH...
じぃーー
JIIII (STARE)

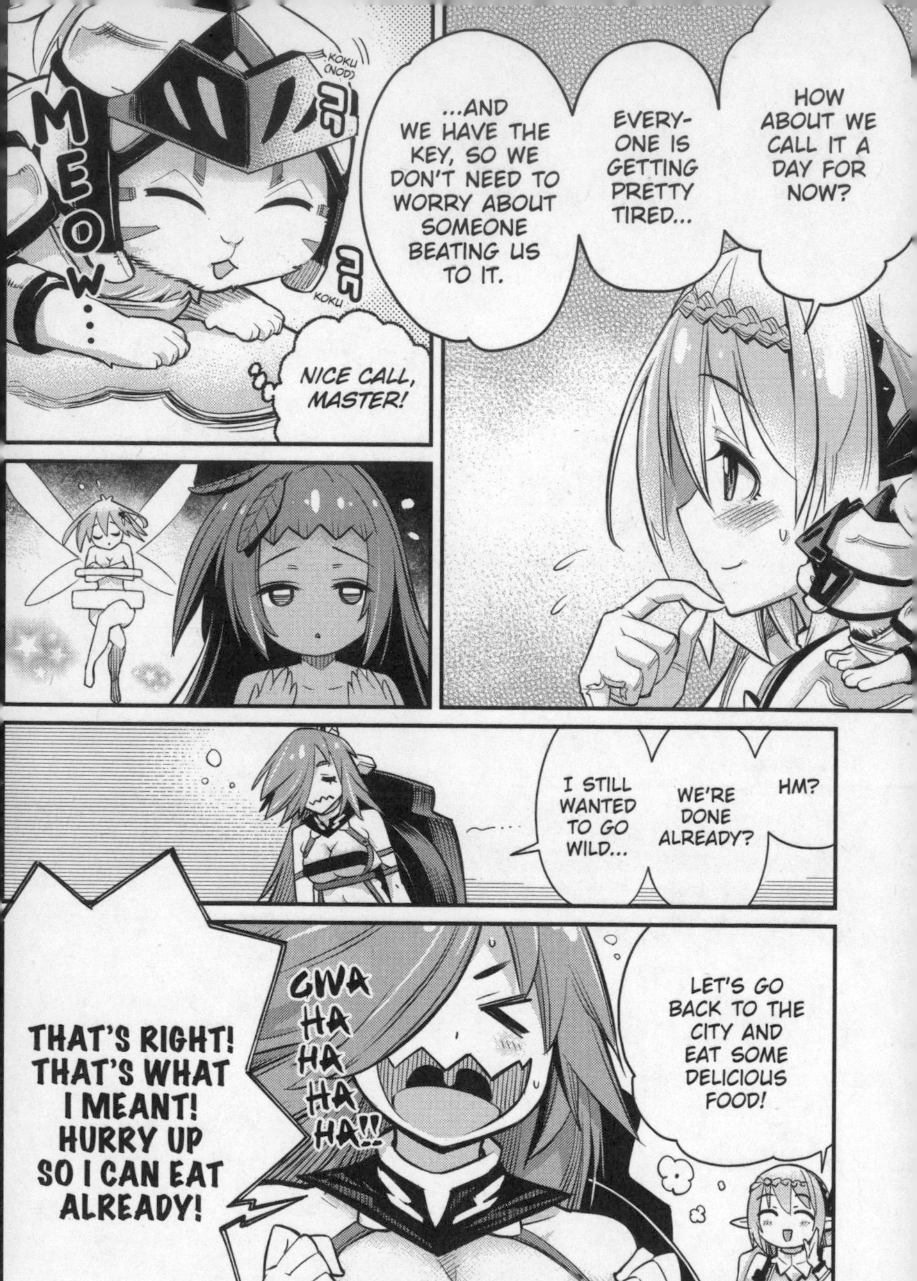
HOW ABOUT WE CALL IT A DAY FOR NOW?
EVERYONE IS GETTING PRETTY TIRED...
...AND WE HAVE THE KEY, SO WE DON'T NEED TO WORRY ABOUT SOMEONE BEATING US TO IT.
KOKU (NOD)
MEOW...
KOKU
NICE CALL, MASTER!
HM?
WE'RE DONE ALREADY?
I STILL WANTED TO GO WILD...
LET'S GO BACK TO THE CITY AND EAT SOME DELICIOUS FOOD!
GWA HA HA HA HA!!
THAT'S RIGHT! THAT'S WHAT I MEANT! HURRY UP SO I CAN EAT ALREADY!

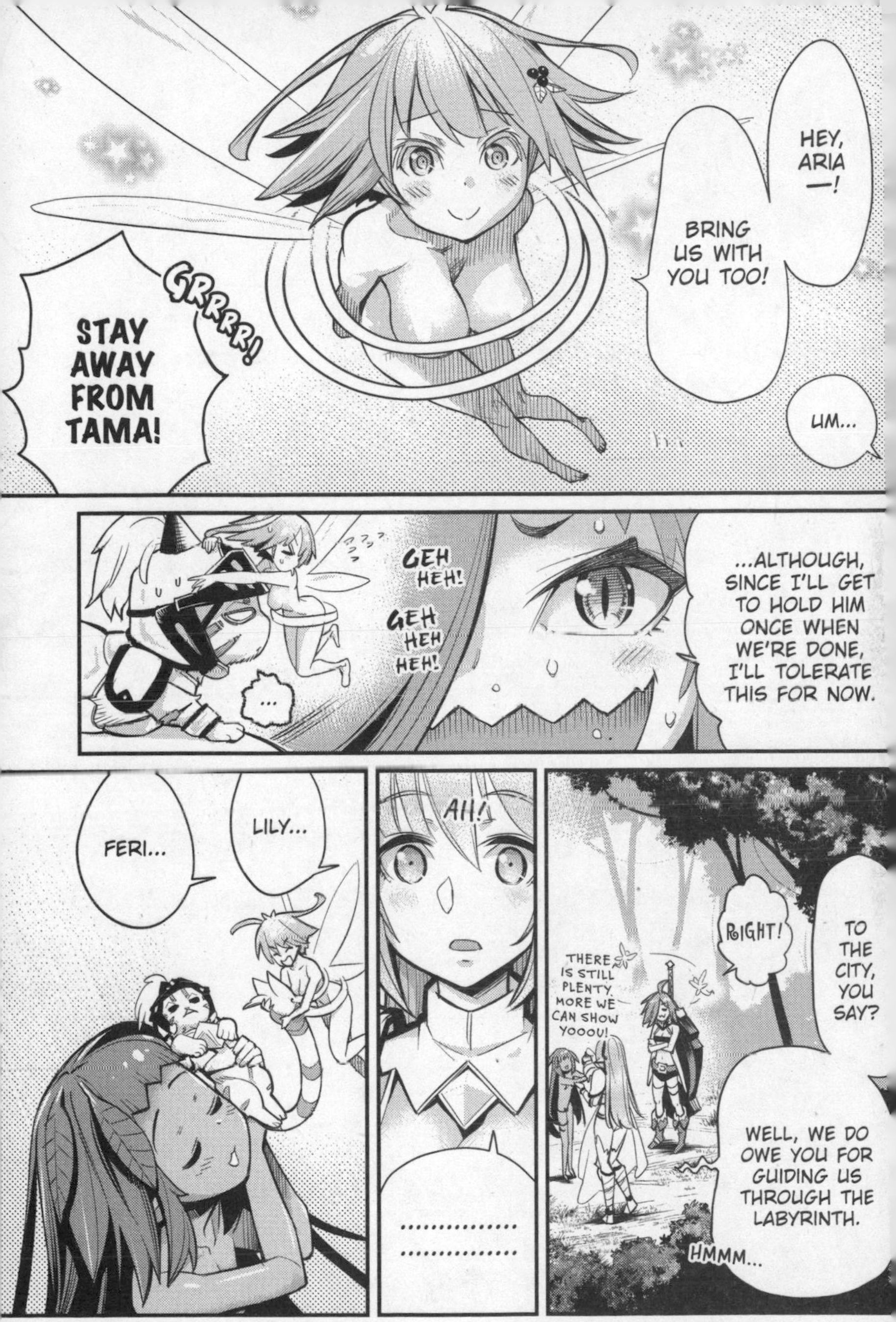
HEY, ARIA—!
BRING US WITH YOU TOO!
UM...
GRRRR!
STAY AWAY FROM TAMA!
...ALTHOUGH, SINCE I'LL GET TO HOLD HIM ONCE WHEN WE'RE DONE, I'LL TOLERATE THIS FOR NOW.
GEH HEH!
GEH HEH HEH!
...
TO THE CITY, YOU SAY?
RIGHT!
THERE IS STILL PLENTY MORE WE CAN SHOW YOOOU!
WELL, WE DO OWE YOU FOR GUIDING US THROUGH THE LABYRINTH.
HMMM...
AH!
....
....
LILY...
FERI...

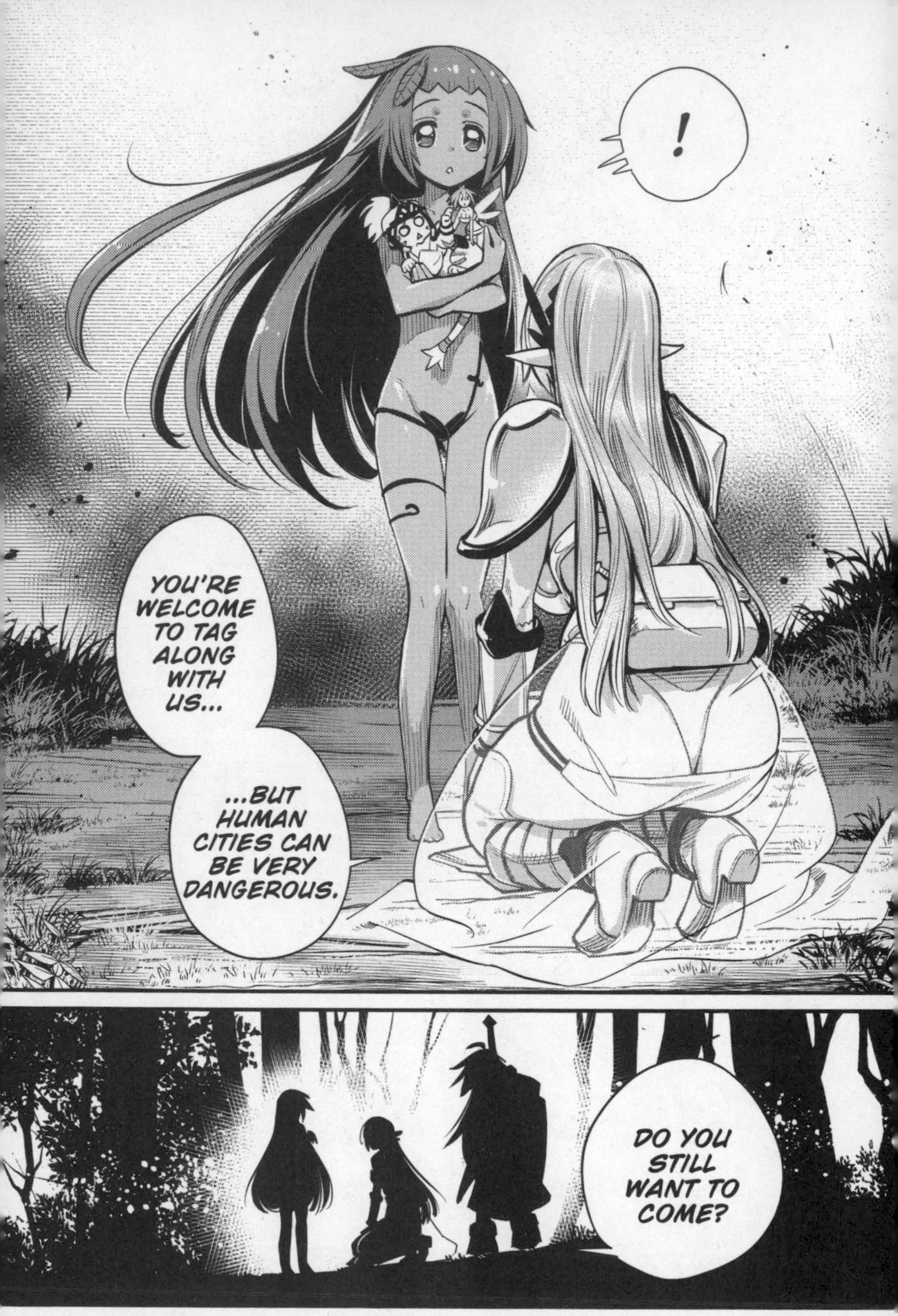
!
YOU'RE WELCOME TO TAG ALONG WITH US...
...BUT HUMAN CITIES CAN BE VERY DANGEROUS.
DO YOU STILL WANT TO COME?

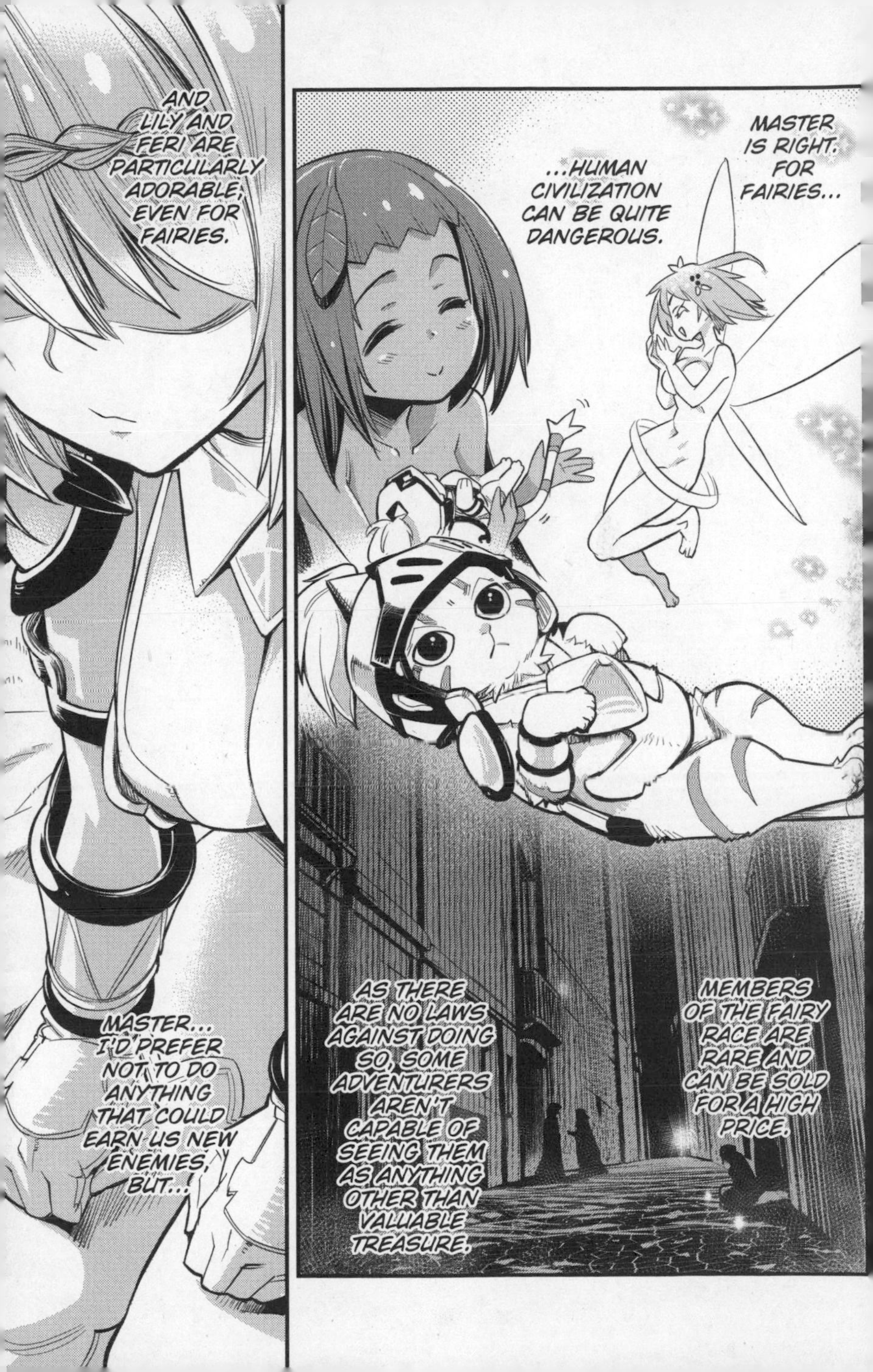
MASTER IS RIGHT. FOR FAIRIES...
...HUMAN CIVILIZATION CAN BE QUITE DANGEROUS.
MEMBERS OF THE FAIRY RACE ARE RARE AND CAN BE SOLD FOR A HIGH PRICE.
AS THERE ARE NO LAWS AGAINST DOING SO, SOME ADVENTURERS AREN'T CAPABLE OF SEEING THEM AS ANYTHING OTHER THAN VALUABLE TREASURE.
AND LILY AND FERI ARE PARTICULARLY ADORABLE, EVEN FOR FAIRIES.
MASTER... I'D PREFER NOT TO DO ANYTHING THAT COULD EARN US NEW ENEMIES, BUT...

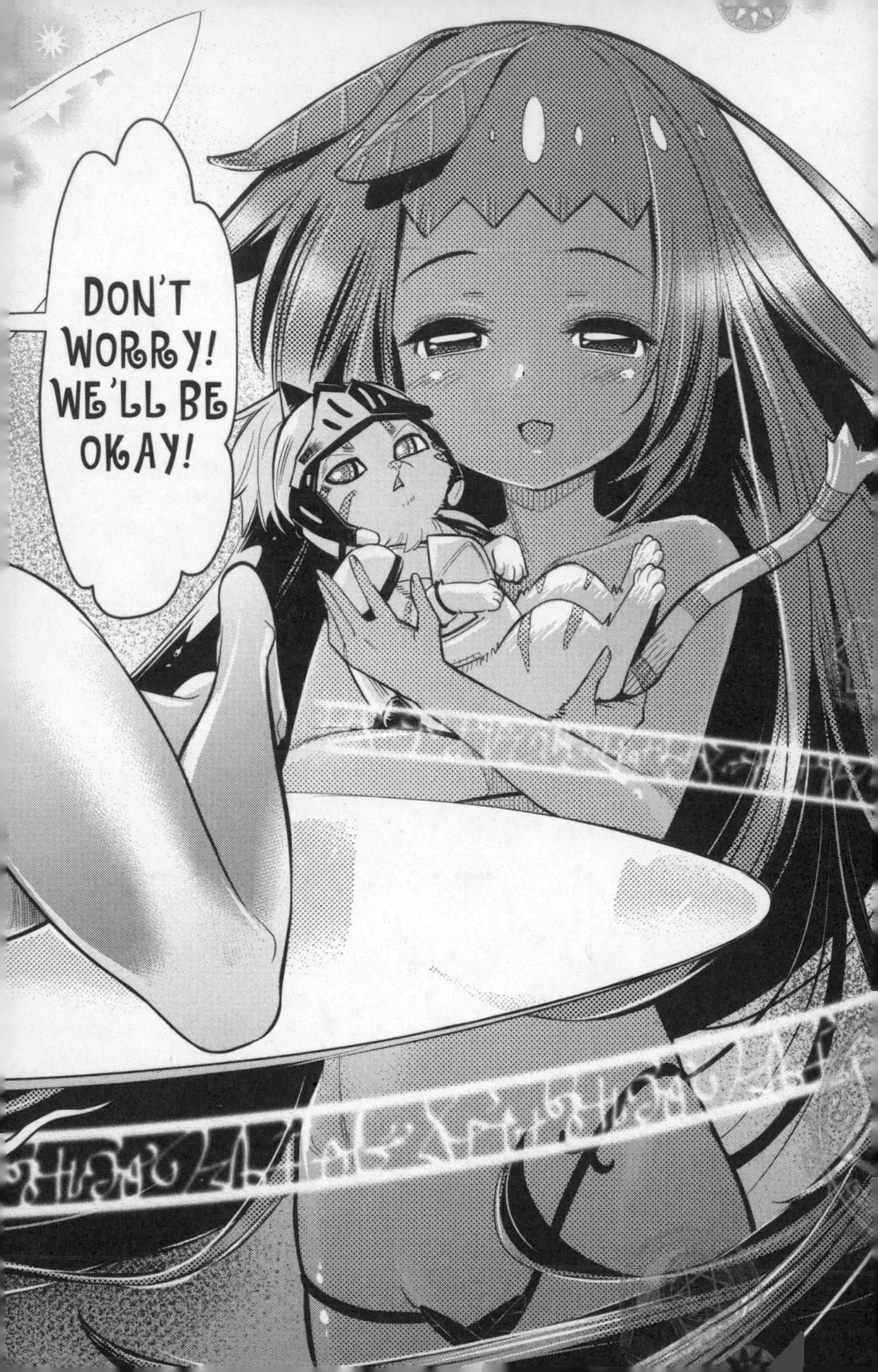
DON'T WORRY! WE'LL BE OKAY!

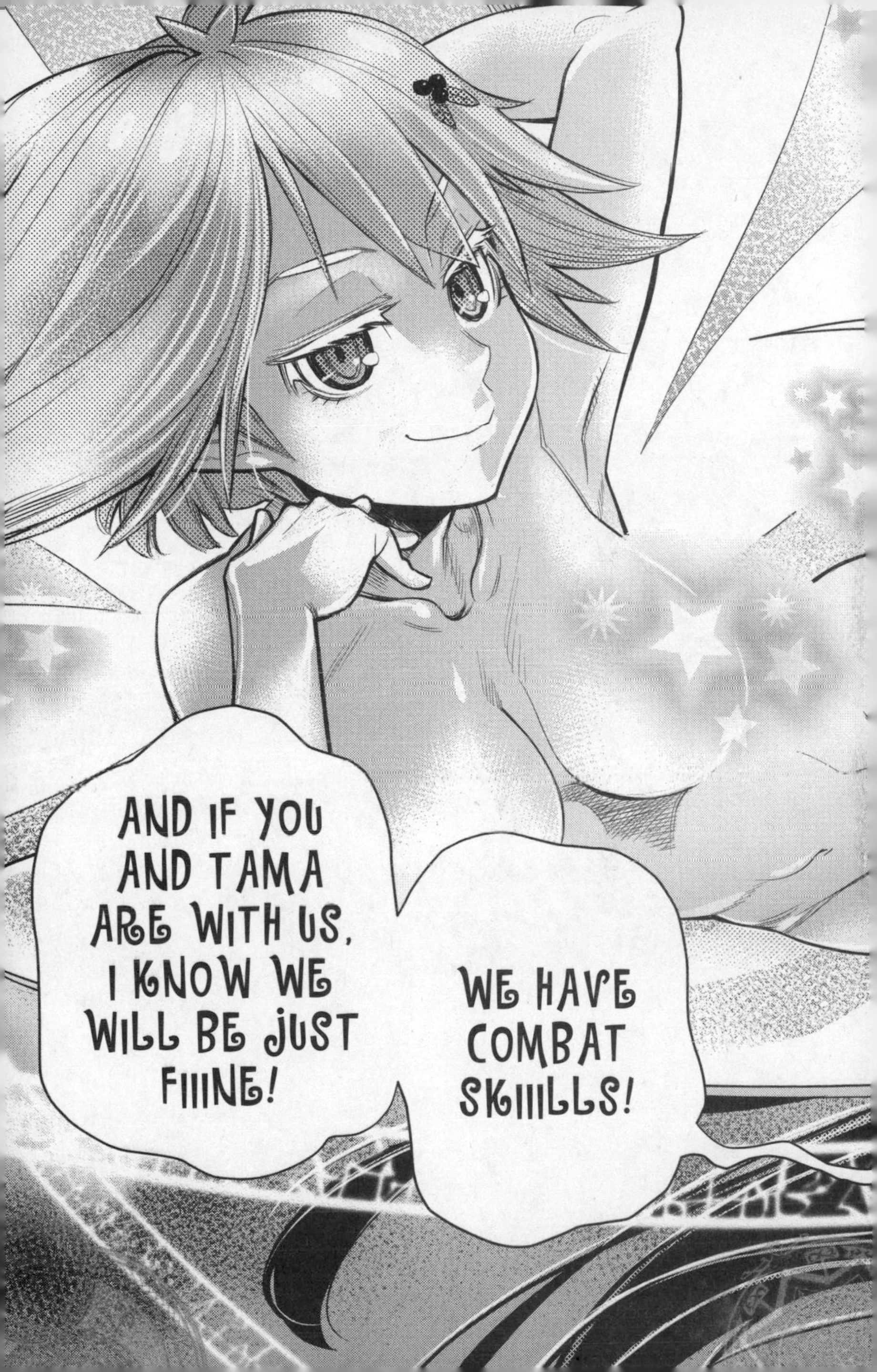
WE HAVE COMBAT SKIIIILLS!
AND IF YOU AND TAMA ARE WITH US, I KNOW WE WILL BE JUST FIIINE!

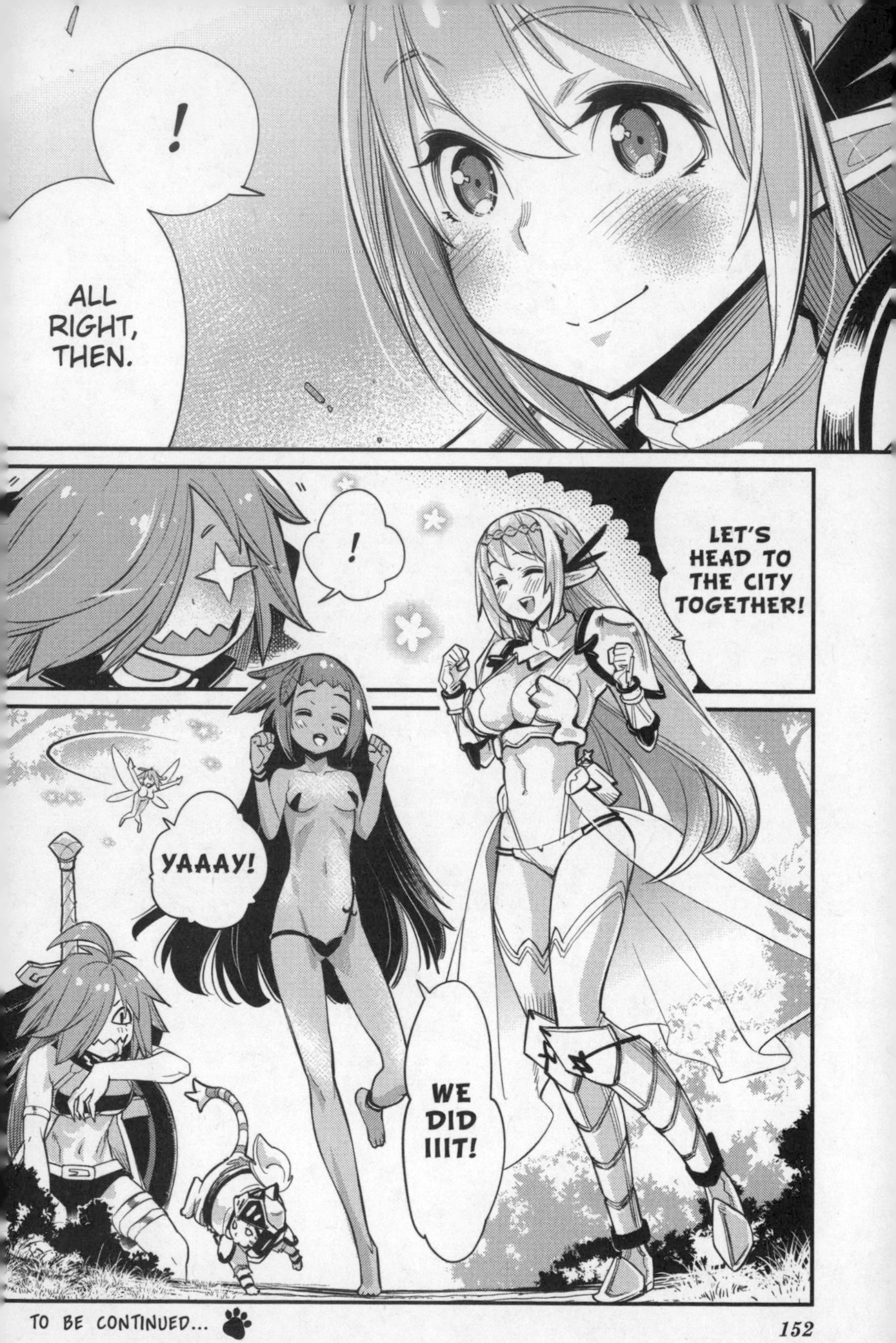
!
ALL RIGHT, THEN.
LET'S HEAD TO THE CITY TOGETHER!
!
WE DID IIIT!
YAAAY!

TO BE CONTINUED...

Turn to the back of the book for a short story by **Nozomi Ginyoku!**

Feri

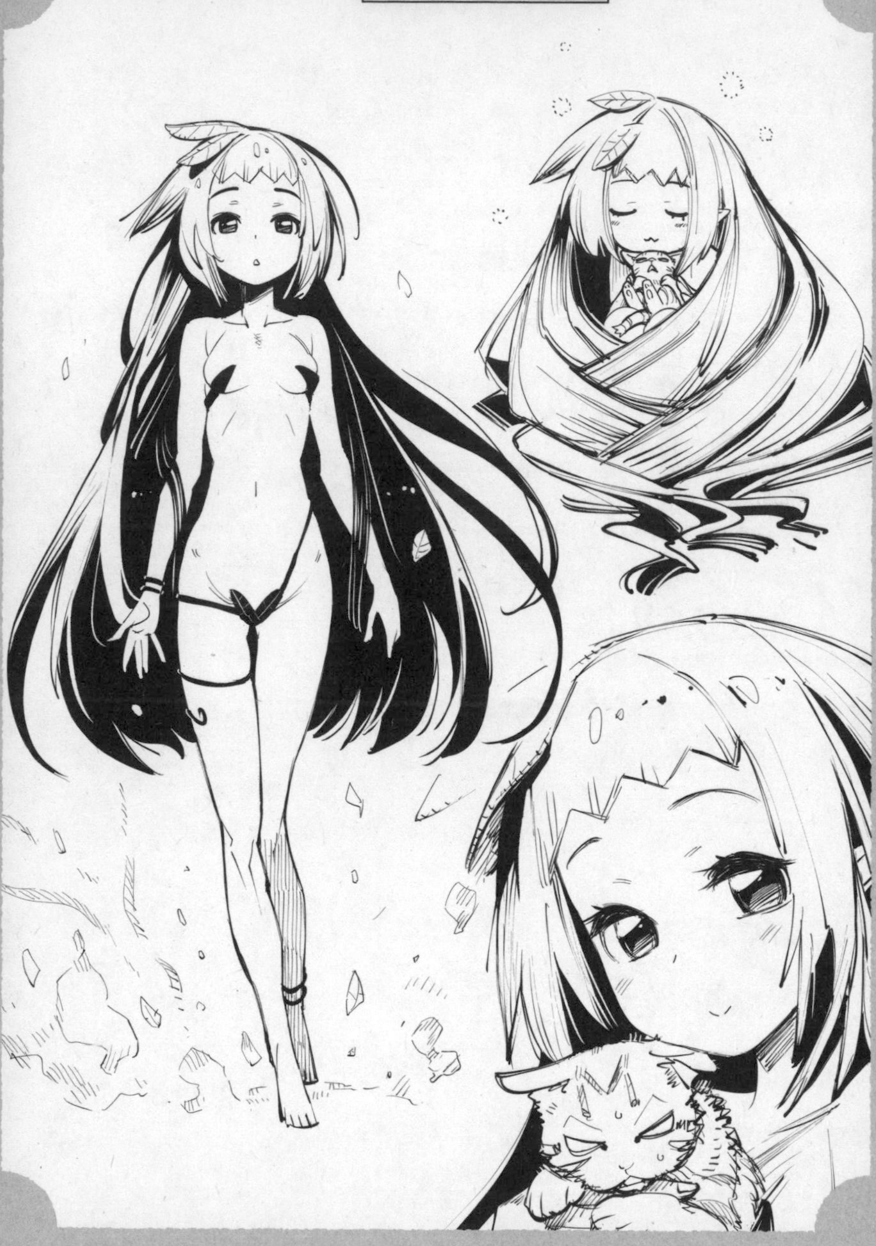

Lily

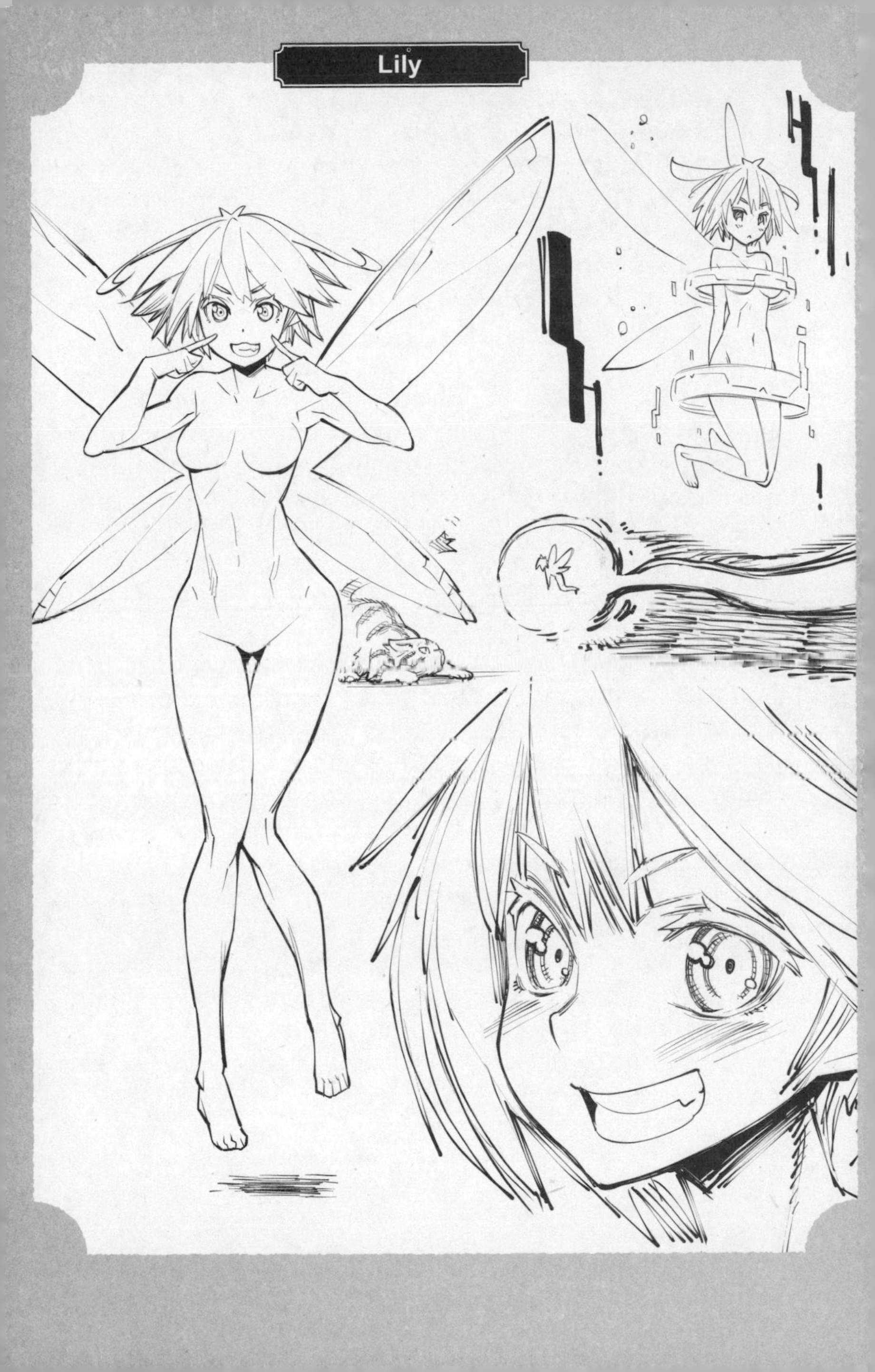

Another thing I realized recently...is that Vulcan may be hiding her true capacity. Or maybe it's more accurate to say that she's not currently capable of displaying it?

Sometimes during battle, she gives off this sense of pressure that's intense enough to even shock me a little, like she's having to try to hold back her true power... The idea that someone would do that is so strange that I can barely understand it.

If my hunch is correct, then I definitely want to see Vulcan's true potential on display someday!

At any rate, Aria is so compassionate, Vulcan really looks after me, and Tama is so strong. I'm not completely sure, but I think I was very lucky to get to be reincarnated as a humanlike being and spend my days around people like them. There are any number of things I'm not fully satisfied with, but even then, every day is enjoyable.

You're looking awfully happy today, Stella.

Ohhh! It makes me so glad whenever you send me a telepathic message on your own, Tama!

However, the fact that I'm starting to enjoy spending time with the others is still a secret to Tama. I don't really know why, but I'd feel a little embarrassed if Tama knew how I felt.

Yes, I think you're making a step in the right direction, Tama thinks at me before cutting off our telepathic connection.

Grrr! I'm pretty sure Tama is seeing straight through me! It's just as embarrassing as I thought it would be!

That said, even this minor embarrassment is somehow making me happy.

When I was a dragon...when I was back in the labyrinth and all I wanted was even greater strength, I never knew these feelings.

Once you get used to it, life as a human isn't so bad.

So in order to keep spending my time like this, I have to keep working hard as an adventurer. That's how I feel these days.

The Dragonewt Girl's Change of Heart

One early morning—

"Hee-hee! Good morning, Tama."

"Meooow!"

These two voices are the first thing that I, Stella, hear as I wake up. I rub my heavy eyelids and open my eyes to the sight of Tama tucked in between Aria's breasts with a blissful look on his face.

Grrr... Why does Tama obey a weakling like Aria anyway?

I may be much stronger than her, but my strength hasn't helped me solve that mystery. However, my perception of Aria has changed a bit recently. I can't really put it into words, but when I'm with her, it's like I feel warm and fuzzy inside. Even though Aria is weaker than me, somehow I feel all relaxed when I spend time around her. When I asked Tama why I felt this way, he told me it's because Aria is "kind to me." At first, I didn't really understand what "kindness" was, but I think I'm starting to get it now.

Aria took me in, even though she didn't know me at all, and took care of me. She feeds me delicious food and showed me how to use the bath. By watching Aria, I realized that I want to feed and hold Tama too. I think all that is part of what..."being kind" is like.

Even now, when Aria realizes I'm awake and greets me with a smile, it makes me feel warm.

Just when I was ruminating on this feeling again—

"Ariaaa! Are you awake meow?"

I can hear Vulcan's voice from the floor below. Come to think of it, we had planned to eat breakfast together today before heading down into the labyrinth.

"Meeeow! Stella, good meowning to you, too!" Vulcan greets me as I follow Aria and Tama downstairs. I think I get along with her fairly well. Because we both fight in the party's vanguard, I think we have a silent understanding in some ways.

Aria once told me that Vulcan is something like her mentor. It seems like Tama respects her too, and lately I've been making an effort not to resist too much when she tells me to do something.

I'M A BEHEMOTH, an S-Ranked MONSTER, but MISTAKEN for a CAT, I Live as an ELF GIRL'S PET

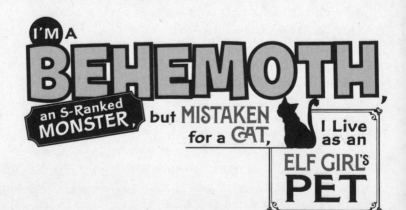

AFTERWORD

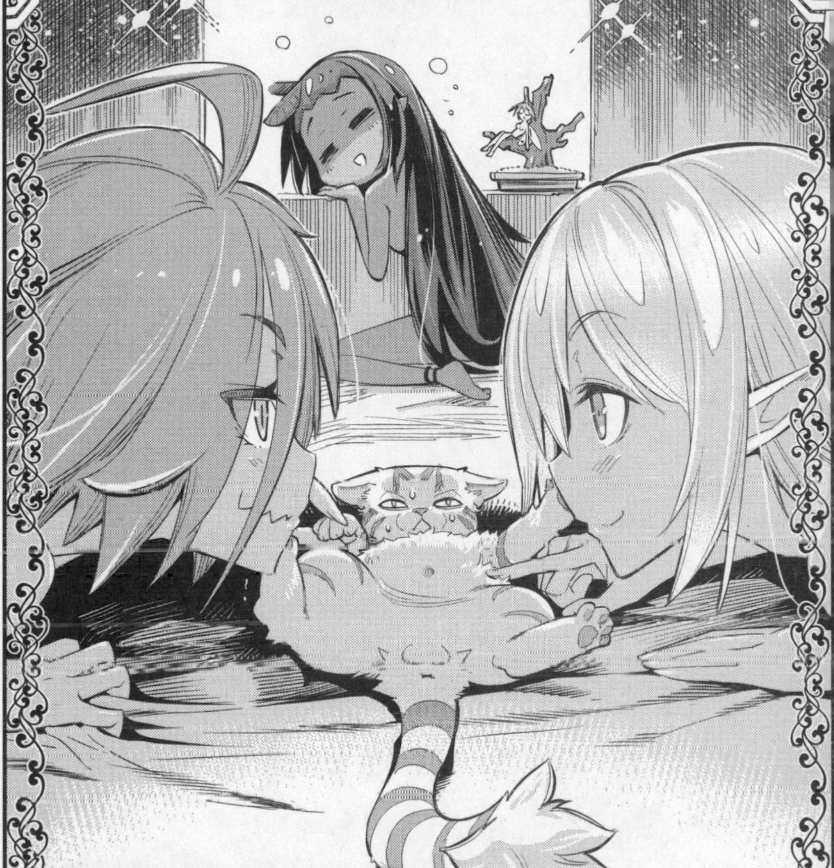

THANKS TO YOU, THE FIFTH VOLUME IS COMPLETE! TAMA'S PARTY HAS BECOME QUITE LIVELY. HOW WILL THEY FARE AGAINST THE BOSS OF THE FOREST LABYRINTH...? I WOULD BE HONORED IF YOU CONTINUED ALONG WITH OUR JOURNEY TO FIND OUT!

TO NOZOMI GINYOKU-SENSEI, MITSUKI YANO-SENSEI, TOSHIHIRO NOZAKI-SENSEI, NATSUKI KUBO-SENSEI, MICRO MAGAZINE, AND HAKUSENSHA, INC. AND AS ALWAYS, THANKS TO EVERYONE WHO SUPPORTED THIS VOLUME!

SPECIAL THANKS: LEE

TARO SHINONOME

東雲太郎

Taro Shinonome

ORIGINAL STORY:
Nozomi Ginyoku

CHARACTER DESIGN:
**Taro Shinonome
Mitsuki Yano**

Translation: Caleb DeMarais

Lettering: Carolina Hernandez

S-RANK MONSTER NO BEHEMOTH DAKEDO, NEKO TO MACHIGAWARETE ELF MUSUME NO PET TOSHITE KURASHITEMASU by TARO SINONOME, NOZOMI GINYOKU, MITSUKI YANO
©TARO SINONOME 2020
©2018 NOZOMI GINYOKU · MITSUKI YANO
All rights reserved.
First published in Japan in 2020 by HAKUSENSHA, Inc., Tokyo.
English language translation rights in U.S.A., Canada and U.K. arranged with HAKUSENSHA, Inc., Tokyo through Tuttle-Mori Agency, Inc., Tokyo.

English translation © 2022 by Yen Press, LLC

Yen Press
150 West 30th Street, 19th Floor
New York, NY 10001

Visit us at yenpress.com
facebook.com/yenpress
twitter.com/yenpress
yenpress.tumblr.com
instagram.com/yenpress

The publisher is not responsible for websites (or their content) that are not owned by the publisher.

Yen Press is an imprint of Yen Press, LLC.
The Yen Press name and logo are trademarks of Yen Press, LLC.

First Yen Press Edition: October 2022

Library of Congress Control Number: 2019956797

ISBNs: 978-1-9753-3455-0 (paperback)
      978-1-9753-3456-7 (ebook)

ScoutAutomatedPrintCode

LSC-C

Printed in the United States of America